The early and middle decades of the nineteenth century in Europe (1815–81) have long been regarded as the major period of assimilation in post-medieval Jewish history. Moreover the established historiography dealing with those years has tended to focus on the processes of accommodation and communal disintegration.

Moving across the continent from west to east, the forces of modernization – unprecedented growth in the economy and population, migration, urbanization – ground down the defences of traditional society. Yiddish, the vernacular shared by the vast majority of European Jewry, was displaced progressively. Hitherto seen as a nation condemned by divine decree to long exile, the Jews began to define themselves in strictly religious terms as Frenchmen, Germans, and so on, by nationality, but of 'the Mosaic persuasion'. Religion, as practised traditionally, was in turn hard pressed by competition with the ideologies of the Enlightenment and Reform Judaism, or treated with simple indifference. Change even made marked inroads into the Russian Empire of Alexander II.

However the historical processes as analysed in this collection of essays emerge as multi- rather than uni-directional, far more variegated and complex than usually described hitherto. Contradictory trends were associated with different localities, levels of development and ideological allegiances. Traditional loyalties, new socio-ethnic structures, communal cohesion, romantic rediscoveries of the past and the political solidarity engendered by the struggle for emancipation across Europe, all served to counterbalance the homogenizing forces of modernity.

Bringing together the work of fourteen leading historians, this book represents a major contribution to the revision, which has gained momentum in recent years, of the traditional historiography.

This book is published in cooperation with the Institute of Jewish Studies, University College London.

Assimilation and community

Assimilation and community

The Jews in nineteenth-century Europe

Edited by JONATHAN FRANKEL

and STEVEN J. ZIPPERSTEIN

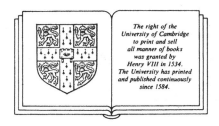

The right of the
University of Cambridge
to print and sell
all manner of books
was granted by
Henry VIII in 1534.
The University has printed
and published continuously
since 1584.

CAMBRIDGE UNIVERSITY PRESS

Cambridge

New York   Port Chester

Melbourne   Sydney

PUBLISHED BY THE PRESS SYNDICATE OF THE UNIVERSITY OF CAMBRIDGE
The Pitt Building, Trumpington Street, Cambridge, United Kingdom

CAMBRIDGE UNIVERSITY PRESS
The Edinburgh Building, Cambridge CB2 2RU, UK
40 West 20th Street, New York NY 10011–4211, USA
477 Williamstown Road, Port Melbourne, VIC 3207, Australia
Ruiz de Alarcón 13, 28014 Madrid, Spain
Dock House, The Waterfront, Cape Town 8001, South Africa

http://www.cambridge.org

First published 1992
First paperback edition 2004

A catalogue record for this book is available from the British Library

Library of Congress Cataloguing in Publication data
Assimilation and community: the Jews in nineteenth-century Europe
edited by Jonathan Frankel and Steven J. Zipperstein.
          p.   cm.
Includes papers presented at a conference held at University
College London, June 1985, organized jointly by the Institute of
Jewish Studies at University College and by the Oxford Centre for
Postgraduate Hebrew Studies.
'Published in cooperation with the Institute of Jewish Studies,
University College London' – T.p. verso.
Includes index.
ISBN 0 521 40284 0 (hardcover)
1. Jews – Europe – History – 19th century – Congresses.   2. Jews –
Europe – Cultural assimilation – Congresses.   3. Jews – Emancipation –
Congresses.   4. Europe – Ethnic relations – Congresses.   I. Frankel,
Jonathan.   II. Zipperstein, Steven J., 1950–   .   III. Institute of
Jewish Studies (London, England)
DS135.E83A85   1991
305.8′92′40409034–dc20   90-15015   CIP

ISBN 0 521 40284 0 hardback
ISBN 0 521 52601 9 paperback

Contents

Contributors

Phyllis Cohen Albert (Harvard University) is the author of *The Modernization of French Jewry: Consistory and Community in Nineteenth-Century France* and co-author of *Essays in Modern Jewish History: A Tribute to Ben Halpern.*

Richard I. Cohen (The Hebrew University of Jerusalem) is the author of *The Burden of Conscience. French–Jewish Leadership during the Holocaust.* He edited Raymond-Raoul Lambert, *Carnet d'un Témoin (1940–43)* and co-edited the symposium 'Art and its Uses: The Visual Image and Modern Jewish Society', in *Studies in Contemporary Jewry*, vol. VI.

Todd M. Endelman (The University of Michigan) is the author of *The Jews of Georgian England, 1714–1830: Tradition and Change in a Liberal Society* and *Radical Assimilation in English Jewish History, 1656–1945.* He edited *Jewish Apostasy in the Modern World.*

Israel Finestein (President of the Jewish Historical Society of England) is the author of *A Short History of Anglo-Jewry* and edited J. Picciotto, *Sketches of Anglo-Jewish History.*

Jonathan Frankel (The Hebrew University of Jerusalem) is the author of *Prophecy and Politics: Socialism, Nationalism and the Russian Jews 1862–1917.* He edited *Vladimir Akimov on the Dilemmas of Russian Marxism 1895–1903* and is an editor of *Studies in Contemporary Jewry.*

Michael Graetz (The Hebrew University of Jerusalem) is the author of *Les Juifs en France en XIXe Siècle* and *The French Revolution and the Jews* (in Hebrew, forthcoming).

Paula E. Hyman (Yale University) is the author of *From Dreyfus to*

Vichy and *Country Jews, City Jews: Emancipation, Acculturation, and Tradition in Nineteenth Century Alsace* (forthcoming). She co-edited *The Jewish Family: Myths and Realities.*

Marion Kaplan (Queens College and the Graduate Center of the City University of New York) has written *The Jewish Feminist Movement in Germany: the Campaigns of the Jüdischer Frauenbund, 1904–1938* and *The Making of the Jewish Middle-Class: Women and German-Jewish Identity in Imperial Germany* (forthcoming). She edited *The Marriage Bargain: Women and Dowries in European History*, and co-edited *When Biology Became Destiny: Women in Weimar and Nazi Germany.*

Hillel J. Kieval (The University of Washington, Seattle) is the author of *The Making of Czech Jewry: National Conflict and Jewish Society in Bohemia, 1870–1918.*

Eli Lederhendler (The Hebrew University of Jerusalem) is the author of *The Road to Modern Jewish Politics: Political Tradition and Political Reconstruction in Tsarist Russia.*

Marsha Rozenblit (University of Maryland, College Park) is the author of *The Jews of Vienna, 1867–1914: Assimilation and Identity.*

Michael K. Silber (The Hebrew University of Jerusalem) edited *Jews in the Hungarian Economy, 1750–1945* (forthcoming).

David Sorkin (The University of Oxford) is the author of *The Transformation of Germany Jewry 1780–1840*. He co-edited *From East and West: Jews in a Changing Europe, 1750–1870.*

Steven J. Zipperstein (The University of California, Los Angeles) is the author of the *The Jews of Odessa: A Cultural History, 1794–1881*, and the co-editor of *Jewish History: Essays in Honour of Chimen Abramsky*. His book, *Ahad Ha'am: An Interpretative Study of His Life*, will appear next year.

Preface

In June 1985 a conference was held at University College London on the subject of 'Assimilation and community in European Jewry, 1815–1881'. Organized jointly by the Institute of Jewish Studies at University College and by the Oxford Centre for Postgraduate Hebrew Studies, it produced two days of exceptionally vigorous give-and-take. The conference had been prepared at short notice and without thought of publication. But given the interest revealed during – and between – the sessions, we decided to try to organize a book on the subject. As is not unusual in such cases, a number of years (too many, no doubt) have had to pass between the inception and completion of the project. It should be noted, however, that of the fourteen essays included in this volume, only four (those of Phyllis Cohen Albert, Israel Finestein, Paula Hyman, and Michael Silber) were among those presented to the conference, and they too have in the meantime undergone varying degrees of revision.

It became clear to us as the work progressed that it would not be possible to keep the book strictly within the original chronological framework of 1815–1881. A number of the authors felt that these dates forced them into something of a Procrustean bed and we therefore opted in the end for the more general period of the nineteenth century. None the less, the fulcrum of the book clearly remains that period in modern Jewish history which preceded 1881 when issues related to Jewish emancipation and integration were generally seen to be of predominant importance and the 'post-liberal' phenomena (Judeophobia, exclusivist nationalism, proto-Zionism, Jewish socialism) were for the most part perceived to be, variously, of declining or of marginal significance.

Finally, we wish to take this opportunity to thank those friends who did so much to make the preparation of this book possible: Dr Manfred Altman, the Chairman of the Institute of Jewish Studies, whose unflagging and dedicated work – backed up loyally as it is by an active board of governors – has made the Institute the vigorous institution which it now is; Dr Mark Geller and Mrs Anita Wall, who together organized the original conference so efficiently and with such wonderful good humour and patience; and Mrs Katie Edwards (Mrs Wall's replacement at the Department of Hebrew and Jewish Studies at University College) who has been much and enthusiastically involved in the final stages of the book's production. We wish to thank the Center for Russian and East European Studies at the University of California for helping to defray the cost of the index. As copy-editor for Cambridge University Press, Mrs Jean Field, however sorely tried, displayed throughout a meticulous care for detail, tact and good humour – in short, great professionalism – for which we wish to express our great appreciation and thanks.

Jonathan Frankel
Steven J. Zipperstein

Assimilation and the Jews in nineteenth-century Europe: towards a new historiography?

JONATHAN FRANKEL

The life and thought of the Jewish people in nineteenth-century Europe is rarely described today, in accord with the basic concept which dominated the history books until some twenty years ago. True, the process of revision has been anything but dramatic. Among the historians who write on nineteenth-century Jewry there have been no great public disputes over method or content, nothing comparable to the fierce debates engendered by the cliometric studies of American slavery, for example, or by the structuralist and deconstructionist schools in contemporary literary criticism. No revisionist school of historiography has proclaimed its existence in this field; nor, in many, perhaps even most, cases, were the individual historians involved aware (at least initially) of being engaged in a broader revisionist trend.

A major contribution to the change of perspective has undoubtedly been made by a number of American historians. But the re-mapping of modern Jewish history has not been confined to any one country (Israeli historians, too, have been strongly represented) nor to any one generation.

What became the historiographical orthodoxy in this field for a number of decades – in most marked form from the 1930s until the 1960s – had its origins in the Tsarist Empire. In general terms, it was a major by-product of the modern Jewish nationalism which surged up in the Pale of Settlement following the pogroms of 1881–2 and which, despite ebbs and flows, sustained its momentum throughout the reigns of Alexander III and Nicholas II.

More specifically, what can be called the Russian-Jewish school of history was, to all intents and purposes, initiated, inspired by one man, Simon M. Dubnov. In an extraordinary burst of energy and creativity during the decade 1888–98, he laid down the basic guidelines for his own work during the rest of his life and for that of mainstream historians over a number of generations.[1]

In those years, Dubnov marked himself off from the great German-Jewish historian, Heinrich Graetz (even while fully acknowledging his own discipleship). Where Graetz had written history from a theological and metaphysical perspective,[2] his own point of view would be secular and anthropocentric, taking as its ideal the empiricism of natural science. Where Graetz had seen the religious and national strands of Jewish history as inextricably and eternally intertwined, Dubnov came to regard it as axiomatic that the Jews were primarily a nation and that Judaism, the religion, was a secondary attribute which could be safely transformed, or even abandoned, according to circumstance.

Graetz had concentrated attention largely on intellectual and literary themes; Dubnov now emphasized communal history, the forms of autonomous self-government which had sustained the Jewish people through the millennia of exile. (And, of course, he linked this thesis to his own political ideology which demanded Jewish national self-government, autonomy within multinational and democratized states.)[3] Or, to take yet another divergence, where Graetz had been critical of all forms of Jewish mysticism, Dubnov now wrote his remarkable history of Hasidism, which described the movement as a socio-psychological response to mass distress, thus justifying it (at least during its period of genesis) in populist terms.[4]

Many factors combined to entrench and bring about the diffusion of the historiographical school which, although launched by Dubnov, soon took on a vigorous life of its own. With its stress on national politics, avowed secularism and the search for scientific certainty, it gave voice to, reinforced and in turn was sustained by the radicalism of the Russian-Jewish intelligentsia in the late Tsarist period. This mode of history could appeal to Zionists, Territorialists, Bundists and Folkists alike, for even though their respective movements were bitterly divided over issues of means and ends, they shared a common faith in the triumphant power of modern nationalism.

By 1914, the increasing interest in Jewish history (above all Russian and Polish) had led to the establishment of a high-quality journal (*Evreiskaia Starina*);[5] of higher educational courses (the so-called Oriental Studies organized under the auspices of Baron David Gintsburg);[6] and of the Historical–Ethnograhical Society (in which

S. An-sky played so conspicious a role).[7] The monumental sixteen-volume encyclopedia (*Evreiskaia entsiklopediia*)[8] and the first part of Dubnov's *History of the Jews in Modern Times* had already been published.[9] Increasingly, contemporary political issues were linked in the Hebrew, Yiddish and Russian-language (Jewish) press in the Tsarist Empire, as well as in Palestine and America, to discussions of possible parallels, precedents and cautionary tales to be found in the national past.[10]

Again, many of the leading scholars of the next generation had by then been drawn into the field of modern Jewish history: B. Z. Dinaburg (Dinur), Z. Rubashev (Shazar), Elyohu Cherikover, Avrom Menes, to name just a few. And some of these, then still very young *intelligenty* would, in turn, exert a powerful influence on contemporaries, future historians, in Central Europe – the most famous example being, of course, Gershom Scholem who like many other German Zionists of his generation looked eastward for inspiration in his search for an authentic, uncompromised form of Jewish life. (Scholem himself would later note that in his circles 'there was something like a cult of Eastern Jews'.)[11]

In the interwar years, with the decline and eventual elimination of Jewish scholarship in the Soviet Union, the historiographical enterprise initiated in Tsarist times was able to re-root itself elsewhere. Two institutions in particular now developed as the central foci in this effort of reconstruction and renewal: the YIVO Institute (or Jewish Scientific Organization) in Vilna which established branches in Warsaw, Berlin and New York, and the Hebrew University of Jerusalem – both founded in the same year, 1925. It was during the 1920s, too, that Dubnov, who was closely associated with YIVO, first published his ten-volume *Weltgeschichte des Jüdischen Volkes* which was very widely read (a Russian edition came out in Latvia in the 1930s)[12] and which, with its clear nationalist message, exerted increasing influence in the wake of the Nazi triumph in Germany.[13]

With the destruction of the Jews in Europe during the Second World War, the Hebrew University found itself almost the sole heir to the Russian (or by now, more exactly, Eastern European) school of modern Jewish historiography. YIVO survived in New York, the depository of a major library and archive, much of it salvaged from postwar Europe, but its research staff was very limited in size. And yet the rapid growth of the Hebrew University following the establishment of Israel in 1948, and the expansion of Jewish studies in the new state generally, meant that the tradition of historical scholarship

leading back to Dubnov was able not only to sustain itself, but was
also revitalized to a remarkable extent, carried forward by new
academic journals, specialized monographs and major works of
synthesis.

It is a remarkable fact that all the major books which seek to analyse
the history of the Jews across the entire expanse of the modern world
belong within that tradition. Nearly all of them have long been
available in English translation: the final volumes of Dubnov's *History
of the Jewish People*;[14] Raphael Mahler's *A History of Modern Jewry*[15]
(which, despite initial aims to the contrary, covers only a limited
period) and Shmuel Ettinger's section in the Harvard *History of the
Jews*.[16] To this list can be added Ben-Zion Dinur's collected essays
(still not translated) in the volume *Bemifneh hadorot*.[17] These works
have by now all attained classic status: they are painted on a vast
canvas, based on extraordinary erudition and informed with im-
passioned concern.

Each of these historians, of course, had his own very distinctive
viewpoint, method and style. Both Ben-Zion Dinur, for example, who
was committed to a thoroughgoing Zionist ideology (including the
concept of the 'negation of the Exile' – *shlilat hagalut*) and Raphael
Mahler, with his Marxist version of Zionism, were inevitably in
profound disagreement on key issues with Dubnov, the Diaspora
nationalist, autonomist and bitter opponent of class-war ideology.
And, none the less, beyond all these very real distinctions they shared
with each other and with the mainstream historians at large, a
number of basic perceptions which resulted, ultimately, from one
overarching concept.

As they saw it, modern Jewish history was best understood in
essentially dichotomous terms. Bipolarity served as the key, the
paradigmatic principle which supplied these works with their
underlying structure. On the one hand, there was the Jewish nation
which had tenaciously survived almost two millennia of exile and
dispersion by dint of its internal solidarity, faith and inventiveness.
On the other, there were the combined forces of change which, unless
creatively absorbed and organically integrated by the nation, could
only set in motion a process of inexorable erosion and a process of self-
destruction.

Ultimately, in the era after 1881, this existential collision would (in
this view of things) be transformed by the emergence of the new
nationalist movements which had found the way to combine tradition

and modernity in a new, a viable, synthesis. The national ideologies did not undermine but rather reinforced the unity of the Jewish people. The clash between the centrifugal and the centripetal forces, between disintegration and solidarity, between assimilation and community remained no less fundamental, but henceforward the scales would no longer be as heavily weighted against the group survival of the Jews.

In his analysis of modern European history, Dubnov developed the theory that during the periods of governmental liberalism and of a more open society the danger of national disintegration increased; while conversely reaction and resurgent Judeophobia acted to revitalize Jewish group solidarity:

> The internal processes of *assimilation*, on the one hand, and of *national consciousness* on the other, are closely tied to the external processes of emancipation and of reaction. The term 'assimilation' can be used to describe both the way in which either Jews are swept along, unconsciously as it were, into the current of the surrounding culture and also the way in which Jews consciously renounce their national identity – with the exception of the religious dimension – and come to include themselves in any given country as members of the dominant nation.[18]

Both Raphael Mahler and Shmuel Ettinger accepted the logic of this reasoning. Mahler placed particular emphasis on 1848. The revolutions of that year, he maintained, 'which for the world as a whole spelled progress, did not bring a Jewish rebirth, but on the contrary heralded a period of national disintegration and assimilation'.[19] And although Ettinger preferred to be less specific in dating the dynamics of assimilation he, too, could argue that,

> On the one hand, we find the centripetal force drawing individual Jews and various groups within the people to identify themselves with the Jewish past and with all Jews throughout the Diaspora, and on the other hand we see the centrifugal tendency pulling them apart and bringing them closer to their alien surroundings . . . There were periods, particularly in the second half of the nineteenth century and at the beginning of the twentieth century, when the centrifugal forces predominated. But the spread of modern antisemitism and the Nazi Holocaust led to a radical change.[20]

For his part, Ben-Zion Dinur likewise interpreted the modern history of the Jews in terms of challenge and response, disintegration and reintegration, although it should be noted that he specifically

disassociated himself from Dubnov's concept of an almost regular ebb
and flow:

> The feeling which was of such vital importance for all generations past
> – that the Jews constitute one people – now in modern times simply, as
> it were, evaporated. That uniform way of life which had made a Jew
> feel comfortable anywhere in the world from the moment that he set
> foot in a Jewish home was severely undermined, and in some countries
> it was reduced to little more than a memory from the lost past. The
> cultural co-operation which had linked the various communities had
> to all appearances come to a stop . . . The Hebrew which had acted as
> the cultural language of the united nation . . . had ceased to fulfil that
> function in most Jewish communities . . . And it is erroneous to
> associate these developments with specific periods of modern history,
> with particular periods of assimilation, of self negation. Rather, these
> phenomena represent permanent processes at work in all recent
> generations.[21]

The bipolar concept which was of such central importance here,
then, in many ways served the historian well. It had a very strong
emotive and political appeal; and as such it undoubtedly provided
him with a source of inspiration, of energy. But, no less significantly, it
acted as a compass, permitting him to orient himself in the vast and
infinitely complex expanses of modern Jewish history. It made it
possible to produce a coherent map of an otherwise all but
incomprehensible terrain, to create order out of chaos.

However, at the same time, this concept encouraged the tendency
to focus the spotlight on the extremes, thus leaving the middle
ground, although certainly not out of sight, still in the shadows. And,
likewise, it brought with it a view of the fundamental conflict as
ultimately a clash of opposing beliefs, ideologies, ideals. Even Mahler
concentrated attention primarily on ideology, even though as a
Marxist he insisted that this dimension of history was the by-product
of warring class interests.

It is above all, perhaps, in his analysis of two major themes in the
development of the Jewish people during the nineteenth century (or,
more accurately, during the hundred years from 1780 to 1880) –
enlightenment and emancipation – that the historian first finds
himself confronted by the clash between tradition and modernity. For
the members of the nationalist school of history, this was no simple
challenge, and the result was often paradoxical. As secular Jews,
dedicated to the cause of critical scholarship, and no less as committed
liberals or socialists they were obviously committed to the side of

'progress' against that of 'reaction'. But as nationalists analysing an era when tradition was in almost constant disarray and Jewish nationalism had as yet hardly emerged, they were pulled in exactly the opposite direction. If change spelled the end of community, or group survival, then even continued immobility was, in the last resort, to be preferred.

As a result, the Jewish Enlightenment movement – or Haskalah – was depicted in the classic works as positive in its original intentions but as profoundly flawed in its subsequent development. In so far and as long as the Haskalah movement, for example, employed Hebrew as its primary means of communication and even sought to bring about a literary renaissance in that language, it was seen as clearly acting within the communal, the national, framework. It represented a genuine attempt to combine the ancient and the modern in a new synthesis.

However, to the extent that the movement encouraged the replacement of Yiddish as the spoken, and Hebrew as the literary, language of the Jewish people by German (or whatever the official language was in any given state), it was treated in highly critical terms.

The linguistic issue was one of a number of the factors which combined to reduce sharply the status of Moses Mendelssohn, the dominant and founding figure in the German Haskalah movement. In the pre-nationalist era (or more specifically, until the publication of Peretz Smolenskin's attacks on the 'Berlin Haskalah' in such essays as his 'Am Olam' of 1872),[22] Mendelssohn had been almost universally admired within modernized Jewish circles ranging from that of neo-Orthodoxy led by Samson Raphael Hirsch to that of extreme Reform. He had combined (such had been the perception) all that was best in European and in Jewish culture, displaying absolute loyalty both to humanity and to the Jewish people, to the universal and to the particular.[23]

Dubnov, himself, in the early 1880s, before his conversion to the nationalist ideology, had still shared this view of Mendelssohn as the all but mythical figure, proud and harmonious, who had demonstrated to the Jews in the modern world how best to combine the old and the new.[24] But in his *History*, Dubnov, while acknowledging, *inter alia*, that Mendelssohn had been able to 'preserve an organic bond with his people whom he was anxious to enlighten and humanize',[25] was in many ways highly critical. In particular, he saw in Mendelssohn's translation of the Bible into German a major causal link in a process which was bound eventually to undermine the very foundations of the community. By the early nineteenth century, he wrote:

> The number of Jews drawn into the process of assimilation was already most significant and was growing year by year. One of the signs of this process was the fact that the German and French Jews in Alsace had repudiated their own national [*narodnyi*] language, encouraged by the propaganda which had been conducted by the Mendelssohnian school ever since the translation of the Bible into German. The state language found its way into every sphere of the people's life, into the family and the school, into literature and even into the synagogue. The new generations steadily alienated themselves from Jewry: first the generation of Henrietta Herz, of Mendelssohn's daughters . . .; and then that of Börne and Heine, Marx and Lassalle – such were the stages of the cultural Reformation.[26]

On the subject of Yiddish, Raphael Mahler was if anything even sharper, although he was ready enough to acknowledge that Mendelssohn (among other things, one of the founders of the Enlightenment journal, *Hameasef*) had sought to raise the level of Hebrew as a classical language. But, as he saw it,

> [Mendelssohn's] contempt for the spoken language of the people expressed the view of the new Jewish middle class, its hope of resembling the country's ruling classes in all things . . . Neither he nor any of the other *maskilim* . . . realized that by jettisoning Yiddish, they were destroying one of the chief foundations of a distinct Jewish culture.[27]

The extremely rapid transition made by the Jews in Central Europe from Yiddish and Hebrew to German was to be regarded, then, as only one among many symptoms of a profound malaise. The Berlin Haskalah had proved itself incapable of mastering the spiritual forces required to assure Jewish group survival in the modern age. It was thus no wonder that nearly all Mendelssohn's children converted to Christianity or that the Berlin community was hit by a veritable 'plague' of baptism by the end of the eighteenth century. The ultimate act of self-degradation (always strongly emphasized in mainstream historiography) was the notorious suggestion made in 1799 by David Friedländer, one of the community's most prominent leaders and an associate of Mendelssohn's in the 1780s, that the Berlin Jews should consider entering the church *en masse* (albeit freed from the obligation to recognize some of the more supernatural articles of the Christian faith).[28]

In contrast to the Berlin Haskalah, the *maskilim* in Galicia and in the Tsarist Empire retained the use of Hebrew (and even, at times, of Yiddish) in many of the journals, newspapers and books (both scholarly and literary) which they published throughout the pre-nationalist era ending in 1881, and beyond. This fact was, of course, fully recognized by the historians of the national school, but none the less the Haskalah movement in the Habsburg and Romanov Empires was also subjected to critical scrutiny. It was perceived as lacking roots in its own ancient soil. 'The Haskalah influences that infiltrated East European Jewry', as Shmuel Ettinger put it, 'came from the cultural centres of the West, and above all from Berlin'.[29]

As an isolated group of would-be reformers, the *maskilim* frequently found themselves forced to seek an alliance of one type or another with the autocratic regimes in Vienna or St Petersburg. The readiness to look for support from this source of power could only be described in negative terms by historians who perceived the Austrian and Russian despotisms as fundamentally hostile to the interests, and ultimately even to the survival, of the Jewish communities in their countries (the only major exception to this rule being the government of Alexander II in his early years).

Thus Dubnov was scathing in his description of the *maskilim* who co-operated with Joseph II in an attempt to impose a state school system on his Jewish subjects. The Emperor, he wrote, sought to impose his experiments on 'the Jews of Galicia whom he undertook to "correct" by harsh police measures [aided by the *maskil*] . . . Homberg whose task it was to execute the "policy" '.[30] Mahler noted that the 'Galician Jews adopted innumerable schemes to evade the decrees of "dictated enlightenment" ',[31] and that the net effect of the support offered to Joseph II by the *maskilim* was to 'precipitate a conflict between Haskalah and ultra-Orthodoxy that raged throughout the nineteenth century'.[32] And Ettinger described the policies of Nicholas I and the response of the Jews in very similar terms: 'Various *maskilim* suggested to him [Uvarov, the Minister of Education] that he introduce these changes by coercive methods.' However,

> the authorities did not have Jewish interests at heart but intended rather to manipulate the beliefs and concepts of the Jews and even to induce them to convert . . . [And] the Jews protected themselves by every means at their disposal.[33]

The result was to arouse 'doubts in the Jewish mind regarding the loyalty of the *maskilim* to their people'.[34]

Surveying the Haskalah as a whole, Shmuel Ettinger saw it as a

transitional movement which had understood what was perhaps the
basic issue facing the Jews in the modern world – 'how to preserve
their Jewish identity within . . . a society that was abolishing
corporative frameworks'[35] – but had failed to resolve it: 'The *maskilim*
were the first to seek solutions to this problem, and although they did
not achieve their aim, they induced Jewish society to seek out new
ways for itself.'[36]

The subject of Jewish emancipation brought with it, if anything,
even greater problems for the nationalist historian than that of the
Haskalah. After all, the cause of equality before the law, full civil and
political rights for the Jews, was one which made not only a rational
but also a profoundly emotional appeal to Dubnov and those who
followed him. Indeed, Dubnov and Dinur had both actively participated in the Russian revolution of 1905 which they had seen as aimed
at liberty for all, regardless of nationality or religion. Their commitment to the cause of liberation, of emancipation, was absolute.

However, here again the same paradox was at work. The greater
the liberty, equality and fraternity, the more powerful would become
the centrifugal forces threatening the survival of the Jewish people –
everywhere a small and scattered minority – at least until counter-
balanced by new forms of national education, consciousness, autonomy, sovereignty. As already noted, Dubnov even saw in this logic a
basic law governing the rhythm of modern Jewish history. The
outcome tended to be that the historians described in detail and in
highly positive terms the process of Jewish emancipation; and yet, at
the same time, focused attention on the extremely negative impact
which that process could exert on the will and ability of the Jews to
survive as a collectivity in the modern era.

If Berlin dominated the historiography of the Haskalah, it was
Paris which came to represent, to symbolize, the dangers inherent in
the politics of liberation. In fact, Dubnov saw German thought and
French political radicalism as the joint cause of crisis. Or, as he put it:
'The epoch of Mendelssohn and of the French Revolution developed
in the upper strata of Jewish society a tremendous centrifugal force.'[37]

Two chapters above all in the story of the revolutionary period
came to illustrate this theme. First, there was the long-drawn-out
struggle, which lasted some two years, until the National Assembly
finally decided in September 1791 to grant the Jews of France equal
rights. From the many speeches delivered on this controversial
subject in the Assembly, one in particular has been assigned special
significance by the historiographical tradition: the statement made in

December 1789 by Clermont-Tonnerre in support of Jewish emancipation:

> Everything must be refused to the Jews as a nation; everything must be granted to them as individuals. Each of them should individually be a citizen. But it is claimed that they do not want this. Very well, let them say so and they will have to be expelled . . . There cannot be a nation within a nation.[38]

As Dubnov understood it, here was the key message, the unwritten contract, which made the grant of civil rights acceptable to the French state. 'The Jews', he wrote, 'were granted equality in civil rights on the assumption that in the given country they constituted not a national, but only a religious, group within the ruling nation.'[39] Shmuel Ettinger summed up the debate of the years 1789 to 1791 in similar terms:

> Their opponents claimed that the Jews were a separate nation and not only a religious entity and, therefore, unable to claim any political rights. Their supporters, on the other hand, agreed to accept them into society as individuals who would be expected, to a greater or lesser extent, to disavow their heritage.[40]

Second, particular attention was likewise concentrated on the Assembly of Jewish Notables and the Sanhedrin brought together respectively in the years 1806 and 1807 by Napoleon in Paris. It was there and then that the leadership of the Jewish people in France (and in French-controlled Europe) was called upon to pay the belated price, as it were, for the civil equality ceded in 1791. Several declarations made by the Jewish representatives have been considered particularly humiliating, among them the statement that 'their religion commands them [the Jews] to regard the law of the land in all civil and political questions as the law of Israel'; and, still worse, the assurance given that 'today . . . the Jews no longer constitute a nation and have been privileged to be included in this great [French] nation'.[41]

Of this latter and similar resolutions Dubnov wrote:

> Taking its stand from the first on the slippery slope of concession and utility the Assembly fell even further. And when the issue arose of the relationship between civil patriotism and Jewish national sentiment, . . . the servility of the Assembly knew no bounds . . . With apparent light-heartedness (although in all probability it cost the better delegates a real inner struggle), [it] renounced all pretensions to broad communal self-government.[42]

And for his part, Mahler was more scathing still, seeing here the joint effort of a counter-revolutionary despotism and of the established Jewish bourgeoisie. The assertion that the Jews had ceased to be a nation was, as he put it, 'an undisguised betrayal of the unity, dreams and historic efforts of the Jewish people'.[43]

Interpreted along these lines, enlightenment and emancipation, Berlin and Paris, had combined to set their stamp on the history of the Jewish people in the century which separated Mendelssohn from the proto-Zionism of Pinsker. They set in motion the dynamics of change which were to predominate until 1881. The result (as seen by the mainstream historiography) was a fundamental metamorphosis – an ever-widening gulf which came to mark off the Jews of Western Europe from the Jews of Eastern Europe. It was in the light of this process that the historians surveyed the unfolding of events over the entire continent for the best part of the century. The division between West and East became an explanatory key of central importance.

Here, too, ideological polarization served as a main theme. At one extreme stood the religious reform movement which first emerged in Germany during the late Napoleonic years but only developed a clearly defined theology and philosophy of history in the 1840s. And at the other, primarily in the Pale of Settlement, Congress Poland and Galicia, stood the world of traditional Judaism, still devoted to age-old religious practice and still ruled by deep loyalty to the Jewish nation.

Reform Judaism which, once entrenched as a major force in Germany, spread to the United States, Hungary and to a number of countries in Western Europe, was understood to be the archetypical product of the Haskalah and of the emancipation process combined. From the Enlightenment movement it took its extreme rationalism and naive universalism. And it was the fierce political struggle to obtain equal rights in Prussia and the lesser German states in the decade leading up to 1848 which had propelled the movement to undertake nothing less than a root-and-branch reformation of its theology. In order to prove the absolute loyalty of the Jews to state and country they were ready to remove from the prayer-books any reference to the age-old hope for a return to the ancient homeland in Palestine and to interpret the dispersion of the Jews across the world not as Exile but as of positive value, as the way for the Jews to carry the message of monotheistic ethics to all of mankind, as a divinely ordained mission. Thus, the Reform movement made it possible to claim that the Jews constituted a strictly religious community divested of all national attributes, that they were Germans (or Poles or Frenchmen, as the case might be) of the 'Mosaic persuasion'.

In this way, reformed Judaism became the symbol, as it were, of a readiness to trade in age-old beliefs in exchange for civil equality and social acceptance. Writing of Abraham Geiger, one of the founding fathers of the movement (as well as of Samson Raphael Hirsch who, although neo-Orthodox, likewise stressed the strictly religious nature of the Jewish people), Dubnov argued that he had erred in denying

> the idea of the eternal [Jewish] *nation* . . . Geiger and Hirsch negated the Jewish people [*evreistvo*] as a national *individuum* and defined it as only a religious entity. In so doing, they reconciled themselves to *national* assimilation which, in the final resort, is bound to lead to the total dissolution of the Jews among the other nations – to the disappearance of that vital organism which sustains Judaism.[44]

The remark, by now much quoted, made by Geiger in a letter to Darenbourg in 1840 during the affair of the Damascus blood libel could be seen as typical. 'It is quite honourable', he then wrote, 'that eminent people are manifesting solidarity with their persecuted brethren, but . . . in my eyes it is more important that Jews in Prussia should be allowed to become pharmacists or lawyers than that Jews in Asia or Africa be rescued'.[45]

In contrast to the essential pusillanimity thus exemplified by the Reform movement was the stubborn refusal of the traditional Jews to desert their own way of life. Mahler could, for example, describe the struggle for the soul of Hungarian Jewry set in motion by the reforming theories of Aaron Chorin in the 1820s as 'a conflict that was to continue for several decades between the Orthodox and the Enlightened Hungarian Jews – between religious conservatism and national Jewish loyalty, on the one hand, and assimilation, on the other'.[46]

The two modes of Jewish life, however, were seen as divided not only by ideological and geographical but also by sociological factors. There was a major strand of populism in the thinking of Dubnov which was shared in large part by his students and successors; while, for his part, Mahler translated the general concepts of the 'people' or the 'masses', as opposed to the social elites, into specifically class terms. In his interpretation, the economic interests of the German-Jewish bourgeoisie lay at the root of its active 'assimilationism' and its antinational Judaism. (In so far as the Italian or American Jewish middle class did not feel pressured similarly by state and society to

prove its loyalty demonstratively, it could therefore remain 'undis-
turbed in its loyalty to the Jewish people's historical goal'.)[47]
However, it was Dinur, perhaps, who provided the sharpest formulation of a Jewish world divided in two:

> between, on the one side, a Jewish world conscious of its own worth
> and, on the other, a form of Jewish existence characterized by self-
> negation; between on the one side the maximal degree of Jewishness
> possible in the Diaspora – with a mass population of Jews closely
> concentrated together in townlets, towns and metropolitan centres
> and united by a common way of life, by self-consciousness and
> confidence in their own world; and on the other, a minimal degree of
> Jewishness; small numbers; a diffused minority with no clearly distinct
> way of life; highly self-effacing and ready to make do with only the very
> vaguest traces of the ancestral heritage.[48]

Broadly speaking, Dinur concluded, this division was that dividing
the Eastern European Jews from the Western Jews.[49]

Of course, Dinur hastened to qualify this statement. Things were in
reality by no means as neat. In so far as the dichotomy was partially
rooted in socio-economic factors, the 'Western' pattern was carried
eastward by the spread of capitalism and modern enterprise. And,
conversely, the 'Eastern' way of life was carried to the West by the
massive emigration in the latter years of the nineteenth century. The
two worlds were profoundly alienated from each other but none the
less increasingly came into contact and interacted. What is more,
Dinur by no means neglected the fact that from the 1830s onwards, at
least, the communities in the West displayed a marked measure of
political activism in defence of their own group interests and those of
the Jewish people at large. He noted the systematic campaigns
mounted in Prussia and England, for example, to win equal rights.
And he described the way in which the representative Jewish bodies
in England and France developed interventionist policies on behalf of
communities in many parts of the world during their moments of
crisis and danger – a mode of political behaviour which culminated in
1860 in the foundation of the Alliance Israélite Universelle.

His analysis of the factors which made possible political action of
this type was detailed and most convincing. He emphasized the key
role played by the growth of a modern Jewish press in many countries;
by the increased self-confidence of the *haute bourgeoisie*; and by the
emergence of an influential stratum of writers, journalists and
politicians (Heine, Börne, Riesser, Crémieux) whose experience in
the world at large could be harnessed at times to defend specifically
Jewish interests.[50]

Dinur was certainly no exception here: the politics of Western Jewry in the era of emancipation was assigned an honourable place by the mainstream historiography.[51] The problem, though, was how to explain the underlying motivation which had produced and sustained this phenomenon in the first place. After all, as defined by Dinur himself, the period from 1789 to 1881 was primarily – and here the Jews of the West had set the pattern – the era of 'national disintegration and religious adaptation'.[52] Given this overriding trend, the emergence of Jewish political activism in the West in the middle decades of the century presented the historian with something of an anomaly.

In consequence, the politics of this type, and at that time, was generally treated as the exception which proved the rule. It was explained partly as a residual traditionalism, as the persistent survival – despite, and in opposition to – modernity of age-old modes of response; as 'intercessionism' of one kind or another (*shtadlanut*, perhaps, or *pidyon shvuim* – the ransom of prisoners). But the assertion of world-wide Jewish solidarity was also attributed at times, para-doxically, to the very assimilationism which it seemed so crassly to deny. ('It is possible', suggested Shmuel Ettinger, for example, 'that . . . the concern of the Jews of Central and Western Europe . . . emanated from their realisation that as long as the "Jewish question" existed even in some remote location they could not be sure of their own total integration.')[53]

Finally, the Western model of Jewish politics was seen, too, as a hesitant and tentative reassertion of the group spirit, as a centripetal force, which was best to be understood as an early, inchoate and still not conscious anticipation of modern nationalism. 'Here was the beginning', wrote Dubnov of the response to the Damascus case of 1840, 'of future attempts to consolidate Jewry – at first for philan-thropical, cultural and political mutual aid, but later on an avowedly national basis'.[54] (However, he none the less insisted that the Jews of the West in the 1840s were still strongly opposed to the few overtly proto-Zionist plans published at the time 'anonymously', by authors who feared 'being dubbed utopians'. 'The assimilated leaders of Western Jewry', he concluded, 'distanced themselves from this national idea.')[55]

When viewed retroactively, it is possible to discern a clear contrast between the historiographical tradition which leads back to Dubnov and the kind of historical studies which have become characteristic in recent decades. It is not that one overarching architectonic paradigm has replaced another. On the contrary, the changing perceptions and methods have resulted in a process of fragmentation. If a powerfully reductionist force acted to give shape and direction to the classic works, the contemporary mood is antireductionist.

The historical process is thus perceived in terms not of bipolarity but of multiplicity. Instead of the one basic conflict between centrifugality and centripetality, now a great variety of autonomous processes, independent variables, are traced as they interact in constantly new permutations. It is as if in this sphere, too, Newton's fixed laws of physics had been undermined and replaced by the apparently random unpredictability of quantum mechanics. Or, in other words, the focus has shifted from the extremes, from the dichotomous archetypes, to that middle ground where it is no easy task to distinguish the exceptions from the rules.

There are, no doubt, many factors which have combined to bring about this changing intellectual climate and it is certainly far too early to enumerate – let alone evaluate – them in any but the most tentative terms. But it is clear enough that the decline in the bitter dispute between the Jewish nationalists and the antinationalists (or 'assimilationists' as their opponents termed them) has been of key importance. The Holocaust and the establishment of the State of Israel were developments of such momentous, indeed incredible, proportions that together they brought an abrupt halt to this conflict that had divided the Jewish world against itself in the years from 1881 to 1939. It was a powerful and exclusive ideological commitment which had inspired Dubnov and his successors and provided their work with its imposing structure. They were historians *engagés*.

With the schism between the nationalists and their opponents becoming a thing of the past, Jewish historiography was bound to turn in new directions – and this was doubly true given the fact that Europe and the Americas since 1945 have proved to be relatively free of violence, thus encouraging if not an actual 'end of ideology', then at least more latitudinarian attitudes not only in the present but also towards the past. As a result, the way was open for a wide variety of institutional and methodological factors to assert or reassert themselves.

Thus it is possible, for example, to perceive a resurgence, particularly in the United States of the traditions of German-Jewish scholarship. The Hebrew Union College of the Reform, and the Jewish Theological Seminary of the Conservative, movements which in varying degrees were both modelled on and influenced by similar institutions established in nineteenth-century Germany, now invested much greater efforts in the teaching and research of modern history. At the same time, German-Jewish scholars, such as Alexander Altmann and Nahum Glatzer, who had emigrated from Nazi Germany, took up teaching positions at American universities; from among their students came many future scholars. And the Leo Baeck Institute established in both New York and London after the Second World War gradually built up a major reputation as a research centre through its many high-quality publications on German Jewry.[56]

Of course, German-Jewish historiography was no more all of a piece than that of Eastern Europe. Mention, for example, has already been made of Gershom Scholem's affinity for the world-outlook of the Russian Zionists, the *Ostjuden*, which went together with his antipathy for the attitudes exemplified, as he saw it, in the *Wissenschaft des Judentums* (although, as David Biale has pointed out, his own work in many ways followed, paradoxically, patterns of scholarship familiar from Germany).[57]

But, none the less, German-Jewish historiography, so powerfully influenced by the genius of Heinrich Graetz, was marked by its own distinguishing characteristics. In contrast to the Dubnov school, it manifested a deep interest in theology and theological thought for their own sake; and this fact, in turn, reflected a tendency to see the Jews as inextricably constituting both a religion and a people (however variously that latter term was defined). It carried with it the stamp both of the German philosophic school and of the Rankean faith in an objective and detached mode of historical scholarship. Alexander Altmann's *magnum opus* was his authoritative (and admiring) biography of Moses Mendelssohn;[58] while Nahum Glatzer devoted much of his research to Leopold Zunz (the leading figure in the first generation of the *Wissenschaft des Judentums*) and to Franz Rosenzweig (existentialist, philosopher, theologian).[59]

Of greater influence still in stimulating historiographical change has been the growing impact exerted by the social sciences on the historians in recent times. For the student of modern Jewish history, the study – both 'empirical' and theoretical – of ethnicity, national consciousness and nationalism by sociologists and cultural anthropologists has acted to change perceptions to a remarkable extent.[60] Sociology and anthropology have, likewise, combined to encourage the growth of microcosmic studies, local and urban histories, as well as the examination of everyday life as lived in the past in a particular time and place.[61] Again, economics and demography have similarly stimulated research beyond the boundaries of political, ideological and cultural history.[62] (A noteworthy side-effect of this particular development has been a renewed interest in a substratum of the Eastern European school of Jewish historiography: the socio-economic research associated initially with the socialist territorialist movement. With its emphasis on world-wide migrationary trends and the universal laws of the market, it had from the first acted to counteract the concept of a Jewish people divided qualitatively between East and West.)[63]

Finally, it can certainly be argued that the mainstream historio-graphical tradition had itself prepared the ground in many ways for its own revision. It is sufficient here perhaps to suggest two examples. First, Dubnov himself, from his middle years onward, declared it as his aim to write 'sociological' history;[64] he can hardly be said to have succeeded, as Salo Wittmayer Baron has pointed out,[65] but he laid down the challenge which others (for example, Baron himself and Jacob Katz)[66] soon took up.

Again, as we have noted, the political activism of the 'assimilated' Jews in the West was not ignored in the classic works but rather treated as something of an aberration, an anomaly or an anachron-ism, thus stimulating new research on this subject which could hardly be contained for long in an explanatory framework so paradoxical and ultimately unsatisfactory. (Indeed, when it came to this and similar issues, Shmuel Ettinger in some of his later research had clearly moved away from the bipolar perspective in favour of more dialectical, more complex theories. And he encouraged his students and colleagues to do likewise.)[67]

If the classic historians sought the underlying laws of development, the grand generalizations, then the newer history rests more on differentiation. Indeed, its major contribution can, perhaps, be said to lie in making distinctions between concepts and processes previ-ously seen as part of a single causal chain.

A clear example of this trend is the fact that in recent studies the Haskalah movement is no longer treated as necessarily a – let alone the – basic centrifugal force in a process leading from community to assimilation. Thus, once modernization is perceived as primarily a socio-economic phenomenon, ideology becomes only one among the many varied factors of change. Urbanization, industrialization, migration, market forces and the opportunities (educational, occu-pational, cultural) available all combined to undermine the tra-ditional life of the Jewish people in nineteenth-century Europe. The

Haskalah movement was, of course, in part the product of such forces and, depending on time and place, itself contributed to the momentum of change. But, in recent studies, its significance has been much reduced. There is little argument today with the view of those sociologists who describe 'modernisation . . . as a kind of tidal wave sweeping out from the West across the globe and bringing in its train industry, science and their social and political consequences'.[68] (Of course, it should be added at once that even tidal waves break when they come up against natural barriers of sufficient height and strength, but that is a subject which will be discussed separately below.)

In his history of Jewish life in Georgian England, Todd Endelman reached the conclusion that the integration of the Jews into the society at large was not only very rapid but actually had very little to do with issues of ideology, theory and faith.[69] Or as he has summarized his findings elsewhere:

> Most Jewish historians until recently looked to the German Jewish experience as the paradigm for the transformation of European Jewry . . . [But] to paraphrase Marx – and to put the matter crudely – German Jews were thinking what Jews elsewhere, and in England in particular, were already doing . . . In England acculturation and integration were well advanced before the 1770s.[70]

And Steven J. Zipperstein in his studies of the Jews in Odessa has reached very similar conclusions. The breakneck development of the Russian port-city in the early nineteenth century generated the demands for modern education and cultural activity which sought many outlets; the Germanizing *maskilim* from Galicia had not produced this situation and they were by no means alone in responding to it. 'The assumption', he has written,

> that the development of this [the Haskalah] movement is synonymous with the modernisation of Russian Jewry focuses attention primarily on the history of ideas and allows little attention to be paid to the social components of the transformation.[71]

Modernization theory, however, has proved to be only one of the factors leading to a different perception of the Haskalah and its contribution to assimilation. The concentration on regional studies (whether of a specific city, locality or country), rather than on overall analysis, has made it logical to emphasize the high degree of autonomy which characterized the movement in different areas. What has emerged as a result is a picture painted less in black and

white and more in various shades of grey. The *maskilim* in Bohemia, in
particular, but also in Hungary and in the Tsarist Empire, are now
described for the most part as far removed in their thinking from the
more radical representatives of the Berlin Haskalah.

The authors contributing to the recent collection of essays edited by
Jacob Katz, *Towards Modernity*, nearly all chose to elaborate on this
theme. Emanuel Etkes, for example, emphasized that the Russian
maskilim, admirers though they were of Berlin, 'did not envision
themselves breaking down barriers and throwing off the yoke of
Torah'.[72] And of the movement in Hungary, Michael Silber wrote
that 'the boundaries between rabbinic and Haskalah cultures were
not sharply defined'.[73] Similarly, Hillel Kieval could argue that the
maskilim in Prague

> confidently pursued a policy of accommodation weaving together
> European rationalism, respect for religious sensitivities and loyalty to
> Jewish traditions.[74]

Again, despite the support that Trieste Jews gave to Wessely and
Homberg (who lived in that city from 1782 to 1787), 'their sense of
cultural continuity with their own, and with medieval Sephardic
traditions', concluded Lois Dubin, 'permitted them to see harmony
between old and new'.[75]

Finally, the relationship between the *maskilim* and the despotic
regimes of Central and Eastern Europe, both of the 'enlightened'
and the unenlightened variety, has, likewise, come in for its share of
re-examination in recent years. Even the most extreme case, the
Tsarist government, always seen with reason as the bastion of
violently anti-Jewish policies in Europe, has emerged from this
process of revision as motivated less by the desire to uproot, persecute
or forcibly convert its large Jewish population and more by
mercantilist and utilitarian strategies inevitably distorted by, and
contradictorily interpreted within the bureaucratic labyrinth.[76]

The belief of the *maskilim* that they, in principle, shared certain
common ground with the regime thus comes to look not so much like
crass self-delusion bordering on betrayal, but rather as grounded on a
calculated risk. In his book on the Jews in the period of Nicholas I,
Michael Stanislawski even argues that in some way the gamble of the
maskilim on the regime paid off. The leadership of Russian Jewry
(including Leon Pinsker) which emerged during the reign of
Alexander II had been educated to a large extent, after all, in the
schools, and in the rabbinical seminaries in Vilna and Zhitomir,

established by the state during the reign of Nicholas I. In Stanislawski's words:

> Despite the intense opposition of the Orthodox, and hence the modest enrollments, the schools . . . educated a large part of the next cohort of the Russian-Jewish intellectual elite and provided the *maskilim* with employment opportunities and financial security. Confident of their eventual victory and the inevitable liberation, the *maskilim* became, by the end of Nicholas's rule, a self-conscious and self-confident intelligentsia, dedicated to creating a new life and culture for Russia's Jews.[77]

The tendency to uncouple the Haskalah (a cultural and elitist movement) from the socio-economic process of modernization reflects, in part, a more fundamental distinction absorbed by the newer historiography – the differentiation made between the concepts of 'acculturation' and 'assimilation'.

To national historians such as Dubnov and Mahler it seemed a truism that the replacement of Hebrew and Yiddish by modern European languages was bound to carry the Jewish people very far towards its complete assimilation, towards its total disappearance, its self-destruction. Deprived of state and territory, the Jews had only their language in which to maintain and develop a coherent and separate national life. The division in the nineteenth century between the Jews of Eastern Europe and those of Western Europe, between community and assimilation, was understood primarily in terms of linguistic dynamics; on the one side, the historic languages of the Jewish nation had been not only preserved but also cultivated and developed; on the other, they had been set aside, abandoned.

But as the concept of 'acculturation' established itself, so the language issue was bound to lose its exclusive significance and become only one among the many factors taken into account by the historians in analysing the metamorphosis undergone by Jewish group consciousness.

It appears to be widely acknowledged that it was the sociologist Milton M. Gordon who, with his book of 1964, *Assimilation in American Life*,[78] did more than anybody else to win acceptance for the idea that 'acculturation' should be clearly distinguished from 'assimilation'. And there is no question that Gordon has been highly influential in disseminating both his sociological lexicon and his methods of analysis.

However, Gordon's work is only part of a much broader and

growing tendency among sociologists, anthropologists, political scientists and historians (apparent since the 1960s) to re-examine such phenomena as ethnicity, nationality and nationalism. As a safe generalization, it can be said that many, although by no means all of the scholars involved, have concluded that national and ethnic consciousness is best understood not as the product of external forces, whether socio-economic, political or linguistic, but rather as an independent factor in its own right.[79] In other words, they reject the unidirectional, reductionist and determinist interpretations common to much of the Marxist, neo-Marxist and sociological (functionalist, structuralist; developmental) writings on this subject.

For the Jewish historians, this growing corpus of scholarly investigation has proved to be of the greatest significance. It encourages a view of group consciousness as developing in open-ended, unpredictable and idiosyncratic ways. Thus the loss of linguistic and cultural distinctiveness is not seen as necessarily bringing with it a loss of ethnic identity. Substitute forms of cohesion can be forged round new institutions, ideologies and causes, be they religious, philanthropic or political.

The studies of Gordon and many other sociologists have focused attention on structural factors which, under certain circumstances, prevent acculturation from leading on to 'complete assimilation'.[80] As long as Jews (or, for that matter, the members of any other *ethos*) tend to live in the same neighbourhoods, attend the same schools, work in the same very specific branches of the economy, attend the same clubs and above all find their friends and marriage partners within the same group, they can be expected to survive indefinitely as a separate entity. There is no guarantee that these conditions will always hold. Even in nineteenth-century Europe they did not prevail universally, but recent studies have emphasized how frequently they were of great importance almost everywhere, whether in Vienna, Berlin, Paris or London.[81]

For their part, cultural anthropologists have sought to explain the tenacity, the sheer will to survive, often demonstrated by ethnic groups when threatened by the homogenizing forces of modernization. They have emphasized the weight of the past on the present; the power of what they term 'primordial' loyalties; the instinctive mechanisms of 'boundary maintenance'; the persistent attraction exerted by historically rooted symbols and myths; and the ultimately subjective nature of ethnic or national identities.

And these theories, too, have influenced our perceptions of Jewish history in the nineteenth century, bringing with them as they do a heightened awareness of the fact that group loyalties in modern society tend to overlap in a wide variety of complex and even contradictory ways, and that the responses to a multicultural environment will be highly differentiated. Here is an issue, after all, touching on the deep inner core of the individual self.

All in all, the thesis that acculturation does not necessarily lead to assimilation has served to undermine the conception of Jewish history in nineteenth-century Europe as bipolar, sharply divided between East and West. In recent years, historians have focused the spotlight more on the modernizing processes gaining momentum within the Jewish communities of Eastern Europe; and, at the same time, on the forces of reintegration, group cohesion, historical continuity and ethnic consciousness at work in the West.

The process of historiographical re-examination has, by now, reached and, in varying degrees, undermined many of the other theses once regarded as all but axiomatic. It will suffice to mention two additional areas of particular interest to the historian of nineteenth-century Jewry: those of theology and scholarship, on the one hand, and of Jewish politics, on the other.

For the nationalist school of historiography, as already noted, the consolidation of the Reform movement was generally seen as organically linked to the struggle for emancipation. The acquisition of equal rights could not be obtained in the German states unless a price was paid; and according to the terms of this implicit social contract, the Jews had, therefore, to renounce all mention of an eventual national restoration to Zion, to their own homeland. Once consolidated in Germany, the movement, with its antinational ethos, spread to other countries in Central and Western Europe as well as to the United States (although not to the Tsarist Empire).

Again, in a very similar way, the extraordinarily influential school of modern Jewish scholarship in Germany, the *Wissenschaft des Judentums* was treated with much greater sympathy than the Reform movement; but it, too, was accused of adopting an 'apologetic' tone and tendentious methods of selectivity in order to facilitate (or, later, consolidate) the process of emancipation.

However, here too the tendency today is to disentangle processes previously regarded as organically united. And as a result, these two movements are increasingly analysed as following their own paths of development, as interacting with their environment according to their own inner logic. The history of the Reform movement has, thus, been subtly redrawn. Today, for example, much more emphasis is put on the fact that the radical reforming wing represented by Holdheim never, in fact, succeeded in becoming anything other than highly marginal within the organized life of German Jewry.[82]

In general, the Jewish communities in Germany remained united (although there were, of course, exceptional cases, the most notable of which was Samson Raphael Hirsch's *Austrittsgemeinde*) and, in consequence, there was strong pressure to maintain a minimal degree of consensus. The fact that the communities were granted the power of taxation by the state and thus enjoyed quasi-governmental status served to reinforce this tendency, as did the predominantly conservative political environment which prevailed in Germany after 1848. To the extent that reformers in Central Europe succeeded in winning truly significant support, they did so by concentrating on issues of style rather than of theological substance. The famous rabbi Isak Noah Mannheimer of Vienna who followed this path and exerted great influence throughout the Habsburg Empire, above all in Hungary, has come to replace Holdheim for the historians as the archetype of the reform leader in Germany and in the Habsburg Empire.[83]

In contrast, it was in the United States, where the question of equal rights had long been settled (if it had ever really existed), that radical Reform truly took hold, carried across the seas by the great German-Jewish emigration of the middle of the century. In the rabbinical declaration issued in Pittsburgh in 1885,[84] Holdheim's theology enjoyed its triumph. This startling development, though, resulted not from the struggle for emancipation, but rather from its absence, from the internalization of the liberal credo with its belief in the inevitability of progress, in the imminent triumph of human brotherhood and in the universality of ethical absolutes.

However, it is typical of the newer historiography that, even when it comes to the American Reform movement, attention is paid as much to the limitations as to the extremes of change. Benny Kraut, for example, has made the point that

> while Felsenthal alone among the radicals became an outspoken advocate of Zionism, by the turn of the century, even [Samuel] Hirsch and Kohler employed terms like 'Jewish people', 'Jewish race' and 'Jewish nation' . . . [which] seems almost contradictory to the standard dichotomous stereotype of an antiethnic or antinational classical Reform Judaism.[85]

For the most part (to repeat ourselves), the revisionism under discussion here has developed cumulatively, hesitantly and almost imperceptibly. But this has not been the case when it comes to the issue of the *Wissenschaft des Judentums*. in the mid 1970s, two historians, Ismar Schorsch and Gershon Cohen, published articles defending the school of nineteenth-century German-Jewish scholarship in the most outspoken terms. They therein responded directly to Gershom Scholem's argument that the *Wissenschaft des Judentums* had (in part consciously, in part not) served the cause of apologetics, accommodation, assimilation.

Men such as Zunz and Geiger, in Scholem's view, had repudiated the romanticism without which the historian of a nation cannot respond creatively to the past. Their ideology of rationalism was motivated by an obvious anxiety to uphold universal values in the face of the German nationalist Judeophobia which drew so much of its strength from romanticism. In thus cultivating the values of detachment and (a spurious) objectivity, they demonstrated that they had reconciled themselves to the continued decline and disintegration of the Jewish people. To have written in a spirit of rebellion against accommodationism, to have aroused new life and hope in the nation, would have cut them off from the established Jewish community in Germany; and that was a risk which they were not prepared to take. The entire enterprise recalled the mortuary and Scholem saw as typical Steinschneider's remark to one of his students that 'we have no other task but to provide all this with a "decent" burial'.[86] 'You see before you', wrote Scholem,

> giants who for their own reasons have turned themselves into grave-diggers, embalmers and even eulogizers; giants who act as dwarfs collecting plants in the fields of the past, drying them to make sure that the sap of life is eliminated and then putting them into a book – or is it a grave?[87]

As Schorsch saw it, this critique was not only 'harsh and tendentious', but actually bore almost no relationship to the facts. 'If', he wrote,

> the motive of giving Judaism a decent burial is verifiable anywhere in the *Wissenschaft* movement, it is only in the early work of Isaak Jost, where the mood fluctuates between animosity and ambivalance. It is this pervasive antagonism which is so conspicuously absent from the work of Zunz.[88]

For his part, Gershon Cohen maintained that the archetypal representative of the movement was in reality Hermann Graetz. For Scholem, Graetz was merely the remarkable exception who proved the rule – the historian who, despite his belief in the illusory liberal 'utopia', none the less, with his loyalty to romanticism, had played a 'constructive' role. But Cohen now argued that:

> if anyone pretended about his real motives it was not Zunz, Geiger, Frankel, Graetz or David Hoffman . . . but Moritz Steinschneider the would-be Jewish mortician of Jewish learning and literature. If Steinschneider deserves any reproach, I submit, it is for his *dissimulating* that his work aimed at giving Judaism a decent burial. But [he] . . . was a maverick in many ways . . . and why should a culture be evaluated by its eccentrics? . . . German-Jewish scholarship was a massive effort at reinfusing vitality into what many Jews had understandably come to regard as a fossil.[89]

In his insistence that the history of the Jews was the history not simply of a religion, but also of a people, a nation, Graetz spoke not for himself alone but for the entire circle associated with the Jewish Theological Seminary in Breslau (founded by Zacharias Frankel in 1854). 'Von Treitschke', concluded Cohen,

> may well have been a Jew-hater but he . . . understood very well what Graetz's gut conception of Jewish history and the Jewish people was. Graetz could not sunder Judaism from the Jewish people, and his monumental *Geschichte* will forever remain not only one of the classic expositions of Jewish history, but one of the great nineteenth-century affirmations of the national and religious integrity of world Jewry.[90]

(Note should be taken here, perhaps, of the fact that Cohen and Schorsch would both be appointed in later years, and in succession, to the post of chancellor of the Jewish Theological Seminary in New York which in many ways has, throughout, taken Breslau as its model.)

If the history of Reform Judaism and of the *Wissenschaft des Judentums* has understandably become a subject of great interest to scholars in America, the study of modern Jewish politics has, for equally obvious reasons, attracted especial attention from historians who teach at Israeli universities. In this area of research, what has been directly challenged is the assumption that Jewish politics as a fully fledged and truly modern phenomenon was produced by the nationalist upsurge of – and thus post-dates – the year 1881. (To permit myself a personal note, I should perhaps point out that in my own work I have, albeit with qualification, elaborated on the idea that 1881 did represent a major turning-point in Jewish history and so must declare myself here as among those now subject to the revisionist critique.)[91]

The bipolar model – sharply dividing the nationalist from the pre-nationalist era – has come under fire from two opposing flanks. On the one side, there are a number of Israeli historians (Yaakov Kaniel and Arye Morgenstern, for example)[92] who argue forcefully that the factor of tradition in the making of Jewish nationalism has been much underestimated; that Palestine – the land of Israel – had been resettled steadily by Jews since the eighteenth century or even earlier; and that the waves of immigration to that country after 1881 were made up largely of religious Jews hardly different in type or motivation from those who had come earlier.

In short, continuity was more important than change. (This thesis was, no doubt, implicit in Dinur's emphasis on the explosive proto-Zionism of the traditional world, but he none the less gloried in the immense power of the revolutionary forces unleashed by modernity.) The attempt of recent years to blur, in this way, the dividing line separating the old from the new has proved to be highly controversial,[93] but it touches only tangentially on the theme of this book.

In contrast, it is possible to identify an opposing group of historians whose work clearly falls within the revisionist framework described here. When historians such as Michael Graetz, and Eli Lederhendler (both contributors to this volume) and Israel Bartal subvert the dichotomous concept, they do so by asserting the primacy not of tradition, but of modernity. They describe how novel forms of Jewish political activism and organization took shape gradually but with growing momentum throughout the course of many decades before 1881.

The new politics, as depicted in studies of this genre, was *sui generis* neither anachronistic nor anomalous, and cannot be reduced conceptually either to a residual traditionalism or to a proto-, or precocious, nationalism. Thus, in his book on the origins of the Alliance Israélite Universelle, Michael Graetz demonstrated that, founded in 1860, it was the creation of highly acculturated, and (even in many cases) marginal Jews, acting as such. They were impelled by a complex amalgam of motives: an abiding commitment to liberal and universalistic values; and alienation from the French intelligentsia which in their eyes hardly appeared to be living up to those values; a revival of Jewish ethnic consciousness (partly in

consequence of that alienation); and a renewed sense of solidarity
with the Jewish people in France and world-wide. Eventually, they
found themselves allied to equally modernized members of the
French-Jewish establishment, among them leading figures in the
financial elite of the country.[94]

In the fight for equal rights at home and for the security of Jews
endangered abroad, the Jewish communities in the West had found a
cause which combined the dominant ideology of the middle of the
century (the doctrine of human rights and constitutionalism) with
loyalty to the ethnic group (variously defined in religious, populist or
quasi-national terms). I have suggested elsewhere that this specific
form of Jewish political activism, which is associated with such figures
as Crémieux, Riesser and Montefiore and with such organizations as
the Alliance, the Board of Deputies and the Anglo-Jewish Association, can, perhaps, best be termed 'emancipationist' as distinct from
the 'traditional' and from the 'auto-emancipationist' or national
models of Jewish politics.[95] (In this field as in others already discussed,
revisionism has brought with it the 'rediscovery', as it were, of
historians whose topics of interest fell outside the area spotlighted by
nationalist historiography. Such diverse names as Cyrus Adler and
Lucien Wolf immediately come to mind.)[96]

Israel Bartal's work on early Jewish nationalism (or 'national
consciousness') as it developed in the middle decades of the
nineteenth century, can be seen as complementing that of Michael
Graetz. He has consistently argued that such nationalism was in the
making from the 1830s; was engendered primarily by the joint impact
made on the Jewish world by the Enlightenment, by emancipation,
by romanticism and by Christian millenarianism; and that, to no
small extent, it had to 'rediscover' the traditional community, motifs
and symbols.[97]

The political activism of Western organizations such as the Board
of Deputies and the Alliance Israélite Universelle, even though their
own ideology was not nationalist, none the less inspired the self-
confidence, the optimism and the faith in resurgent Jewish power,
which alone made possible the plans formulated from the 1830s
onwards for the resettlement of the Jewish people in Palestine. Within
the emergent nationalist circles, the traditional and the modern
groups acted on totally different premises but, none the less, coexisted
uneasily in a dialectical relationship; influencing now the one, now
the other; mutually dependent. Or as it was put in the essay of 1981

published jointly by Bartal and Shmuel Ettinger (who, as already noted, was ready enough to re-examine established formulas):

> The processes of interaction between tradition and innovation; between the pre-modern and the acculturated worlds; between the hopes inspired by emancipation and the sense of alienation, of being rejected – all made themselves strongly felt during the three different periods in which modern national consciousness, then emerging, discovered the pull of Palestine – the forties, the sixties and the early eighties of the nineteenth century.[98]

In such passages as these, then, the emphasis is not on the opposing poles *per se*, but on their points of contact, on the overlap of continuity and change, on 1881 as culmination rather than revolution.

In his recent book, *The Road to Modern Jewish Politics*,[99] as well as in a number of his articles on the political activism of the Russian Jews, Eli Lederhendler has suggested a similar redrawing of the map. At one level, it is true, he has simply undertaken to analyse the role of the modernizing Jewish intelligentsia in the Tsarist Empire during the reigns of Nicholas I and Alexander II from a more empathetic vantage point; or, in other words, to add his contribution to the rehabilitation of the Haskalah movement. He argues that the *maskilim*, in their attempt to recruit the support of the regime, not only had much logic on their side but had actually proved able to appropriate and redefine traditional political functions. 'If by 1881', writes Lederhendler,

> men like Gordon, Lilienblum, Leon Pinsker and their fellow *maskilim* were playing leadership roles in Russian Jewish politics, it is clear that somehow the *maskilim* were able, over the course of two generations, to transform a position on the extreme periphery of Jewish life into a beachhead of considerable strategic advantage and even a certain degree of legitimacy. It is also clear that they must have accomplished this not simply by dint of cultural or literary activity but through a political struggle.[100]

Or, as he put it elsewhere:

> For the *maskilim*, the defense of the Jews' human dignity was a way in which they could declare their unequivocal affinity to their community, while allowing them scope to promote the value of enlightened religious tolerance, the importance of learning the language of the land and earning the trust of the state . . . Their political activities were the factor that transformed them from literati to public figures.[101]

At another level, though, Lederhendler goes further. The rapid growth during the years 1860 to 1880 of the Jewish press (published variously in Hebrew, Yiddish, Russian and Polish) brought with it, in his estimate, a qualitative change in the politics of Russian Jewry. Control over this medium rapidly conferred on the intelligentsia the power to disseminate their ideas on a totally new scale; to appeal alike to the Jewish public, Russian opinion and governmental authority; to earn prestige and influence on a scale hitherto utterly denied to them; and to establish themselves as a political leadership group. They developed novel modes of political rhetoric (part traditional, part radical) and ambitious strategies of change.

The strong focus thus directed on to the period of Alexander II sharply reduces the scale of 1881 as the great watershed year. 'In other words', asks Lederhendler,

> can ideological change really be best understood as a self-generating and self-explaining process or ought one to look for underlying structural changes in the political life of [the] society?[102]

Conclusion

Any attempt such as that made here to isolate and sharply define major trends of thought in a particular area of scholarship must, by its very nature, be flawed. A high degree of selectivity and subjectivity is unavoidable. For any statement chosen from the historiographical canon as representative, quintessential, another can be found (if so desired) to prove the opposite. None the less, the essays collected in this volume do, surely, in varying degrees, reflect a changing mood as well as changing methods. And an attempt to set that change in context can possibly serve to clarify issues otherwise left undefined.

It has been our contention here that there is an historiographical school that can be defined as Eastern European, or as nationalist, or as following the tradition of Dubnov; that it achieved a dominant or mainstream status for some two generations (from the 1930s until the late 1960s); and that today for many reasons it is under challenge. In the older historiography, the clash between community and assimilation, Eastern and Western European Jewry, centripetal and centrifugal forces served as the key, the paradigmatic theme. It permitted order to be brought out of chaos. It was the source of extraordinary vitality. It made it possible to survey the entire history of the Jewish people in the modern age *sub specie aeternitatis* and yet in wholly secular terms.

The more recent historiography, in part represented in this volume, is no longer informed by a bipolar world-view. In one sense, therefore, a more unified view of Jewish history is implicit in its underlying assumptions. East is no longer clearly divided from West. Greater credence is lent to the survivalist strategies of Western Jewry; and less romanticism is employed to describe the masses of Eastern Europe. And Jewish political activism, as it developed in the nineteenth century, is seen as transcending the East–West divide.

But in another sense, we are left with a sub-world subjected to a multiplicity of conflicting forces interacting in unpredictable ways. Acculturation is no longer seen as leading necessarily to assimilation; in many cases it did; in others it did not. The Jewish masses are no longer seen as necessarily loyal to the community; sometimes they were; sometimes they were not. Every place, every time, every group, could manifest different results in different permutations. Order has been replaced by flux; one law of motion by a myriad of contexts, and by a multiplicity of responses.

Notes

1 For a full list of Dubnov's publications, see his *Kniga zhizni*, vol. III (New York, 1957), pp. 163–89.

2 On Graetz's philosophy of history: H. Graetz, *The Structure of Jewish History and Other Essays*, edited and introduced by I. Schorsch (New York, 1975).

3 See, particularly, S. M. Dubnov, *Pisma o starom i novom evreistve (1897–1907)* (St Petersburg, 1907). For an abbreviated English edition: S. M. Dubnov, *Nationalism and History: Essays on Old and New Judaism*, edited and introduced by K. S. Pinson (Philadelphia, 1958).

4 Dubnov's history of Hasidism was first published in the monthly *Voskhod* during the years 1888 to 1892. A Hebrew edition, *Toldot hehasidut betkufat zmihatah vegidulah* was published in three volumes in Tel Aviv, 1930–1.

5 *Evreiskaia Starina: trekhmesiachnik Evreiskogo istorikoetnograficheskogo obshchestva* (St Petersburg/Leningrad, 1909–30).

6 On Baron David Gintsburg, in general, and the Courses in Oriental Studies in particular, see *He'avar* 4 (1958), 77–165. (Among the essays published there note Zalman Shazar, 'Raboteinu beveit midrasho shel baron Ginzburg (5666–5672)', ibid., pp. 88–100.)

7 I.e., The *Evreiskoe istoriko-etnigroficheskoe obshchestvo* founded in St Petersburg in 1908.

8 The *Evreiskaia entsiklopediia* was published in St Petersburg, 1906–13.

9 S. M. Dubnov, *Noveishaia istoriia evreiskogo naroda* (St Petersburg, 1914).

10 See e.g. S. Almog, *Zionism and History: The Rise of a New Jewish Consciousness* (Jerusalem, 1987), particularly pp. 23–83; and J. Frankel, 'The "Yizkor" Book of 1911: a Note on National Myths in the Second Aliya', in H. Ben Israel, A. Goren, O. Handlin, M. Heyd, G. Mosse and M. Zimmerman, (eds.), *Religion, Ideology and Nationalism in Europe and America: Essays Presented in Honor of Yehoshua Arieli* (Jerusalem, 1986), pp. 355–84.

11 G. Scholem, *From Berlin to Jerusalem: Memories of My Youth* (New York, 1988), p. 44.

12 *Weltgeschichte des Jüdischen Volkes*, 10 vols. (Berlin, 1925–9); *Vsemirnaia istoriia evreiskogo naroda*, 10 vols. (Riga, 1936–9).

13 E.g. Dubnov, *Kniga zhizni*, vol. III, p. 120.

14 Dubnov, *History of the Jews*, vols. IV–V (New York, 1971–3).

15 R. Mahler, *A History of Modern Jewry 1780–1815* (London, 1971). See, too, R. Mahler, *Divrei yisrael: dorot aḥaronim*, 7 vols. (Merhavia/Tel Aviv, 1961–80).

16 S. Ettinger, 'The Modern Period', in H. H. Ben-Sasson (ed.), *A History of the Jewish People* (Cambridge, Mass., 1976), pp. 725–1,096.

17 B.-Z. Dinur, *Bemifneh hadorot: meḥkarim veiyunim bereshitam shel hazmanim heḥadashim betoldot yisrael* (Jerusalem, 1972).

18 Dubnov, *Noveishaia istoriia evreiskogo naroda*, vol. I (also counted as vol. VIII of the *Vsemirnaia 'istoriia*) (Riga, 1937), p. 57 (English edition: p. 496.) (This and subsequent translations from Dubnov's *World History* are my own, made directly from the Russian edition.)

19 Mahler, *A History of Modern Jewry*, p. ii.

20 Ettinger, 'The Modern Period', p. 731.

21 Dinur, *Bemifneh hadorot*, pp. 31–2.

22 P. Smolenskin, 'Am olam', *Hashaar* 3 (1872), 3–16, 73–84, 145–52, 201–8, 377–84, 433–40, 505–12, 553–66, 643–50, 659–84.

23 E.g. Ben Uziel (S. R. Hirsch), *Igrot Zafon: Neunzehn Briefe über Judenthum* (Altona, N.Y. 1836), p. 93; H. Graetz, *Geschichte der Juden*, vol. XI (Leipzig, 1900), pp. 1–92.

24 E.g. Dubnov, 'Mendelson russkikh evreev: ocherk zhizni i deiatelnosti I.B. Lebenzona', *Razsvet* 30 (24 July 1881), 1,192.

25 Dubnov, *Istoriia evreev v evrope*, vol. IV (also counted as vol. VII of the *Vsemirnaia istoriia*), p. 294 (English edition: vol. IV, p. 336).

26 Dubnov, *Noveishaia istoriia*, vol. I (*Vsemirnaia istoriia*, vol. VIII), p. 59 (English edition: vol. IV, p. 498).

27 Mahler, *A History of Modern Jewry*, p. 162.

28 E.g., Dubnov, *Noveishaia istoriia*, vol. I (VIII), pp. 159–61 (English edition: vol. IV, 595–7). Mahler, *A History of Modern Jewry*, pp. 207–9.

29 Ettinger, 'The Modern Period', p. 841.

30 Dubnov, *Istoriia evreev v evrope*, vol. IV (VIII), p. 297 (English edition: vol. IV, p. 339).

31 Mahler, *A History of Modern Jewry*, p. 338.

32 Ibid., p. 166.
33 Ettinger, 'The Modern Period', pp. 817–18.
34 Ibid., p. 842.
35 Ibid., p. 788.
36 Ibid.
37 Dubnov, *Noveishaia istoriia*, vol. I (VIII), p. 57 (English edition: vol. IV, p. 497).
38 Mahler, *A History of Modern Jewry*, pp. 32, 744; Ettinger, 'The Modern Period', p. 744; Dubnov, *Noveishaia istoriia*, vol. I (VIII), p. 74 (English edition: vol. IV, pp. 513–14).
39 Ibid., p. 58 (English edition: vol. IV, p. 497).
40 Ettinger, 'The Modern Period', p. 749.
41 Mahler, *A History of Modern Jewry*, p. 65.
42 Dubnov, *Noveishaia istoriia*, vol. I, (VIII), pp. 115–16 (English edition: vol. IV, pp. 552–3).
43 Mahler, *A History of Modern Jewry*, p. 66.
44 Dubnov, *Noveishaia istoriia*, vol. II (IX), p. 68 (English edition: vol. V, p. 82).
45 'Abraham Geigers Briefe an J. Derenbourg', (ed. L. Geiger), *Allgemeine Zeitung des Judenthums*, 24 (12 June 1896), 284. (For references to this letter: e.g. Dinur, *Bemifneh hadorot*, p. 31; Ettinger, 'The Modern Period', p. 848.)
46 Mahler, *A History of Modern Jewry*, p. 278.
47 Ibid., p. xxii.
48 Dinur, *Bemifneh hadorot*, p. 50.
49 Ibid.
50 Ibid., pp. 37–46, 55–62.
51 E.g. Ettinger, 'The Modern Period', pp. 847–52.
52 Dinur, *Bemifneh hadorot*, p. 64.
53 Ettinger, 'The Modern Period', p. 848.
54 Dubnov, *Noveishaia istoriia*, vol. II (IX), p. 241 (English edition: vol. V, p. 250).
55 Ibid., pp. 242–3. (English edition: vol. V: pp. 251–2).
56 The Leo Baeck Institute of Jews from Germany, founded in 1954 (with branches in New York, London and Jerusalem) has published a very large list of scholarly books and brings out periodical publications, notably the *Leo Baeck Institute Year Book* and the *Bulletin für die Mitgleider der Gesellschaft der Freunde des Leo Baeck Instituts.*
57 D. Biale, *Gershom Scholem: Kabbalah and Counter-History* (Cambridge, Mass., 1979), pp. 5–12.
58 A. Altmann, *Moses Mendelssohn: A Biographical Study* (London, 1973).
59 E.g. N. N. Glatzer (ed.), *Leopold Zunz: Jude-Deutscher-Europäer: ein jüdisches Gelehrtenschiksal des 19. Jahrhunderts in Briefen an Freunde* (Tübingen, 1964); and N. N. Glatzer, *Franz Rosenzweig: His Life and Thought* (New York, 1953).

60 See note 79, below.

61 E.g. the impact exerted by the *Annales: économies-sociétés-civilisations* and by *Past and Present: Journal of Scientific History*.

62 For one example, see the publications of Peter Laslett and the Cambridge Group for the History of Population and Social Structure.

63 The attempt to examine the socio-economic development of the Jewish people as a subject transcending narrow geographic limits can be traced back to the early efforts of such Marxist territorialists as Jacob Lestzchinsky (as well as to the efforts of Arthur Ruppin and other German-Jewish scholars who founded the *Zeitschrift fur Demographie und Statistick der Juden*).

64 S. M. Dubnov, 'Obshchee vedenie', in *Vsemirnaia istoriia*, vol. I, pp. xi-xx. (English edition: vol. I, pp. 25–33). This introduction was concluded by Dubnov with the note 'St Petersburg, 1910/Berlin, 1924), ibid., p. xxxii (English edition: p. 44).

65 E.g. 'Dubnov . . . proclaimed the need for a sociological interpretation . . . But in his actual description of the Jewish past he has no more succeeded in realising his program than had Graetz in avoiding the pitfalls of the *Leidens und Gelehrtengeschicte* which he himself had so bluntly denounced' (S. W. Baron, *History and Jewish Historians: Essays and Addresses* (Philadelphia, 1964), p. 78).

66 See, for example: S. W. Baron, *The Jewish Community: Its History and Structure to the American Revolution*, 3 vols. (Philadelphia, 1942): S. W. Baron, *A Social and Religious History of the Jews*, 18 vols. (New York, 1952–83); J. Katz, *Out of the Ghetto: The Social Background of Jewish Emancipation 1770–1870* (New York, 1973); J. Katz, *Tradition and Crisis* (New York, 1961).

67 See, for example, S. Ettinger and I. Bartal, 'Shoreshei hayishuv hehadash beerez-yisrael', in *Sefer ha'aliyah harishonah*, ed. M. Eliav, vol. I (Jerusalem, 1981), pp. 1–24 (for the English version, see *The Jerusalem Cathedra*, vol. II, (Jerusalem, 1982), pp. 197–210). Cf. the excellent article of B. Mevorah, 'Ikvotehah shel 'alilat damesek behitpathuta shel ha'itonut hayehudit beshanim 1840–1846', *Zion*, 23–4 (1958–9), 46–65.

68 A. Smith, *Theories of Nationalism* (London, 1971), p. 117. (In this quotation, Smith is summarizing the viewpoint of Ernest Gellner.)

69 T. M. Endelman, *The Jews of Georgian England 1714–1830: Tradition and Change in Liberal Society* (Philadelphia, 1979), particularly pp. 272–93.

70 Idem., 'The Englishness of Jewish Modernity in England', in J. Katz (ed.), *Toward Modernity: The European Jewish Model* (New Brunswick, N.J. 1987), pp. 225–6.

71 S. J. Zipperstein, 'Haskalah, Cultural Change and Nineteenth Century Jewry: a Reassessment', *Journal of Jewish Studies* 35, no. 2 (1983), 193.

72 E. Etkes, 'Immanent Factors and External Influences in the Development of the Haskalah Movement in Russia', in Katz (ed.), *Toward Modernity*, p. 29.

73 M. Silber, 'The Historical Experience of German Jewry and its Impact on Haskalah and Reform in Hungary', ibid., p. 113.

74 H. J. Kieval, 'Caution's Progress: the Modernization of Jewish Life in Prague, 1780–1830', ibid., p. 83.

75 L. Dubin, 'Trieste and Berlin: the Italian Role in the Cultural Politics of the Haskalah', ibid., p. 209.

76 See, e.g., H. Rogger, *Jewish Policies and Right-wing Politics in Imperial Russia* (London, 1986); M. Aronson, 'The Attitudes of Russian Officials in the 1880s Toward Jewish Assimilation and Emigration', *Slavic Review* 34 (1975), 1–18; M. Aronson, 'The Prospects for the Emancipation of Russian Jewry During the 1880s', *Slavonic and East European Review* 55 (1977), 167–82.

77 M. Stanislawski, *Tsar Nicholas I and the Jews: The Transformation of Jewish Society in Russia 1825–1855* (Philadelphia, 1983), pp. 187–8.

78 M. M. Gordon, *Assimilation in American Life: The Role of Race, Religion and National Origins* (New York, 1964). Cf. M. M. Gordon, *Human Nature, Class and Ethnicity* (New York, 1978).

79 See, e.g., J. Armstrong, *Nations Before Nationalism* (Chapel Hill, N.C. 1982); G. P. Castile and G. Kushner, *Persistent Peoples: Cultural Enclaves in Perspective* (Tucson, Ariz., 1981); G. De Vos and L. Romanucci (eds.), *Ethnic Identity: Cultural Continuities and Change* (Chicago, 1975); E. K. Francis, *Interethnic Relations: an Essay in Sociological Theory* (New York, 1976); G. Geertz (ed.), *Old Societies and New States: The Quest for Modernity in Asia and Africa* (New York, 1963); J. Krejci and V. Velinsky, *Ethnic and Political Nations in Europe* (London, 1981); J. Roths-child, *Ethno-politics* (New York, 1981); H. Seton-Watson, *Nations and States: An Enquiry into the Origins of Nations and the Politics of Nationalism* (London, 1977), A. D. Smith, *The Ethnic Origins of Nations* (Oxford, 1987).

80 Gordon, *Assimilation in American Life*, pp. 60–83, Cf. C. Goldscheider, *Social Change and Jewish Continuity* (Bloomington, 1985); F. Kobrin and C. Goldscheider, *The Ethnic Factor in Family Structure and Mobility* (Cambridge, Mass., 1978).

81 See, e.g. M. L. Rozenblit, *The Jews of Vienna, 1867–1914: Assimilation and Identity* (Albany, N.Y. 1983); D. Sorkin, *The Transformation of German Jewry, 1780–1840* (New York, 1987); R. S. Wistrich, *The Jews of Vienna in the Age of Franz Joseph* (Oxford, 1989).

82 See, e.g., M. Meyer, *Response to Modernity: A History of the Reform Movement in Judaism* (Oxford, 1988), pp. 138–42; 180–91.

83 E.g. R. S. Wistrich, 'The Modernization of Viennese Jewry: the Impact of German Culture in a Multi-Ethnic State', in Katz (ed.), *Toward Modernity*, pp. 46–9. (Cf. M. Rozenblit in this volume, pp. 230–4.)

84 On the historical context from which the Pittsburgh declaration emerged: Meyer, *Response to Modernity*, pp. 264–95.

85 B. Kraut, 'A Unitarian Rabbi? The Case of Solomon H. Sonneschein',

in T. Endelman (ed.), *Jewish Apostasy in the Modern World* (New York, 1987), pp. 296–7.

86 G. Scholem, 'Mitokh hirhurim al hokhmat yisrael', in G. Scholem, *Devarim bego: pirkei morashah utehiyah* (Tel Aviv, 1975), p. 393.

87 Ibid., p. 392.

88 I. Schorsch, 'From Wolfenbuttel to Wissenschaft: the Divergent Paths of Isaak Markus Jost and Leopold Zunz', *Leo Baeck Institute Year Book* 32 (1977), 144.

89 G. D. Cohen, 'German Jewry as Mirror of Modernity', ibid. 20 (1975), xxv, xxvii.

90 Ibid., xxviii.

91 J. Frankel, *Prophecy and Politics: Socialism, Nationalism and the Russian Jews* (Cambridge, 1981), pp. 49–132; J. Frankel, 'The Crisis of 1881–82 as a Turning Point in Modern Jewish History', in D. Berger (ed.), *The Legacy of Jewish Migration: 1881 and its Impact* (New York, 1983), pp. 9–22.

92 Y. Kaniel, *Hemshekh utmurah: hayishuv hayashan vehayishuv hehadash betkufat haaliyah hashniyah* (Jerusalem, 1982); A. Morgenstern, *Meshihiut veyishuv erez-yisrael bemahazit ha-rishonah shel hameah ha-19* (Jerusalem, 1985).

93 See, for example, I. Bartal's responses to Morgenstern's book: 'Messianic Expectations and their Place in History', in R. Cohen (ed.), *Vision and Conflict in the Holy Land* (Jerusalem, 1985), pp. 171–81; and 'Meshihiut vehistoriah', *Zion* 52 (1987), 117–30. For Morgenstern's rejoinder: 'Al bikoret hameshihiut bemeah ha-19', ibid., 371–89.

94 M. Graetz, *Haperiferiyah haitah lemerkaz: perakim betoldot yahadut zarfat bemeah ha-19* (Jerusalem, 1982). For a more critical appraisal of the politics pursued by the Jewish leadership in France (as well as in Germany), see Michael R. Marrus, 'Jewry and the Politics of Assimilation: Assessment and Reassessment', *The Journal of Modern History* 49 (1977), 88–109. (Cf. Michael R. Marrus, *The Politics of Assimilation: A Study of the French Jewish Community at the Time of the Dreyfus Affair* (Oxford, 1971).)

95 J. Frankel, 'Crisis as a Factor in Modern Jewish Politics: 1840 and 1881–82', in J. Reinharz (ed.), *Living with Antisemitism: Modern Jewish Responses* (Hanover, N. H., 1987), pp. 42–58.

96 E.g. C. Adler and A. A. Margalit, *American Intercession on Behalf of Jews in the Diplomatic Correspondence of the United States* (New York, 1948); L. Wolf, *Notes on the Diplomatic History of the Jewish Question* (London, 1919).

97 E.g. I. Bartal, 'Moshe Montefiori veerez-yisrael', *Katedra letoldot erez-yisrael veyishuvah* 33 (1984), 149–60.

98 Ettinger and Bartal, 'Shoreshei hayishuv headash beerez-yisrael', in Eliav, *Sefer haaliyah harishoneh*, p. 6.

99 E. Lederhendler, *The Road to Modern Jewish Politics: Political Tradition and Political Reconstruction in the Jewish Community of Tsarist Russia* (New

York, 1989). Cf. Lederhendler's article in this volume, pp. 324–43; and E. Lederhendler, 'Interpreting Messianic Rhetoric in the Russian Haskalah and Early Zionism', *Studies in Contemporary Jewry*, vol. VII, *Jews and Messianism in the Modern Era: Metaphor and Meaning*, ed. J. Frankel (New York, 1991), pp. 14–33.

100 Lederhendler, *The Road to Modern Jewish Politics*, p. 88.
101 Ibid., p. 110.
102 Ibid., p. 4.

Jewish emancipationists in Victorian England: self-imposed limits to assimilation

ISRAEL FINESTEIN

Acculturation is not the same as absorption. The former consists of increasing the levels of similarity in the way of life between individuals (or a group) on the one hand and the larger body within which they live on the other hand. It is a mood as well as a process. It has its own momentum, whether by design or by the sheer impact of fashion.

Similarity in speech, dress and public behaviour may be the instant objective, which itself will be directed towards fuller and easier acceptance into the wider society. But the immediately aimed-at similarities can in time come to reflect and induce deeper inner changes in outlook and aspiration. The fuller the acceptance, the more pervasive and more effective those changes.

The long-term results may endanger the remains of any distinctiveness, subject only to the impact of any outside hostility or some dramatic resurgence of ethnic interest or historical pride. In the Victorian era the conventional wisdom was that for the most part hostility would wither with the expansion of education and improved social conditions. Nor did Victorian Jewry experience any dramatic resurgence of ethnic self-consciousness.

Meanwhile, those who consciously advocated a high degree of integration were often acutely concerned not to be acculturated to the point of total absorption, by which I mean the loss of transmissible distinctiveness. The leading Jewish emancipationists assumed that the wider society was both ready for Jewish assimilation and would, on the whole, not misconstrue the setting of limits to that process. Their campaign for Jewish civic and political equality was conducted within this framework.

Jewish separateness was presented by Jews as a religious requirement. Historical recollections and inherited mores inevitably intertwined with and strengthened the social effects of religious difference.

There were special features of the Anglo-Jewish experience which constituted a strong moving force towards the cultivation at one and the same time of pride in being English and of pride in Jewishness.

Among the most important of those features was the growing social emancipation of the Jews since the late seventeenth century. The retention of a distinct Jewishness was part of a continuing style of living amidst a surrounding public which seemed to expect it. The influence of the Bible on English life and thought made that distinctiveness seem the more natural to Christian as well as to Jew. It had the character of a long-standing convention. Furthermore, the highly personalized form of Jewish communal government, associated with habits of centralization and lay power, encouraged the leadership to treat the measure of difference as a matter of family pride and public duty.

These considerations, some conscious, some instinctive, were reinforced by the nature of the thirty-year public debate in the nineteenth century on the case for and against Jewish civil emancipation. It was a debate in depth, conducted largely between Christians of whom many, whatever their opinions on the particular issue of Jewish emancipation, were unalterably and favourably impressed by Jewish survival, and by the role of Jews and Judaism in the world. There was also on the Jewish side of the debate a universal conviction as to the virtues of Britain's hegemony and British procedures.

There was a strong attachment among Jewish emancipationists to the institutions which embodied Jewish separateness – the synagogues, the schools, the welfare agencies and family cohesion. It went beyond nostalgia. They were eager to sustain, and to be seen to sustain, the nature of the Jewish community as a community of faith. It was axiomatic that it was as a religious community that the Jews were presented as worthy of the full rights of citizenship. The pervasiveness of religion in the public life of Victorian England gave Judaism (whether in its Orthodox, that is normative, style, or in its Reformist model) the character of an emblem of self-conscious patriotism and normality.

If the English Jews took on the colour of their environment, they did so even in the very fashioning, conscious and subconscious, of their own responses to the danger of absorption. The combination of their leaders' attachment to the institutional life of the Jewish community with a high degree of proud and articulate assimilation, became and long remained a distinctive feature of Anglo-Jewish life, and was an example widely followed in the community.

The Victorians would have been at a loss to grasp any assumption concerning the availability of a secular Jewishness. As far as they entertained the Jewish national idea, it had wholly different connotations. For them Jewish continuity was worthwhile in so far as it was rooted in, and defined by, reference to religion. If religious faith, for historical reasons, gave expression to certain national ideas, they regarded this as either a subject for rabbinic eschatological exposition or as essentially an anachronism. What a remote future might be thought to have in store would be, if anything, a matter not only for Jews but for the whole world, even if there were some current philosophies related to an inscrutable particular role for the Children of Israel within the supposed eventual universal transformation.

The concern of the emancipationists for the transmissibility of their distinctive qualities as Jews, was no less real for being in many cases an offshoot of family commitment. There was room, within their own world outlook, for an anxiety to preserve points of Jewish difference. The far-reaching acculturation of their households, and of those who followed their examples, was relied on initially to justify the claim for emancipation and once that was attained, to evidence its propriety and good sense. The envied accolade was the acceptance of Jews as Englishmen. As long as full civil rights had been withheld, that title, so it was felt, had been visibly, hurtfully and in defiance of reality, denied to them. These sentiments were shared by Jewish middle-class families in the provincial cities, many of whose members were prominent in municipal life and in local literary and philanthropic activity.

The extent of British power and wealth and the strength of Britain's liberal image were such that, to the Jews of Britain, it seemed that fortune had smiled upon them in the distribution of the Jews in the world. These considerations heightened the sense of an Anglo-Jewish duty to intercede on behalf of less fortunately placed Jews abroad. Any such intercession was a reflex of Jewish self-esteem. It was both a counterpart to Jewish acculturation and a parallel to the Whig- and Liberal-related popular British policy of public sympathy (and sometimes diplomatic and other practical support) for liberationist movements abroad. Anglo-Jewish leaders responded both as Englishmen and as Jews.

The Jewish pride in their capacity as Englishmen likewise sharpened the Jewish desire to have what was called 'a native ministry'. The needs of the day – Anglicization of the broad Jewish community, improved standards and techniques in Jewish education, a more Westernized and sophisticated synagogal service, regular addresses in

English to the increasingly integrated congregations – pointed to the imperative nature of the call for Englishmen to occupy the pulpits and for the creation of a modern pastorate. It was an internal Jewish desideratum, a postulate of being English and an earnest of the sincerity of Jewish emancipationist polemics. These motivations were seen as one. Long-standing social emancipation and the pragmatic habits of English public life gave the Jews not only an assured sense of liberty but also, so to speak, a sense of unpressured timelessness. In this condition they lacked the spur needed to invest real effort in higher Jewish learning or intense Jewish study.

The outward religiosity of English domestic life – largely Bible-based and Evangelically inspired – was reflected in the fashionable religiosity of the more prominent Jewish communal leaders. In such matters genuine sentiment was allied to public prudence and social convention.

It was believed that the Anglo-Jewish community had attained a beneficent balance. This was viewed as a goal, which either under divine providence or through historical evolution awaited other Jewish communities. Time, effort and patience would be required. The British example was considered important in the unfolding of this dispensation. England was held to be in the van of what was regarded as the rapidly advancing moral and cultural regeneration of the Western world. Even the Tsarist Empire was not regarded as permanently immune to relevant changes.

Anglo-Jewry experienced no radical break with the past. For them, historical perceptions, common sense and contemporary Jewish needs combined to warrant their integration and to require and justify their attempted limitations upon it. Their leaders (unlike those of French Jewry under Napoleon) at no time felt called upon by public events to declare the precise principles of their civic creed. Nor were there sudden changes – now towards liberalism and now towards autocracy – by which public policy and Jewish responses were pulled hither and thither, as in Central Europe. Nor was there that particular sense of utopia achieved, which deeply affected and affects American Jewish reactions. It was always far easier for an American Jew to declare 'Philadelphia is my Jerusalem' than for a Jew in England to announce 'London is my Jerusalem'.

The Jews in England did not feel it incumbent upon themselves to evince their modernity by a public rejection of the distinguishing attributes of Judaism and Jews. Their circumstances and often their inward faith told against their so doing. The place of the Bible in

English thought and sentiment would in any event have made it difficult and artificial for the Jews to repudiate expressly their characteristics as a people with a special and an awaited providential role. The founders of Reform Judaism in England did not in principle reject the authority of the Mosaic law. They challenged the obligatory authority of its interpretation and development in the Oral Law. Nor did they disown the Jewish Messianic hope.[1] They shared with the generality of Jewish spokesmen a preference for allowing it to be classified, by way of a public intellectual analogy, with a Christian's belief in the Second Coming.

The long-term influence of Puritanism as an outward religious discipline and as a factor in the advancement of economic individualism and industrial expansion was a major element in British public life. With that influence were involved assumptions concerning chosenness, grace, divine favour and personal moral accountability. The Old Testament was a living influence on Christian life and thought, affecting attitudes to the Jewish people. Among the implications for Jews was that their own degree of separateness was the more readily perceived by Anglicans (notably the Evangelicals) and especially by the Nonconformists as divinely ordained. St Paul had proclaimed (whatever else he may have said) that the old promises had not been overturned. For whatever purposes, their one-time chosenness was widely taken for granted. There remained a residue of speciality about the Jews not only in the public mind at large but also in the Jewish mind. However assiduously their uniqueness might be defined in terms of utterly remote eventualities, it was by its nature and by its widespread acknowledgement a limitation upon easy, absorptive assimilation. It reflected and seemed to give a meaning and even a sense of pride to differences.

Jewish publicists carefully avoided associating themselves with Disraeli's doctrine of Jewish superiority. But this did not prevent them from giving expression to their sense of the Western world's indebtedness to the moral teachings of the Jews. It fell to them from time to time to rebut attacks upon the moral standards of the Talmud. Morris Raphall, the *maskil* who was the Minister of the Birmingham Hebrew Congregation in the 1840s, was in his day the main and self-appointed defender of the rabbinic tradition against such detractors.[2] Jewish apologetics in the middle of the century rested upon assumptions and contentions as to the moral and practical value of Jewish distinctiveness from the point of view of the societies in which they lived.

One Jewish writer in the *Voice of Jacob* (edited by Jacob Franklin) on 28 April 1843 reflected a Jewish mood of unconscious irony. He urged the need for a Jewish movement not only to press for advances in the civil status of the Jews but also to advance their moral standing in the public mind. He presupposed that the latter advance needed to be made and that it would be conducive to the success of the movement for emancipation. His concern was that the Jews should demonstrate to the public their readiness for the high role expected of them in society. 'England', he commented, 'religious England is perhaps the only country which would afford us free scope' for a movement directed to these ends. While preaching the virtues of emancipation and the value of measures directed to its attainment, there was characteristically purveyed an inbuilt particularist philosophy.

No clerical party arose, as in France, to disturb Jewish equanimity. No *Volk*-type xenophobic romanticism, as in Germany, stirred their peace of mind. Their self-esteem was satisfied by their evidence of good citizenship, their care for their own poor and their acknowledgement through practical measures of the international Jewish kinship. Such insignia were taken seriously. An active respect for them was inculcated into the succeeding generation.

Ideological debate was as little Anglo-Jewish as it was English, but the sound administration of communal institutional life was as important to the communal leadership as was the sensible administration of the new Victorian public Boards to the rising caste of bureaucrats. The cessation of immigration during the long French wars had greatly increased the native element within Anglo-Jewry. The Jewish community was as much affected by a kind of insular pride as were the self-made men of Christian faith in the emerging middle classes. As Todd Endelman has observed, 'the transformation of Anglo-Jewry at all levels . . . took place largely in terms of new patterns of behaviour rather than new lines of thought'.[3]

A behaviourist acculturation, largely concerned with a search for indistinguishability out of doors and in club and market-place, did not alter the fact that inner traditions died hard. There was no sense of haste for inner change. If it was to come, the pace could be left to whatever emancipation might reasonably require or induce.

In 1830 the unreformed House of Commons rejected a Bill which would have placed the Jews on a par in law with the Roman Catholics. It would have included their admissibility to Parliament, a reform not achieved until the Jewish Relief Act of 1858. In his influential emancipationist pamphlet in 1831, Francis Goldsmid referred to the Jewish dismay at the rejection of the Bill. His language of surprise has the ring of truth. There was, he wrote, 'so little' in the measure that seemed likely to alarm the staunchest opponent of change. 'Parliament', he added,

> had so solemnly sanctioned the principles of religious liberty [by the Acts of 1828 and 1829 relating to Protestant Dissenters and Roman Catholics respectively] that – any very serious opposition – was regarded as an impossibility.

Goldsmid's essential point is clear. The Jews submitted their claim as a religious communion, one of the Dissenting bodies, even though Jewish distinctiveness raised special questions concerning the nature of the Jews as a body and the purposes of their retained identity. Goldsmid rested his case on the broadest principles of religious liberty, as did the Whig and Radical supporters of the Jewish cause. They were presented as entitled to civil rights in spite of, as well as because of, their faith and qualities.

In his survey of the Jewish community entitled *The British Jews* (1853), John Mills, the Welsh Calvinist preacher, observed: 'Just as many [Englishmen] attribute the prosperity and happiness of this country to its Saxon blood and pride themselves upon it, so do the Jews in the same spirit pride themselves upon being still the chosen people of Heaven.' No representative Jew would have challenged the proposition. When Mills averred that 'the Jew's faith and his nation are synonymous', he was expressing a widespread belief, shared by Jews. It was not in its day held to be a pejorative formulation.[4]

When in the next generation Goldwin Smith, the historian and Liberal polemicist who was deeply averse to the policies and style of Disraeli, presented to the reading public a renewal of the equation between Jewish faith and nation, it was hotly resented. Jews were no longer aspirants but highly self-conscious *arrivistes*, alert to the implication of the growing anti-Jewish movement on the continent and watchful of the effects of the expanding Eastern European Jewish immigration into Britain. Smith contrasted the reality of Jewish inwardness and cohesion, on the one hand, with the outward conventionality of Jews and their public influence on the other. For all the differences in motivation between the philanthropic and conversionist-minded Mills and the antisemitic Smith (who propounded a Zionist remedy for 'the Jewish question'), there was some degree of common ground between them, if unwittingly.

During the decades leading up to 1858, the special suffering of the Jews over the ages was prayed in aid as imposing upon Christian society a liability to make redress by the granting of civil rights. It was a point made more by Christian supporters than by Jews, who none the less welcomed the notion. Allied to that argument was the assertion made, in this case by Jews, that by reason of their history they were especially conscious of the value of religious freedom unfettered by penalties. In his election address to the voters of Reading in 1860, Francis Goldsmid described himself as 'descended from a race and belonging to a religious community which for centuries was the object of persecution'. He went on to attribute to that fact his own attachment 'by feeling and conviction to the great value of religious freedom' for all in society.[5]

Goldsmid's words were typical of the age. Not only did he thereby add a personal element to his electoral praise of liberty, but he also thus used his Jewishness and the special history of his people (he makes no reference to 'nation') to further his candidature, which was successful.

In the 1860s Francis Goldsmid again and again raised in the House of Commons the treatment of Jews abroad, especially the denial of fundamental rights in Romania, despite the undertakings of authoritative Romanian spokesmen. His successor as the Jewish 'representative' in the House in the 1870s was his fellow-founder of the Reform congregation, Sir John Simon. Like Goldsmid, Simon was a prominent member of the Liberal party. He actively supported many progressive reforms in Parliament and was among Gladstone's most forceful lieutenants in the House. On the issue of the Jews overseas, he was at public odds with his leader. He upbraided Gladstone for seeming to ignore the plight of Eastern European Jewry, notably in the Tsarist Empire, in pursuit of his pro-Russian policy and in the context of his protracted attack on Disraeli's pro-Turkish foreign policy. Simon publicly warned Gladstone that, while the safety of the Christian communities within the Ottoman Empire was a laudable and necessary objective, he risked the loss of some Jewish support for the party because of his apparent indifference to the condition of the Jews under the Tsar.

It was in connection with these issues that in December 1879 an extensive correspondence appeared in *The Times* on the motivations of the Jews in politics. Letters from leading Jewish figures demonstrated their concern to equate their attachment to the cause of Britain and her honour with their advocacy of Jewish interests.

However, the crucial public debate over the ideology of Jewish emancipation had taken place in the 1840s. Once the municipalities were opened to professing Jews by the Act of 1845, the way to Parliament was clear, save for a rearguard action by inveterate opponents and the gambits of politics. This was fully appreciated by most people on all sides of the argument.

In those circumstances the Jewish responses to the Act of 1845 are of considerable interest. No Jewish statement was more indicative than that of the *Voice of Jacob* on 1 August 1845. 'We Jews', commented the editor,

> who claim first rank for our nation as the chosen one before God, may well afford to be indulgent towards Christian prelates, peers and other legislators whose preconceptions would have been revolted and whose sensitivities would have been wounded by any broad proposition that religious profession is not a needful qualification for offices of trust and authority.

This bland and practical approach was not entirely in accord with the more robust ideas on which the Goldsmids had acted. They consistently protested on principle against any Jewish exclusion from full civil rights; but it was the attitude expressed by Franklin which prevailed within the Jewish community – supported as it was by Peel and Lyndhurst who, as Prime Minister and Lord Chancellor respectively, adopted in the form of the Act of 1845 a pragmatic stage-by-stage approach. Admission to Parliament would take its course.

The above editorial pronouncement related to much more than tactics. Jews were reluctant to press their claim on the basis that religion did not matter for public office, despite the eminent sponsorship by Macaulay and others of that very doctrine. Jews had no wish to face the charge of encouraging the transformation of society by advancing the cause of its secularization.

What in the end won the day for the campaign for admission to Parliament, as earlier to the municipalities, was the recognition of the impracticability of exclusion, the political nuisance of seeking to sustain it, the shifting of the burden of proof to its opponents and the persistent demonstration of services to state and society by Jews. The Jewish case had to be presented on practical grounds relating to practical grievances, unjust anomalies, party considerations and public needs.

When Christian opponents of Jewish emancipation argued that the Jews in London had more in common with Jews in the continental capitals than with their local Christian neighbours, there were respects in which the claim was true. When they spoke of Jewish international links, they were referring to what the editor of the *Jewish Chronicle*, on the occasion of the Queen's Jubilee in 1887, called 'Jewish solidarity'. This was a solidarity which the emancipationists were not minded to deny. Hermann Adler described the links as being those which tie together people who have a common history and a common hope. If he were thus concerned to depoliticize the character and the appearance of such linkage, his expressions nevertheless enhanced to the ears of Jew and gentile the sense of bonding. On the lips of gentile critics, solidarity was a pejorative term. To Jews it represented a self-evident virtue and responsibility.

Typical of the inward-lookingness of the Jews – even when no less concerned to procure civil emancipation – was the discussion in the *Voice of Jacob* in 1843 of the idea of a Jewish 'conclave'. Abraham Benisch, who later took control of and edited the *Jewish Chronicle*, was an enthusiast for the proposed scheme, which had the encouragement of Franklin. The phrase was presumably adopted from Vatican practice and certainly implied that such an assembly should enjoy a degree of international authority within Jewry. The proposed body was discussed as possibly exercising 'spiritual authority' over the Jewish people. One motive mooted for such a convocation was to stem Reform. Another was that, speaking for Jewish communities from many lands, it might be able to exercise a proper persuasion on governments to improve the Jewish lot.

The suggestion was also related to the fact that in some countries 'representative' Jewish assemblies were growing in self-confidence. It seemed appropriate that they should consult together on common interests. On 14 March 1843, Franklin referred to the effect of the Jewish press on both sides of the Atlantic on the increasingly organized and cohesive Jewish communities in the West.

An important feature throughout these discussions was the Damascus Affair of 1840. The suddenness of that episode, the resurgence of the ritual murder charge and the apparent credence given to it in high places in the capitals of Europe, were in stark contrast to the rationality and libertarianism which the eighteenth century was thought to have bequeathed. The cross-frontier co-operation in reaction to the events in Damascus, together with the related and influential public meetings of protest in major capitals in the West in which Christians were as prominent as Jews, encouraged both the notion and the practice of international Jewish consultation and, when necessary, co-ordinated action.

The Jewish avowal of a mutual Jewish responsibility was a

distinctive particularist phenomenon. To describe this phenomenon simply in terms of 'spiritual authority' within Jewry would be misleading, for it had a quasi-political quality in defence of Jewish rights. Before the creation of the Alliance Israélite Universelle in 1860, there were many calls for, and much discussion in Jewish counsels on the need for, such machinery. The Anglo-Jewish press was a regular forum for discussion of this type. Benisch was in the forefront of the debate.

If the leaders of the Board of Deputies of British Jews preferred to act independently, that was not inconsistent with the co-ordination of efforts. Their preference was related to their own sense of *noblesse oblige*, the pre-eminence of British power, the comparative antiquity of the Board and perhaps its deliberative procedures, a sense of British insularity and the personality of Sir Moses Montefiore. In so far as the Jewish leaders regarded themselves as acting as Englishmen as well as in their capacity as Jews, one may therein detect some response by them to the ever-recurring strictures by critics of the Jews both before and after their admission to Parliament on the score of Jewish internationalism.

The Anglo-Jewish Association, of which Benisch was the principal founder in 1871, came into being (with the declining power of the Alliance following the defeat of France) in order to sustain international Jewish consultation and action, especially in the face of what was considered to be the slow operation of the Board. Many of the most prominent emancipationist activists became leading members of the Association from the start. Just as the Damascus Affair led to the marshalling by Jews of sympathetic gentile opinion in Western capitals and precipitated the creation of international Jewish co-ordinated action, so too in the 1870s and later such action was undertaken in response to the plight of Romanian and Russian Jewries.

Anglo-Jewish leadership had evolved out of a group of families with a highly cultivated sense of responsibility for a community whose members they had initially tended to regard in the last resort as dependants. It represented the psychology of patron and retainer, and owed much to English class-consciousness. It was reinforced by a sense of religious duty, compassion, habit and enlightened self-interest. No one can read, for example, the memoirs and journals of the Cohen and Rothschild ladies without being struck by the strength of personal and family commitment arising from such attitudes and instincts, including those who married out of the faith.[6] A somewhat formal relationship with Judaism, even in some instances a marked and conscious attenuation of attachment to its forms, was combined at times with strenuous involvement in communal administration.

Directly and indirectly, such states of mind gave to a large array of ruling families, as well as to those who adopted their kinds of communal action, a strong sense of pride in being involved in the sustaining of Jewish institutional life. There having been no ghetto, there was none of the continental drive to demonstrate that they had left the ghetto, even though a high priority was accorded to the nurture of Anglicization. The process of Westernization was gentler in Britain.

The existence and the entrenched privileges of the Established Church encouraged establishmentarianism within the Jewish community. It was seen as a bolster to tradition, a force for moderation, and an 'in-fashion' device for control. The creation of the United Synagogue in 1870 through the union of the main Ashkenazi congregations in London, provided the founders of the organization with an English-style instrument against deviation from received ritual and liturgy. The union rested on the principle of rationalized mutual support between the synagogues. In practice it also rested upon the personal influence and communal power of the lay heads of the parent congregation, the Great Synagogue, notably Sir Anthony de Rothschild (who became the first President of the United Synagogue) and more especially his kinsman, Lionel Louis Cohen who had led the way towards union and who personified the outlook of the Jewish emancipationists and their immediate successors.[7]

The formation of the union by Act of Parliament which was passed upon the initiative of those men, was a remarkable event. They had prided themselves upon the voluntary nature of their religious community and upon the 'Nonconformist' character of Anglo-Judaism within the pattern of religions in the kingdom; yet they hinged their institution to statute, and expressly provided in its deed of foundation that the religious administration was to be under the sole control of the Chief Rabbi. No less striking was the provision that the synagogues were to follow the German and Polish ritual. That requirement retains its especially striking character in the historical context, even when one allows for the importance of the wish of the founders to exclude Reformism and even when one takes account of their respect for the example of their senior and prestigious sister community, long known as the 'Spanish and Portuguese' congregation.

Each one of the above provisions ran counter in one way or another to the public case defended by the emancipationists. They become more intelligible when set within the totality of communal thinking. It was always an inherent part of their public campaign that the Jews should be free to cultivate those elements in Jewish life which were deemed necessary to ensure their distinctive survival – and in particular to do so free from the anxiety that such an approach might come to be looked upon by themselves or by others as constituting or implying some unacceptable self-isolation. The success of the campaign for emancipation was taken as an indication that their acceptance in society as Englishmen arose in spite of their necessary exclusivity.

The principal founder of the United Synagogue was the banker, Lionel Louis Cohen, prominent in the Great Synagogue and the Central Synagogue. In January 1885, Cohen, a vice-president of the United Synagogue, addressed the Council of that body on the subject of foreign Jews in London. His words expressed attitudes which had long been prevalent in his school of thought. 'It is a mistake', he declared,

> to suppose that a radical difference exists between persons coming from Eastern Europe and the English Jews. Differences do exist, but they are less than formerly, and are rubbed off by the responsibility which comes when persons . . . are brought into contact with each other.

This practical, if also patronizing, approach lay behind the efforts of the United Synagogue and related organizations to exert an English and West End influence over the expanding immigrant Jewish community after 1881. Such control was particularly difficult to impose in the decades of rapidly increasing immigration, but it had not been an easy task even in the 1870s when the independent-minded Jewish congregations in and around the East End, although still relatively small, were often imbued with their own distinctive enthusiasms and a brittle pride.

However much Cohen's policy was motivated by the desire to anglicize the newcomers (and later to help stem anti-immigration agitation), his stance strongly reinforced the general image of Anglo-Jewry as a closely knit community, within which newer and older elements influenced each other and which could retain its character as Jewishly traditional, English in style and mutually supportive.

Long before he succeeded his father as Chief Rabbi in 1891,

Hermann Adler was the senior exponent of the views of the Anglo-Jewish leadership. He came to be so regarded from the 1860s in the early course of his long tenure as Minister of the Bayswater Synagogue. To that synagogue were attached many of the leading families in the hierarchy of communal leadership. Hermann Adler is often portrayed as the epitome of the Anglicized Victorian Jewish pastor. Until near the close of his career, he failed to promote study for the rabbinic diploma among the pastorate of which he was the head.[8] He was a frequent public advocate in effusive terms of pride in England and all things English. It was both a form of self-conscious patriotism and a part of the Westernizing process in which religious and lay leaders were consistently engaged. His consistent public discouragement of Yiddish had the eager support of Lord Rothschild. It was held to be a needlessly separatist jargon, even though many of those who spoke it were likely to regard the language as semi-hallowed by time and by usage in religious study. Adler was the major public advocate of Jewish attendance at the Local Authority schools newly established under the Education Act of 1870.

At the same time he consistently upheld rabbinic Judaism. His public identification with the Jewish cause was equally eloquent and consistent. He frequently gave expression to the official disapproval of the growing practice in the older families of exogamous marriage. He was an influential advocate of the creation of Jewish houses at the public schools attended by children of the Jewish upper middle classes. He publicly argued again and again that separateness was necessary to ensure that the Jews could continue to serve mankind by their dedication to an ideal of moral duty.[9] He publicly deplored any falling away in the readiness of adequate numbers in the Jewish 'upper classes' to succeed to positions of leadership in Jewish institutional life.

Whatever divergencies there may have been between the religious principles which the Chief Rabbinate sought to uphold, and the outlook and practices in some sections of the lay leadership with which he worked, there was seen by all to be communal benefit and public desirability in retaining an 'official orthodoxy'. That term came readily to the lips of critics of the system, from the religious 'right' as well as from the religious 'left'; but its implications were not disowned by those against whom the criticism was levelled. The point was often made that the Chief Rabbinate was highly suited to the temperament of British Jewry, especially in respect of the principles and attitudes evinced from the 1860s by Hermann Adler, the undoubted 'Crown Prince'. What was meant was the preference for the practical, a contentment with the public forms of piety and the non-ideological spirit of their performance, an ultimate moderation in contentious debate, deference to established authority and the assumption as to the value of comprehensiveness and union.

Adler discerned no contradictions in his policies. This devout ecclesiastic was devoted to the task of assisting the integration of the Jewish community into the life of the nation while retaining as its ethos the principles of traditional Judaism and sustaining the transmissibility of that cause.

The Jewish community could not be immune to influences affecting the whole of society. In his *The Secularization of the European Mind in the Nineteenth Century*, Professor Owen Chadwick wrote of the 'elusive shift in the European mind' which gained momentum in the 1860s.[10] It was a long-maturing shift away from beliefs and outlook resting upon metahistorical interpretations of history. Since Anglo-Jewry prided itself upon its denominational character and since the image of the Jews as a nation was increasingly shunned, the consequences of the advance in the secularized outlook gave particular pause to those who looked ahead. Thus, the sophisticated leaders of the Jewish community remained religionists. For many it was a matter of conviction. Where it was not, or where the issues were encased in inward personal debate, few were ready to make a conscious withdrawal from the religious system by which the community was defined and within which it operated.

The growing respectability of secular philosophies was not the only erosive factor impinging upon the Jewish community. There were ever more opportunities for public service outside that community. Furthermore, the advancing social fraternization between the Jewish and gentile middle classes, especially in the upper echelons, tended to broaden the gulf between the cadres from which Jewish leadership had traditionally come and the expanding base of the Jewish community. However, communal policy required that the gulf be bridged and this fact in many instances encouraged the privileged to retain communal responsibilities and personal communal involvement regardless of social distance and ideological divergence.

In 1852 the City of London School, following the example of University College School in Hampstead, opened its doors to all, subject to fees, regardless of religion. On 6 August the *Jewish Chronicle* in classic Victorian terms welcomed this liberalization. 'Our surest hope', wrote the editor, of enlisting the future sympathies of our educated fellow-citizens is to make ourselves more worthy of their friendship and respect by raising up in the next generation a body of Jewish gentlemen who shall be equal to their Christian fellows in intelligence and mental acquirements no less than in pecuniary means.

The enlisting of the 'sympathies of our educated fellow-citizens' continued to be an important objective and in its own way required that the above-mentioned gulf be bridged.

The comparison between Henry Keeling and Samuel Montagu is picturesque and instructive. The former was a jeweller in the City of London and a vocal member of the Western Synagogue and the Board of Deputies. His easy manner and charitableness made him a popular figure among Jews and Christians. In 1853 he allowed himself to be elected Churchwarden of St George's in the City, stipulating only that he should be excused from taking part in the religious services. His condition was accepted. His election, which was unanimous, was hailed as evidence of the folly of the scare that the admission of Jews to Parliament would 'unchristianize' the legislature.

Keeling was also among the leading Jewish spokesmen against opportunities of excessive fraternization between Jewish and Christian children in the schools. In the *Jewish Chronicle* on 23 July 1869 he sternly warned against the risks of Christian influence at school. Asserting his own liberal outlook ('I have always been liberal in my ideas'), Keeling added,

I have always considered the prime purpose in the struggle to attain civil and religious liberty was to secure the Jewish community in its exclusive right of upholding our institutions distinct from those of other creeds.

Sir Samuel Montagu (later the first Lord Swaythling), the banker who in 1887 founded the Federation of Synagogues out of the intensely Orthodox bethels (or *shtiblekh*) of the East End, was from the 1870s the most resolute layman in metropolitan Jewry in defence of firm Orthodoxy. He was also among the most outspoken critics of Jewish day schools, save for the children of the immigrant poor. For the latter they would be a valuable Anglicizing factor. For the children of the Jewish middle classes, Jewish schools would, he stated, cause narrow-mindedness and foster inhibitions in the relationships between Jews and their fellow-citizens of the Christian faith in later life.

Throughout the nineteenth century, Anglo-Jewish opinion retained the paradoxes involved in the non-merging of the Westernized Jews. Those paradoxes are the stuff of which modern Jewish life is made. Many issues which were debated in the middle decades of the century remained in the public consciousness – the nature and purpose of Jewish identity, the meaning of the Jewish national idea, the character of Jewish kinship, the forms and extent of Jewish integration. Such issues became more highly charged around the turn of the century. However, if in the twentieth century the mid-Victorian scene takes on the remote air of distant familiarity, it is familiarity none the less.[11]

Notes

1 Prior to Claude Montefiore, the most vocal Anglo-Jewish advocate of the kind of advanced Reform well known in Germany was Alfred Henriques. On 7 August 1906, the *Jewish Chronicle*, in its obituary notice which was in personal terms sympathetic, rightly observed that 'his ideas were not palatable to many members of the community'. While the implications of the Reform Synod convened in Leipzig in 1869 were much discussed in Anglo-Jewry, it was noted that the Reform congregation in Britain was not represented there. See D. W. Marks, Consecration Discourse at West London Synagogue of British Jews, 1842, in *Collected Sermons* (London, 1851), p. 132; D. W. Marks, *The Jews of Modern Times* (two lectures London, 1871); and D. W. Marks and A. Lowy, *Memoir of Sir F. H. Goldsmid* 2nd edn (London, 1882).

2 See in particular the correspondence between M. Raphall and Charles N. Newdegate, M.P., in M. Raphall, *Jewish Dogmas* (London, 1849).

3 T. M. Endelman, *The Jews in Georgian England 1714–1830: Tradition and Change in a Liberal Society* (Philadelphia, 1979), p. 9.

4 The emancipationist spokesmen, regardless of their differing opinions on the proper pace of emancipation and integration, were aware that, on the whole (the optimistic hopes of the conversionists apart), society did not expect the total absorption of the Jews. They were looked upon by many as an irretrievably surviving ancient people whose role, character and external relations were bound up with a particular faith. Absorption would require the erosion of that faith, especially its national elements. See, too, for example, I. Finestein, 'Anglo-Jewish Opinion during the Struggle for Emancipation', Jewish Historical Society of England, *Transactions*, 20 (1964), 113–43; I. Finestein, *Post-Emancipation Anglo-Jewry: The Anglo-Jewish Experience* (Oxford, 1980); I. Finestein, 'The Uneasy Victorian: Montefiore as Communal Leader', in V. D. and S.

Lipman (eds.), *The Century of Moses Montefiore* (Oxford, 1985), pp. 45–70;
I. Finestein, 'Some Modern Themes in the Emancipation Debate in
Early Victorian England', in J. E. Sacks (ed.), *Tradition and Transition,
Essays Presented to the Chief Rabbi* (London, 1986), pp. 131–46; L. P.
Gartner, *The Jewish Immigrant in England, 1870–1914* (London, 1960; 2nd
edn 1973); V. D. Lipman, *Social History of the Jews in England, 1850–1950*
(London, 1954); V. D. Lipman (ed.), 'The Age of Emancipation', *Three
Centuries of Anglo-Jewish History* (Cambridge, 1961), pp. 69–106; and H.
Pollins, *Economic History of the Jews in England* (London, 1982).

5   For Goldsmid's electoral address, see D. W. Marks and A. Lowy, *Memoir
of Sir F. H. Goldsmid*, appendix 5 to part 1.

6   See in particular: Lucy Cohen, *Arthur Cohen, a Memoir* (London, 1919);
Lucy Cohen, *Lady de Rothschild and her Daughters* (London, 1935); Lucy
Cohen, *Some Recollections of Claude Goldsmid Montefiore* (London, 1940);
Lady Battersea, (Constance Flower, née de Rothschild), *Reminiscences*
(London, 1922); and Hannah F. Cohen, *Changing Faces* (London, 1937).

7   For the emergence and growth of the United Synagogue, see S. S. Levin
(ed.), *A Century of Jewish Life* (London, 1970), and A. N. Newman, *The
United Synagogue 1870–1970* (London, 1976). Cf. Geoffrey Alderman, *The
Jewish Community in British Politics* (London, 1983); Geoffrey Alderman,
The Federation of Synagogues (London, 1987); Stephen Sharot, 'Religious
Change in Native Orthodoxy in London, 1870–1914', *Jewish Journal of
Sociology* 15, no. 2 (1973), 167; and Steven Singer, 'Jewish Religious
Observance in Early Victorian London', *Jewish Journal of Sociology* 28,
no. 2 (1986), 117.

8   For Adler's personal and public explanation of this policy and of his late
change of attitude in terms of the changing needs and character of the
community, see his important published lecture (1905) 'The Sons of the
Prophets', in *Jews' College Jubilee Volume* (London, 1966), part 2, p. 1.

9   The idea of the Jewish mission was stressed in the mid-Victorian era as a
justification for Jewish separateness. In the following generation it was
stressed as an explanation of a moral justification for Jewish dispersion in
face of political Zionism. In widely noted sermons at the Bayswater
Synagogue in 1869 (published in London in that year), Adler ex-
pounded the doctrine of Jewish Messianism and explored its biblical and
rabbinic sources. He rejected Christian assertions that the ruined
condition of Jewish Jerusalem was by its nature permanent and later
advocated support for Jewish settlements in the Holy Land. He was less
to the fore with these ideas when confronted with political Zionism,
which he vehemently opposed. The influx of Eastern European Jews into
Britain from 1881 (totalling almost 150,000 entrants by 1914 into a
community which in the 1870s barely totalled 60,000) presented Adler
and his lay associates with ready-made centres of resistance to the style of
Anglicized, centralized and anti-Zionist Judaism of which he was

deemed the main exponent. See, for example, I. Jakobovits, 'The
Attitude to Zionism of Britain's Chief Rabbis as Reflected in their
Writings', in his *'If Only My People . . . ': Zionism in My Life* (London,
1984), p. 209.

10 O. Chadwick, *The Secularization of the European Mind in the Nineteenth
Century* (Cambridge, 1975), p. 17.

11 A telling demonstration is afforded by the efforts of some members of the
Sephardi Synagogue in 1852 to discover from the congregation's
religious heads (David Meldola and Abraham Haliva) whether it was
'inimical' to their religion for them 'to associate for the purpose of
adopting constitutional measures to promote the idea of our nation
regaining possession of Palestine'. This interest was in the wake of Judah
Alkalai's famous efforts to arouse support for his proto-Zionist endeavours. With the concurrence, if not at the request of, the Mahamad,
Meldola and Haliva avoided giving a reply. In response to publicly
expressed dismay at this seeming abdication of authority, Meldola wrote
to the *Jewish Chronicle* on 23 July that the 'future deliverance' will be by
divine intervention as distinct from human agency. The spokesman of
the enquiring members, Solomon Sequerra, wrote to that journal in the
next issue that they made their enquiry as 'Englishmen' and that their
object was 'to see the Jewish nation assume rank and standard amongst
the nations of the earth, that millions of our suffering brethren may be
released from the despotism and unheard-of oppressions and national
degradation'. Meldola's reply and Sequerra's rejoinder were typical of
that age, and are not necessarily mutually exclusive in their implications.
The aforementioned 'object' was pursued by the emancipationists and
their early successors but without any express cultivation of the Jewish
national idea.

German Jews in Victorian England: a study in drift and defection

TODD M. ENDELMAN

At the accession of Queen Victoria to the throne in 1837, there were, at most, 30,000 Jews living in England, approximately half of them in London.[1] They were overwhelmingly of Ashkenazi origin, themselves immigrants or the descendants of immigrants from Holland, the German states and, to a lesser extent, Poland. Most had come to England to escape the poverty and degrading restraints on freedom of movement, residence, occupation and marriage that embittered Jewish life in most of old-regime Europe. In the Victorian period, Jews from German-speaking Central Europe continued to migrate to England, even after Jewish legal status there began to improve. However, it is impossible to know how many came, since the British census, while recording country of origin of persons of foreign birth, failed to distinguish between Jews and Christians at a time when there was a substantial German commercial colony in England. In addition, because this immigration stretched over many decades, beginning soon after the end of the Napoleonic wars and continuing until almost the end of the century, and burdened neither native Jewry nor the larger society, as the later Eastern European wave did, it attracted little attention at the time. At best, one can say that several thousand – but certainly no more than 10,000 – German Jews moved to Britain during this period.[2]

German Jews who settled in Victorian England differed from their eighteenth-century predecessors in a number of critical ways. Most immigrants in the Georgian period, like the majority who remained behind, were poor. They came with few material resources or skills and on arrival took to low-status street trades to earn a living: hawking goods about the streets, buying and selling old clothes and other second-hand goods, peddling notions, gimcracks and inexpensive jewellery in the countryside.[3] These trades required little capital or knowledge of English and were already familiar to the immigrants before their migration. Some were eventually able to improve their economic situation, entering the ranks of small shopkeepers and manufacturers; a fortunate few became overseas merchants and dealers in luxury goods; others remained mired in poverty, frequently dependent on communal relief to make ends meet. The immigration from German-speaking lands in the Victorian period, on the other hand, was largely middle-class in character – in part, a reflection of the rapid social and economic transformation of German Jewry which occurred in the nineteenth century. Those who arrived at this time came with greater resources – a secular education, prior experience in large-scale commerce, access to capital – and a broader cultural outlook than their predecessors and were thus better positioned from the start to make their way into the English middle class.

Most of the new arrivals were merchants and commercial clerks with current links to or previous experience in large-scale trading ventures, attracted to England by its unrivalled mercantile and industrial pre-eminence. A number of immigrants who rose to prominence in the textile trade in the Midlands, like Moritz Rothenstein and Jacob Moser in Bradford, served apprenticeships in Jewish merchant houses in Germany before settling in England. Others, like Emanuel and Philip Freud in Manchester (half-brothers of Sigmund Freud) and Jacob Behrens in Bradford, gained experience in family firms before their migration. Some were sent to England for the specific purpose of establishing branches of already flourishing ventures. The story of Jacob Behrens is typical (though the extent of his success was not). His father Nathan headed a merchant house in Hamburg that imported woollen and cotton goods from England, then the centre of world textile production, and in turn distributed them in northern Germany. Jacob visited England a number of times during the years 1832–4 to buy textile goods in Leeds for the family firm. His inability each time to persuade local manufacturers to make up goods to his exact specifications convinced him of the advantage of setting up a permanent branch in England. In 1834, he rented a small factory and warehouse in Leeds; at first he manufactured and shipped woollen goods for the firm in Hamburg but later he set up as an independent manufacturer and exporter, eventually becoming one of the great textile magnates of the region.[4]

Most immigrants from Germany in the Victorian period, then, could at a minimum read and write German; in many instances, they were literate in other European languages as well. A very small number had attended university and acquired professional training. The laryngologist Felix Semon had completed his medical studies in Berlin; the industrialist Ludwig Mond had studied chemistry at Marburg and Heidelberg; the journalist Karl Marx had studied history and philosophy at Bonn, Berlin and Jena. One indicator of the cultural status of the immigrants, whatever the level of their formal education, was their ability to take part in musical, literary, artistic and political activities outside the Jewish community – either in the company of gentile German merchants or native English merchants and professionals. In Manchester, for example, the prosperous calico printer Salis Schwabe (a convert to Unitarianism) moved easily in middle-class philanthropic and political circles. He took an active role in the anti-corn-law campaign, became a close friend of Richard Cobden and Elizabeth and William Gaskell, entertained them and other middle-class notables at his country home in Wales, served as Chopin's host when he visited Manchester, chaired a meeting of German residents at the time of the 1848 revolution to express their sympathy with the Frankfurt Assembly and in general made his mark on liberal philanthropic activity in the city.[5] In Bradford, Birmingham and Manchester, German Jews and German gentiles banded together to establish social and cultural clubs where they could eat heavy, multi-course, two-hour meals in the German fashion, read German periodicals, gossip about politics and business in their native tongue, nap and play cards. The first two chairmen of the Schiller Anstalt in Manchester (a library, newspaper reading room and dining club) were Jews, as were many of the members – a fact that led Friedrich Engels to refer derisively to the institution as 'the Jerusalem Club'. In London, the merchant banker Isidore Gerstenberg and the orientalist Emanuel Deutsch were members of the German Association for Science and Art, founded in 1864 by the political exile Gottfried Kinkel.[6]

Those German Jews who settled in England were not typical, however, of German-Jewish migrants in general in the nineteenth century, the vast majority of whom settled in the United States. Most of the latter came with far fewer resources of any kind with which to launch themselves. They were overwhelmingly young and poor, without prior experience in large-scale commerce or family connections to established mercantile firms. Many of them, particularly those who left in the first decades of the migration, had their fares paid by communal charities eager to be rid of persons who might otherwise become a long-term fiscal burden. Without sufficient capital to start their own businesses, the great majority became pedlars, in the cities and the countryside, along the Atlantic seaboard and in newly settled regions of the Mid-West, South and Far West.[7] Most did not remain pedlars for the remainder of their lives, however, but, after ascending the various rungs of the peddling ladder, became shopkeepers, wholesale merchants and, in some instances, manufacturers, primarily in various branches of the clothing trade. Indeed, by the turn of the century German Jews in America had become a solidly middle-class community, their rise from poverty to prosperity being the most rapid of any immigrant group at the time.

Immigrants to England in the Victorian period also differed from earlier Jewish arrivals in their pattern of settlement. In the eighteenth and early nineteenth centuries, almost all newcomers settled in London, where the great bulk of the Jewish population was concentrated, although some, after a stay in London and a stint peddling in the provinces, set up as shopkeepers in ports on the south and east coasts, like Chatham, Portsmouth, Plymouth and Yarmouth, or in pre-industrial county towns, like Exeter, Canterbury, Oxford and Ipswich. In the Victorian period, however, substantial numbers of immigrants settled immediately in what had become the industrial heartland of the country, in manufacturing cities like Manchester, Leeds, Bradford and Nottingham. Representatives of Jewish trading houses in Germany that imported and distributed English textiles and other manufactured goods came to establish permanent branch offices that would allow them to circumvent local brokers and ensure a steady flow of goods at favourable prices.

The Behrens family came to the Midlands under such circumstances, as did scores of others. To cite only two examples: Jacob Weinberg arrived in Nottingham at the age of twenty to establish a branch of the well-known Hamburg firm of Simon, May and Co. and succeeded in making it one of the most flourishing in the city; Isidore Gerstenberg came to Manchester, also as a twenty-year-old, to represent the Hamburg textile merchant Abraham Bauer, though he moved to London several months later. There he continued to work for Bauer, until setting up on his own four years later, first as a merchant and then as a banker and stockbroker.[8] Young men without capital or connections also migrated to the Midlands with the intention of working as clerks and managers in the offices, warehouses and factories of their fellow immigrants. After a number of years they frequently went into business on their own.

Immigrants continued to settle in London as well, certainly in numbers equal to those who went to the Midlands, for it remained a major centre of small-scale manufacturing and a dynamic commercial and financial capital, despite the concentration of heavy industry elsewhere. Thus London continued to attract persons with entrepreneurial drive, capital and commercial experience: cigar importers, antique dealers, toy manufacturers, wool brokers, grain brokers, investment bankers, fancy goods merchants, etc. Several Jewish banking families in Germany sent their sons to London (and Paris and New York as well) to take advantage of rapidly growing opportunities in government loans, international trade and railroad, mining and industrial securities. Jakob Stern of Frankfurt, a brother-in-law of Nathan Rothschild, sent two of his eight sons – David and Herman – to London. Another Frankfurt brother-in-law of Nathan Rothschild, Benedikt Moses Worms, sent his three sons to London to open a merchant bank. When Ralph von Erlanger, a Frankfurt agent of the Rothschilds in the period after the Napoleonic wars, launched his own concern, he too sent a son to the City. Speyer Brothers, Bischoffsheim and Goldschmidt and Schuster, Son and Co. – likewise offshoots of Frankfurt family concerns – also began in the same way.[9]

Although the immigrants of the Victorian period were motivated chiefly by economic considerations, they were also moved, if not to the same degree, by the pervasive anti-Jewish hostility of their homeland. Some were in flight from discriminatory statutes that limited freedom of settlement and occupation; a handful were refugees from the political repression that followed the abortive revolutions of 1848 (but they were no more representative of the migratory stream as a whole than their counterparts who fled to America). But most were not so much attempting to escape this or that obstacle to advancement, many of which were removed with the spread of legal emancipation, as seeking to flee a milieu in which Jews were routinely treated with contempt and derision. In his memoirs Jacob Behrens repeatedly recalled the indignities he suffered while growing up in Hamburg. He described, for example, how he and his father, when travelling to fairs, would be refused lodging because they were Jews. He also related how his friendship with Ferdinand David, a young Jewish pupil of the Cassel orchestra conductor, was abruptly terminated when the latter insisted that David convert and sever all relations with Jews in order to advance his career. 'This was typical of the times and such experiences fixed an indelible impression on my mind', Behrens wrote.

Felix Semon, who grew up in Berlin several decades later, also cited the intolerance of German society as a motive for migrating to England. In his autobiography he recalled the difficulty of choosing a profession when he was a gymnasium student in the 1860s. All the careers he was most inclined towards – the diplomatic corps, the army, the civil service – were closed to Jews. Commerce held no interest for him; history and science did, but a university career without baptism was also an impossibility. Thus Semon was led by a process of elimination to medicine. When he completed his training, he chose to leave Germany, in part because of the widespread dislike of Jews there. Sigmund Freud considered settling in England several times for similar reasons and never ceased to envy his half-brothers in Manchester, whom he visited in 1875, for being able to raise their children far from the daily indignities to which Viennese Jews were subject. A few months after becoming engaged to Martha Bernays, he recalled for her 'the ineffaceable impressions' of his trip to England and asked, 'Must we stay here, Martha? If we possibly can, let us seek a home where human worth is more respected.'[10]

Immigrants in the Victorian period differed from their predecessors in one other important respect as well: they did not grow up in a traditional Jewish milieu, segregated socially and culturally from the surrounding society. Although legal emancipation was incomplete before 1871, the corporate and national character of Jewish life was well on the way to dissolution before then. German Jews were embracing gentile patterns of thought and behaviour and abandoning traditional religious customs. Old loyalties and allegiances were weakening and new identities being forged. Thus the new immigrants from Central Europe, unlike those who migrated earlier, were accustomed to participating in spheres of activity outside the confines of Jewish social and business networks. Few had received a traditional Jewish education or grown up in homes in which regular synagogue attendance and observance of the dietary laws were the norm. Jacob Behrens, for example, who grew up in Hamburg in the 1810s, received no Jewish education except for some last-minute preparation for his bar mitzvah in the Reform synagogue. Ludwig Mond's upbringing in Cassel in the 1840s and 1850s was not too different. He was educated at non-Jewish schools, learned only enough Hebrew to go through the bar mitzvah ceremony and as he grew to maturity gave up all religious practices, declaring himself an agnostic.[11]

The immigrants' prior acculturation to gentile standards and habits and complete or partial estrangement from Jewish beliefs and customs, as well as their exposure to the pervasive antisemitism of their homeland, profoundly influenced their communal and religious behaviour once settled in England. Many held aloof from any formal identification with Judaism, while those who affiliated with synagogues remained for the most part haphazard in their attendance at services and lukewarm in their observance of domestic rituals. (Because the German immigrants were few in number in relation to the native Jewish community and synagogues already existed in the towns where they settled – with the exception of Bradford – they did not form congregations of their own, as did their counterparts who migrated to the United States at this time.) Most either passed out of the Jewish community altogether, through conversion or intermarriage, or established such a weak connection to it that their children or grandchildren eventually did so. To be sure, none of this can be established with statistical certainty, but contemporary testimony, as well as non-quantifiable evidence, makes abundantly clear that the majority of immigrants from Central Europe in the Victorian period took advantage of their new surroundings to shed or dilute their Jewishness.

Contemporaries commented frequently on the disinclination of the immigrants to identify themselves publicly as Jews. When the newly appointed Chief Rabbi, Nathan Adler, surveyed the congregations under his authority in 1845, the New Synagogue in Glasgow replied that many 'respectable' German Jews lived in the city who did not belong to or attend the synagogue. The *Jewish Chronicle* noted in April 1859 that there were hundreds of foreign-born, prosperous Jews in the country, especially in London, Liverpool and Manchester, neither belonging to synagogues nor subscribing to communal charities. In Manchester, in particular, there were numbers of German Jews who were not even known as Jews. When Chaim Weizmann arrived there in 1904, he recalled in his memoirs, 'The great majority of German Jews . . . were disassociated from their people, and many of them were converts to Christianity.' In August 1865, the *Jewish Chronicle* reported that there were many wealthy Jews in Bradford but no congregation, not even a burial ground. These German Jews, according to the newspaper, did not want to be known as Jews (although apparently everyone knew they were). They failed to circumcise their sons or educate them in any way as Jews. They buried their dead in a Christian cemetery and married their children to gentiles in church ceremonies. Efforts on the part of the Leeds congregation to stimulate the formation of a synagogue in Bradford in the early 1860s failed. When the Chief Rabbi himself visited the city in 1865, six Jews showed up at the meeting he called and told him that he was wasting his time in attempting to create a congregation. Five years later, when there were two to three hundred German Jews in the city, the one service held that year – on Yom Kippur – attracted only fifteen people. The following year, when services were held on both Rosh Hashanah and Yom Kippur, thirty to forty people attended on the latter day. When the community's first rabbi, Joseph Strauss – German-born, German-educated, and Reform in outlook – arrived in 1873, he found the older and wealthier Jewish residents 'indifferent to Judaism'. Chief Rabbi Adler charged him with bringing these families back into the fold, dubbing him a 'missionary for Judaism'.[12]

Some of those who distanced themselves from Judaism remained equally aloof from Christianity out of contempt for revealed religion of any kind. Jacob Behrens, who failed to establish even nominal links with the Anglo-Jewish community (despite his marriage to a Jewish woman, whom he brought from Germany ten years after his arrival in England), resembled an eighteenth-century deist in his religious outlook. His exposure to religious bigotry as a boy and young man in Germany made membership in any religious body impossible for him.

> All forms of service conducted on lines strictly laid down and according to dogma find no response in me, even if they do not repel me. When either Christian minister or Jewish rabbi calls on the inscrutable God with the audacity and familiarity of an old acquaintance, I can see nothing but a hollow lie or an unfathomable depth of stupidity.

Reasonable men, he felt, could not believe in the personal God of organized religion. Thus he refused to give his children any religious training, convinced that it was hypocritical to educate children in a faith in which one did not believe.[13] However, his descendants and those of his brothers Louis and Rudolf drifted contentedly into the Established Church. For them and other English-born offspring of German Jews, free-thinking anticlericalism was neither attractive nor relevant to their own experience. They were eager to get on in polite English society and principled opposition to institutional religion was simply not socially respectable.

The religious outlook of Ludwig Mond was as sharply deistic as that of Behrens. For him there was no such thing as a reasonable religion. He and his German-born Jewish wife were completely alienated from Jewish practices. They did not celebrate Jewish holidays in their home. They failed to circumcise their sons Robert and Alfred or make any effort to raise them as Jews – or, for that matter, as Christians. For Mond's alienation from Judaism was fuelled by a principled objection to revealed religion, not by social ambition, as evidenced by his unwillingness to acclimatize himself to English ways. He preferred to speak German at home, for example, and his sons grew up speaking that language better than English. In addition, despite his wealth, he never acquired the trappings that would have eased his way into upper-class society, such as a fashionable London address, a country estate (his home, Winnington Hall, Cheshire, adjoined his chemical factory), a racing stable, a hunting pack or a yacht. He even declined a peerage when it was informally offered. He also did not seek to make socially advantageous matches for his sons.

Alfred married Violet Goetze, daughter of a London coffee merchant, in 1892; the officiating clergyman almost refused to perform the ceremony when he discovered that the bridegroom was neither a professing Jew nor a Christian. Robert married Edith Levis, daughter of a wealthy Manchester rubber importer of German-Jewish origin, in 1898. Her family, including aunts, uncles and cousins, had drifted away from the Jewish community earlier in the century and she had converted to Christianity following her parents' deaths. The third generation of Monds in England, not surprisingly, were raised as members of the Established Church, although two of Alfred's children, much to their mother's distress, later embraced Judaism and Zionism. Their grandfather Ludwig also experienced some uneasiness late in life about his earlier rejection of his ancestral faith and on his deathbed sent for a rabbi and made arrangements for a Jewish burial.[14]

Felix Semon also espoused views similar to those of Mond and Behrens. While believing in 'divine government' and claiming to be 'by nature of a religious turn', Semon refused to join any religious body, for he thought that all religions, each alone claiming to possess the truth, were too exclusive. Like the deists of the previous century, he cited the suffering and bloodshed engendered by religious differences throughout history as an obstacle to faith and affiliation. Yet he raised his children in the Church of England, in part because his wife was a Christian (although he did not cite this as a reason), and in part because he did not want 'to close many careers open to them, by mere obstinate adherence to the old tradition'.

Whether adherence to Judaism in fact was a serious obstacle to career advancement in early twentieth-century England is doubtful. Perhaps Semon was led to believe that this was so by his upbringing in Germany, where, indeed, being Jewish was frequently an absolute barrier to occupational mobility. In any case, his children merged into the English mainstream – so much so that when his son Henry, a dermatologist, was asked in 1926 to supply biographical information for an entry in the *Jewish Year Book*, he indignantly replied, 'I cannot imagine where you could have read that I am a member of the Jewish community – much as I respect both it & many of its members, who are my friends.'[15]

A principled refusal to affiliate with any religious body was not characteristic of German Jews who failed to affiliate with Anglo-Jewish institutions. More common, at least in provincial cities, was membership in a Unitarian chapel. In justifying his decision to preach on the differences between Judaism and Unitarianism, S. M. Schiller-Szinessy, rabbi of the Reform congregation in Manchester, explained in 1859:

> Our attention is due to Unitarianism on account of the fortuitous circumstance that it is *that* form of Christianity to which such Jews as feel themselves induced to abandon their brethren and to turn their backs on the religion of their fathers are in the first instances chiefly attracted.

Most of the German-Jewish merchants who arrived in Manchester between 1790 and the mid 1830s abandoned Judaism, and most of them became Unitarians. The most prominent in the group, Salis Schwabe, apparently took his new faith seriously. At home, for example, he would lead the servants, assembled in the library, in prayer and read to them the Bible and sermons by Unitarian divines. According to an obituary in the *Christian Reformer*, 'sincere and deliberate conviction' had led him to Unitarianism, not the hope of 'worldly advantages', which were available only to members of the Church of England. Unlike most Jewish apostates in the nineteenth century, whose attachment to Christianity was nominal, 'he adhered with quiet and honourable firmness to the forms of worship of Unitarian Christianity'. His children remained active in the Cross Street Chapel after his death, serving as trustees for many years.[16]

In Nottingham the majority of the German immigrants, most of whom were active in the city's hosiery and lace trade, became Unitarians. The most prominent was Lewis Heymann, a native of Teterow in Mecklenburg-Schwerin, who settled in Nottingham about 1834. He began business as a lace manufacturer but later became primarily a shipper. He and his German-born Jewish wife joined the High Pavement Chapel not long after their arrival, for their two oldest children, who were born in November 1835 and January 1837 respectively, were both baptized there in June 1837. Like Salis Schwabe in Manchester, his attachment to his new faith was not a matter of mere convenience. He and his family attended worship regularly and he served as a warden of the congregation several times. He also occupied a prominent place in local politics, serving as alderman and then, in 1857, becoming the town's first foreign-born mayor. His fellow Unitarian, the silk merchant and brewer Edward Goldschmidt, who migrated from Hamburg to Nottingham in 1851, was active in politics a generation later. He was elected a member of the town council in 1870, served as alderman from 1876 until he retired in 1895, and was nominated as Liberal candidate for Parliament in 1890 but refused to accept.[17]

The tendency of newcomers who settled in the provinces and then abandoned Judaism to affiliate with Unitarianism was a departure from the usual pattern of apostasy in Anglo-Jewish history. In general, when Jews in England embraced Christianity, they joined the Church of England – for obvious reasons. Their motives for becoming Christian were almost always pragmatic. They were seeking to escape the stigma attached to Jewishness and complete their absorption into the mainstream, to improve their social fortunes and, before emancipation, gain entry to institutions, such as Parliament, which were closed to professing Jews.[18] In these circumstances, Jews in flight from their Jewishness naturally joined the high-status Established church rather than low-status Nonconformist chapels, whose members were themselves often objects of scorn and were also barred from certain offices and honours. If the object of conversion was social advancement rather than spiritual salvation, it hardly made sense for Jews to become Baptists or Methodists.

However, in the manufacturing cities of the Midlands and the North, the reference group for upwardly mobile Jews was not the same as it was in London or in the countryside. The elite to whom the recent arrivals from Germany looked for guidance in matters of deportment and style and with whom they sought to merge was Unitarian and industrial-mercantile, not Anglican and landed (as it was for Jews who made their fortunes in finance and international trade in the City of London). In Manchester, for example, the membership of the Cross Street Chapel included opulent merchants

(many with country estates purchased out of the profits of trade),
affluent professional men and bankers. Its members played a key role
in establishing the major educational and cultural institutions of the
new liberal order in the city, such as the Literary and Philosophical
Society and the Mechanics Institute. They were well-educated and
culturally sophisticated men and women, not dour Philistines, as
literary caricatures of dissenters frequently suggest. On the contrary,
they subscribed to the substantial quarterly reviews, spent considerable sums of money on oil paintings and ardently read the latest
poetry. The Unitarians in Manchester were, in the words of a
contemporary observer, 'as a body, far away superior to any other in
intellect, culture, and refinement of manners, and certainly did not
come behind any other in active philanthropy and earnest efforts for
the social improvement of those around them'.[19]

Yet the attraction of Unitarianism to German-Jewish immigrants
in the provinces was not entirely social. Although rooted in Calvinist
Presbyterianism, Unitarianism had become relatively broad-minded
by the early nineteenth century. It was theologically relaxed,
spiritually undemanding and politely rationalistic. Its ministers were
frequently men of wide secular learning, intellectually sophisticated
and tolerant of diverse opinions. Most importantly, its anti-
trinitarian stance removed what was to Jews the most baffling and
objectionable aspect of Christianity and made sincere acceptance of
the faith possible. To immigrants critical of traditional religion in any
form, this was an immense advantage. They could enjoy the social
benefits of belonging to a religious body whose members were
wealthy, dynamic and influential without having to accept supernatural theological doctrines repugnant to their own outlook.

In London, where Unitarians did not occupy the same position as
they did in Manchester and other industrial cities, German-Jewish
immigrants did not join Unitarian chapels in substantial numbers.
The records of the Rosslyn Hill Chapel in Hampstead, which drew its
upper-middle-class membership from neighbourhoods throughout
northwest London (the major area of German-Jewish settlement),
indicate that only four or five families of German-Jewish origin
belonged to the congregation in the 1860s and 1870s and only eight or
nine families at any one time from the 1880s to the start of the First
World War. If German Jews in London formally abandoned
Judaism, they were likely to be baptized – or have their children
baptized – in the Church of England, which was the religious
affiliation of the dominant strata of society there. Thus, the novelist
Cecily Sidgwick's father, David Ullman, who married outside the

Jewish community after settling in London in 1848, raised his children as members of the Established Church, as did the laryngologist Felix Semon. Louis Heinemann, father of the publisher William Heinemann, married within the community, but he and his Manchester-born wife, Jane Lavino, both abandoned Judaism for the Church of England.[20]

An even smaller number of Central European Jews in London chose yet another religious alternative to membership of the Established Church – affiliation with a universalist ethical society or ethical church. Hungarian-born Maximilian Loewe, a follower of Louis Kossuth who settled in London following the collapse of the 1848 revolution, was an enthusiastic supporter and close friend of Charles Annesley Voysey, the heretical Anglican priest who established his own congregation, the Theistic Church, in London in 1871. Loewe (or Low, as he eventually spelled his name) and his wife, daughter of an Austrian rabbi, discarded all Jewish practices soon after their marriage and at some point were attracted to Voysey's anti-supernatural theism, which rejected fundamental pillars of Christian belief like the divinity of Jesus and the divinely revealed character of scripture. When Voysey launched his own church, Low was one of the wealthy Londoners who backed him financially. The publisher William Swan Sonnenschein and his wife, a descendant of an old Huguenot family, were members of the London Ethical Society, the first to be established in England, and his firm issued its literature, including many volumes in the Ethical Library series, mostly at a financial loss. His father Albert, a native of Moravia, had migrated to England in the middle of the century, opened a school in Highbury, and married the daughter of the Revd Edward Stallybrass, a missionary in Siberia for many years. The educator Samuel Sigmund Fechheimer joined an ethical society when sixteen years old and later helped to found the Ethical Church in Queen's Road, Bayswater, in 1909. As an honoured founder, his ashes were kept in a funeral urn in a niche in the wall of the church. Of the various ethical churches and societies in London, the Hampstead Ethical Institute, which was established at the turn of the century, drew the largest group of Jews of Central European origin. In later years it attracted Jews from other backgrounds as well and after the First World War, in fact, became predominantly Jewish in its make-up. One sociologist has even suggested that its largely Jewish membership in this century endowed it with longer life and greater cohesion than other ethical societies.[21]

In general, though, the ethical movement in Britain, unlike its counterpart in the United States, attracted relatively few Jews, native or immigrant. At first, this may seem surprising, for the ethical movement offered Jews who were alienated from Jewish tradition the possibility of religious affiliation without the acceptance of supernatural doctrine. It spared them the hypocrisy of endorsing, even nominally, Christian beliefs that were as irrational and fantastic as those they were rejecting. Felix Adler's Ethical Culture Society attracted widespread support from German Jews in New York and other American cities precisely because it forged a progressive, high-minded path between Judaism and Christianity. It allowed its adherents to escape the ritualism and supernaturalism of existing religious bodies and yet proclaim, at the same time, their commitment to universal religious ideals.

In England the ethical movement did not have the same appeal to Jews, largely due to its historical associations with radical political culture. There secularism was part and parcel of a broader stream of causes that threatened the established order in state and society: attacks on private property, republicanism, anti-clericalism. The secularist movement brought to mind the sight of atheists haranguing large, unruly crowds in parks; it suggested working-class infidelity and moral laxity. Secularists were, in Susan Budd's phrase, 'perpetual outsiders', frequently suffering social ostracism and occupational discrimination. Genteel men and women, whatever their true religious views, did not go in for this sort of thing, as Felix Adler himself discovered when he toured England in 1892. After failing to obtain a hearing for his ideas at Oxford, he wrote home to his wife that the atmosphere there was suffused with conservatism: 'Even the scientific men are more or less pledged to conventionalism, and are constrained to all sorts of subtle compromises.'[22] It is not surprising, then, that few German Jews in England – or native Jews, for that matter – cast their lot with the ethical movement. Only those with strong personal convictions and equally strong personalities were likely to become members. Most who wanted to escape the stigma of Jewishness but felt uncomfortable with supernatural religion swallowed their reservations and settled into nominal conformity with the Established Church or, in some provincial cities, a Unitarian chapel. Others, generally those who were not eager to better their social standing in gentile circles, remained quietly outside any religious body.

The tendency of German Jews to shed their Judaism after settling in England contrasts sharply with the religious behaviour of their native-born middle-class counterparts, who did not disaffiliate with the community in great numbers in the Victorian period.[23] To a limited extent, the high rate of defection can be explained by the fact that the newcomers were leaving a Jewish environment in which religious observance and knowledge had already declined precipitously. In other words, they came to England without a strong prior attachment to home observance and synagogue attendance and once there simply carried their disengagement one step further. On the other hand, native middle-class Jews, while perhaps more diligent in some matters of observance than Jews elsewhere in the West, were not on the whole pious practitioners of their ancestral faith. Yet most were content to remain within the boundaries of the community of their birth, even if they felt little attachment to traditional rituals and beliefs. In others words, alienation from Judaism as a system of doctrines and practices need not necessarily lead to estrangement from the Jewish group – as should be abundantly clear from the history of the Jewish community in the United States in this century.

The German environment shaped the behaviour of Jewish immigrants to Victorian England in another, more profound, way, however. The new arrivals carried with them attitudes towards Jewishness that bore the impress of conditions quite different from those they encountered in their new home. In German-speaking lands, Jews had remained second-class citizens until the last third of the century, and even after emancipation they still faced widespread social and occupational discrimination. In addition, ideological antisemitism was virulent, deep-rooted and far from being a marginal element in high culture or respectable society. German Jews who identified strongly with the majority culture frequently experienced their Jewishness as a misfortune or burden; in some instances, bitterness and resentment at the accident of Jewish birth developed into pathological self-hatred. (It is no coincidence that studies of Jewish self-hatred utilize examples from German-speaking lands almost exclusively.)[24] Those who migrated to England at this time often behaved in regard to their Jewish identification as if they were still living in their homeland, where conversion was a common response to discrimination and denigration. Once settled, they took advantage of their new surroundings to jettison that part of their past with which they were uncomfortable. Migration became for them not only a means of improving themselves materially but also an opportunity for refashioning their identity. To be sure, it is possible that they found integration into their new surroundings blocked by their Jewishness – although there is little evidence that this happened – and that they remained apart from the Anglo-Jewish community in order to expedite their acceptance. However, we know that prosperous native-born Jews were able to break into gentile circles and institutions without rejecting communal bonds.[25] (The relatively few native English Jews who converted at this time did so largely to escape the psychological burden of belonging to a stigmatized minority, rather than to gain access to offices and circles that in other lands were closed to professing Jews.) This suggests that it was not primarily antisemitic discrimination in England that encouraged their flight but the formative impact of conditions in their homeland in the period before their migration. The experiences of their early years made it difficult for them to assess the character of Jewish status in Britain dispassionately, and thus they failed to realize that worldly success and advancement were attainable there without abandoning the Jewish community.

In the case of those immigrants who settled in the provinces, the small size of some communities and the absence of well-developed communal institutions – synagogues, charities, schools – may also have contributed to the tendency to choose a different religious affiliation. Bradford, for example, had no Jewish institutions of any kind when German-Jewish merchants began settling there in the 1830s. In nearby Leeds there were a mere handful of Jewish families in the first half of the century – seventy persons at most by 1850; a cemetery was acquired only in 1840 and a synagogue (a converted room) established only in 1846. There the presence of a disproportionate number of single men and the absence of a substantial Jewish middle class encouraged intermarriage and a falling away from Judaism among both native and immigrant residents. Still, the Jews of Leeds were more numerous and better provided for than those in Bradford, and thus by the 1860s Jewish merchants from Germany who settled there were more likely to establish Jewish connections than those who went to Bradford.[26] On balance, however, the underdeveloped character of Jewish life in the provinces, while contributing to drift and defection, was not the decisive element, for German Jews in London were no more steadfast in their allegiance to Judaism, although the London community was more numerous and better organized by far than any other in the country.

In regard to the Manchester community, Bill Williams suggests that the absence of a Reform synagogue (before 1856), with decorous worship, enlightened preaching and progressive ideas, contributed to the apostasy of German-Jewish merchants who arrived there in the first half of the century. He points out that the Reform congregation was established at a time when many Manchester Jews were hesitating between Unitarianism and Judaism and, while failing to recapture families whose assimilation was far advanced, did succeed in keeping the allegiance of those whose distaste for Orthodoxy would otherwise have led them to depart. It became, in his words, 'a religious safety-net for the future'.[27] The argument Williams advances is not novel. Enthusiasts for Reform everywhere in the West argued that the creation of an up-to-date Judaism would stem the tide of apostasy by offering young men and women a way of being Jewish consonant with their secular cultural and educational attainments. The German-born American Reform rabbi David Einhorn termed the Reform movement 'the liberation of Judaism for the sake of preventing an estrangement from Judaism', while his German contemporary Samuel Holdheim called the radical Reform congregation in Berlin that he headed 'an alliance against apostasy'.[28] The assumption they and other champions of Reform made – and that Williams himself makes as well – is that Jews who became Christians in the nineteenth century were fleeing Judaism – that is, primitive rituals, lengthy and disorderly services, unenlightened doctrines. In truth, while these aspects of Judaism repelled increasingly secularized and acculturated Jews, those who left the community altogether were more in flight from the social and pyschological strain of being Jewish, as well as concrete obstacles to career advancement, than from Judaism *per se*. No amount of reforms, no matter how radical, would have kept such men and women within the community.

Not all immigrants from Germany in this period deserted Judaism, of course. Most of the religious functionaries of the Victorian community were German-born and German-educated – a reflection of the intellectual poverty of the native community. The most notable were Nathan Adler, Chief Rabbi from 1845 until his death in 1890; Gustav Gottheil, rabbi in Manchester for thirteen years before his departure for New York City in 1873; Michael Friedländer, principal of Jews' College for more than forty years; and Samuel Marcus Gollancz, reader at the Hambro Synagogue in London and progenitor of an intellectually distinguished Anglo-Jewish family. In addition, there were also, here and there, lay persons who were loyal to traditional practices before their migration and remained so afterward. The Nottingham lace shipper Jacob Weinberg, a native of Hamburg, for example, was meticulously observant. He shut his office on the sabbath and festivals and maintained a private synagogue in his own home. He took no active part in political or civic affairs but instead devoted his leisure hours to Jewish learning. In Highbury, Canonbury and Stoke Newington, a small community of strictly orthodox Central European immigrants – followers of S. R. Hirsch's so-called neo-Orthodoxy – coalesced around the North London Beth Hamedrash in the last decades of the century.[29]

But such immigrants were clearly exceptional. Most of those who chose to identify themselves with Anglo-Jewish institutions did not perpetuate traditional practices and beliefs. Their attachment to Judaism was lukewarm, and the profession of their ancestral faith was limited in some instances to being married and buried according to Jewish rites.[30] Their homes were largely devoid of Jewish ritual and their attendance at synagogue rare and irregular. Their efforts to provide the next generation with the learning that would allow them to live as Jews were half-hearted and minimal, if not altogether absent. Their children, who were educated in English schools, grew up feeling far more English than German or Jewish. They mixed with non-Jews in a variety of formal and informal settings and participated in spheres of activity outside the social boundaries of English Jewry. Yet, however attenuated their sense of Jewish identity, to the larger society they remained somehow different, not quite English. Thus many found their Jewishness to be a burden that was not worth bearing and ceased to have any contact with Jewish institutions or social circles after they entered the adult world.

In two volumes of memoirs, the poet and critic Humbert Wolfe recorded with great sensitivity the anguish of growing up Jewish in such circumstances in Bradford at the end of the century.[31] Wolfe's father, a native of Germany who had been in business in Milan before settling in Bradford, was a prosperous wool merchant. The family maintained a loose attachment to Judaism. They visited the synagogue, which was Reform, on Rosh Hashanah and Yom Kippur, and Humbert attended religious school classes there on Sunday mornings for a number of years, but nothing in his upbringing fostered warm feelings toward Judaism. Attendance at High Holiday services left him emotionally unmoved. The rabbi (Joseph Strauss, a German import) had no message to impart; the Hebrew hymns made no impression. 'There was nothing here to inspire or excite the young worshipper.' Strauss's position in the community brought home to Wolfe how little his parents and their friends valued religion, for the wealthy merchants who managed the synagogue treated Strauss like a clerk in one of their warehouses, bullying him into 'a state of sullen stupidity'. They brooked no interference with their consciences by someone they considered their paid servant. His business was 'to interpret the ways of God to man in general, but to avoid the particular at all costs'. Their contempt for Strauss was infectious; Wolfe learned from his elders to sneer at him.

Although Wolfe felt unmoved by Judaism, he could not forget he was Jewish. At school and university he was acutely sensitive about being set apart from his fellow students by his origins. Regularly taunted by a group of urchins as he made his way to the synagogue school on Sunday mornings, he felt bitterly ashamed of being different, envying the church- and chapel-goers on their way to worship. As he wrote of himself, 'Each Sunday the boy ran this gauntlet, hating not his persecutors but the object of their persecution.' Overt attacks such as these, however, were rare and less destructive of his confidence than a host of small signs, not always conscious, reminding him that he belonged to a minority, 'edged on the one side, excluded, different'. That the English were too 'easy-going and good-humoured' to carry their antisemitism to extremes only made matters worse, for 'when the taint of Jewry means only exclusion from garden-parties, refusal of certain cherished intimacies, and occasional light-hearted sneers, it is difficult to maintain an attitude of racial pride'. Had he been secure in his faith or taken pride in his Jewishness, he later realized, he would have been better able to withstand the sense of being different.

In his last years at school, Wolfe developed strong literary interests and simultaneously began to think seriously about religious questions. The 'faint shamefaced Judaism of Bradford' offered him no answers or solace and so he turned to Christianity. He discussed the desirability of being baptized with a friend, George Falkenstein, who had himself become a Unitarian. Falkenstein admitted that Unitarianism was a compromise, 'a sort of half-way house'. To Wolfe, the budding poet and prospective Oxford man, this choice seemed 'well enough for unadventurous or doubtful spirits' but 'a little too mild' for himself. Yet he could not bring himself to embrace Christianity. He repeatedly slunk in to evening services at St Jude's and found himself pleased with the eloquence of the preacher and the light streaming in through the stained-glass windows. He realized that it would be 'comfortable' to feel himself 'numbered among those to whom these spiritual elegances belonged' and 'advantageous' to the career he envisioned. 'But something – probably no more than a mixture of shyness and apathy – had held him back.' He arrived at Wadham College, Oxford, still concerned about the fate of his soul – and his career – but unsure about what religion he was committed to. He had no doubt that Judaism was unsatisfactory but still could not take the plunge into the Church of England – 'a step which a desire to be like other men tempted him to take' – for he was concerned about what his mother would think (his father was dead) and restrained by 'something stubborn in his blood, which remembered Zion'. When Wolfe left Oxford, he passed by examination into the civil service and went on to a distinguished career in a number of departments, in addition to writing and editing over forty books. In 1910, he married a gentile, the daughter of an Edinburgh schoolmaster, and as an adult maintained no affiliation to the Anglo-Jewish community.

The painter William Rothenstein grew up in a German-Jewish home in Bradford similar in its Jewish loyalties to Wolfe's. His father, who arrived in Bradford in 1859 at the age of twenty-two, was a rationalist in religious matters and attended the Unitarian chapel in Chapel Lane – though he also subscribed generously to the needs of the Jewish community. However, his mother, also a native of Germany, remained faithful to Judaism. Before a synagogue was erected, she attended High Holiday services conducted by a visiting rabbi in a rented hall, and when a building and rabbi were later acquired, she took the children with her. They greatly disliked the experience and irreverently mocked the Hebrew prayers when they returned home.

The Judaism of the Rothenstein home did not reach very deep. One summer, when the family was on holiday at Scarborough, a handsome evangelist from Oxford holding children's services on the sands captivated young William and baptized him. William took his new faith seriously, solemnly discussing with the family maids the almost certain damnation of his parents. With the approach of his thirteenth birthday, he faced a personal religious crisis, for his mother insisted that he celebrate his bar mitzvah, while he believed in the saving grace of Jesus of Nazareth. He refused to learn the Hebrew blessings, so they were transliterated for him. In the end he went ahead with the ceremony, convinced that Jesus would not allow him to utter blasphemy and would appear in person to save him from wrongdoing. As he waited to be called to the Torah, he thought he saw the shadow cast by the *ner tamid* sway a little and took this as a sign that Jesus was coming to his rescue. But when he went forward to recite the blessings, nothing happened. He experienced intense disappointment and afterward came to the conviction that no one religious system was better than another.[32]

As an adult, Rothenstein held to this conviction; neither he nor his wife, a lapsed Roman Catholic, affiliated with any religious community, although they were not opposed to religion on principle. Yet, when their son John was born in 1901, they had him baptized in the parish church of the Norfolk village where they were spending the summer. Clearly they felt that even if they found no solace in organized religion their son might and, at the very least, should be able to enjoy the benefits of membership in the established faith. When he was five or six, they asked a close friend, the Revd Henry Woods of the Temple Church, London, to come to the house to explain God to John because they were constitutionally unable to do so, that is, they simply could not express whatever religious sentiments they felt in dogmatic terms. In time, as can happen with the children of irreligious parents, John moved dramatically in the opposite direction, becoming a fervent Catholic. However, he postponed his formal conversion for many years because his father, the lapsed Jew, objected. William Rothenstein was not troubled by the supernatural doctrines of the Roman Church, for religious doctrines of any sort meant little to him, but by the minority status of the religious community John proposed to join. 'What he intensely disliked', John recalled in his autobiography,

> was the propensity of English Catholics – far more pronounced then than it is today [1965] – to form a closed world within a world; the idea of my becoming a member of a society that might make me sectarian, cut off from the mainstream of national life, and above all from . . . upper-middle-class Liberal tradition.

Having himself emerged from a 'sectarian' group 'cut off from the mainstream of national life', William did not want his son to join a similarly marginalized group. John waited until he was financially independent and then, in 1926, was received into the Catholic Church. Towards the end of his life, William was also drawn to Roman Catholicism and during the Second World War attended mass with his son and daughter-in-law, but he could not accept the necessity of dogma so he remained unbaptized. When he died in 1945, he was buried in the parish churchyard near his Gloucestershire country home.[33]

Children of German-Jewish immigrants who grew up in circumstances similar to those in which William Rothenstein and Humbert Wolfe were raised tended to disassociate themselves from Jewish life once they reached adulthood. The ambiguous religious and ethnic character of their home life – part Jewish, part Christian, part English, part German – left them without a firm inner sense of who they were and thus unable or unwilling to cope with even low levels of contempt and exclusion. That is, because they did not follow a recognizably Jewish regimen nor affirm distinctively Jewish beliefs nor mix primarily in Jewish social circles, they were not prepared to endure even modest slights on account of their identification with the Jewish group. Humbert Wolfe, it should be recalled, felt that he had been especially sensitive to the taunts of other children because he had been brought up in a lukewarm Jewish atmosphere and lacked the pride that would have allowed him to withstand their contempt. He concluded that a Polish Jew, secure in his faith, was better able to withstand virulent antisemitism than a deracinated English Jew, ever alert to the least suggestion of being different, the occasional social sneer or jibe.

The poet E. H. W. Meyerstein, who was raised in such circumstances, felt that he became the target of wounding schoolboy taunts precisely because he was neither fully Jewish nor fully Christian. His father, Sir Edward William Meyerstein, was a wealthy London stockbroker whose parents had migrated from Germany in the middle of the century. Sir Edward and his wife practised no religion at any time in their lives, but brought up their children from an early age in the Church of England, presumably for pragmatic reasons. According to Meyerstein, his father, 'if he believed in a deity, never mentioned the fact', while his mother 'often mentioned God, as a being, apparently immaterial, in whose sight she was justified in whatever she did'. Although the children attended Church of England services, they were not formally baptized until 1903, just prior to Meyerstein's departure for Harrow.

There he suffered greatly as a newly minted Christian of German-Jewish origin. Boys would shout at him in the streets of Harrow; athletes would roar out behind him a musical comedy ditty about a Mr Rosenstein. The music master told another boy that Meyerstein liked Mendelssohn's piano music because he was a Jew; when Meyerstein won the school music prize, the music master refused to post the announcement on the school board. As Meyerstein later recalled, a boy from a well-established Jewish family who was proud of his religion and believed he was as good as anyone else got through school just fine, but a boy of Jewish antecedents who had been baptized and also had a German name was 'due for hell'. He felt he would have been much happier had he been able to boast 'I am proud of my race!' and then bash his tormenters with his fists. His father tried to assure him that there was no prejudice against Jews in England, but, as Meyerstein realized, his father's experience and his own were entirely different, since his father had been educated at a day school (University College School) with few social pretensions and a sizeable Jewish enrolment and had passed most of his life among bankers and brokers.[34]

Meyerstein's experience at Harrow haunted him his entire life, influencing both his self-confidence (or, rather, his lack of it) and his attitudes to Jews. At Oxford, he participated enthusiastically in chapel (more for aesthetic than spiritual reasons), but later he ceased to identify himself in any way with the Church of England. Indeed, he felt he did not fall within any denominational pale. Yet he realized, however reluctantly, that he would always be viewed as a Jew, regardless of his formal religious status. His reputation as a poet, he believed, had suffered because the English would not tolerate 'a bloody German Jew' in their poetic pantheon. Had he been a pianist, an impresario, or a financier – or had his name been different – there would have been a place for him, or so he claimed. Yet he protested, in vain, that he was not a Jew and not particularly proud of the race that had persecuted Spinoza and crucified Jesus. He did not like Jews or 'the Jewish genius' (he made exceptions for Felix Mendelssohn and Heinrich Heine) and was never at ease in their company, believing that they were always expecting 'some sort of display or exhibitionism' that he could not give them.[35]

The reactions of a Meyerstein were not typical, however. For most offspring of German-Jewish immigrants who abandoned or drifted away from their ancestral origins, entry into gentile society was a less troublesome experience. Anguish and anxiety were not the usual accompaniments of radical assimilation in England, particularly since most Jews were content with modest levels of social integration (unlike Meyerstein, who yearned for literary apotheosis). For the second generation, the break with Judaism was frequently not even the outcome of a premeditated scheme for social advancement but rather the unintended consequence of prior social integration and religious secularization.

In families with weak or nominal Jewish commitments, the choice of a spouse – itself subject to the vagaries of sexual attraction and financial calculation – frequently determined the Jewish fate of the next generation. If a young person from a home that was only nominally Jewish took a partner from a similar background, they might remain attached to the Jewish community, though in a tenuous way. But if this young person happened to choose a spouse from a Christian background – which was equally possible, given the ease with which the offspring of German-Jewish merchants moved in gentile society – the couple and their descendants would almost certainly have no contact with the Jewish community. In either case, the Jewish fate of the family would depend not on any prior commitment to or strategy for radical assimilation but on chance circumstances and, of course, prior indifference to traditional religious practices.

How this worked out in practice can be seen in the Jewish affiliations of the London branch of the Warburg banking clan. Fredric Elias Warburg emigrated from Sweden to London around 1860. (The Swedish Warburgs were not, strictly speaking, German Jews, but in the context of this discussion can be considered as such, for they had only recently settled in Sweden and were similar in their religious habits to family members who remained in Germany.) The founder of the English branch made a fortune in the City, largely through financing London's first underground railways in association with Ernest Cassel. He and his wife never attended synagogue or in any way practised Judaism. Two of their three sons married Christian women and ceased to be even nominal Jews on their marriage, raising their children eventually in the Church of England.

A third son, John Cimon Warburg, happened to marry a woman of German Jewish origin, Violet Amalia Sichel, and so consequently he remained a Jew, that is, he was married in a synagogue service and buried in a Jewish cemetery. His Judaism did not go much further than that. His son, the publisher Fredric John Warburg, explained in a memoir that the family's Jewishness was largely a matter of inertia. The Warburgs, he wrote, were Jews 'because they were born of Jewish parents and believed themselves to be Jews', but 'their religious feeling was slight and their racial exclusiveness negligible'. They were both too proud and too lethargic to disaffiliate themselves formally from the Jewish group through conversion; thus they remained Jews until something unintended occurred to make them leave their Jewishness behind. 'Then they changed with as little fuss as a man changing from one lounge suit to another of a slightly different colour. So they remained basically the same, substituting for the practice of not going to synagogue the rather similar practice of not going to church.'[36]

Unlike her husband, Violet Amalia Warburg felt that religion was important. In the view of her son Fredric, she turned to Judaism because she was unhappy and lonely: her husband ignored her and her in-laws bullied her. Whatever the reason, she found some relief in the consolations of religion. She gave her children religious instruction, hiring a tutor to come to the house to teach them Judaism. There were also periods when she and the children attended sabbath services with some regularity. But her approach to Judaism was decidedly non-traditional. For example, she never fasted or had her children fast on Yom Kippur (a practice then common even among otherwise lax Jews) because her 'fondness' for her children would not allow 'the smallest degree of religious fanaticism', and thus they ate substantial meals that day without qualm.[37]

Her son Fredric did not share her interest in Judaism, however easygoing its character. As a boy, his main concern was to be so like his schoolmates as to be indistinguishable from them. At Westminster School, where he was enrolled at the age of thirteen, he gladly would have attended chapel (actually divine service at Westminster Abbey), but his mother was adamant that he, like the other Jewish boys, be excused. Non-attendance marked him out as a Jew, so 'to the horrors of being a new boy at public school was added the horror of being known as a Jew'. The 'substantial if superficial' antisemitism of his upper-class schoolmates caused him to suffer 'profoundly'.[38] The source of his suffering, however, was not entirely persecution from without. Herbert Samuel's son Edwin started Westminster School at the same time as Warburg, but apparently did not suffer greatly from anti-Jewish taunts and jibes during his years there, for he makes no mention of antisemitism at school in his memoirs.[39] This is not to say that he never heard unpleasant remarks about his origins. To claim so would be patently absurd. But for Samuel, who came from a family whose Jewish commitments were firm and unambiguous, the level of antisemitism he encountered at school was not sufficiently powerful to disturb his equilibrium or subsequently merit inclusion in his memoirs. Warburg, on the other hand, was in a situation similar to that of a Humbert Wolfe or an E. H. W. Meyerstein: he was not prepared, by virtue of his background, to withstand even moderate levels of anti-Jewish sentiment. Thus, precisely because he was eager to flee his Jewishness, he was unable to brush off remarks that reminded him of it. As an adult, not surprisingly, he had no contact with Judaism or Jewish communal affairs. He married twice, both times non-Jews, and effectively left the community.

The absorption of German Jews and their offspring into English society progressed steadily in the years before the First World War. Although it is impossible to gauge their incorporation in any quantitative way, the available evidence seems to indicate that with every year more and more of them ceased to be identifiable as Jews. Their departure was not a dramatic affair for the most part. This was because their numbers were not great by comparison with the native community and even more by comparison with the new Eastern European immigrant community, which became the focus of wide-spread public attention from the 1880s. Their absorption also failed to attract public notice because the host society, which, after all, determined the pace of integration, put few obstacles in their way and for the most part welcomed them with open arms, thus obviating the need to wage a public campaign to secure access to new circles and institutions. Moreover, those who left their Jewishness behind them were already so indifferent to Jewish concerns that they seem to have experienced little remorse or inner discomfort; if so, they left few records of it. For them, taking on a new religion was not a momentous decision; for many, if not most, it was no more emotionally charged than changing from one suit of clothing to another of slightly different colour (to borrow Warburg's metaphor).

During the First World War, the pace of assimilation among families of German-Jewish origin received an unexpected boost. The anti-German hysteria of the war years caused hundreds of families to Anglicize their names in order to avoid suspicion of disloyalty to Britain. Auerbachs became Arbours; Meyers, Merricks; Rothen-steins, Rutherstons; Schlosses, Castles; Waldsteins, Walstons; etc. Although the immediate motive for these changes was the desire to obscure German, rather than specifically Jewish, origins, the effect was the same. Stripped of their German names, the children and grandchildren of Jewish immigrants from Central Europe could blend even more easily into the larger society. As Albert Rutherston explained in urging his brother William Rothenstein to join the rest of the family in changing his name: 'A German name will be a hindrance and an inconvenience so long as we live. It is not giving the children a fair chance because the bitterness will never go.' He emphasized, moreover, that the Rothensteins – or Rutherstons, rather – were 'a new family'. Changing the family name would help the family sink its roots in the country. 'Why not whilst we can make them [the children] as strongly planted as we can?'[40]

The wholesale name changing of the war years made possible the virtual disappearance of the German-Jewish group in the 1920s and 1930s. Individual families here and there continued to identify as Jews, of course, but they were the exceptions. When J. B. Priestley returned home to Bradford in 1933, he discovered, to his regret, that there was 'hardly a trace now of that German-Jewish invasion' of the previous century. That same year, when Jewish refugees from Nazi Germany began arriving in Great Britain, they found no circles or associations of Jews of German origin to help them in their resettlement. Indeed, the rise in anti-Jewish agitation and discrimination in the country at that time discouraged persons of Jewish origin without strong Jewish commitments – regardless of when their ancestors arrived in England – from asserting their links with Jewry. Stephen Spender, whose maternal grandfather, Ernest Joseph Schuster, came from a Frankfurt-Jewish banking clan, recalled that when he was growing up in the 1910s and 1920s both his Jewish and German origins were 'passed over in silence or with slight embarrassment' by his family. As a child, he had no idea that he was 'a quarter Jewish'. From the conversation of nurses and governesses, he had gathered the impression that Jews were 'a strange race with hooked noses' and 'avaricious manners', with whom he had no reason to imagine that he had any connection.[41]

The assimilation of the descendants of the German immigration of the Victorian period was more or less complete by the outbreak of the Second World War. Their disappearance from the stage of English-Jewish history was rapid, occurring within one or two generations after the arrival of their forebears in England, and quiet, attracting almost no attention from friendly or hostile observers. Unlike their more numerous counterparts in the United States, they left no collective mark on the institutional structure or religious temper of the English-Jewish community. They were too few in number and too eager to distance themselves from their religious origins to do so. For however successful their social and economic integration in their new home, they were unable to escape the formative impact of their earlier experiences in a much less hospitable clime. For some, attachment to the Jewish group remained a matter of indifference at best, while for others it was an unnecessary burden or an outright embarrassment, an association just as well left behind or forgotten. In the relatively benign climate of England, this was easily done.

Notes

1 Vivian D. Lipman, *Social History of the Jews in England, 1850–1950* (London, 1954), pp. 6–8.

2 C. C. Aronsfeld estimates that of the 250,000 Jews who left Germany between 1830 and 1930 only 'a very few thousand' chose Britain. 'German Jews in Victorian England', *Leo Baeck Institute Year Book* 7 (1962), 312. Aronsfeld's essay, which is essentially a survey of prominent Victorians of German-Jewish birth, is the only extended treatment of the topic.

3 Todd M. Endelman, *The Jews of Georgian England, 1714–1830: Tradition and Change in a Liberal Society* (Philadelphia, 1979), ch. 5.

4 Jacob Behrens, *Sir Jacob Behrens, 1806–1889* (n.p., *c.* 1925).

5 Bill Williams, *The Making of Manchester Jewry, 1740–1850* (Manchester, 1976), pp. 93, 168–9; Rosemary Ashton, *Little Germany: Exile and Asylum in Victorian England* (Oxford, 1986), p. 207; *The Christian Reformer* n. s., 9 (1853), 596–7.

6 J. B. Priestley, *English Journey* (London, 1934), p. 160; Oswald E. Stroud (ed.), *The Story of the Stroud Family* (Bradford, *c.* 1974), p. 83; Zoe Josephs, *Birmingham Jewry, 1749–1914* (Birmingham, 1980), pp. 23–4; Williams, *The Making of Manchester Jewry*, pp. 169, 260, 412, n. 95; Ashton, *Little Germany*, p. 164.

7 Rudolf Glanz, *Studies in Judaica Americana* (New York, 1970), pp. 96, 109–11, 126–7; Allan Tarshish, 'The Economic Life of the American Jew in the Middle Nineteenth Century', in *Essays in American Jewish History to Commemorate the Tenth Anniversary of the Founding of the American Jewish Archives* (Cincinnati, 1958), pp. 264–5; Avraham Barkai, 'German-Jewish Migrations in the Nineteenth Century', *Leo Baeck Institute Year Book* 30 (1985), 311, 314.

8 *Jewish Chronicle*, 23 March 1900; Alexander Behr, 'Isidore Gerstenberg (1821–1876) – Founder of the Council of Foreign Bondholders', Jewish Historical Society of England, *Transactions*, 17 (1953), 208–9.

9 Stanley Chapman, *The Rise of Merchant Banking* (London, 1984), pp. 45, 50, 54, 136.

10 Behrens, *Sir Jacob Behrens*, pp. 20–1; Felix Semon, *The Autobiography of Sir Felix Semon*, ed. Henry C. Semon and Thomas A. McIntyre (London, 1926), pp. 31–2, 60; Ernest Jones, *The Life and Work of Sigmund Freud*, 3 vols. (New York, 1953), vol. I, pp. 13, 24, 178–9.

11 Behrens, *Sir Jacob Behrens*, pp. 11–13; J. M. Cohen, *The Life of Ludwig Mond* (London, 1956), pp. 16, 62.

12 Bernard Susser (ed.), Statistical Accounts of All the Congregations in the British Empire, 5606/1845, MS 104, Office of the Chief Rabbi, London, printed in *Provincial Jewry in Victorian Britain*, ed. Aubrey Newman (London, 1975); *Jewish Chronicle*, 8 and 15 April 1859, 11 August 1865,

21 and 28 October 1870, 6 October 1871; Chaim Weizmann, *Trial and Error* (New York, 1949), p. 115; Stroud, *The Story of the Stroud Family*, pp. 26–7.

13 Behrens, *Sir Jacob Behrens*, pp. 91, 93–4; *Jewish Chronicle*, 21 March and 4 April 1913.

14 Cohen, *Ludwig Mond*, pp. 189–247; Jean Goodman, *The Mond Legacy: A Family Saga* (London, 1982), pp. 30, 31, 34, 39, 68, 69, 75; Hector Bolitho, *Alfred Mond, First Lord Melchett* (London, 1933), pp. 44, 92, 358.

15 Semon, *Sir Felix Semon*, pp. 33–4; Henry C. Semon to S. Levy, 21 October 1926, AJ/151/1/B/14, Cecil Roth Papers, Anglo-Jewish Archives, London.

16 Solomon Marcus Schiller-Szinessy, *Harmony and Dis-harmony between Judaism and Christianity: Two Sermons Preached on the Sabbaths Shemot & Va-eira 5619 (December 25th 1858 and January 1st, 1859) at the Manchester Synagogue of British Jews* (Manchester, 1859), p. 9; Williams, *The Making of Manchester Jewry*, pp. 82–3, 93; *The Christian Reformer*, n. s., 9 (1853), 596–7; Malwida von Meysenbug, *Memoiren einer Idealisten*, 10th edn, 3 vols. (Berlin, 1906), vol. II, 38–9; Cross Street Chapel, Manchester. *Proceedings on the Occasion of the Bi-Centenary of the Chapel, June 24–25th 1894* (Manchester, 1894), p. 67.

17 C. C. Aronsfeld, 'German Jews in Nottingham', *AJR Information* (Dec. 1955), 8; Roy A. Church, *Economic and Social Change in a Midland Town: Victorian Nottingham, 1815–1900* (London, 1966), pp. 76–7, 182; register of births and baptisms, High Pavement Chapel, Nottingham, 1828–37, RG4/2674, Public Record Office, London; High Pavement Chapel, Nottingham, *A Biographical Catalogue of Portraits* ([Nottingham], n.d.), p. 28; William Blazeby, *My Year's Ministry at the Old High Pavement Chapel, Nottingham* (London, [c. 1906]), p. 8.

18 Todd M. Endelman, *Radical Assimilation in English Jewish History, 1656–1945* (Bloomington, 1990).

19 John Seed, 'Unitarianism, Political Economy and the Antinomies of Liberal Culture in Manchester, 1830–50', *Social History* 7 (1982), 1–25; Margaret J. Shaen (ed.), *Memorials of Two Sisters: Susanna and Catherine Winkworth* (London, 1908), p. 26.

20 Rosslyn Hill Chapel, list of members, 1 January 1875, RNC 38, 189; subscriptions, 1886–96, RNC 38.154; minutes, 1907–22, RNC 38.132, Dr William's Library, London; Cecily Sidgwick to Cecil Roth, 16 October 1926, AJ/151/1/A/4/54, Anglo-Jewish Archives, London; Frederic Whyte, *William Heinemann: A Memoir* (London, 1928), pp. 30, 38–9.

21 John Carswell, *The Exile: A Life of Ivy Litvinov* (London, 1983), pp. 21–3; *Dictionary of National Biography*, 1922–30, s.v. 'Sonnenschein, Edward Adolf'; F. A. Mumby and Frances H. S. Stallybrass, *From Swan Sonnenschein to George Allen & Unwin Ltd.* (London, 1955), pp. 13–15, 36;

The Ethical Message, special number: *A Souvenir of the Ethical Church* 2, nos. 7–8 (1917), 30–1; Susan Budd, *Varieties of Unbelief: Atheists and Agnostics in English Society, 1850–1960* (London, 1977), p. 205.

22 Budd, *Varieties of Unbelief*, pp. 36, 84–5, 110; Horace L. Friess, *Felix Adler and Ethical Culture: Memories and Studies*, ed. Fannia Weingartner (New York, 1981), p. 114.

23 Endelman, *Radical Assimilation in English Jewish History*, ch. 3.

24 See, for example, Theodor Lessing, *Der judische Selbsthass* (Berlin, 1930); Peter Loewenberg, 'Antisemitismus und judischer Selbsthass', *Geschichte und Gesellschaft* 5 (1979), 455–75; and Sander L. Gilman, *Jewish Self-Hatred: Anti-Semitism and the Hidden Language of the Jews* (Baltimore, 1986). Of course, there were also English Jews in the Victorian period who regarded their background with contempt and even loathing – the writers Amy Levy and Julia Frankau and the politician Edwin Montagu are well-known examples. But it is my impression that self-hatred was a less prominent feature of their make-up than that of their counterparts in Germany. It was milder and less pyschologically crippling. I also believe that this kind of self-hatred was less common in the Anglo-Jewish community, although further research on this interesting question may disprove what is, in truth, a mere impression.

25 Endelman, *Radical Assimilation in English Jewish History*, ch. 3.

26 A. S. Diamond, 'A Sketch of Leeds Jewry in the 19th Century', in *Provincial Jewry in Victorian Britain*; *Jewish Chronicle*, 11 August 1865.

27 Williams, *The Making of Manchester Jewry*, p. 262.

28 *Jewish Chronicle*, 8 April 1859; Michael A. Meyer, *Response to Modernity: A History of the Reform Movement in Judaism* (New York, 1988), p. 131.

29 *Jewish Chronicle*, 23 March 1900; Bernard Homa, *A Fortress in Anglo-Jewry: The Story of the Machzike Hadath* (London, 1953), pp. 10–11, 70.

30 See, for example, the comments of the novelist Cecily Sidgwick about German Jews in North London in *Isaac Eller's Money* (London, 1889), pp. 46, 110.

31 Humbert Wolfe, *Now a Stranger* (London, 1933); Humbert Wolfe, *The Upward Anguish* (London, 1938).

32 Robert Speaight, *William Rothenstein: The Portrait of an Artist in His Time* (London, 1962), pp. 5–6.

33 John Rothenstein, *Summer's Lease: Autobiography, 1901–1938* (New York, 1965), pp. 9, 30, 37, 123; Speaight, *William Rothenstein*, pp. 151, 405–6, 410.

34 E. H. W. Meyerstein, *Of My Early Life (1889–1915)*, ed. Rowland Watson (London, 1957), pp. 17–19; E. H. W. Meyerstein, *Some Letters of E. H. W. Meyerstein*, ed. Rowland Watson (London, 1959), pp. 240–1.

35 Meyerstein, *Some Letters*, pp. 131, 138, 241–3.

36 Fredric Warburg, *An Occupation for Gentlemen* (Boston, 1960), pp. 31–2; David Farrer, *The Warburgs: The Story of a Family* (New York, 1975), pp. 226–7.

37 Warburg, *An Occupation for Gentlemen*, p. 32.

38 Ibid., pp. 30, 32–3.

39 Edwin Samuel, *A Lifetime in Jerusalem: The Memoirs of the Second Viscount Samuel* (London, 1970).

40 Albert Rutherston to William Rothenstein, 2 April 1916, William Rothenstein Papers, BMS ENG 1,148 (1,296), Houghton Library, Harvard University.

41 J. B. Priestley, *English Journey* (London, 1934), pp. 160–1; Stephen Spender, *World Within World* (London, 1951), p. 13.

Israelite and Jew: how did nineteenth-century French Jews understand assimilation?

PHYLLIS COHEN ALBERT

Words often obscure more than they clarify. The problem is not intrinsic to the terms, but lies with the inconsistent ways they have been employed, and the myths fostered by indiscriminate use. In Jewish historiography, particularly problematic words have included 'emancipation', 'assimilation', and 'Israelite' (used as an alternative to 'Jew'). Happily for contemporary historians, Jacob Katz's thorough study of the history of the word 'emancipation' and other terms related to the concept has provided us with a more rigorous approach to this essential aspect of modernity.[1]

There remain, however, conceptual and linguistic problems with other terms, such as 'assimilation', frequently used to describe the modern Jewish historical experience. Ideologies and emotions have prompted polemical usage of 'assimilation', and thereby prevented dispassionate historical analysis. Zionists' disillusionment with emancipation as a solution to antisemitism readily led to scorn for nineteenth-century 'assimilationists', who had believed emancipation ideology and had assumed that acculturated Jews would be allowed to combine equality with particularism. Jewish nationalism branded such goals as delusions leading to collective ethnic and cultural suicide. These critics of emancipation railed against 'assimilationists', whom they accused of having rejected their historical past and their national identity, in favour of a new, narrowly religious definition of Judaism.

French Jews are often cited as the prime example of the inexorable rush of Western European Jewry from emancipation to collective self-denial. A relentless centralizing Jacobinism is deemed to have mandated a culturally homogeneous nation-state which crushed both territorial and non-territorial deviants. According to this view,

Bretons, Alsatians and Jews were all flushed out of their particularist, cultural enclaves and into the melting pot of French civilization.[2]

Like all myths, the depiction of assimilation in France contains some accurate observations, but as is also the case with myths, it distorts more than it illuminates. Studies of nineteenth-century French society by Theodore Zeldin, Eugen Weber and Gérard Noiriel have successfully challenged the old view of a unified French cultural and political allegiance. We now know that regional identities resisted the growth of the idea of a broader 'nation', a term and concept first introduced in the eighteenth century, and that immigrants were not systematically processed by the 'Frenchification machine' until the Third Republic.[3]

Yet, despite evidence that schoolchildren in parts of France in the middle of the nineteenth century did not even know that they lived in France, many Jewish historians continue to believe that the country's Jewish population quickly abandoned their group allegiance in favour of total identification with the French nation and state. This view produces the distorted cliché of the nineteenth-century French-Jewish experience as consisting of the rapid succession of emancip-ation, assimilation and the shock of the Dreyfus Affair. According to this interpretation, assimilationist ideology became the guiding principle of French Jews after their emancipation in 1791, as they sought to transfer their primary identification from a Jewish sub-group to the French nation through the assimilatory process that would ultimately eliminate all particularisms. Although religious differences would be retained temporarily, religion would occupy an increasingly narrow sphere, and Judaism would eventually be replaced by a new universalist religion in ultimate fulfilment of the Jewish mission to the nations.

It is the contention of this chapter, however, that this conventional analysis is based on a misunderstanding of the history and con-temporary connotations of the various terms used to discuss Jews in the nineteenth century. Concentrating on France, I will show that an understanding of the actual usage of these terms reveals that until late in the century Jews believed that emancipation (or equality of opportunity in the legal, civil and economic spheres) was fully compatible with their own desire to retain a Jewish social and cultural specificity. Their utilization of the term *Israélite* as an alternative to *Juif*, for example, lacked the antiethnic implications it acquired in the twentieth century.

Because French Jews understood emancipation as having granted them the right to be fully French, while retaining the freedom to develop and express their Jewish identity, they did not perceive a need for a conscious programme of assimilation. The assimilation that did take place was therefore spontaneous rather than programmatic. As one observer put it, 'The progressive disappearance of Jewish separateness came about without conscious choice.'[4]

The reasons for the misreadings of French-Jewish history are not difficult to pinpoint. They include the use of the optic of German-Jewish historiography; the reading of Jewish history backwards, in which twentieth-century realities are applied to the nineteenth century; and the selective and uncritical reading of nineteenth-century sources, without paying adequate attention to the changing meanings of words.

Elsewhere I have mustered linguistic and institutional evidence to demonstrate that French Jews maintained ethnic sentiment and solidarity during the nineteenth century.[5] Here I will summarize the indications that the community was not assimilated, and then focus on the key concepts which have been misunderstood by the propagators of the assimilationist myth. The terms I will analyse are, first, the word pair *Juif–Israélite*, and then 'assimilation' itself, together with the related terms 'fusion', 'identification', and 'affiliation'.

No sooner had French Jews received political emancipation than they began to seek ways of extending it to their 'brethren' living under less liberal regimes. From Michel Berr's abortive attempt of 1801 to use the forum of an international congress to achieve emancipation for European Jewry, until and beyond the establishment of the Alliance Israélite Universelle in 1860, a series of political activities brought French Jews together and gave expression to their solidarity.[6] At the same time a full range of ethnic institutions at home provided structures in which French Jews not only exercised their religion, but gave or received charity, were educated, received job training and work, were cared for when ill, all without leaving a Jewish milieu.

Participation in these Jewish associations was, of course, voluntary, and members of the socially mobile elite did loosen their ties, and in some cases even broke entirely with organized Jewish life. This was the case, however, for only a small minority. Because emancipation came early to French Jewry, and because the terms of that emancipation, in practice, if not always in theory, were lenient in regard to Jewish particularism, French Jews were not required to deny the social and cultural aspects of their Judaism. Clermont-Tonnerre's observation that the Jews deserved everything as individuals, but nothing as a nation, has been misunderstood almost as often as it has been quoted. What Jews were required to give up was not their ethnicity, but their corporate structure, their set of privileges and obligations as an officially recognized, unified body within French society.

Once the principle of individual citizenship with personal accountability to the state was established, no more was asked of the Jews. They were free to retain their social and cultural specificity (as were the many regional and linguistic groups within the country). Because no demands for assimilation were made, Jews were under no pressure to shed their identity. Their process of adaptation began to take the form of what has been called additive, rather than substitutive, acculturation.[7] Jews adopted the French language, norms and values, and merged them with their own traditions. They did not rush to disappear into the general French society, or to divest themselves of their own associations.

Religious observance, on the other hand, did decline significantly after the emancipation. This slackening in the religious sphere was chastised by the rabbis, who were the first to accuse Jews of putting the French above the Jewish aspect of their identity. Symbolic of this unfortunate reversal of emphasis, the rabbis complained, was the transformation of the term *Israélite Français*, common in the early nineteenth century, into the opposite formulation, *Français Israélite*, which had gained ground by the middle of the century.[8]

Discourse on the declining Jewish aspect of the dual French-Jewish identity was thus an invention of rabbis who feared the decline of Judaism as a religion. Only at the end of the century did the Jewish component of the dichotomy come to have a secular meaning, with social, cultural and national facets. What would later be transformed into the controversial 'double loyalty' of French and Jewish identification started life as the 'double love' for France and for Judaism that the rabbis preached in France in the middle of the nineteenth century.[9]

In support of the assimilationist myth, historians often claim that in the wake of the Revolution emancipated French Jews began calling themselves *Israélites*, in preference to *Juifs*, thus indicating that they had denationalized their Jewish identity, and limited it to a newly narrowed definition of the religious sphere. They are said to have thus set themselves apart from non-emancipated Jews of their own or previous generations.[10] Neat, appealing and popular as this theory is, it is unfortunately not supported by the evidence. All indications of nineteenth-century usage of the terms *Juif* and *Israélite*, in fact, refute the idea that any distinction existed between the two terms until the last few years of the century.

Only in the twentieth century did the language pattern contrasting the unacculturated ghetto *Juif* with the socially integrated *Israélite* crystallize. Such usage became popular during the four decades before the outbreak of the Second World War and lasted even into the 1960s. During these years *Israélite* was the polite term, favoured by Frenchmen anxious to prove their lack of prejudice and by Jews eager to demonstrate their integration and socio-economic success. A popular saying of the time had it that *Juifs* earned less than 300,000 francs a year, *Israélites* earned more than 300,000, *Français d'origine sémitique*, more than one million, and Christians more than 10 million.[11] A work of fiction popularizing this difference between the two terms appeared in Paris in 1930.[12]

During the interwar period, when the commitment of French Jewry to emancipation was being challenged by Zionism, the two terms expressed this political conflict. *Juifs* were nationalist Jews, whether Zionists or Diaspora autonomists, and *Israélites* were Jews who viewed their Jewishness as a religious category, while their nationalism was determined by the country of their citizenship. It has been a mistake, however, to read this dichotomy of terms and their significance, characteristic of the first half of the twentieth century, back into the nineteenth century.

The usage of *Israélite* took on new turns after the Second World War. Dominique Schnapper, in her book of 1980,[13] characterizes *Israélite* in a fivefold way: (1) it is a neutral term; (2) it refers to Jews born in France of parents born in France (and whose French ancestry might go back even an additional generation or more); (3) it designates those whose Jewish observance is either totally lacking or is limited to the bar mitzvah and Yom Kippur; (4) *Israélites* are not politically active, but do contribute money to Israel in times of crisis; and (5) they are fully acculturated and behave similarly to the non-Jews of their social class.

Although the many reincarnations of the term *Israélite* have served only to promote confusion about its meaning at any given time, no change in its meaning took place between the eighteenth and the nineteenth centuries. The great political watershed that occurred with the emancipation of French Jews in 1791 produced no comparable linguistic watershed on which to pin theories of changing notions of Jewish identity. Both terms, *Juif* and *Israélite*, had already existed in the eighteenth century,[14] ;and both continued to be used by Jews after the Revolution. Occasionally Jewish leaders did propose to abandon *Juif*, and use only *Israélite*, but the suggestion was never implemented.

The first to urge that *Juif* be eliminated from the French lexicon was Berr Isaac Berr, who would later represent Nancy at Napoleon's Assembly of Jewish Notables. In an essay written in 1805, Berr argued that the long-standing negative associations of the word *Juif* presented a serious obstacle to the Jews' regeneration. 'The Bible calls them the Children of Israel; their language is the Hebrew language', he argued. 'Should they not, then, be called Israelites or Hebrews?' Yet, this eloquent plea for a conscious substitution of *Israélite* for *Juif* is contained in an essay whose very title includes the rejected term *Juif*.[15] It is hardly surprising that those who followed Berr found it as difficult as he did to rid themselves of this controversial word.

It must be emphasized that Berr's favouring *Israélite* was not motivated by the view that it was a non-national, narrowly religious, term. Rather, he preferred it because the word was relatively free of the centuries of opprobrium connected with *Juif*. He hoped to induce the French to look with a fresh perspective on Jews by designating them by the less prejudicial term. *Israélite*, far from being non-national, connoted the politically independent *Israélite* citizen, living in his own historic homeland.

There are strong indications that we have been wrong in believing that an *Israélite* was someone who saw his primary identification as French, and who relegated his Jewishness to a narrowly 'religious' segment of his existence. One such indication is the controversy over the nineteenth-century popular term, *Israélite Français*. Jewish spokesmen who wanted to promote the integration of Jews into French society objected to this phrase, arguing that it must be reversed to *Français Israélite*, in order to demonstrate that the Jews' first loyalty was to France. Clearly, they objected to using *Israélite* as a noun, precisely because it conveyed an ethnic meaning, whereas the adjectival form had the reduced connotation of a religious affiliation.[16]

By the middle of the century the re-ordered term, *Français Israélite*, had, indeed, been created, although not to the exclusion of the older version. Some religious leaders, such as Rabbi Lazare Wogue, then complained that the new version indicated that the Jewish component of the double identity had been relegated to second place.[17] It was in this way that the charge of disloyalty to the Jewish heritage was first introduced, although for the time being the issue was seen as one primarily of religious observance. Wogue was accusing the Jews, not of assimilation, but of laxity in their religious behaviour. In its adjectival form, *Israélite* implied less religiosity than it did as a noun.

The use of *Israélite*, perhaps because of Berr Isaac Berr's encouragement, did expand rapidly. By 1808 it was in common parlance, both as a noun and as an adjective.[18] The first French-Jewish periodical, published briefly in 1817–18, used *Israélite* as a noun in its title (*L'Israélite Français*). When the press re-established itself on firmer ground more than twenty years later, the principal journals made use of the adjectival form of the word (*Archives Israélites, Univers Israélite* and *La Vérité Israélite*).

The word *Juif* continued, however, to be employed as both noun and adjective. Napoleon's 1806 Assembly of Notables referred to 'Notables professing the Jewish religion' (*la religion Juive*). The 1808 census counted the Jewish population (*la population Juive*). When the abortive attempt was made in 1813 to establish the first Jewish periodical, the proposed title was *Annales Historiques et Littéraires du Peuple Juif*.

A small number of French Jews, intellectuals and leaders, continued to believe that anti-Jewish hostility was furthered by the continued use of the word *Juif*. They periodically took up the pen in a vain attempt to convince Jews and non-Jews alike to eliminate the word from the French vocabulary.[19] Despite such attempts, *Juif* maintained its place next to *Israélite* in the literary output of the century. The two terms were used concurrently and interchangeably, often by a single writer, in the same paragraph, as a way of varying the style.

An examination of the nineteenth-century periodical press readily confirms the simultaneous and fully equivalent use of the two words. Articles in *La Vérité Israélite* during 1860 and 1861, for example, talk of *la race Israélite, le peuple Juif*, and *des Juifs*. One article, entitled 'Le Nom Juif', exhorts Jews to be proud of the term *Juif*. Jews should never give up their great heritage, and eventually the Jewish faith, alternately called *la foi Juive* and *la foi Israélite*, will be embraced by everyone. The name *Juif*, which was formerly disparaged, will be glorified.[20] Other issues of the journal furnish additional examples of the interchangeability of these terms. In an article of 1869, for example, the three terms *Israélitisme*, *Judaïsme*, and *Mosaïsme* are used without distinction.[21]

Published books of the period reveal the same language pattern as the periodical literature. In Israel Bédarride's 1859 publication, *Les Juifs en France, en Italie et en Espagne*, the words *Juif* and *Israélite* alternate, with *Juif* apparently being used slightly more frequently. Even as late as 1900 Henri Luicen-Brun's book *La Condition des Juifs en France depuis 1789* uses the two terms alternately and with the same meaning.

It remains true that antisemites did not speak of *Israélites*. Their publications bore titles likes *Les Juifs, Rois de L'Epoque*, *L'Anti-Juif*, *La France Juive*, etc. The reverse, however, was not true; *Juif* was by no means consistently a negative term, and this fact explains why Jews did not cease using it. *Israélite* became the more formal term and tended to be used in the names of organizations and periodicals.[22]

The distinction between *Juif* and *Israélite*, as it has been known in the twentieth century, was first introduced into the French language in 1890 by Bernard Lazare, who defined the difference in his article entitled 'Juifs et Israélites'. In this publication, and in other writings of 1890–4, before he modified his views under the impact of the Dreyfus Affair, Lazare blamed non-assimilated Jews, especially Eastern European immigrants, whom he labelled *Juifs*, for the rise of political antisemitism in France. He prescribed assimilation as both the prevention and the cure for antisemitism. Jews who met the required standard of assimilation were approvingly designated *Israélites*.[23]

According to Lazare's imaginative and unfounded distinctions (which appear to have been modelled on Sephardic emancipation rhetoric that had successfully promoted a more favourable treatment of Sephardim than of Ashkenazim), *Israélites* had inhabited France for two thousand years, and were productive people who earned modest incomes. He contrasted them with *Juifs*, newcomers from Central and Eastern Europe,[24] whom he described as thoroughly unscrupulous capitalists, bankers and money-lenders. He drew the classic socialist conclusion that it was the economic behaviour of the Jews which gave rise to antisemitism.

With this article, Bernard Lazare provided the discourse about the Jews in France with an entirely new vocabulary. Yet, despite the growing distinction between the polite and the impolite terms, and although *Juif* was the term preferred by antisemites,[25] and despite the fact that the official communications generally used *Israélite*, Jews, themselves, never abandoned the term *Juif*. Theodore Reinach, in his encyclopedia article of 1894 on Jews, defended this linguistic practice by explaining that the word *Juif* no longer had the negative meaning previously attached to it. Reinach, himself, used the two words interchangeably.[26] Examples of such use in the Jewish press likewise abound.[27] During the very last years of the century, although the distinction had become more solidified, even those who called themselves *Israélites Français* were still willing to identify as *Juifs*; 'Nous, Israélites Français, nous sommes Français d'abord, Juifs ensuite.'[28]

The same tendency to read history backwards that has distorted nineteenth-century meanings of *Juif* and *Israélite* has caused several additional words frequently used in Jewish polemical texts to be wrongly construed. By anachronistically applying later definitions to several terms found in nineteenth-century texts, including 'assimil-ation', 'fusion', 'affiliation' and 'identification', historians have concluded that French Jews were extreme assimilationists who passionately believed that their salvation lay in being pure French-men, and who therefore sought to destroy all remnants of Jewish group consciousness. It has further been said that not even the collective threat posed by political antisemitism was able to arouse French Jews from their complacent sense of individual security within French democracy. A different reading of the texts suggests an opposite interpretation, emphasizing lack of confidence in the future of emancipation, and a consequent persistent fear.

In order to allay their fears and encourage acculturation and integration into French society, Jewish leaders urged members of the community to 'affiliate with the larger French family',[29] or to 'identify with the surrounding society'.[30] Although terms like 'affiliation' and 'identification' can easily be construed as suggesting extreme assimil-ation, the context of such statements makes it clear that neither affiliation nor identification was seen as impinging on Jewish ethnic consciousness.

Similarly misleading is the erroneous reading of the word 'fusion'. French Jews continuously sought 'fusion' with the general French population. One recent article, for example, quotes Léon Halévy's call in 1828 for the 'complete and definitive fusion of the followers of Moses with the rest of the French'.[31] Although it is tempting to believe that the Saint-Simonian Halévy did, indeed, have syncretistic aims, what are we to make of the call for fusion when it emanates from Chief

Rabbi L. M. Lambert? This conservative religious leader, who in 1840 called for both civil and religious fusion of the Jews with the rest of the French population,[32] could not have been advocating the abandonment of Judaism. He declared explicitly that after the attainment of 'fusion' religious distinctions would remain between Jews and Frenchmen, deriving from 'the obligations to our Creator according to the Bible and the tradition'. But Lambert was not sacrificing ethnicity, nor even national aspirations, in favour of a narrowly defined Judaism. He argued, in fact, that Jews are as much entitled to their nationality as are Poles, Greeks and Italians![33]

Examples abound of this use of the word 'fusion'. In 1852 a journalists called 'for the complete liberation [of Jews from] . . . barbaric prejudice . . . [by] a complete and sincere fusion of the Jewish race with the great French family.[34] Toward the end of the century an employee of the organized Jewish community, writing about the Napoleonic period, said that the 'fusion' of Jews with the rest of the population had taken place without interfering with the 'family spirit that characterized the Jewish race'.[35]

Clearly, 'fusion', 'identification' and 'affiliation', as urged by these nineteenth-century writers, meant nothing other than emancipation (or legal equality), and social acceptance. Polemicists who used these words sought harmonious coexistence of French and Jewish values and traditions, without prejudice to either.

Even the word *Judaïsme*, has been misunderstood, contributing to the erroneous idea that French Jewry had narrowed its collective identity to that of believers in a religious faith. The French word *Judaïsme*, unlike its English cognate, did not refer only to the Jewish religion, but also embraced the concept of the community as a whole. Until 1962, when Albert Memmi suggested limiting the meaning of the word to the religion, and introduced the word *Judaïcité* to refer to the community,[36] the two ideas were normally represented by the single word.

This utilization of *Judaïsme* to mean the community was common in the late nineteenth-century writings of Theodore Reinach. Sometimes incorrectly viewed as an assimilationist, Reinach's works on the history of the Jewish people stressed the continuity of its sense of community, not only immediately after the destruction of the ancient Jewish state, and throughout the history of the Diaspora, but even after Jewish emancipation. Reinach often used the word *Judaïsme* to refer to the community, speaking, for example, of the geographic, demographic and economic transformation of *le Judaïsme*.[37]

As for the term 'assimilation' itself, it was used only rarely during most of the century,[38] and it was not until around 1860 that it began to contain even a hint of its future connotation. 'Assimilation', as nineteenth-century French Jews applied it to themselves, generally meant emancipation, or legal equality as citizens. When these insecure Jews called for assimilation they were not recommending collective self-destruction, merging without trace into an open-armed France. They were seeking, rather, to bolster and complete their emancipation by encouraging an ambivalent and potentially hostile France to eliminate the legal inequalities still remaining.[39] And sometimes, in using the term, they were calling for socio-economic mobility to be achieved through 'regeneration', constructive philanthropy such as job-training programmes and small-business loans.[40]

A full history of the word 'assimilation' remains to be written, and such a study would have to be comparative, encompassing the usage in all places of Jewish settlement. For our purposes, I will limit myself to some aspects of the historical development of the term and some speculations on the dissemination of both the word and the idea.

The English verb, 'to assimilate', can be used both transitively and intransitively, and the two uses correspond roughly to the French active and passive forms, *assimiler* and *s'assimiler*. Depending upon which form is used, it is possible to talk either of Jews assimilating surrounding cultures, or of their *being* assimilated or absorbed into the surrounding culture. Nineteenth-century French-Jewish assimilation was almost exclusively of the first kind. This distinction has been well captured in a recent account of the French rabbinate, in which the author shows that the rabbis tried to implement the tacit consensus, 'Assimiler oui, s'assimiler non.'[41] Failure to discriminate between these two ideas can lead to serious errors in historical evaluation.

The earliest known use of 'assimilation' in English, in the sense of the national assimilation of people into the nation where they live, dates from 1677.[42] By 1774 it was being used in Canada, where during the early nineteenth century it was applied to Frenchmen who acquired the British language, customs and outlook.[43] Perhaps it was from this context that the word entered the French language with the meanings of acculturation and the equal rights of foreigners. It was only towards the end of the nineteenth century, however, that assimilation became – for a short time – the major doctrine of French colonial policy.[44]

In regard to Jews, 'assimilation' was used to mean 'emancipation', both before and after the introduction around 1830 of the word 'emancipation' itself.[45] An early example of this use of 'assimilation' as 'emancipation' can be found in Léon Halévy's 1828 history of modern Jews. Halévy writes that Abraham Furtado, testifying before the Malesherbes Commission in 1788, asked them 'to assimilate the Jews to other subjects in regard to their civil and political rights'.[46]

The myth about Jewish assimilation in France may have its origin in German-Jewish misperceptions. Nineteenth-century German Jews were fascinated by French Jews, whose comparatively fortunate situation was enviable. German Jews marvelled at their co-religionists in France, fully fledged citizens of a modern state, where Jews were allowed to hold important public offices, and where synagogues were even built at public expense. Inevitably the truth became exaggerated. German Jews who visited Paris, even those who stayed for long periods, were prone to overstate the integration of French Jews into general society, while considering them as the model of what German Jews should strive either to achieve or to avoid, depending upon the observer's ideological perspective.

Heinrich Heine and Moses Hess figured among those German Jews, resident in Paris, who feared that France's integration of her Jewish citizens would destroy Jewish bonds. In 1840 Heine wrote that:

> the Jews in France have been emancipated too long for the bond of their race not to have become loose and slack; they have all been sunk in – or to express it more correctly – have been raised to French nationality; they are Frenchmen like the rest.[47]

Heine did not yet employ the term 'assimilation', as the word only began to be used twenty years later to describe a social and cultural integration of serious enough proportions to be seen as the enemy of Jewish national sentiment. One of the earliest examples of such usage in French appeared in a Jewish periodical of 1861, in which the journalist, specifically rejecting Jewish nationalism, favoured the 'universal assimilation' of 'human families'.[48] Writing in German the following year, Moses Hess introduced what would later become the standard Jewish nationalist rejection of assimilation. In his *Rome and Jerusalem* he wrote, 'the Frenchman assimilates every foreign racial element with an irresistible power of attraction. Even the Jew is considered here as a Frenchman.'[49]

Hess's rejection of assimilation was later echoed by other Jewish nationalists,[50] who sometimes argued that assimilation could not succeed, and at other times rejected it as undesirable. In his pamphlet of 1882, Leon Pinsker attributed antisemitism to the fact that Jews remain aliens everywhere.[51] He described Jews as 'form[ing] a distinctive element which cannot be assimilated, which cannot be readily digested by any nation'.[52]

Immediately after Pinsker's pamphlet appeared, the word 'assimilation' became common currency in Jewish polemics of all persuasions. When religious Jews condemned it, they were referring to the abandonment of Jewish law and ritual.[53] When Alexandre Weill, an intimate of Heine's circle, attacked assimilation, he was rejecting the tendency of the Jewish elite to adopt the manners of upper-class Frenchmen. Weill exhorted Jews to make their own distinctive contribution to France as Jews, rather than to supply France with yet more racehorse owners and small-game hunters. If assimilation proved to be the result of emancipation, he declared, it would have been better to have remained in the ghetto, where Jewish creativity had flourished.[54]

The word 'assimilation' had thus gradually undergone a broadening of its meaning. Originating as a synonym for emancipation, it had already been enthusiastically urged as a code-word for total integration as early as 1861, and had been as vehemently rejected as a programme the following year. The early Zionists had rejected it as unworkable even before they rejected it as undesirable. Those with a respect for Jewish identity as a religious or cultural phenomenon had rejected it as antithetical to their own values. Yet it once again fell to Bernard Lazare, who had shortly before established the dichotomy between *Juif* and *Israélite*, to establish the terms of the discourse about assimilation that would become standard in the twentieth century.

Lazare first urged 'assimilation' as a goal, but later came to believe it was a serious historical error. In his *L'Antisémitisme* of 1894, he blamed the unassimilated Jews, mainly the Eastern European immigrants, for the outbreak of the antisemitic movement. This publication contained the first ideological statement calling for extreme assimilation as a means of ensuring the security of French Jewry.[55] Even though Lazare soon beat a retreat from international socialism, and as a Zionist condemned the very assimilationist ideology he had previously advocated, his polemics continued to promote the extreme definition of assimilation, which now acquired pejorative associations.

The use of 'assimilation' with this extreme meaning, by its champions and critics alike, became common after 1900. Yet, even in the twentieth century, writers also used the word in the far less radical sense of emancipation and equal treatment. Thus, when the historian

Henri Lucien-Brun wrote in 1900 of 'the complete assimilation of Jews and Frenchmen, religiously, civilly and politically', he was referring to equality in all these areas.[56]

It is noteworthy that Bernard Lazare's about-face on the issue of assimilation, which was prompted primarily by the Dreyfus Affair, occurred at just the time that France was debating the wisdom of assimilation as the central doctrine of its colonial policy. Jewish nationalism struggled to win a place for itself in a France that was gradually rejecting its *mission civilisatrice* in favour of cultural relativism. Thus, the early failure of Zionism in France was hardly a result of the supposed Jacobin, monolithic, cultural imperialism.

If assimilation is a relatively recent concept, incorrectly read back into the nineteenth century, we are still left with the question, to what extent did it subsequently take place as the result of a conscious programme? The height of French-Jewish assimilation occurred in the interwar years, and first-hand observers have offered conflicting views of the extent to which it was planned. Writing in the 1950s, Pierre Aubéry and Arnold Mandel took opposite sides on this issue. Aubéry wrote that 'the generation that reached manhood in France before 1939 was assimilationist and, in fact, assimilated'.[57] Mandel, on the other hand, argued that the assimilation of French Jews 'was a natural and spontaneous kind of assimilation, almost never the result of deliberate decision'.

In defence of this position, which denies the existence of an assimilationist ideology, even for the period when it was far more likely to have existed than during the nineteenth century, Mandel quotes the French-Jewish philosopher Leon Brunschwicg, professor at the Sorbonne, who died in 1944. Brunschwicg's personal observations seem convincing for his own time, as well as applicable to the nineteenth century:

> The polemical shafts of the Zionists and other Jewish nationalists against the French-Jewish assimilators miss their mark. My father was a rabbi and I am an assimilated professor, but I am not an assimilator at all; I never made the decision to be a Frenchman. I became one all alone and quite naturally.[58]

Notes

I would like to thank the following people who read earlier drafts of this paper and who made helpful suggestions: Philippe Boukara, William Brinner, Jonathan Frankel, Nancy Green, Raphael Loewe, Norman Stillman and Daniel Swetschinski.

1 Jacob Katz, 'The Term "Jewish Emancipation"': Its Origin and Historical Impact', in Alexander Altmann (ed.), *Studies in Nineteenth-Century Jewish Intellectual History* (Cambridge, Mass., 1964), pp. 1–25.

2 Phyllis Cohen Albert, 'Ethnicity and Jewish Solidarity in Nineteenth-Century France', in *Mystics, Philosophers, and Politicians: Essays in Jewish Intellectual History in Honor of Alexander Altmann*, ed. Jehuda Reinharz and Daniel Swetschinski (Durham, N.C., 1982).

3 Zeldin writes that . . . 'the French were not only confused about what held them together, but . . . they consistently exaggerated their differences and . . . emphasis on diversity was an essential part of their society . . . France was one of the first "nation-states" in Europe, but for long its unity was felt consciously more by its rulers than by its people' (Theodore Zeldin, *France, 1848–1945* (Oxford, 1977, vol. II, p. 4). See also the important works by Eugen Weber, *Peasants into Frenchmen: the Modernization of Rural France, 1870–1914* (Stanford, 1976); and Gérard Noiriel, *Le Creuset Français: Histoire de l'Immigration, XIXe–XXe Siècles* (Paris, 1988). The phrase, *machine à franciser*, is Noiriel's.

4 Arnold Mandel, 'French Jewry in a Time of Decision', *Commentary*, December 1954, p. 539.

5 Cohen Albert, 'Ethnicity and Jewish Solidarity'.

6 Ibid.

7 J. Milton Yinger, 'Toward a Theory of Assimilation and Dissimilation', *Ethnic and Racial Studies* 4, no. 3 (July 1981), 252.

8 Lazare Wogue complained of this new term in an 1853 article that was later reprinted in his *La Predication Israélite en France* (Paris, 1885), pp. 9–10. Cited by Jean-Marc Chouraqui, 'Le Corps Rabbinique en France et sa Prédication: Problèmes et Desseins (1808–1905)', in *Histoire, Economie, et Société* 3, no. 2 (1984) 312–13.

9 Ibid.

10 Although these meanings of *Juif* and *Israélite* are accurate for the twentieth century, scholars have erred in attributing them also to the nineteenth century. See, for example, two recent accounts: (1) 'Tout au long du dix-neuvième siècle, Juif et Judaïsme continuèrent à désigner l'adepte d'une religion et celle-çi. Israélite était couramment employé pour désigner de façon élogieuse les émancipés par opposition à ceux qui demeuraient sous le joug de lois discriminatoires' (Patrick Girard, 'Les Doctrines de l'Assimilation en France au Dix-Neuvième Siècle', in *Aspects du Sionisme*, proceedings of College de France workshop, ed. Institut National des Langues et Civilisations Orientales (Paris, 1982), p. 187); (2) 'Le terme d'israélite fut forgé au cours du dix-neuvième siècle et jusqu'à la Deuxième Guerre mondiale par les juifs embourgeoisés qui tenaient à manifester leur complète assimilation aux autres français et à marquer ce qui les différenciat, culturellement et socialement, des juifs pauvres, récemment arrivés en fuyant les persécutions de l'Europe

centrale et orientale' (Dominique Schnapper, *Juifs et Israélites* (Paris, 1980), p. 189).

11 *Univers Israélite*, 20 October 1933, quoted in David Weinberg, *A Community on Trial: The Jews of Paris in the 1930s* (Chicago, 1974), p. 64, n. 10.

12 Edmund Cahen, *Juif, Non! . . . Israélite*, referred to by Weinberg, *A Community*, p. 64, n. 10.

13 Schnapper, *Juifs et Israélites*, p. 189.

14 A full study of the history of the terms used to designate Jews would be a worthwhile undertaking. For our purposes, I will briefly note some of the highlights of the terminology used in Jewish, Christian and Muslim contexts. The Old Testament speaks of 'Hebrews', 'Children of Israel', and *Yehudim* (Jews). Negative associations with the word 'Jew' are introduced by Christianity, and are visible in the Gospel of John, which repeatedly assails the 'Jews'. The synoptic gospels, on the other hand, confine their attacks to 'Pharisees', 'tax collectors' and 'priests'. The distinction between the bad 'Jew' and the neutral, or even positive, 'people of Israel', is first visible in Acts. (Compare Acts, 17, 14:2 and 19.)

Some people have assumed that the Latin equivalent of Jew, *judaeus*, which derived from the Hebrew *yehudi* via the Greek *ioudaios*, acquired its negative associations by its similarity 'with the name of the villain of the Gospel story, Judas Iscariot, who was linked with the Devil (Luke 22:3)' (*Encyclopedia Judaica*, 'Jew', vol. x, column 22). In the years following the Roman destruction of the Jewish state, those who remained in residence in the Holy Land referred to themselves as Israelites, in preference to *judaei*, with its pejorative connotation. In places of the Jewish Diaspora, 'Jew' and related terms were used with opprobrium, while 'Hebrew' and 'Israelite' were more likely to be positive, or at least neutral.

Christians disdained the Jewish (literal) interpretation of the Bible, which they called *sensus judaicus*, because it contradicted their own mystical exegesis which supported Christological belief. Raphael Loewe has said of the attitude towards Jews in the early church, 'When you agree with them they are *Hebraei*; when you don't they are *Judaei*' (personal communication, 26 November 1985). The positive connotations of 'Israelite' probably derive from medieval usage, when the church was often designated 'the new Israel' and Christians called themselves 'new Israelites'.

Early Muslims oscillated in their usage between the terms *Yahud* (Jew) and *Banu Isra'il* (children of Israel), yet attempts to demonstrate that in the Koran *Yahud* is used negatively and *Banu Isra'il* positively are not entirely convincing (Norman A. Stillman, personal communication, 5 February 1986; see also his *The Jews of Arab Lands* (Philadelphia, 1979); William Brinner, personal communication, 4 May 1986). Rather, the two terms often seem to distinguish between the Israelites of biblical times and the Jews who were contemporaries of Muhammed (S. D. Goitein, 'Banu Isra'il', *Encyclopedia of Islam*, new edition (Leiden, 1958), vol. I, pp. 1,020–22). Although it is true that Muhammed lost no love on the 'Jews' of Medina, who rejected his message and whom he accused of falsifying scripture, the Koran speaks very harshly also of the 'Israelites' of the Bible who defied Moses and created the Golden Calf. In the Middle Ages *Isra'ili* did become the Muslims' polite term for Jews (*Goitein*), but after the establishment of the state of Israel it generally lost that connotation and became a negative epithet. (Norman Stillman relates a personal incident which shows that even recently the term has been used in the Muslim world for politeness. Writing of an encounter which took place in Sefrou, Morocco, in 1972, he says, 'One day a local shopkeeper asked me if I was an *Isra'ili* . . . I was startled and replied rather insistently that I was an American. He rejoined, "Yes, yes, but your religion is *Isra'ili*." It was clear that he was using the term for the sake of politeness' (personal communication, 5 February 1986).

It seems difficult, then, in both the Christian and the Muslim traditions, to anchor the bad 'Jew', good 'Israelite' distinction in antiquity. Throughout the ages, to be sure, 'Israelite' was a neutral or a positive term, and antisemites used only the word 'Jew'. It does not follow, however, that all ancient and medieval usage of 'Jew' and related terms are negative.

Nor is it true that only under the impact of emancipation and the struggle to attain it, did the modern usage of 'Israelite' emerge. One can find numerous examples of the term in early modern publications from the seventeenth century, in various languages, including Portuguese, French and English. It was used to designate both ancient Israelites, living in the land of Israel, and post-destruction Diaspora Jews. In both cases the term had full national implications.

Examples of this usage include the well-known plea by Menasseh ben Israel for the readmission of Jews to England, published in 1650 in Portuguese and translated as *The Hope of Israel* in 1652. In 1681 Claude Fleury published his *Les Moeurs des Israélites*, the 'most widely known book on ancient Judaism to appear in France before the Revolution . . . [it was] reprinted at least 60 times in the eighteenth-century' (Arthur Hertzberg, *The French Enlightenment and the Jews* (New York, 1968), p. 41). The popularity of the volume, together with its essentially positive attitude toward ancient Judaism, created a positive climate in France for *Israélites*.

'Israel' was also the collective term used throughout the eighteenth century in Christian-Jewish Polemics. See, for example, *Israël Vengé*, the title given to the 1770 French translation of Isaac Orobio de Castro's seventeenth-century Jewish refutation of Christian anti-Jewish polemic (originally called *Prevenciones Divinas Contra la Vana Idolatria de las Gentes*, or 'Divinely Inspired Critique of the Worthless Idolatry of the Gentiles'

(Yosef Kaplan, *From Christianity to Judaism: The Story of Isaac Orobio de Castro* (Oxford, 1989), pp. 451–7.

In England the words 'Israel' and 'Israelite' were frequently employed during the eighteenth-century debates over Jewish rights. William Arnall's work *The Complaint of the Children of Israel* (London, 1736) depicted the Jews' grievances regarding the Penal Laws. Several years later an anonymous book appeared with the title *The Full and Final Restoration of Jews and Israelites* (London, 1753).

15 Berr Isaac Berr, *Réflexions sur la Régénération Complète des Juifs en France* (Paris, 1806).

16 Throughout the nineteenth century the words *Israël* and *Israélite* continued to have as much ethnic connotation as did *Juif*. Thus, in 1866, concluding a textbook of Jewish history, Moïse Schwab could write that when Jews everywhere achieve emancipation and all the nations benefit from progress, 'Israël, dispersé aux quatre coins de la terre selon la prédiction de Jacob, formera, par ce lien nouveau, une unité sans bornes' (Moïse Schwab, *Histoire des Israélites Depuis l'Edification du Second Temple Jusqu'à Nos Jours* (Paris, 1866), p. 299).

17 Wogue, *La Prédication Israélite*, pp. 9–10; quoted in Chouraqui, 'Le Corps Rabbinique', pp. 312–13.

18 See, for example, Antoine Toussaint D'Esquiron de Saint Agnan, *Considérations sur l'Existence Civile et Politique des Israélites* (Mayence, 1808), cited in Zosa Szajkowski, *Judaica-Napoléonica*, no. 43.

19 See, for example, Ben Lévi, in *Archives Israélites* (1841), 'Juif est un adjectif vide de sens . . . c'est que le Juif dont l'âme est à Jérusalem tandis que son corps est en France n'existe plus guère de nos jours; c'est que la nation juive ne se trouve plus sur le sol français' (quoted by Patrick Girard, 'Les Doctrines de l'Assimilation', p. 187).

20 *La Vérité Israélite* 4 (1861), pp. 270, 277.

21 Ibid, 8 (1869), 400–1.

22 The fact that *Israélite* became the official word when Jewish institutions were in the process of crystallization is attributable to the campaign in favour of the word carried on by Berr and others.

23 'Juifs et Israélites', in *Entretiens Politiques et Littéraires*, September 1890, *L'Antisémitisme, son Histoire, et ses Causes* (Paris, 1894). Lazare also wrote several articles and book reviews on antisemitism between 1890 and 1894. Cf. the bibliography of Bernard Lazare's works in Nelly Wilson, *Bernard Lazare* (Cambridge, 1978), pp. 326–32.

24 Lazare does not distinguish between newcomers of recent or less-recent origin, and he includes the Rothschilds as examples of unscrupulous capitalist newcomers.

25 In addition to the self-declared antisemites, the general press was also guilty of offensive use of the term *Juif*. See, for example, *Archives Israélites* 51, no. 2 (9 January 1890), 13–14, 'L'Abus de Mot Juif', which decries the press's habit of designating Jewish criminals as *Juifs*.

26 Theodore Reinach, 'Juif', in *La Grande Encyclopédie*, 1894, vol. 12, p. 256.

27 Several examples from the *Archives Israélites* will demonstrate the interchangeability of the terms *Israélite* and *Juif*. In the obituary of Dr Louis Philippson, a journalist wrote, 'Le journalisme israélite et la littérature juive viennent de faire une perte . . . irréparable' *Archives Israélites* 51, no. 1, 2 January 1890, 7). Throughout other issues of the same volume we find such phrases as: *Les défenseurs des juifs, Montpellier est redevable aux Juifs, les juifs de Romainie*, but *les Israélites du Russie* (pp. 156, 157, 267). In another volume we find: 'La tradition des médecins israélites s'est continuée jusqu'à nos jours à Francfort, où l'art de guérir est pratiqué par les Juifs distingués', *Archives Israélites* no. 3 (8 September 1887, 285.)

28 Louis Lévy, *L'Univers Israélite* (1897), quoted by Girard, 'Les Doctrines de l'Assimilation', p. 182.

29 'Depuis que l'ère des persécutions a cessé, l'empressement des Juifs à s'affilier à la grande famille est venu protester contre les reproches qu'on leur avait injustement adressés; une régénération complète s'est opérée' (Israel Bédarride, *Les Juifs en France, en Italie, et en Espagne* (Paris, 1859), p. 11).

30 *La Vérité Israélite*, 1 (1860), 38:'les Israélites se sont identifiés avec la société environnante.' The approving observer of this phenomenon informs us that he is proud to belong to 'cette race Israélite, à ce peuple choisi par Dieu'. Although this author clearly uses 'identify' to mean only 'acculturate', *s'identifier* was understood by others as too strong, tantamount perhaps to the later usage of 'assimilation'. Thus, in 1856, expressing the same idea of integration and fusion without assimilation, the journalist Isidor Cahen had rejected the term in favour of *unité*. He had urged Jews to '*s'unir et non s'identifier*' (quoted by David Cohen, *La Promotion des Juifs en France à L'Epoque du Second Empire (1852–1870)* (Aix-en-Provence, 1980), p. 837).

31 Girard, 'Les Doctrines de l'Assimilation', p. 185.

32 L. M. Lambert, *Précis de L'Histoire des Hebreux depuis le Patriarche Abraham jusqu'en 1840* (Metz, 1840).

33 Ibid.

34 Ibid.

35 Léon Kahn, *Les Juifs à Paris Depuis le Sixième Siècle* (Paris, 1889), p. 192.

36 Albert Memmi, *Portrait d'un Juif* (Paris, 1962), p. 17.

37 See, for example, Theodore Reinach, 'Juif', pp. 258–9.

38 In comparison, it is interesting to note that Jacob Katz has observed that in Germany also the word 'assimilation' was not used in regard to the Jews in the first half of the nineteenth century. The word 'amalgamation' served the purpose. Jacob Katz, 'The German Jewish Utopia of Social Emancipation', *Studies of the Leo Baeck Institute*, ed. Max Kreutzberger (New York, 1967).

39 This idea is further developed in my article 'Ethnicity and Jewish Solidarity', cited n.2 above.

40 In its most common usage, before 1890, the word 'assimilation' had two major meanings in both French and English. It meant making things (or people) alike or equal, and it also meant comparing things (or people) in order to point out their similarities. (For the English meanings see the *Oxford English Dictionary*.)

For the French usage, note the following examples culled from the *Archives Israélites* (January 1856): (a) Judaism's doctrines do not permit 'l'assimilation entre l'homme et Dieu' (p. 34); (b) speaking of the similarities and differences between rabbis and Catholic priests, the journalist approves of 'l'assimilation du rabbin et du prêtre' (p. 45); (c) writing of the extremely conservative Catholics (Ultramontanes) who consider heresy a crime, the author uses the phrase 'assimiler l'hérésie au crime' (p. 46).

41 Jean-Marc Chouraqui has shown that rabbis in the middle of the nineteenth century saw it as their job to reconcile the spirit of the century with traditional Jewish teachings. They tried to encourage Jews to assimilate the mentalities and ideologies of the nineteenth century into Judaism and Jewish life, without assimilating themselves into the surrounding society ('Le Corps Rabbinique', pp. 303–4).

42 ' . . . total assimilation to the country where they thus are mingled': *Oxford English Dictionary*; cf. Charles Price, 'The Study of Assimilation', in J. A. Jackson (ed.), *Migration* (Cambridge, 1969), p. 182.

43 Price, 'The Study of Assimilation', pp. 181–2.

44 During the last two decades of the century the French wavered between the two policies of 'assimilation' and 'association' in regard to the colonies. The newly developed idea of *mission civilisatrice* supported assimilation. In response, advocates of association urged a relativist approach which would respect cultural differences, rather than trying to remake everyone in the image of the Frenchman. The discussion about cultural imperialism abroad eventually raised the issue of pluralism at home. Yves Guyot, who opposed assimilation, pointed out that, contrary to popular theory, French regional differences remained strong. Despite the diversity, he said, all were Frenchmen. The French-Jewish sociologist, Emile Durkheim, was among the promoters of the idea of *association* as colonial policy. See Price, 'The Study of Assimilation'; Yves Guyot, *Lettres sur la Politique Coloniale* (Paris, 1885), ch. 40: 'L'Assimilation des Indigènes'; Raymond Betts, *Assimilation and Association in French Colonial Theory, 1890–1914* (New York, 1961).

45 Katz, 'The Term "Jewish Emancipation".'

46 Leon Halévy, *Résumé de l'Histoire des Juifs Modernes* (Paris, 1828), p. 300. This shows that for Halévy's contemporaries, 'assimilation' meant making Jews equal in regard to some specific legal rights, an idea which

would later come to be called 'emancipation'. Even today this meaning of 'assimilation' is frequently found in France, especially in discussions of salaries. Teachers, for example, might be 'assimilated to engineers', in which case they would receive the same salaries and benefits.

47 Heinrich Heine, Paris, 3 June 1840, in Hugo Bieber and Moses Hadas, *Heine, A Biographical Anthology* (Philadelphia, 1956), p. 381. Anka Muhlstein (*Baron James: the Rise of the French Rothschmidt* (New York, 1982), pp. 119–20) cites an identical passage from *Lutèce* (Paris, 1855), p. 8.

48 *La Vérité Israélite* 4 (1861), 13.

49 *Rome and Jerusalem* (1862), English translation by Maurice Bloom (New York, 1958), p. 33. Moses Hess claimed that he had already written this in 1840, but his most recent intellectual biographer finds no evidence to support the claim (Schlomo Avineri, *Moses Hess: Prophet of Communism and Zionism* (New York, 1985), p. 238).

50 Edward Lasker is said to have used the word during the same decade, although I have not been able to find the citation. (The use was signalled by a participant at the London conference on which this volume is based, 2–3 June 1985.)

51 Arthur Hertzberg, *The Zionist Idea* (New York, 1959), pp. 186–7.

52 Ibid., p. 182.

53 One of the earliest examples of orthodox polemics against assimilation is a German-language booklet, published in Poland, by Berisch Goldenberg, *Die Assimilation der Juden* (Tarnopol, 1883).

54 Alexandre Weill, *Le Centenaire de l'Emancipation des Juifs* (Paris, 1888); *Moïse, le Talmud et l'Evangile* (Paris, 1875), p. xxiv; *Cris d'Alarme, Epîtres aux Juifs* (Paris, 1889). Weill's ideas in all these works are well studied and abundantly quoted in Joë Friedemann, *Alexandre Weill: Ecrivain Contestataire et Historien Engagé* (Strasbourg, 1980), pp. 113–15.

55 Bernard Lazare, *L'Antisémitisme* (Paris, 1894). Karl Kautsky has sometimes been credited with being the father of the idea of assimilation, and he, indeed, spoke of it, using the very term, at least as early as 1902. His writings from 1885 already suggested the concept, although he may not yet have used the word. Kautsky, like Lazare and other socialist thinkers, drew on Marx in arguing that the problem of antisemitism would best be solved by the Jews' merging into a socialist society. Kautsky's contribution to these ideas has been discussed by Jack Jacobs in 'On German Socialists and German Jews: Kautsky, Bernstein and their Reception, 1914–1922', in *Studies in Contemporary Jewry*, vol. IV, *The Jews and the European Crisis, 1914–1921* ed. J. Frankel (New York, 1988), and in 'Marxism and Antisemitism: Kautsky's Perspective', in *The International Review of Social History* 30 (1985), part 3: *Contributions on Antisemitism*. Robert Wistrich has also discussed Kautsky's and other socialists' ideas of assimilation in his books, *Revolutionary Jews from Marx to Trotsky* (London,

1976); and *Socialism and the Jews: The Dilemmas of Assimilation in Germany and Austria-Hungary* (Rutherford, N.J., 1982).

In contrast with Lazare's early view that assimilation would prevent or cure antisemitism, stands Alexandre Weill's contemporaneous view that assimilation is a mere decoy, impotent to prevent antisemitism: 'L'assimilation est un leurre, l'antisémitisme en est la preuve patente' (Friedemann, *Alexandre Weill*, p. 115).

56 Henri Lucien-Brun, *La Condition des Juifs en France depuis 1789* (Lyon, 1900), p. 273. In the same publication, Lucien-Brun also wrote of the remaining legal barriers to complete equality of treatment for Catholicism and Judaism. A specific legal advantage favoured the Catholics, and he declared, 'C'est le seul point sur lequel l'assimilation entre le culte catholique et le culte israélite soit demeurée incomplète' (p. 288). Similarly, Léon Kahn, writing in 1889 about the French Revolution, labelled his chapter, 'La Révolution – Les Juifs résidant à Paris demandent leur assimilation aux autres citoyens' (*Les Juifs á Paris*, p. 64).

57 Pierre Aubéry, *Milieux Juifs de la France Contemporaine à Travers Leurs Ecrivains* (Paris, 1957), p. 303.

58 Arnold Mandel, 'French Jewry', p. 539.

The social contexts of assimilation: village Jews and city Jews in Alsace

PAULA E. HYMAN

The nineteenth century witnessed the creation of the modern Jew. In the wake of political emancipation, Western European Jews took advantage of new economic and educational opportunities to acculturate to the host society and sought integration into the economic, social and institutional life of their respective nations. They succeeded so brilliantly that by the end of the century they had become symbols of the currents of change, no longer seen as socially backward and culturally laggard but rather as agents of capitalism and purveyors of modernist culture. They had assimilated into the European bourgeoisie.

Although we know much about the outcome of the century of assimilation that followed the first act of emancipation of European Jewry during the French Revolution, we know less about the process of assimilation itself. Jewish historians have focused primarily upon the legal, institutional and ideological components of Jewish integration into European societies.[1] In doing so, they have inevitably studied the proclamations, actions and reflections of Jewish elites, particularly urban ones. It was the elites that first internalized the critique of traditional Jewish society offered by both proponents and opponents of Jewish emancipation and impressed upon their reluctant constituents the need for self-improvement. It was the elites that broke most radically with traditional patterns of Jewish life and reshaped the Jewish communal institutions of their time. Finally, it was the elites that defined and articulated an emancipationist ideology which emphasized inculcating the values of citizenship to a new generation of Jews. According to that ideology a new Jewish identity would emerge, in which civic consciousness would be harmonized with Jewish religious sensibility. Jewish citizens would abandon their ethnocentrism and define their fellow citizens as their brethren. They would realize the moral degradation inherent in the traditional Jewish occupations of petty commerce. And they would place the acquisition of secular culture at the centre of their concerns and relegate traditional Jewish learning to an ancillary position.

This focus upon the emergence of new attitudes to gentile culture and society, particularly among intellectuals, professionals and businessmen, who asserted a new claim to communal leadership, has been important. But to understand the diversity in patterns of Jewish accommodation to the new conditions offered by nineteenth-century European societies, it is necessary to investigate closely the social contexts in which assimilation occurred.[2] Jews differed by class, gender, place of residence and level of education, and those differences affected their responses to emancipation. Both those who took the lead in promoting change and those who lagged behind in their acceptance of the new canons of belief and behaviour were shaped by specific social forces and not merely by ideological influences.

The Jews of Alsace offer an ideal vehicle for exploring the processes of social change and the complexities of assimilation among the inarticulate Jewish masses. Unlike the Jews of Bordeaux or Paris or the *maskilim* of Berlin, the Jews of Alsace on the eve of the French Revolution, and even considerably thereafter, constituted a traditional Jewish population, largely untouched by secular culture. Alsatian Jews were not an atypical Western Jewry. Indeed, they were more like the masses of Jews in the south German states and East Prussia than were the Jews of Berlin or Hamburg. They were religiously observant, spoke their own Yiddish dialect and lived in no fewer than 183 villages that dotted the Alsatian landscape. In fact, until the emancipation, Jews were not permitted to reside in the largest cities of Alsace, including Strasburg. In the nineteenth century the urban centres of Alsatian-Jewish life were therefore new communities.[3]

In economic terms Alsatian Jews served in a limited range of roles as middlemen in the rural economy. They were pedlars and dealers in old clothes, commercial brokers and petty merchants, cattle and horse dealers, traders in grain and money lenders – all occupations which brought them into contact, and produced conflict, with the peasant populations.[4] Constituting more than half of the French-Jewish population in 1789, Alsatian Jews were the first large traditional Jewish community to experience the benefits and challenges of emancipation. Living in a region plagued by sporadic antisemitic incidents, they saw in emancipation an opportunity to improve their personal fortune and to attain limited integration into French society while retaining a distinctive Jewish identity.

Although it remained the heartland of French Jewry throughout the century and a major exporter of Jewish youth to Paris and abroad, Alsace produced few local Jewish luminaries. In this the social historian is perhaps fortunate, for figures of the stature of a Moses Mendelssohn or his disciples in the Berlin Haskalah or *Wissenschaft des Judentums* movement so dwarf their contemporaries that the activity of their less-illustrious fellow Jews is often overlooked. The Jews of Alsace were distinctly ordinary individuals, with a modest lay and religious leadership.

The inarticulate and unexceptional are often difficult to study. They give us few specific indications of their motivations and ideological predispositions. However, they often leave behind, in the course of their daily routine, records of their behaviour which, when carefully examined, can reveal as much as ideological pronouncements. The Jews of Alsace emerge in all their variety from local manuscript censuses taken halfway through the century, which list addresses, occupations, household size and composition and occasionally places of birth. Through civil marriage records their choice of marriage partners, migratory patterns, intergenerational social mobility and growing literacy in French can all be examined. Local notarial records provide evidence of the kinds of wealth the more successful Jews had acquired by the middle of the century. Finally, as a commercial group, Jews figure prominently in the commercial court records of Strasburg. Although constituting some 3 per cent of the Alsatian population, Jews appear in no fewer than 25 per cent of the cases of the Strasburg court from the 1820s to the 1860s. From this litigation, the economic activity of otherwise anonymous Jewish cattle dealers, small merchants and wholesale businessmen is available for investigation.[5] Thus, the methods and sources tapped by European social historians can be put to good use to track down the types of Jews who are otherwise absent from more traditional documents.

For information on the Jews of Alsace I have drawn upon the manuscript censuses and marriage records of the entire Jewish population of Strasburg as well as the three smaller communities of Bischheim, Niederroedern and Itterswiller, located in different areas of the department of the Lower Rhine. I have also examined scattered census data from other towns in both Alsatian departments. When supplemented by governmental reports, records of the Jewish consistories, minute books of *hevrot* (confraternities) and local communities, memoirs and literature, the bare bones of quantifiable data yield a flesh-and-blood portrait of a community in transition from the status of the westernmost outpost of traditional Ashkenazi Jewry to an acculturated modern Jewish population.

While the dominant picture of the impact of emancipation upon European Jewry is of a rampant assimilation, a profound and rapid disruption of the traditional Jewish way of life, Alsatian Jewry presents an altogether different image. Within Alsace the village sustained traditional patterns of Jewish behaviour, language, values and identity for at least two or three generations after emancipation. Only the decline of the village economy and the widespread introduction of modern educational institutions, both of which did not occur until the second half of the nineteenth century, stimulated cultural assimilation among the masses of Alsatian Jews.

The urban environment of Strasburg and Mulhouse, on the other hand, offered economic and cultural opportunities which promoted adaptation to French bourgeois standards. As the home of bourgeois Jewish leaders, both cities provided direct contact with their social authority and their model of acculturation. Moreover, the very act of migration to the city loosed the social bonds which had facilitated continuity in the countryside. Finally, the migrants were a self-selected group, predisposed to innovation in matters of economic activity and cultural behaviour. Their removal from the village and insertion into an urban milieu helped preserve the cultural conservatism of the Jewish village while stimulating cultural change in their new places of settlement. In both the village and the city alike the economic, cultural and social adaptation of Jews was a product of the interaction of a specific set of actors with their particular environment.

Village Jews were rooted in a setting in which they played a vital, if resented, economic role. Although the economic opportunities available to village Jews were narrow, they were sufficiently attractive to keep most Jewish offspring in the village at least to the end of the 1850s. Moreover, traditional Jewish occupations demanded little acquisition of secular culture or accommodation to new values. Despite efforts to channel rural Jews into 'productive' occupations, the socio-economic composition of Jewish villages barely altered in the years between the Napoleonic period and the German annexation of Alsace in 1870. In the three Alsatian villages which I studied intensively, during Napoleon's time fully 40 per cent of the heads of household supported themselves in the typical Jewish street trades of peddling, dealing in old clothes and petty brokerage. Another 28 per cent were engaged in the cattle, horse and grain trade, and 9 per cent each were butchers, leather and textile merchants and scrap-metal dealers. Only 2 per cent were artisans. In 1846, 5 per cent of the employed residents of these villages had learned a trade, while 78 per cent were engaged in commerce. Pedlars, second-hand dealers and petty agents still accounted for approximately 40 per cent of all Jewish occupations. Twenty years later a similar pattern emerges: pedlars and hawkers predominate (36 per cent), the cattle, horse and grain trade retain their significance, and artisanry and industry attract a meagre 6 per cent of village Jews.[6]

This economic stability (or, to be less charitable, stagnation) was accompanied in the countryside by a steadfast adherence to the traditional features of Alsatian Jewish life: the use of Yiddish, a high degree of religious observance and a penchant for what we might call the practices of folk religion.

The Judeo-German dialect persisted throughout much of the nineteenth century, for knowledge of French was not necessary for the conduct of daily business. (The Alsatians, it should be noted, spoke a German dialect.) Official consistorial documents may have been carefully kept in French, but correspondence with village residents had to be conducted in Yiddish. As late as 1847 an inquiry into the administration of Jewish communal affairs in Hattstatt (Upper Rhine) was held and recorded entirely in Yiddish, since the residents could not have understood proceedings in French.[7] The correspondence of the Bischheim Jewish community in the 1840s was largely in Yiddish; the few letters written in French were replete with errors of grammar and spelling.[8] A report of 1844 indicated that most children entered Jewish communal schools in the countryside with no prior knowledge of French whatsoever.[9] In his stories of Jewish life in rural Alsace in the 1850s, Daniel Stauben described the very beginnings of change – the awkward courting by an educated French-speaking youth of a young lady who 'as is so frequent among us . . . was scarcely at home in the national language'.[10] Yet village communal leaders often saw no need to make the transition to the national language in their records. The small community of Odratzheim, for example, kept its *pinkas* (minute-book) in Yiddish until the end of 1889.[11]

The civil marriage records of Alsatian Jews also give testimony to the slow diffusion of French in the countryside. In my three villages and one town the use of signatures in Hebrew characters was frequent: in the 1820s and 1830s, 27 per cent of the grooms and 58 per cent of the brides could not sign their names in French; in the 1840s 10 per cent of the grooms and 37 per cent of the brides still signed in Hebrew letters. Only in the years between 1850 and 1862 did that number decline to 5 per cent of the grooms and 23 per cent of the brides. (And, of course, in each period, the number of parents of the bridal couple unable to sign their names except in Hebrew was considerably higher.)[12] Thus, more than two generations after emancipation a sizeable minority of individuals in this literate population had not begun to master writing in Latin characters.

Acculturation to gentile taste can be measured not only by the acquisition of the rudiments of the French language but also by the adoption of French names. That process, too, was a gradual one, especially in the case of men's names. Jewish men living in villages and small towns retained a high proportion of traditional Jewish names. In fact, there was no statistically significant decline in Jewish names between the cohort born in the 1770s and 1780s (76 per cent Jewish names) and that born in the 1830s (69 per cent Jewish names). Only in the 1860s was there a shift from Jewish to French names.[13]

The persistence of traditional usages may be accounted for, in part, by the observation that village Jews had no higher status group into which they might assimilate. On the level of popular custom, they were acculturated to their rural milieu, for they often adapted practices found among the gentile peasantry (though they did not consciously look to the peasantry for social acceptance). Too often, when we speak of assimilation, we look only for assimilation into the bourgeoisie and overlook assimilation to the mores of other social classes. Thus, like their Christian peasant compatriots, Alsatian Jews were no strangers to the nuptial charivari, a ritualized mêlée enacted as part of village wedding festivities. In 1823 the Consistory of Wintzenheim formally abolished 'the established custom . . . by virtue of which young bachelors demanded or rather extorted certain sums or food and drink from the newlyweds'.[14] That formal ban appears to have been of limited success, for in *Couronne* Alexandre Weill describes, halfway through the century the persistence of a Jewish nuptial charivari:

> It is the custom in Alsace that . . . the fiancée offer all the young girls of the village a collation composed of fruit cakes, sweets and gentle liqueurs while the groom, if he is of the same village, treats all the young men to drink. This custom is so *de rigueur* that the young persons, without being invited, come on their own to the house of the fiancée to pay their compliments and seat themselves at the table.[15]

Like the Christian peasants, village Jews in Alsace believed in
'miracle workers', consulted local faith-healers (Jewish ones, such as
Reb Moshe, the wise man of Uttenheim), purchased talismans and
drew circles around women in childbirth to protect them from evil
spirits.[16] Just as the entire Christian population of a village took part
in religious processions, so the entire Jewish population turned out for
funerals and marched in disarray behind the coffin, much to the
distress of the bourgeois leaders of the Strasburg Consistory. As late as
1860 the latter sought to ban such funeral processions because they
lacked dignity.[17] Within the context of village life, however, such
ritual behaviour was not an affront to local sensibilities.

In the realm of patriotism, village Jews also differed from the
bourgeois emancipationist model but, again, resembled the Christian
rural population. While patriotic themes began to appear in the
nineteenth century in Alsatian Torah wrappers,[18] and while bourgeois Jewish leaders promoted army service as a sign of Jewish
patriotism, ordinary Jews, like their Christian countrymen, continued to prefer that their own sons do without that particular
honour. In Léon Cahun's tales of rural Jewish life, Chmoul, an
observant man living in a tiny hamlet, tells his son: 'The profession of
soldier is the profession of an assassin.'[19] Traditional attitudes towards
army service surived also in the Judeo-Alsatian dialect, which used
the term '*rek*' (empty or poor one) to refer to a soldier.[20] And Alsatian
Jews used magic rituals to improve their chances of escaping
conscription in the draft lottery.[21]

While grateful to the French government for its granting of
citizenship, village Jews did not remake their Jewish identity to fit the
emancipationist model. Although recent studies have pointed to the
survival of ethnic solidarity among post-emancipation Western
Jews,[22] such Jews are still most often pictured as acquiring a national
French or German identity at the expense of a Jewish consciousness
which transcended international borders. Alsatian Jews, however,
continued to express a sense of shared fate with their brethren.
Despite efforts of consistorial leaders and the French government to
stem the flow, the wandering poor, including those from across the
Rhine, could count on the assistance of Alsatian Jews, especially those
in small towns and villages.[23] The victims of the Damascus blood libel
also found their place in the *Memorbukh* of the Haguenau Jewish
community, together with Jewish martyrs from as far back as the
Crusades.[24] Thus, the Jews of Haguenau in 1840 used a traditional
form of commemoration to express their sense of continuity, their

linkage, both to the martyrs of Damascus and also to the Jewish victims of persecution throughout the ages.

The persistence of traditional values and forms of identity and the slow pace of assimilation to bourgeois standards among village Jews in Alsace is intimately linked to the local social structure. Even the post-emancipation Jewish community excerised considerable constraints, both formal and informal, upon the Jewish population. Most Jews in Alsace lived in communities of between 100 and 400 Jews, where anonymity was hardly the order of the day. Moreover, even after 1831 when membership of the local Jewish community became theoretically voluntary, failure to support the synagogue was met with denial of all religious privileges, including burial in the Jewish cemetery. The tight-knit village society thus promoted conformity and continuity. It is of interest that in villages where the concentration of Jews was especially high (more than 25 per cent) relative to the total population, emigration was discouraged.[25]

There were few agents of social change within village Jewish society. The local notables, for the most part, were men of wealth whose fortune was derived from traditional commercial pursuits in the countryside rather than from new industrial ventures.[26] Moreover, as my study of migration patterns has revealed, the upwardly mobile within the villages were the most likely to leave. From governmental marriage records it is possible to ascertain that both migrating grooms and migrating parents of the bridal couple were two to three times as likely as non-migrants to come from the very highest economic strata; conversely, they were far less likely to be located at the bottom of the socio-economic scale, plying their wares in the traditional Jewish street trades. Migrants were also more likely than their stay-at-home brethren to assume new economic positions, even when they settled in towns no larger than those they left. Finally, while Alsatian Jews as a whole had a high rate of literacy, the migrants tended to be more literate, especially in French, than the stationary Jews. Male Jewish migrants also married later, at a median age of 32.4 years, compared with 28.8 years for those who stayed put.[27] Thus, those with the greatest potential for innovation and with the highest aspirations were siphoned off from village society.

The village rabbinate was also a conservative force. As late as 1870 the majority of Alsatian rabbis belonged to the traditionalist camp. The oldest had been trained before the modern Ecole Rabbinique was established in 1830. In fact, twenty of the thirty-eight rabbis and *ministres-officiants* serving Alsace in 1864 had been born before 1812 and had therefore received much or all of their rabbinic education in traditional yeshivot.[28] Their authority was based upon traditional learning, and they feared the enforcement of governmental requirements of secular education. Even many of the younger rabbis had a superficial knowledge of secular culture. As Phyllis Cohen Albert has pointed out, the French rabbinate attracted primarily those whose social aspirations were limited and whose educational attainments were such as to restrict their possibilities for economic advancement.[29]

The Alsatian situation thus differed substantially from the German scene. There, as Steven Lowenstein has shown, young university-trained rabbis took their first pulpits in villages and small towns, where they often introduced reforms in ritual along with new models of appropriate behaviour.[30] In Alsace, such rabbis were a rarity. One, Moses Nordmann of Hegenheim on the Swiss border, lamented his inability to abolish the sale of honours in the synagogue in the 1840s and conceded that 95 per cent of the Jews of Alsace supported the staunchly traditional views of Rabbi Salomon Klein, who led the opposition to the consistories' attempt to introduce moderate reforms in liturgy and practice.[31]

The village economy itself promoted continuity, for Jewish occupations were independent ones which were not linked to education. Not surprisingly, then, village Jews resisted the modern Jewish primary schools which the Strasburg Consistory and the Academy of Strasburg attempted to establish in every locale with a Jewish population of at least 200 persons. While the government and the consistory sought to close all Jewish schools with unlicensed teachers (i.e., *heders* with traditional *melamdim*), they failed repeatedly in the 1820s and 1830s. Occasionally village Jews, as in Zellwiller in 1826, objected so strenuously to the imposition by the consistory of a new schoolmaster that they physically abused him. Clandestine schools, as the consistory called them, flourished.[32] The writer Alexandre Weill, for one, attended such a school in the 1820s.[33] In 1832, of 110 Jewish communities in Alsace, only seventeen contained authorized primary schools. The following year it was estimated that a mere 365 school-age Jewish children (of a total of 4,000) were receiving a modern education.[34] The survival of traditional Jewish schools represented a form of passive resistance to consistorial-imposed forms of acculturation.

The situation changed in the 1840s and especially during the Second Empire, when modern Jewish elementary schools were established securely in almost every Jewish community in Alsace of more than 200 persons and in some smaller communities as well. In villages lacking Jewish communal schools Jewish children attended Christian public schools, receiving their instruction in Judaism in private lessons with the local cantor.[35]

While the village social structure retarded acculturation to emancipationist values, the urban environment of Strasburg and Mulhouse facilitated acculturation to the bourgeoisie. The city offered new vistas of economic mobility. Settled commerce and regular commercial employment replaced the peddling and irregular petty brokerage that predominated in the countryside. Both Strasburg and Mulhouse boasted respected schools for Jewish vocational education. Moreover, in the middle of the century 16 per cent of Jewish household heads in Strasburg were artisans as compared with 5 per cent of village Jews. While only 1 per cent of village Jews were proprietors or professionals, the figure for the Jews of Strasburg was 7 per cent.[36] As the commercial and cultural centre of Alsace, Strasburg was home to the wealthiest Jewish merchants and bankers of the region as well as those with literary and political aspirations, who often became communal leaders. Its Jewish population of 2,387 in 1854 made Strasburg the second largest (after Paris) Jewish community in France. Mulhouse, dominated by a Protestant industrial elite, was a hub of entrepreneurial activity. Although never the seat of the Consistory of the Upper Rhine, by 1853 Mulhouse's 1,527 Jews comprised the largest Jewish community in the department.[37] Finally, Strasburg and Mulhouse, like Paris, acted as magnets, attracting Jewish migrants who were willing to assume new economic positions and experiment in matters of social, religious and cultural behaviour.

Strasburg and Mulhouse presented Alsatian Jews with a French-speaking bourgeoisie whose ranks they might aspire to join. Accordingly, urban Jews adopted French names far more rapidly than did their country cousins. Sixty-seven per cent of the Jewish males living in Strasburg and born in the 1770s and 1780s bore Jewish names, but that percentage declined precipitously by the 1830s and reached a low of 20 per cent by the 1860s. Women's names, which were less constrained by religious practice and hence always more sensitive to fashion, reflected French taste even earlier. In Strasburg Jewish names virtually disappeared among girls as early as the first decade of the nineteenth century.[38] The rate of minimal literacy in French, as revealed by signatures of marriage contracts, was also far higher in Strasburg and in Colmar than in the villages. Even in the 1820s and

1830s, 89 per cent of the grooms in Strasburg and 96 per cent in Colmar could sign the marriage register in Latin script, as could 83 per cent of the Strasburg brides. By the 1840s 100 per cent male literacy was achieved in both urban seats of the departmental consistories, and close to that (86 per cent in Strasburg and 90 per cent in Colmar) among females.[39]

The public use of Yiddish also declined dramatically in Strasburg two generations before such a decline in the villages. As early as the Napoleonic period all correspondence and records of the Strasburg Consistory were kept in French. Modern Jewish elementary schools were established in Strasburg on a firm footing by the 1820s and were noted for their insistence on conducting education solely in French.[40] The Jewish vocational school (*Ecole de Travail*) in Strasburg also banned the use of Yiddish and caned boys who violated the regulation.[41] Moreover, public *lycées* were available for those seeking upward mobility via education. They brought Jewish students in contact with their gentile peers. Additionally, Mulhouse boasted the only large denominationally mixed primary school where children of different religious backgrounds could study together, reputedly in harmony.[42]

Religious observance was also more relaxed in the cities than in the countryside, and popular ritual was adapted to more cosmopolitan standards. Indeed, Edouard Coypel, a non-Jewish and not particularly sympathetic observer of Jewish practice in Alsace in the 1860s and 1870s, noted that in the cities Jews were more sensitive to gentile opinion and introduced changes in their funerals, for example, 'so as not to present too great a contrast to gentile customs'.[43] Similarly, in his study of Judeo-Alsatian humour, Rabbi S. Debré, writing of his childhood in the 1860s, commented that the Jews in the villages had remained observant while those in the cities had not.[44]

This is not to suggest that observant Jews shunned the city, but that an urban environment offered a measure of anonymity to those eager to relax communal bonds, and subjected those who resisted dominant communal patterns of behaviour to direct pressure. As the seat of the departmental consistory, the Strasburg Jewish community in particular was governed by men who moved in the ranks of the *haute bourgeoisie* and prided themselves on their advanced culture. When selecting a functionary (*commissaire surveillant*) to monitor local communities, the Strasburg Consistory leadership wrote, as early as 1830, 'his opinions and his approach must be as close to our own views as possible . . . [T]he choice must fall on a man of moderate character, endowed with some education and zeal for the general welfare and whose religious sentiments are in no ways exaggerated.'[45] Although the acculturated leaders of the Jewish community could not impose all their ideas immediately upon their less-acculturated constituents – whether traditional newcomers to the city or village Jews in their home communities – they could propose a model of Jewish practice and civility that ultimately became the norm for the masses.

The wealthy and educated lay leaders of the consistory of the Lower Rhine and the *commissaires surveillants* whom they appointed took the lead in promoting a form of Jewish practice consonant with bourgeois aesthetics, definitions of spirituality and norms of decorum. Beginning with the Strasburg community, they instituted a variety of non-doctrinal modifications in synagogue worship designed to meet the needs of a population concerned with its social acceptability.

In 1831 the Strasburg Consistory set up a commission, composed of five imposing members of the communal elite, to 'investigate the obstacles which are still opposed to the complete regeneration of the Jews of Alsace and to indicate the most appropriate means to make such obstacles disappear'. The commission report was replete with proposals to eliminate aspects of traditional Jewish practice which were embarrassing to those who considered themselves enlightened or which had no direct counterparts in Christian culture. The commission suggested, for example, the suppression of the auctioning in the temple of synagogue honours and a ban on the wearing of special robes by laymen on the High Holidays; the setting up of the temple in such a manner that girls could enter the main sanctuary; the regulating of ceremonies in the temple in a 'more seemly' manner; the enforcement of a 24-hour waiting period before interment; abolition of the custom of wearing a beard; a ban on the practice of *kapores* (in which sins are transferred to a chicken on the eve of the Day of Atonement); the administration of the *mikveh* so as not to compromise the health of women; and the introduction of weekly sermons by rabbis and laymen to inculcate morality and social responsibility.[46]

Most of the recommendations of the commission for modifying distinctive customs, not to mention its more radical proposals for abridging the liturgy and abolishing the second day of festivals, found no receptive audience in 1831 even in Strasburg, where much of the Jewish population then retained a sentimental attachment to traditional custom. Within the decade, however, the Strasburg community introduced reforms that touched upon the aesthetics of worship. Its major success was the abolition of publicly auctioning the honour of being called to the Torah and the insistence upon quiet worship following the lead of the cantor rather than the spirited anarchy which characterized traditional Jewish communal prayer.[47]

In the 1840s the pace of change accelerated. In 1842 the Consistory of the Lower Rhine mandated that a ceremony of religious initiation for both boys and girls be instituted in all the temples in the department.[48] The following spring, in response to a petition seeking significant changes in the observance of the Ninth of Ab, the traditional day of mourning for the destruction of the First and Second Temple in Jerusalem, the Strasburg Consistory accepted a proposal for draping the sanctuary in black – a substitution of the Western colour of mourning in place of the traditional Jewish colour, white. It also agreed to refuse admission into the synagogue to worshippers who were not decently attired. (Traditionally mourners were not to pay attention to the state of their clothes.) The tactic of a petition failed, however, in 1845, when the consistory refused to consider the demand for the introduction of an organ.[49]

The reluctance to introduce an organ into the synagogue as well as the failure to adopt in their entirety the proposals of the 1831 commission reflected the fact that a small segment of the Jewish elite of Strasburg was far more distant from Jewish tradition than the rest of the consistorial leadership, not to mention the Jewish masses. In fact, the absence in the 1820s and 30s of a critical mass of enlightened and well-educated Jews in Alsace had led a few Jewish leaders – most notably the Ratisbonne brothers – to convert to Catholicism; later it led others to withdraw from Jewish communal life. Thus, in 1853 the secretary of the Strasburg Consistory chose dismissal from his post rather than to have his son circumcised. Another lay member of the consistory, a physician, resigned in frustration when his proposals to initiate religious reforms and to increase the pastoral function of the rabbis were met with disdain by the moderate Grand Rabbi Arnaud Aron, who saw in them a desire to Christianize Judaism.[50]

The acculturated, largely non-university-educated and non-radical elite of businessmen who comprised the majority of Jewish communal leaders in Strasburg gradually succeeded in transforming the public expression of Judaism because of the power wielded by the Consistory within the city and the impact of the general social milieu. When in 1858 an observant Jew in Strasburg protested at the exclusion of his son from reading the Torah in the synagogue because his son had not participated in the religious initiation ceremony (limited to those with a modern Jewish education), he could not rely upon a social network to support his rejection of a modern education for his son.[51] The progressive lay leadership in Strasburg found an appropriate rabbi in the urbane Arnaud Aron, who preached in French, edited a French prayerbook replete with pious bourgeois sentiment, welcomed the Revolution of 1848 and promoted secular education. Although he rejected what he perceived as radical reforms, Aron provided clerical legitimation for the moderate acculturation of Judaism to bourgeois standards. Similarly in Mulhouse, Rabbi Samuel Dreyfuss served as a representative of a moderate approach to tradition and self-consciously wrote of the need to present Judaism in a way that would appeal to the educated Jewish youth of his community.[52]

After the middle of the century a combination of economic and social factors diffused new values and patterns of behaviour in the countryside as well as in the city. The inability of the rural economy to absorb the growing Jewish population after 1848 stimulated the emigration of the young – to Strasburg, to Mulhouse, to Paris and abroad. By 1866, for example, only 33 per cent of those Jews who were children in 1846 remained in their home villages of Bischheim, Niederroedern and Itterswiller.[53] Between 1854 and 1863 78 per cent of the Jewish communities of the Lower Rhine declined in size.[54] And by the 1850s the clandestine schools in the villages yielded to a generation of combined consistorial and governmental pressure and gave way to modern Jewish schools, which were supervised by the urban Jewish leadership of Strasburg and whose teachers had to be licensed by the government. Those schools promoted new values – an emancipationist mentality – in the countryside, while their teachers brought urban manners into the villages. Traditional Jewish learning virtually disappeared, replaced by instruction in Bible stories, a bit of Hebrew, moral precepts and the tenets of Judaism as presented in catechisms. As Rabbi Salomon Klein, leader of the traditionalist element in Alsace, noted sadly in an 1861 Hebrew pamphlet: 'Now the ignorant are many and those who desire to know God and thirst for his words are few . . . or the houses of study have ceased in Israel . . . Secular learning has become fundamental and our Holy Torah of secondary importance and relegated to a corner.'[55]

The reforms in the style of Jewish public worship which were initially introduced in Strasburg during the July monarchy were diffused over the course of the succeeding two decades to the towns and villages of the countryside. Information and recommendations

provided by the departmental consistory, occasional regional meetings of rabbis and the gradual acceptance of urban mores as the
desired standard appear to have been the crucial factors in the
adoption of new types of ritual behaviour. Despite initial opposition,
the abolition of the auction of synagogue honours, the practice of
praying quietly and the introduction of ceremonies of religious
initiation became widely accepted in scores of Jewish communities in
Alsace.[56]

By the 1860s bourgeois standards of decorum had penetrated
deeply into the countryside. The *pinkas* (minute-book) of the Jewish
community of Bouxwiller, a small town northwest of Strasburg,
which in 1863 had a population of 3,825 of whom 312 were Jews, on
December 31 1863 recorded in Yiddish a new set of regulations for
proper behaviour in the synagogue. 'Entry into the temple', noted
Article 1, 'should take place without noise, without wandering from
one place to another. Each person should go directly to his own
seat . . .' Once within the synagogue worshippers were enjoined not
to sing along with the cantor; violators were subject to fines. Dress
regulations were also promulgated. On the sabbath and holidays
each male worshipper was expected to attend synagogue services
wearing 'a high black hat'.[57]

Ultimately, then, accommodation to bourgeois culture and aesthetics prevailed among Alsatian Jewry as a whole. But the gradual
process of assimilation had significant consequences for French
Jewry. As the major source of opposition to the reformist tendencies of
the bourgeois leadership of the Central Consistory, Alsatian Jews
acted as a brake upon ideological religious reform. Petition campaigns and a threat of schism emanating from Alsace, the heartland of
France's Jewish population, persuaded the consistorial elite in Paris
to adopt a moderate approach. The traditionalism of Alsatian village
Jews was also reflected in the French rabbinate, for Alsace was
virtually the exclusive recruiting ground for the rabbinate until the
arrival of Eastern European immigrants at the turn of the twentieth
century. Finally, Alsatian Jews rooted in the culture of the village and
the small town retained a traditional definition of international
Jewish solidarity, which later expressed itself in support for Zionism
far surpassing that of the rest of French Jewry.[58]

The experience of Jews in Alsace suggests the importance of social
context, and of the available reference group, in understanding the
pace and style of acculturation and integration. The Alsatian
countryside provided a communal social setting which cushioned the

potentially disruptive impact of emancipation. The city offered avenues of social and economic mobility to those Jews who recognized, and opted for, the new possibilities provided by emancipation; they developed models, and mobilized support, for reconciling Judaism and contemporary bourgeois standards of propriety. City and countryside also interacted. Urban Jewish elites developed and enforced the policies of Jewish communal institutions, introducing them first in the cities, and later disseminating them to town and village. Yet the traditional Jewish village community also influenced urban Jews. Proposals for reform had to take into account the sensibilities of Jews in the countryside. And once Jews had left their villages and small towns for the more stimulating environments of Strasburg, Mulhouse or Paris, and had found a place within the French bourgeoisie, they turned the village communities they had fled into stimuli of Jewish memory. Through the mechanism of nostalgia, parlayed in popular genre tales, the Alsatian Jewish countryside served to preserve a measure of Jewish identity among its emigrant youth.[59] Ideologies helped to define and transmit to the masses those new possibilities, but the social contexts of village and city – and their interaction – determined how, and when, those possibilities would be realized.

Notes

1 For the best general treatment of the political and ideological aspects of Jewish emancipation in Europe, see Jacob Katz, *Out of the Ghetto* (Cambridge, 1973); Reinhard Rürup, 'Jewish Emancipation and Bourgeois Society', *Leo Baeck Institute Yearbook* 14 (1969), 67–91; and Salo Baron, 'Ghetto and Emancipation', *Menorah Journal* 14 (June, 1928), 515–26 and 'Newer Approaches to Jewish Emancipation', *Diogenes* 29 (Spring 1960), 56–81; and Michael Meyer, *The Origins of the Modern Jew* (Detroit, 1967). On the institutional and intellectual developments among French Jewry, see Phyllis Cohen Albert, *The Modernization of French Jewry: Consistory and Community in the Nineteenth Century* (Hanover, N.H., 1977) and Michael Graetz, *Haperiferiah haytah lemerkaz* (Jerusalem, 1982).

2 For good examples of studies which emphasize the socio-economic context, see Jacob Toury, 'Der Eintritt der Juden ins deutsche Bürgertum', in *Das Judentum in der deutschen Umwelt 1800–1850*, ed. Hans Liebeschutz and Arnold Paucker (Tübingen, 1977), pp. 139–242 and Monika Richarz, *Jüdisches Leben in Deutschland, 1780–1871* (New York, 1976) and *Im Kaiserreich* (New York, 1979).

3 On the Jews of Alsace, see Elie Scheid, *Histoire des Juifs d'Alsace* (Paris, 1887), *passim*; and Freddy Raphael and Robert Weyl, *Juifs en Alsace: Culture, Société, Histoire* (Toulouse, 1977) and *Regards Nouveaux sur les Juifs d'Alsace* (Strasburg, 1980).

4 On the economic role of Alsatian Jewry, see Roland Marx, 'La régénération economique des Juifs d'Alsace à l'époque révolutionnaire et Napoléon', *Annales Historiques de la Revolution Française* 223 (Jan.– March 1976), 105–20 and Paul Leuilliot, *L'Alsace au Debut du xixe Siècle* (Paris, 1959–60), vol. II, pp. 176–93.

5 The census data are drawn from Archives Départementales du Bas-Rhin (hereafter, ADBR) VII M 719, 726, 733, 740 (Strasburg, 1846); VII M 720, 727, 734, 741 (Strasburg, 1856); VII M 722, 729, 736, 743 (Strasburg, 1866); VII M 459 (Itterswiller 1836–66); VII M 266 (Bischheim 1836–46) and VII M 267 (Bischheim 1856–66): and VII M 562 (Niederroedern 1836–66). The marriage records used include ADBR 4E 330, Niederroedern (1793–1830; 1831–62); 4E 226, Itterswiller (1793–1830; 1831–62); and ADBR 5M1 852 and 853, Bischheim (1813–32; 1833–42; 1843–52; 1853–62); 5M1 1663, Strasburg (1823–4; 1825–6; 1827–8; 1844–5; 1846–7; 1860; 1861; 1862). All Jewish marriages in Bischheim, Niederroedern and Itterswiller – a total of 368 – were coded. For Strasburg the Jewish marriages of 1823–8, 1844–7, and 1860–2 – a total of 176 marriages – were selected. The notarial records and commercial court records are found in Series E and Series U respectively of ADBR.

6 Lists of Jews applying for patents to engage in business, 1808–13, Patentes des Juifs d'Alsace, HM 2 782a and 782b, Central Archives for the History of the Jewish People, Jerusalem (henceforward: CAHJP); manuscript censuses of 1846 and 1866, ADBR VII M 459, VII M 266 and 267, VII M 562.

7 CAHJP, ZF 212.

8 CAHJP, HM 5519 and HM 5520.

9 'Souvenirs d'un Voyage en Alsace', *Archives Israélites* 5 (1844), 469–70.

10 Daniel Stauben, *Scènes de la Vie Juive en Alsace* (Paris, 1860), pp. 221–2.

11 Archives of the Jewish Theological Seminary of America (JTS), MS. 3834.

12 ADBR 4E 226, 4E 330, and Bischheim (1813–32; 1833–42); (1843–52; 1853–62).

13 Manuscript censuses, ADBR VII M 459, VII M 266 and 267, VII M 562.

14 JTS, Box 18 01924.

15 Alexandre Weill, *Couronne* (Paris, 1857), p. 197.

16 Freddy Raphael, 'Rites de naissance et médecine populaire dans le judaïsme rural d'Alsace', *Ethnologie Française* 1, nos. 3–4, 82–7.

17 Consistoire Israélite de Strasbourg, 'A Messieurs les Rabbins Communaux et Commissaires Administrateurs des Synagogues', 1 November 1860, p. 1, Houghton Library, Harvard University.

18 Freddy Raphael, 'Les Juifs d'Alsace et la Conscription au XIX-e Siècle', in *Les Juifs et la Révolution Française* ed. Bernhard Blumenkranz and Albert Soboul (Toulouse, 1976) and Robert Weyl and Freddy Raphael, *L'Imagerie Juive d'Alsace* (Strasburg, 1979).

19 Léon Cahun, *La Vie Juive* (Paris, 1886), p. 53.

20 Honel Meiss, *Traditions Populaires Alsaciennes à travers le dialecte Judéo-Alsacien* (Nice, n.d.), p. 207.

21 Raphael, 'Les Juifs d'Alsace', pp. 122–3.

22 See Michael Graetz, *Haperiferiah, passim*; Phyllis Cohen Albert, 'Ethnicity and Solidarity in Nineteenth-Century France', in *Mystics, Philosophers, and Politicians. Essays in Jewish Intellectual History in Honor of Alexander Altmann*, ed. Jehuda Reinharz and Daniel Swetschinski (Durham, N.C., 1982), pp. 249–74 and Robert Liberles, 'Emancipation and the Structure of the Jewish Community in the Nineteenth Century', *Leo Baeck Institute Yearbook* 21 (1986), 51–67.

23 S. Debré, *L'Humour Judéo-Alsacien* (Paris, 1933), pp. 273–6.

24 *Memorbukh* of the Jewish community of Haguenau, CAHJP, HM 5010.

25 My calculation, based on population statistics of Alsatian villages and the patterns of migration as calculated from marriage records, which list place of birth of the bridal couple and their parents as well as the current domicile of all of them.

26 See lists of Notables of Bas-Rhin and Haut-Rhin, CAHJP, ZF 464, ZF 655, ZF 659, ZF 744, ZF 745, ZF 746.

27 Paula Hyman, 'Village Jews and Jewish Modernity: The Case of Alsace in the Nineteenth Century', in *Jewish Settlement and Community in the Modern Western World*, edited by Ronald Dotterer, Deborah Dash Moore and Steven M. Cohen, Susquehannah University Studies (Selinsgrove, Pa., 1991).

28 'Tableau du Personnel des Ministres du Culte Israélite', 1864, Archives of the Leo Baeck Institute, New York, AR 2863 80–101.

29 Albert, *Modernization*, pp. 242–59.

30 Steven Lowenstein, 'The 1840s and the Creation of the German-Jewish Religious Reform Movement', in *Revolution and Evolution: 1848 in German-Jewish History* edited by Werner E. Mosse, Arnold Pauker and Reinhard Rürup (Tübingen, 1981), pp. 255–97.

31 *Archives Israélites* 5 (1844), 661 and 8 (1847), 477.

32 Copie des Lettres du Comité Cantonal d'Istraélites du Ressort de l'Académie de Strasbourg (Letter to Rector of Academy of Strasbourg), 28 November 1825, HM 5529, CAHJP.

33 Alexandre Weill, *Ma Jeunesse*, vol. 1 (Paris, 1870), pp. 67–9, 73–5.

34 Consistoire du Bas-Rhin, Comité d'Instruction Primaire, letter to the Minister of Public Instruction, 8 June 1832, HM 5518, CAHJP.

35 *Archives Insraélites* 4 (1843), 280–8; *L'Ami des Israélites* (1847), p. 278; Statistics, Consistory of the Upper Rhine, 1851, JTS, French Documents, Box 26; Statistics, Consistory of the Lower Rhine, 1854, Leo

Baeck Institute (LBI), AR-C 1088, #34–9; *UI*, IX (1853–4), p. 277.

36 ADBR, vii M 719, 726, 733, 740.

37 A.N. F¹⁹ 11.024.

38 Manuscript censuses from Strasburg, ADBR, as cited above, note #5.

39 ADBR, 5Mi (1844–5; 1846–7; 1860; 1861; 1862).

40 Consistoire de Strasbourg, 26 July 1825; Académie de Strasbourg, 6 November 1821, Archives Nationales, F19 11.028.

41 Maurice Bloch, *L'Alsace Juive*, Publication de la Société d'Histoire des Juifs d'Alsace et Lorraine (Strasburg, 1908).

42 'Rapport sur la Situation de l'Enseignement Secondaire, Académie de Strasbourg, 1864', Archives Nationales, F 17 6849.

43 Edouard Coypel, *Le Judaïsme* (Mulhouse, 1876), p. 158.

44 Debré, *L'Humour* p. 291.

45 Commission Administrative, Consistoire de Strasbourg, letter 21 February 1830, ZF 295, CAHJP.

46 Commission report, 6 September 1831, Strasburg Consistory, JTS, French documents, Box 18.

47 In 1839 the Strasburg Consistory discussed means of compensating for the loss of revenue due to the abolition of the sale of honours. Minutes, Strasburg Consistory, 25 June 1839. JTS, French documents, Box 18.

48 Minutes, Consistory of the Lower Rhine, 19 October 1842 and 8 November 1842, CAHJP, HM 5503.

49 Ibid., 10 May 1843 and 17 July 1845.

50 On the conversion of the Ratisbonne brothers, see Jacob Katz, 'Religion as a Uniting and Dividing Force in Modern Jewish History', in *The Role of Religion in Modern Jewish History*, ed. J. Katz (Cambridge, 1975), pp. 6–9 and Natalie Isser and Lita Linzer Schwartz, 'Sudden Conversion: The Case of Alphonse Ratisbonne', *Jewish Social Studies* 45 (1983), 17–30. On the other lay leaders, see Minutes, Strasburg Consistory, 23 June 1853 and 11 November 1853, Archives of Strasburg Jewish community.

51 Archives of the Strasburg Consistory, uncatalogued, Minutes, 13 May 1858. See Albert, *The Modernization of French Jewry*, p. 191.

52 See Aron's prayerbook, entitled *Prières d'un Coeur Israélite: Recueil de Prières et de Méditations pour toutes les Circonstances de la Vie* (Strasburg, 1848), for a revealing look at his social philosophy. Letters from Rabbi Salomon Ullman of Nancy, a future Grand Rabbi of France, to Rabbis Aron and Dreyfuss discuss their agreement on the need for moderate reform under the auspices of rabbinic leadership. See letters of early 1844 (undated), 28 December 1844, 25 December 1846, JTS, MS. 8488. See also Samuel Dreyfuss, *Archives Israélites* 14 (1853), 250–5.

53 Analysis of manuscript censuses, ADBR vii M 459, vii M 266 and 267, vii M 562.

54 List of communities, Consistory of the Lower Rhine, 1854 and 1863, LBI, AR-C 1088, 34–9.

55 Salomon Klein, *Mipne Koshet* (Frankfurt-am-Main, 1861), p. 30.
56 Minutes of the reunion of the Consistories of Metz, Nancy and Strasburg, Jan. 1846, LBI, AR 2863, 629–30; report of rabbinical conference in Colmar, February 1854, *Le Lien d'Israel* 2 (1856), 258–67; on Nieder-roedern, Sierentz and Wintzenheim (HR), see *L'Ami des Israélites* (Strasburg), 2 (June 1847), pp. 77–9; on Bieswiller and Diemeringen, Minutes of Consistory of the Lower Rhine, 22 April 1843 and 28 August 1843; on Rosheim and Bouxwiller, 20 April 1847, CAHJP, HM 5503; on Wissembourg and Mulhouse, *Le Lien d'Israel* 3 (1857), 233 and 204–5; on Habsheim, *Le Lien d'Israel* 4, no. 3 (August 1858), 138.
57 Pinkas of the Jewish Community of Bouxwiller, 1828–1948, CAHJP, HM 1067, pp. 32–3.
58 Paula Hyman, *From Dreyfus to Vichy: The Remaking of French Jewry, 1906–1939* (New York, 1979), pp. 173, 177.
59 Books such as Daniel Stauben's *Scènes de la Vie Juive en Alsace*, Léon Cahun's *La Vie Juive*, illustrated by Alphonse Levy, and Georges Stenne's [David Schornstein's] *Perle* (Paris, 1877) enjoyed great success among acculturated French Jews, especially those of Alsatian origin. Additionally, artefacts depicting scenes of traditional Jewish life in Alsace were preserved by highly assimilated French Jewish families. The Jewish Museum's 1987 exhibit on the Dreyfus Affair, for example, displayed a cloth depicting the observance of the three pilgrimage festivals which Alfred and Lucie Dreyfus hung on the wall in their apartment. See Norman Kleeblatt (ed.), *The Dreyfus Affair: Art, Truth, and Justice* (Berkeley and Los Angeles, 1987), p. 271.

Nostalgia and 'return to the ghetto': a cultural phenomenon in Western and Central Europe

RICHARD I. COHEN

In 1878, Isaac Strauss, a wealthy French Jew, best known perhaps as a composer of popular music for Napoleon III's court balls at Vichy, exhibited eighty-two Jewish ritual objects at the International Exposition in Paris. This exhibition, the first of its kind, was eventually to form the nucleus of the Judaica collection at the Cluny Museum in Paris, where it would spur an interest in the collection and study of Jewish art objects.[1]

What brought Isaac Strauss to assemble this 'curious collection' (as the editor of the catalogue phrased it) after having spent most of his adult life at a distance from the Jewish community? A scion of a rabbinic family from Strasburg, Strauss had moved to Paris in 1827 at the age of twenty-one and then travelled extensively through various countries of Europe in pursuit of general art objects. Only later did he extend his search to Jewish artefacts.

Can we assume that for Strauss this was an excursion back to his childhood? Collecting sabbath lamps, kiddush cups, spice boxes, Hanukkah lamps or Esther scrolls as objects of religious art may have conjured up memories of his early years in Strasburg and reaffirmed his identification with his past. For Strauss, this quest may have been inspired by what Gaston Bachelard has called 'the dream of childhood', the images of his early years which the adult sets against a colourless world. Or as the French poet Paul Chaulot has put it: 'The world totters/when from my past I get/what I need to live in the depths of myself.'[2]

However, beyond its relevance for Isaac Strauss, the exhibition has proved to be a landmark in, and a testimony to, the development of Jewish life in Western and Central Europe since the French Revolution. Now, for the first time, Jewish ritual artefacts were presented in their own associational context as a historical and aesthetic phenomenon, beyond the framework of religion and religious practice. Indeed, with this exhibition, yet one more aspect of Jewish life had been objectified and it too would gradually warrant the attention of the analytical school in Jewish life which had developed since the establishment of the 'Verein für Kultur und Wissenschaft der Juden' in 1819. And here, too, the dialectical force, ever present in the enterprise loosely termed the *Wissenschaft des Judentums*, asserted itself. For by 'deactualizing Judaism' (the phrase is Gershom Scholem's), or in another sense by transplanting the sacred into the profane, one also released lingering feelings of attachment and nostalgia which allowed individuals to renew contact with a Jewish world otherwise so distant.

In the process of emerging from the 'ghetto', Jews were willing to adapt quickly to the language, culture, mores and even at times the religion of European society. However, the rapid move from the relatively slow-moving Jewish community to the pulsating life of Europe's capitals and cities tended to produce feelings of disorientation and emptiness, which certain Jews tried to counteract by re-establishing an attachment to that 'ghetto' world which they or their parents had abandoned. This reconciliation with, and nostalgia for, the 'ghetto' took many forms and encompassed a surprising number of people, Strauss and his collection of Judaica being only one example. In general terms, this is the phenomenon which Erikson has described as

> the collective need of human adults, between the complex process of having been 'brought up' and a certain terminal 'decline', to affirm ceremonially with whom they have grown up and whose standing in the world they now share.[3]

This socio-cultural process – wherein the world of the 'ghetto', the 'authentic' Jewish experience, served as a constant luring attraction – developed within a chronological framework extending from the 1830s to the late nineteenth century and beyond. It had a strong appeal in Western and Central Europe and frequently surfaced where the processes of integration into European society were the most developed. As a cultural phenomenon, it manifested itself in various ways, but at work throughout was the urge to retrieve aspects of a community that could no longer be reconstituted. To touch that world in any way was to help overcome the emptiness of a relentless modernization and to *integrate* the forgotten (or receding) past into contemporary existence. Yet the modern 'enlightened' world, it should be emphasized, was never wholly rejected by the personalities under study here; on the contrary, it continued to be their basic, formulative experience. But it would now coexist with forms of identification which did not neatly fit in to the 'enlightened' scheme of modernization.

Clearly this was the way in which Georges Stenne, who collaborated with Strauss on the exhibition and wrote the introduction to the catalogue, must have perceived their joint enterprise. Like Strauss, Stenne had been born and brought up in Alsace and he, too, moved to Paris, where he became involved in various literary circles and journals, wrote theatrical works and was engaged in the visual arts. None the less, he maintained an association with the Jewish community and must have felt drawn to the Strauss collection, as it complemented his own popularization of Jewish religious and family life in Alsace. The author of several novels (*Perle*; *La Dime*, for example) which highlighted the pristine life of the observant Jewish family hardly perturbed by the processes of industrialization and modernization, Stenne (a *nom de plume*; his original name was David Schornstein) fittingly equated the Strauss collection with 'religious art'.[4]

Re-identification with the past was part and parcel of the romantic revival which swept Europe in the nineteenth century, expressing itself in so wide a range of forms – political, social, cultural. For Jews in Central and Western Europe, a romantic and nostalgic quest was necessarily delayed until the complex, often highly uneven, processes of emancipation and integration were far advanced. In the cultural sphere, it was not until almost half a century after the French Revolution that attempts were made to address the 'vanishing world' and to describe the disintegration of the Jewish community.

Artists were so involved in their own radical break with Jewish traditional society and patterns, so concerned with coming to grips with the new surroundings into which they had been thrown (in Heidegger's sense of *Geworfenheit*) that much time was needed before a return to the past could be contemplated.[5] Solomon Alexander Hart, the English Jewish artist of the nineteenth century, has left us an apt recognition of this dilemma in his *Reminiscences*:

> I wished to avoid the imputation of being the painter of merely religious ceremonies. I felt confident that I could do something of a more definite character in the expression of human emotion and strong dramatic action.[6]

Figure 1 Abraham Abramson (1754–1811), *Enfranchisement of the Jews of Westphalia*, 1808. Medal, silver and bronze. Courtesy of the Israel Museum, Jerusalem. Obverse: a woman in prayer before an altar against which the Tables of the Law rest. Broken chains symbolizing freedom lie at her feet. An inscription above in Latin – To God and Fatherly King. Reverse: Two cherubim representing Christianity and Judaism join hands.

Hart and others vacillated between this desire to evoke universal feelings and situations, and a preoccupation with the Old and New Testament themes which could illuminate their inner religious struggles.

Looking at the collected works of Philipp Veit and Eduard Bendemann, two German-Jewish artists who converted to Christianity, one cannot fail to discern the predominance of religious themes, marked by an overdose of sentimentalism. Veit's *Moses Hidden by his Mother* and Bendemann's portrayal of the Jews in the Babylonian Exile (1832), or his *Jeremiah*, reflect a treatment of the subject through Christian eyes. Veit and Bendemann were not alone in this direction; artists of Jewish origin in Germany and England rarely attempted to integrate a Jewish traditional or Midrashic view of the biblical story into their work. It appears that in the early nineteenth century, the artistic interpretation of the Bible, even of the Old Testament, was bound to be predominantly Christian.

In the first generation, the Jewish artists were so enamoured with the possibilities of emancipation, eloquently depicted by Abraham Abramson in his medal showing Judaism kneeling before the Altar of Reconciliation (figure 1),[7] that they were incapable of a more genuine expression of Jewish life. Moreover, to reach beyond the religious sphere and treat the Jews in the context of their occupational

surroundings also held no attraction for them, even though such
European genre painters as Georg Emanuel Opiz were then depicting themes from everyday life.[8] This type of painting required a sense
of total ease with the environment, which Jewish artists still sorely
lacked.

Whereas the first half of the century failed to produce a Jewish
artist who dealt uniquely with Jewish life, the 1860s saw the
appearance of at least two: Simeon Solomon (1840–1905) and Moritz
Oppenheim (1800–82).[9] Both men sought to describe a vanishing
Jewish past, Solomon by presenting a stereotypical world of decrepit
Jews with few signs of joy and happiness in their lives; Oppenheim by
portraying Jewish religious life as a family experience, exuding
warmth and charm.

Solomon's career was a turbulent one which began with much
promise and terminated in tragedy. Educated in his youth in the pre-
Raphaelite brotherhood (comparable to the Nazarene group which
made a strong impact upon many of the German-Jewish artists,
including Oppenheim), Solomon studied at Dante Gabriel Rosetti's
studio and exhibited at the Royal Academy of Arts in London in the
1850s. In the early 1860s he turned his talents to Jewish topics dealing
with both biblical themes and scenes of Jewish religious life.[10] In 1862,
a series of photographs and woodcuts of his drawings was published
by a London printing company. The series depicted ten religious
ceremonies, ranging from the lighting of the sabbath candles to the
shivah and included the main Jewish holidays. Solomon's series was
the first of its kind since Johann Bodenschatz had published his
Kirchliche Verfassung (1748–9),[11] which had included an extensive
series of engravings on Jewish religious life in Germany. In contrast
to Bodenschatz's book, which was one of the various works by
Christians on Jewish religious life and which reflected the persistent
interest in Jewish ritual noticeable since the seventeenth century,
Solomon's series constituted the first attempt by a Jew to portray
graphically such customs and ceremonies outside the religious
framework.[12] Jewish books and customs, Hagadot, and illuminated
manuscripts abound with depictions of this kind but their 'audience'
and reference point were wholly internal. In contrast, Solomon's
portrayal was directed primarily, although not exclusively, to a
highly acculturated Jewish community, resembling Bodenschatz's
perspective more, perhaps, than that of Jewish religious books.

Solomon's view of Jewish life was standardised: elderly, somewhat
ragged, observant Jews revealing signs of resignation and mel-

ancholy, perform their religious functions with little hope in the future generation. The scarcity of children in these drawings was indicative.[13] Not surprisingly, this rather fossilized view of Jewish life elicited criticism from the major weekly of the English Jewish community, the *Jewish Chronicle*. Having followed his career with enthusiasm and looked forward to a more positive presentation of the Jewish tradition, it now chided Solomon for lacking a sense of idealization in these works and for falsely representing some of its ceremonies.[14] In rejecting Solomon's interpretation of Jewish life, the *Chronicle* failed to recognize that the artist was representative of a cultural current common among Jews of the time – a dialogue with what was seen as a vanishing Jewish world. Some, like Solomon, found it wanting and deteriorating; others, like Moritz Oppenheim, revelled in it as a source of inspiration and saw its demise with a certain anguish.

Moritz Oppenheim's early career followed the path of other German-Jewish artists of the 1820s and 1830s. He studied with the Nazarene group in Rome, executed very fine portrait paintings of Jewish and non-Jewish celebrities and illustrated literary, historical and biblical subject matter, while he personally wrestled with his Jewish background.[15] In contrast to other Jewish artists of the early nineteenth century, Oppenheim not only remained Jewish but also maintained personal contact with leading Jewish figures of his day (among them Gabriel Riesser and Adolphe Crémieux) and felt personally involved in the fortunes of the Jewish community. His '*The Return of a Jewish Volunteer from the War of Liberation*' (figure 2) sympathetically evoked the varied currents within Jewish society – the patriotic fervour of the youth shown side by side with the traditional family. It was painted in 1833, a time when the status of the Jews was under constant public discussion.[16] Eventually the painting would acquire an added significance when it was integrated into Oppenheim's famous series on the Jewish family.

Scenes from Traditional Jewish Family Life catapulted Oppenheim into the limelight, making him a central figure among those seeking to interpret the Jewish past as a source of cultural inspiration. Designated as 'the first Jewish painter', Oppenheim worked within the Biedermeier genre style, eliciting a feeling of *Gemütlichkeit*.[17] Jewish religious life was portrayed as a warm family experience in which children abound. Their eyes were often directed to their elders for guidance and inspiration, while they in turn were seen as called upon to uphold the tradition in the future (figure 3). As observed by

Figure 2 Moritz Oppenheim (1800–82), *Return of a Jewish Volunteer from the Wars of Liberation to His Family Still Living According to the Old Tradition*, 1833–4. Oil on canvas. Collection Edgar F. Rebner, New York and Lugano.

Figure 3 Moritz Oppenheim, *Sabbath Eve*. Picture from *Bilder aus dem altjüdischen Familienleben nach Originalgemälden von Professor Moritz Oppenheim*, Frankfurt-am-Main, second edition, 1886.

Figure 4 Moritz Oppenheim, *The Village Vendor*. Picture from *Bilder aus dem altjüdischen Familienleben nach Originalgemälden von Professor Moritz Oppenheim*, Frankfurt-am-Main, second edition, 1886.

Oppenheim, Jewish tradition blended well with occupational exigencies, while relations with the surrounding society lacked stress and discomfort. Oppenheim consciously showed gentiles watching Jewish practices, performed openly, and integrated them into the framework of Jewish social behaviour (see figure 4, *The Village Vendor*).

Yet, this celebrated series on Jewish life, with all its charm and positive portrayal of the continuing tradition, represented the religious experience as an anachronism, almost as a transient phenomenon left over by a former time. Relocating the observant Jew in a non-urban setting, away from his contemporary environment, Oppenheim implied that this way of life belonged more to the past than to the future. Thus, if the 'Jewish artist' had come of age to portray scenes previously depicted by Christians in the eighteenth century and by Jews working within the traditional framework, it was only because the scenes described no longer reflected a common experience but had become nostalgic memories for a growing segment of Central and Western European Jewry. This becomes all the more clear when one analyses the successful distribution of Oppenheim's paintings, and assesses its impact on future artists.

Oppenheim began to work on the paintings in the 1850s, but in response to the request of the Frankfurt publisher Heinrich Keller he became deeply engaged in a further 'enterprise'.[18] He copied the paintings in grisaille (tones of grey) to facilitate their photographic reproduction and in 1866 six paintings were thus reproduced. Several additions followed, until in 1882 a complete series of twenty such paintings was published in a special elaborate volume edited by the Reform rabbi, Leopold Stein. Produced for a bourgeois Jewish clientele, the volume included Stein's introductory remarks to each painting, geared to readers unfamiliar with Jewish habits and customs. Their rapturous tone indicated that, in his view, the paintings might well arouse a new interest in Jewish life and serve as a guide to the nature of Jewish observance.[19] (The 'Orthodox' representation seemingly did not prevent Stein from encouraging wide interest in the series). Indeed, the Oppenheim series became a common commodity and performed a symbolic function for middle-class Jews in Central and Western Europe: it allowed them to identify passively with their vanishing past and to feel a sense of pride with their recent ancestors.

A cottage industry now developed around the religious themes represented in Oppenheim's work. Pewter plates with scenes from his paintings (the festivals and the marriage ceremony) were produced in Germany and Holland and could be found in many Jewish homes, often exhibited together. Sabbath porcelain trays with the Friday evening scene (together with the benedictions) and Seder plates with the Seder ceremony were similarly manufactured on a large scale. But above all, as Ismar Schorsch has pointed out, the re-publication of the series in several editions made the Oppenheim paintings an unprecedented success in the history of Jewish books in Germany in that period.[20]

This nostalgic interest in the 'authentic' Jewish world – the ghetto – had other interesting offshoots. The search for marketable portrayals of Jewish religious ceremonies led, for example, to the rediscovery of Bernard Picart's series on Jewish life which had first been executed in the 1720s. Again, the medium was a series of pewter plates amenable for display in the home, recalling Oppenheim's themes but broadening their selection. Judaism, in a decorative dress, had become a marketable product among middle-class Jews. Others, possibly of greater means, were among the patrons of the Jewish genre painters of the period, Isidor Kaufmann (1853–1921) and Maurycy Gottlieb (1856–79), who, like Oppenheim, turned to the religious experience as a source of inspiration.

The case of Kaufmann throws particular light on the interaction

Figure 5 Isidor Kaufmann (1853–1921), *Yeshiva Boy at Study*, end of the
nineteenth century. Oil on panel. Judaica Collection of Mr and
Mrs Jacobo Furman. Catalogue no. JAF 75.

between artist and public. A Hungarian Jew, Kaufmann moved to
Vienna at the age of twenty-three, and later began to travel to the
shtetls of Hungary, Galicia and Poland in an attempt to recapture the
way of life of Orthodox Jews in Eastern Europe. His paintings were
earmarked for bourgeois Jewish patrons in Central Europe, who
maintained a lingering desire to touch that 'tottering' world of the
past[21] (figure 5). He thus exemplified the emerging dialogue between
Jewish artists who were willing to rework their early childhood
memories and their Jewish clientele who sought scenes from a
disappearing world. Following Bourdieu, it would appear that the
purchase of such paintings, illustrated pewter plates and the like by
bourgeois, urbanized Jews represented an attempt to appropriate the
tradition embodied in those works; their specific character and detail
were of only secondary significance.[22]

France also produced its nostalgic representation of Jewish religious life in the extensive drawings by Alphonse Lévy (1843–1918).
Lévy returned to the French reservoir of 'authentic' Judaism – Alsace
– and illustrated a book on Jewish life which appeared in 1886.
Although his was a more contemporary and detailed depiction of
religious life than that offered by Oppenheim, his series nevertheless
made a similar emotional appeal. He described his intention in
recording the internal world of Alsatian Jewry as: 'the homage

Figure 6 Alphonse Lévy (1843–1918), *Mother Teaching her son his Blessings,* late nineteenth century, Lithograph on paper. Courtesy of the Library of the Jewish Theological Seminary of America.

rendered by a son of Alsace to the simple ways and rustic customs which are falling by the wayside and disappearing'.[23] Lévy depicted the Jew not in his ever more prevalent urban setting but rather within his normative religious context, returning him to the home, to prayer, to the study of religious texts and the performance of religious acts (figure 6). He did not remove the Jew completely from worldly matters, and in a further series he portrayed him at work (but still removed from the realities of modernized French Jewry). All told, warmth and contentment reign in Lévy's depiction of Jewish life; the elderly and the young (*La promenade du samedi* figure 7) graciously meet each other in a spirit of undivided satisfaction and the old can communicate religious teachings to the young.

The contrast between the 'ideal' or 'authentic' Jewish life and the social realities increasingly characteristic of contemporary French Jewry was not lost on Lévy's audience. Bernard Lazare noted that the strength and appeal of Lévy's drawings lay in his recognition that Jews were not only millionaires. This fact derived, he maintained, from the

> awareness of a man who knows that to reach the true Jew [*le juif véritable*] and not the one from the antisemitic legend, one should not go to a gala evening at the Opera where one meets him with an archduchess on his arm.[24]

Figure 7 Alphonse Lévy, *La Promenade du Samedi* (The Saturday Stroll), late nineteenth century. Lithograph on paper. Courtesy of the Library of the Jewish Theological Seminary of America.

That is, the 'true Jew' still resides in the 'ghettos' of Alsace. Judging from the successful dispersion of Lévy's drawings in reproductions and as postcards at the turn of the century in France, one can assume that Lazare's response reflected a nostalgia not uncommon among French Jews, although just how extensive and profound this sentiment was cannot easily be assessed.[25]

The sense, expressed by Alphonse Lévy, that the artist had a duty to portray a dying Jewish world before its ultimate demise, had similarly prompted another former Alsatian, the writer Daniel Stauben (Auguste Widal), to return to his birthplace more than twenty years earlier to describe the life of 'age-old Judaism' standing on the verge of oblivion. Stauben's *Scènes de la Vie Juive en Alsace*, infused with this sense of urgency, was part of an extensive literary trend among Jewish authors in Western and Central Europe in the middle decades of the nineteenth century.[26] This cultural development reflected a re-evaluation of the 'assimilatory' tendencies in Jewish life, accentuated in part by the defeat of the revolutions of 1848.

In the sixth letter of his *Rome and Jerusalem* (1862), Moses Hess hailed the increased tendency current among enlightened Jews to regard Judaism as a source of inspiration. Hess pointed to the developments in the literary world as most indicative of what he considered a growing

Messianic movement among the Jews. Relying on this phenomenon
to show that his call for a nationalist reorientation was not an
arbitrary act, he had to admit that none of the writers discussed had
actually given voice to his own political ideas. None the less, with his
usual perspicacity, Hess lumped together a diverse group of writers
(and more could have been added), sensing that, despite their
marked differences, they shared an important common denominator
– a proud, positive attitude to Jewish life. And I would add that they
also had in common a deep desire to integrate the experience of the
ghetto, or of their childhood, into their adult life.

Whether fundamental cultural change in the Jewish community
preceded the move to urban centres or only came in its wake is a moot
point,[27] but all agree that the modern development of major urban
centres wrought much havoc in the internal life of the Jewish
communities. One outcome of the urbanization process, however,
which has attracted little attention is the need of individuals to
transform their feelings of displacement, of a lost childhood experience (what I referred to above as Heidegger's sense of *Geworfenheit*),
into a newly integrated whole. The biographies of Berthold Auerbach
and Alexandre Weill can serve here as representatives of this
widespread phenomenon.

Both Weill (1811) and Auerbach (1812) were born into Jewish
families in rural villages, where they received a traditional Jewish
education and were groomed to become rabbis. Within two decades
they had dispensed with religious practice after having immersed
themselves in the humanities at German universities. By the 1830s,
they had embarked upon literary careers which were to develop in
various directions during the next fifty years, while they struggled to
find a meeting point between their Jewish past and modern
civilization. Both were fascinated by the ideals of the revolutionaries
in 1848 but returned dejectedly to their literary pursuits with the
failure of the liberal cause.

Auerbach's early career showed a deep involvement with Jewish
themes and problems: he wrote full-length historical novels on
Spinoza and on the Jewish poet, Ephraim Kuh, as well as studies of
two significant contemporaries, Gabriel Riesser and Gotthold
Solomon.[28] For his part, Weill initially was more concerned with
political problems, contributing articles on politics to various German periodicals. However, while Auerbach gradually reduced the
centrality of outright Jewish themes in his work, Weill increasingly
emphasized Jewish characters and Judaism in his social philosophy.

Yet, the fact that they both put so much emphasis on the same genre – the literary treatment of peasant life in the small villages of Alsace and the Black Forest – brought them together in what was a highly innovative search for the traditional roots of Jewish life. The *Dorfnovellistik*, as Heine called it with little appreciation,[29] was by no means a specifically Jewish creation, but each of these writers brought his own particular approach to an examination of the tensions between the 'ancients' and the 'moderns'.

Considered by Heine as one of the more gifted writers on village life, Weill did not deal exclusively with the Jewish peasant. However, in those stories where Jews appear, constant conflict reverberates between the specific traditions of Alsace and the customs of city life. For example, in 'Couronne', around the hackneyed theme of a tutor falling in love with his student, Weill weaves a tale which describes the traditional observance of the Jewish holidays as celebrated in Alsace. Room is found here to stress not only the social and economic cleavages within the community, but also the tension between the generations as emphasized by the rebellious 'assimilatory' remark coming from the younger generation during the Passover prayer about Jerusalem:

> 'This prayer', said the son of the house, 'should be rewritten. I have not the slightest desire to return to Jerusalem. I say that we should put Paris in its place.'[30]

Weill viewed his village stories as a testament to a vanishing past and thus felt obliged to convey them with perfect authenticity. Recounting in his autobiography, *Ma Jeunesse* (1870), the long deliberations which preceded its composition, Weill emphasized that only a Jew steeped in Talmudic studies from youth could recall a childhood lived in a society unknown to the external world and irretrievable. As an interpreter of that past, he went beyond the usual self-adulation of autobiographers to define his existential status, and that of his contemporaries, in modern society.

He was not alone in trying to fuse the past and present in the autobiographical genre. Leopold Kalisch, for example, in his *Bilder aus meiner Knabenzeit* (Leipzig, 1872), went about the process of reorganizing his childhood experiences by contrasting the modern (or, at least, 'maskilic') education he received in Leszno, Poland, to that provided to most other Jewish children reared in the distorted tradition of martyrology.[31] Kalisch, who was bent on explaining this unique Jewish life to modern German-Jewish readers, revelled in retelling

stories of the Golem and other demonic figures. But at the same time
he sought to impart a definite message: the modern German Jew has
left this closed world, is gradually entering German society, and yet
strives to maintain some continuity with his past. Almost echoing the
words of Eduard Gans, he concluded:

> The Jewish people with its lively intellect will for a long time to come
> still act as a powerful factor of fermentation among all the nations. It
> will not die, but will go forth amidst mankind, having written the most
> remarkable page in the history of man.[32]

The ability of the Jews to merge in the larger society necessitated some
recognition by their contemporaries of their unique Jewish past,
which remained a source of internal strength even though they
themselves were breaking away from it. The Jew no longer had to
hide his past in shame.

It should be noted, however, that Alexandre Weill had made a
more significant step forward. As he showed in his numerous writings
on Moses and Mosaic law, he not only envisaged a central role for
Judaism in modern civilization but also castigated Christianity for its
responsibility in perpetuating anti-Jewish attitudes. Especially in the
extensive prose and poetry he composed in the 1860s and 1870s, Weill
dealt head on with the historical clash between the two religions and
squarely placed the blame for the recurrent cruelties at the doorstep
of Christianity.[33] His bold statements on the subject articulated a
growing tendency among committed, modern Jews (Ludwig Geiger
and Heinrich Graetz being two other examples) to challenge the
surrounding society which had failed to integrate the Jews fully after
the revolutions of 1848.

This approach stood in marked contrast to the one exemplified by
Berthold Auerbach in his village stories. How did Auerbach reconcile
his past experience with his belief in integration into German society?
'Lederherz' is a case in point. Herz, a Jewish pedlar, known by all as
Lederherz, befriended a gentile named Lipp, who had originally
intended to convert him. Though Lederherz rejected the overture,
Lipp maintained the friendship. Later on, Lederherz became mort-
ally ill and turned to Lipp for help. Lipp responded in kind. He
assisted him in putting on *tefillin* and together with a priest read him
portions of the holiest of Jewish prayers, the *Shm'a*. The story ends
with the priest's evoking the feeling that in this act he had served the
will of God in the noblest of ways. The moral was clear. A spirit of
kinship was possible between Jews and gentiles even if the Jew

remained loyal to his past.[34] Moreover, in recreating the life of the gentile peasants of the Black Forest, initially inspired no doubt by his own childhood memories and the death of his father, Auerbach was depicting a community which had allowed the Jew a measure of integration.[35] Yet in nostalgically reverting back to an ideal and trusting society lay an implied dialectical negation: integration was imaginable in the fantasy world of childhood but ridden with complications in the modern urbanized context of adulthood.

Nevertheless, Jewish literati had, of course, been encouraged at the time by the liberal sentiment which had swept Western Europe in the 1840s and had become involved in various national movements of the day. Instilled with the belief that these trends would improve the fortune of the Jews, they had welcomed the coming of the revolution in 1848. Leopold Kompert had expressed this viewpoint in a unique form, arguing that a revolution which denied equality to the Jewish masses was doomed to failure. For the urbanized Kompert, the poor Jew symbolized the spirit of Judaism:

> In him lies our kernel, our power, our Judaism. The beautiful, delicate, and inspiring that we possess is found in these crippled and afflicted creatures. What we have lost in spirit and soul in our conflict with the world, he still possesses untouched.[36]

Kompert had idealized the way of life of the 'ghetto' Jew before the revolutions of 1848 had begun, but his hopes for the future were focused on the struggle for emancipation. This would be the only compensation for sacrificing that personality which embodied the authentic spirit of Judaism. His stories, which revolved around the ghetto life of Bohemian Jews, were well received in non-Jewish as well as Jewish circles and were translated from German into Dutch, Italian, English, French and Czech. They were to exert a strong influence on a number of Jewish writers (K. E. Französ, Stauben and Leopold Weisel, to name only a few).[37]

Like the vignettes from peasant life of Auerbach and Weill, Kompert's plots are simple and his characters one-dimensional, tending toward the banal. Yet the squalid, physical ghetto which Alphonse Lévy had turned into a congenial and attractive quarter, was likewise rendered attractive by Kompert who stressed its human dimension as its uppermost quality. His idyllic ghetto closed out the verdure of the trees, the singing of birds and play in the open air, putting in their stead the sharp, angular Jew, who derived his greatest satisfaction from his family and religious pursuits. However, whereas

Karl Emil Französ was to see the atmosphere of Barnow (the fictional
name of Chortkow, Eastern Galicia) as repressive and intolerable,
Kompert sympathized with the ghetto and its struggle for existence.
He did not shy away from its state of flux, with the young yearning to
leave ('Die Jahrzeit') and tempted by the pull of Christianity
('Rander's Children'), but he was impressed by its authenticity. At a
crossroads in his own evolution, Kompert idealized the ghetto, but
saw beyond it, recognizing the need for an economic transformation
of Jewish life (*Am Pfluge*, 1855) although not the nationalist proposition that would lead to the 'rebuilding of Jerusalem'.[38]

Yet there were some for whom the nostalgia and yearning for
'Jerusalem', nurtured by the changing place of Palestine in the
European consciousness and the romantic orientation of the period,
took on a further significance.[39] One such figure was the Viennese
Jew, Ludwig August Frankl (1810–94), who combined in his work
various strands to be found in the Jewish literary scene of the middle
of the nineteenth century. Well trained in Jewish studies, Frankl
remained active in the Jewish community throughout his lifetime,
notwithstanding his interests in general literature and his involvement in the revolution of 1848 with the publication of 'Der
Universität'. Although his romantic writings on Jewish themes
preceded his revolutionary involvement – it was in his *Sonntagsblätter*
that Kompert's ghetto stories were first published in 1846 – the
outcome of 1848 intensified his interest in this area. Frankl's
treatment of biblical and post-biblical figures took on greater depth;
their lives were to him a prism of the Jewish historical fate. In his
portraits of Rachel, Joseph, Saul, Moses, Jochanan Ben Zakkai,
Chanina ben Teradyon or Moses Mendelssohn, Frankl etched out a
symbolic Jewish characteristic.

But Frankl's Jewish interests also led him in other directions. His
eerie poem on the Jews of Prague in the sixteenth century ('Gedicht in
sieben Gesänger', Vienna, 1862) delved into the mystical tradition of
the Golem, while his *Libanon*, compiled with the Jewish family in mind
('primarily for the young'), was intended to be a universal ode to
Jews, Judaism and Jerusalem.[40] And it was indeed to Jerusalem that
Frankl travelled in 1856, in the service of Elisa Herz. From his trip
Frankl left behind a comprehensive description of the Jewish
community in Palestine, elucidating the nature of the various
societies and their mutual tensions. His stereotypical portrayal of the
Ashkenazic community (the 'Old Yishuv') seems to mirror the
preoccupation of contemporary Jewish writers with the 'ghetto' and

may in fact have been influenced by it.[41] It would appear therefore that an attachment to 'Jerusalem' was in some cases becoming intertwined with the spiritual quest for a more wholesome Jewish life.

Another literary figure who looked to Jerusalem with deep emotion was the German-Jewish poet, Ludwig Wihl. In his 'West-östlische Schwalben' (Mannheim, 1847), Wihl mourned the loss of Jerusalem. Although it was for him in part a sacred memory and in part a source of national inspiration, Wihl shuddered at the thought that Jerusalem remained under Muslim rule. He even remarked that had he an army at hand he would rise to fight for Jerusalem's freedom. According to a contemporary commentator, Pierre Mercier, his major poem was written at a time when Slavs, Italians and Romanians were agitating for their national identity and Wihl sensed that the Jews needed their own homeland.[42] His poetry, which spanned the history of Jewish life from biblical times through the Middle Ages until the Enlightenment, exalted Judaism and placed it on a level with Hellenism, the culture worshipped by all European literati. Is it then any wonder that Hess was exhilarated by his poetry?[43] But he was not alone. Daniel Stauben, who laboured to popularize Kompert's works in France, wrote a glowing essay on Wihl in which he depicted him as a

> poet of heart and faith, above all a lyric poet inspired by the Jewish religion and, in general, by Judaism with its periodic tragedies and immortal grandeur.[44]

Stauben himself chose a different path of idealization by recounting the life and customs of an Alsatian village, Bolwiller. Markedly impressed by the works of George Sand (especially *La Mare au Diable* [1846]), Stauben returned in the mid 1850s to Bolwiller and subsequently began to publish his recollections in the popular literary journal *Revue des Deux Mondes*. He endeavoured to bring to light the religious life of Alsatian Jews in all its detail, emphasizing their unique traditions – language, dress, artefacts – and seeking the deeper meaning within these traditions: the kindling of the sabbath candles symbolized the disappearance of all preoccupations, miseries and worries of the week; the hospitality shown to guests recalled the traditional hospitality practised by the forefathers in Palestine, whereas the customs of mourning, the *shivah*, pointed to the unique sense of loss among Jews born of generations of persecution.[45] In general, Jewish solidarity was a constant feature in all the holidays he witnessed, showing that even in his hour of joy the Jew remembered his less fortunate brothers.

But for Stauben personally, the return to Bolwiller stimulated the romantic fascination with the Orient, which he felt was preserved there in the heart of Alsace. It was again the contrast between modernity and the wholesome life of the 'ghetto' which attracted Stauban. Recalling Wihl's sentiments, Stauban wrote:

> On returning to Paris I recalled the pretty verses which open Goethe's
> *Le Divan* and I thought to myself that it is sweet sometimes, in the midst
> of our troubled and agitated life to go and honour the land of our
> forefathers and breathe in the middle of Europe the pure air of the old
> Orient.[46]

Interestingly enough, together with this nostalgia for and return to, the land of the forefathers, Stauben dabbled with another pastime of Jewish writers of the day – the mystical legends of the Golem of Prague. Here too, the romantic revival of medieval myths, figures and legends, so common in the Germanic lands of the middle of the century, reverberated among the Jewish writers encouraging them to find comparable Jewish tales. This type of folk-literature developed among Czech-Jewish writers from the late 1830s, influenced both by the local interest in myths of the Golem and by Kompert and Ludwig August Frankl.[47]

The group of Jewish writers highlighted here all wrote in either German or French, rejected conversion and in most cases maintained an association with the Jewish community. Well versed in each other's work and often acquainted with one another personally, they formed a kind of coterie of Jewish literati. Though some became very popular in their particular genre, none rose to become an important figure within European literature and hardly anyone made a lasting mark upon the future development of Jewish literature. Their historical significance lies elsewhere. Their writings evoked the difficulties involved in stepping outside the sheltered Jewish world and entering body and soul into the urban setting of European society. In their 'return' to the 'ghetto', in one form or another, they were clearly seeking an anchor in their new context. Moreover, their work found a sympathetic audience in Jewish circles, suggesting that nostalgia was a broad cultural phenomenon.

This is not to say that the nostalgic literature, notwithstanding its wide distribution, was universally well received. Various critics of this mode of literature emerged even during the heyday of this genre. They included leading personalities of German Jewry, among them

Ludwig Philippson and Marcus (Meyer) Lehman, who both engaged in the writing of romantic historical novels. They sought to disparage the genre, fearing that it could prove to be a dead-end for the development of Jewish *belles-lettres* and that it could have a negative impact on the situation of the Jews in Germany at the time. Nevertheless, the predominance of 'ghetto' stories within the German-Jewish newspapers remained uncontested, and it is estimated that almost half of the stories and novels published on their pages during the nineteenth century were of this character. This in itself offers a significant indication of the scope and social attraction of this type of literature.[48]

Culturally speaking, the various expressions of nostalgia that evolved in the middle of the nineteenth century were most brilliantly voiced by Heinrich Heine in his *Geständnisse* (1854). Heine's 'return' to Jewish sources, especially to the Bible, and his reassessment of Judaism and Moses as pillars of moral civilization undermined his former worship of Greek culture and philosophy. Heine had been a central figure for all the writers mentioned here – they had pilgrimaged to his home and kept abreast of his writings – but towards the end of his life these contacts became somewhat more meaningful for him and for them.[49] For them he was not only the formidable poet and writer, but a guiding figure whose Jewish roots were of constant interest and whose disdain for the modern, bourgeois Jew they largely shared. Heine's later inner development, encapsulated symbolically the change that had transpired in the status of the Jewish writer in European society: he no longer needed to yield to baptism as an entry card into European civilization nor feel constrained from writing on Jewish themes and expressing an attachment to the Jewish past.

Notwithstanding the rapid disintegration of traditional Jewish life, Jewish individuals like Isaac Strauss, Moritz Oppenheim, Alphonse Lévy and Alexandre Weill felt compelled to negotiate with the Jewish past. Aware of the growing distance between the 'authentic' Jewish experience and contemporary Jewish life and moved by their own ambivalence to these developments, they returned to childhood memories to formulate their own singularity. The vanishing past was to be recalled and recorded by collecting Judaica, visualizing Jewish religious life, describing its family setting and emotions and even imagining a return to Jerusalem. Their efforts were not totally isolated from Jewish society, but in a sense thrived on the urge of the modernized Jew to acknowledge his historic past. All in all, these cultural expressions illuminate a preoccupation with Jewish tradition that allowed for both integration into European society and insistence on a measure of Jewish particularity.[50]

Notes

1 *Collection de M. Strauss. Description des Objets d'Art Religieux Hébraïques* (Poissy, 1878); Victor Klagsbald, *Catalogue Raisonné de la Collection Juive du Musée de Cluny* (Paris, 1981). For a most enthusiastic response to the exhibition see V. Stassov, 'Art Israélite à l'Exposition Universelle', *Archives Israélites* 41 (1878).

2 Gaston Bachelard, *The Poetics of Revelrie* (New York, 1963), p. 220.

3 Erik H. Erikson, 'Reflections on Dr. Borg's Life Cycle', *Adulthood*, ed. Erik H. Erikson (New York and London, 1978), p. 20.

4 Stenne was born in Alsace in 1826 and died in Paris in 1879. Active on several fronts in the Jewish community, he was one of the founders of the Alliance Israélite Universelle and a frequent contributor to various Jewish journals. In the spirit of romantic nostalgia, he published in *La Vérité Israélite* (1861–2) legends relating to Jewish life in the Middle Ages. See Freddy Raphaël and Robert Weill, *Regards Nouveaux sur les Juifs d'Alsace* (Strasburg, 1980), pp. 227–32.

5 Hans W. Loewald, *Psychoanalysis and the History of the Individual* (New Haven and London, 1978), pp. 19–22.

6 Solomon Alexander Hart, *Reminiscences of Solomon Hart* (London, 1882), p. 13. See Alfred Werner, 'Jewish Artists of the Age of Emancipation', *Jewish Artists of the Age of Emancipation*, ed. Cecil Roth; rev. edn Bezalel Narkiss (Jerusalem, 1971), pp. 200–1.

7 On Abramson and his medals see Daniel Friedenberg, *Jewish Medals From the Renaissance to the Fall of Napoleon (1503–1813)* (New York, 1970), pp. 40–1.

8 Walther Scheidig, *Die Leipziger Messe. Mit bildern von Georg Emanuel Opiz* (Leipzig, 1938); Hansjorg Krug, 'Georg Emanuel Opiz (1775–1841)', *Philobiblion* 16 (1972), 227–59; Richard I. Cohen, 'The Visual Dreyfus Affair – A New Text?', *Studies in Contemporary Jewry*, vol. VI, ed. Ezra Mendelsohn (1990), pp. 71–90.

9 Recent unpublished research by Christiaan Roosen has uncovered several contemporary Jewish artists in the Netherlands who also took up Jewish themes. Probably the earliest was Maurits Leon.

10 Alfred Rubens, *A Jewish Iconography*, rev. edn (London, 1981), pp. 2–3; Steven Kolsteren, 'Simeon Solomon and The Song of Songs', *Journal of Jewish Art* 11 (1985), 47–59.

11 J. Chr. Bodenschatz, *Kirchliche Verfassung der heutigen Juden sonderlich derer in Deutschland* (Frankfurt and Leipzig, 1748–9).

12 The most important works of this genre are: Bernard Picart, *Cérémonies et*

Coutumes Religieuses de tous les Peuples du Monde Représentés par de Figures Dessinées de la Main de Bernard Picart vol. 1 (Amsterdam, 1723); P. Chr. Kirchner, *Jüdisches Ceremoniel* (Nuremberg, 1724). For an evaluation of the intellectual background within which these works appeared see S. Ettinger, 'The Beginnings of the Change in the Attitude of European Society Towards the Jews', *Scripta Hierosolymitana* 7 (Jerusalem, 1961), 193–219.

13 These comments follow the implications of Aries's interpretation of family portraits. See Philippe Aries, *Centuries of Childhood*, trans. Robert Baldick (New York, 1962), part 3; Diane Owen Hughes, 'Representing the Family: Portraits and Purposes in Early Modern Italy', *Journal of Interdisciplinary History* 17 (1986), 7–38.

14 The *Jewish Chronicle* (London, 1 August 1862), p. 8. Interestingly enough, a contemporary non-Jewish critic of Solomon, cited by Kolsteren, 'Simeon Solomon', p. 58, remarked that the artist would do well to limit himself to Jewish themes where his strength lies.

15 Moritz Oppenheim, *Erinnerungen*, ed. Alfred Oppenheim (Frankfurt, 1924).

16 Ismar Schorsch, 'Art as Social History: Oppenheim and the German Jewish Vision of Emancipation', Israel Museum Catalogue, *Moritz Oppenheim. The First Jewish Painter* (Jerusalem, 1983), pp. 31–61; reprinted in Isadore Twersky (ed.), *Danzig, Between East and West: Aspects of Modern Jewish History* (Cambridge, Mass., 1985).

17 See *inter alia* Alfred Werner, 'Oppenheim: A Rediscovery', *Midstream* 20 (1974), 46–57; Elisheva Cohen, 'Moritz Daniel Oppenheim', *Bulletin des Leo Baeck Instituts* 53/4 (1977/8), 42–74; Elisheva Cohen, 'Moritz Oppenheim "The First Jewish Painter"', *The Israel Museum News* 14 (1978), 86–93; Israel Museum Catalogue, *Moritz Oppenheim. The First Jewish Painter* (Jerusalem, 1983).

18 Alfred Oppenheim, 'Nachwort', in Oppenheim, *Erinnerungen*, pp. 115–16; the notion of an artist's enterprise appears in Svetlana Alpers, *Rembrandt's Enterprise. The Studio and the Market* (Chicago, 1988).

19 Stein (1810–82) had been an active participant in the rabbinic conferences of the reform movement during the 1840s. See *Bilder aus dem altjüdischen Familien-Leben nach Original-Gemälden von Moritz Oppenheim* (Frankfurt, 1882). A condensed version of his introduction was translated into English and published independently of the paintings, see L. Stein, *Family Scenes from Jewish Life of Former Days. From Original Oil Paintings by M. Oppenheim* (New York, n.d.).

20 Schorsch, 'Art as Social History', pp. 31, 59. For examples of pewter plates see the Israel Museum Collection, nos. 136/50, 136/86; R. D. Barnett (ed.), *Catalogue of the Permanent and Loan Collections of the Jewish Museum* (London, 1974), no. 465; Jana Doleželová, 'The State Jewish Museum Collection of Wedding Dishes and Plates', *Judaica Bohemiae* 13 (1977), 29–43, plate 4.

21 Yeshivah University Museum, New York, *Families and Feasts. Paintings by Oppenheim and Kaufmann* (New York, 1977); Alfred Rubens, *A History of Jewish Costumes* (London and Jerusalem, 1973), pp. 111–12.

22 Pierre Bourdieu, *La Distinction: Critique Social du Jugement* (Paris, 1979). My thanks to Pierre Birnbaum for the reference. See also Daniel J. Sherman, 'The Bourgeoisie, Cultural Appropriation, and the Art Museum in Nineteenth-Century France', *Radical History Review* 38 (1987), 38–58.

23 Part of this extensive series was used to illustrate Léon Cahun's *La Vie Juive* (Paris, 1886). Many of these were reproduced and published under the title *Scènes familiales juives* (Paris, n.d., c. 1900). The above quotation is from the latter. Cf. an anti-Jewish treatment along similar themes in E. Coypel, *Le Judaisme Esquisse des Moeurs Juives* (Mulhouse, 1876).

24 Bernard Lazare, 'Introduction', Lévy, 'Scènes familiales'.

25 See the extensive collection in the Prints Department of the Library of the Jewish Theological Seminary, New York.

26 'We have tried our best to portray this contemporary form of ancient Judaism, which is alas on the verge of disappearing . . . Already, in more than one place, it is being obliterated like everything that ages. Thus, we must hasten to record quickly the most characteristic traits' (*Scènes de la Vie Juive en Alsace* (Paris, 1860), p. v).

27 See *inter alia* Jacob Toury, ' "Deutsche Juden" in Vormärz' *Bulletin des Leo Baeck Instituts* 8 (1965), 65–82; Steven M. Lowenstein, 'The Pace of Modernisation of German Jewry in the Nineteenth Century', *Leo Baeck Institute Yearbook* 21 (1976), 41–56; Steven M. Lowenstein, 'The Rural Community and the Urbanization of Germany Jewry', *Central European History* 13 (1980), 218–36; David Sorkin, *The Transformation of German Jewry, 1780–1840* (New York and Oxford, 1987), pp. 149–55. For France, see Michael R. Marrus, *The Politics of Assimilation* (Oxford, 1971); Christine Piette, *Les Juifs de Paris (1808–1840). La Marche vers L'Assimilation* (Quebec, 1983).

28 Anton Bettelheim, *Berthold Auerbach. Der Mann, Sein Werk, Sein Nachlass* (Stuttgart, 1907).

29 Heine's introduction to A. Weill, *Sittengemälde aus dem elsassischen Volksleben*, vol. 1, 2nd edn (Stuttgart, 1847). Recent studies on Heine have put this introduction into the context of the poet's need to allay pressures that Weill had put on him. See, *inter alia*, S. S. Prawer, *Heine's Jewish Comedy. A Study of His Portraits of Jews and Judaism* (Oxford, 1983), pp. 493–7.

30 Quoted from Alexandre Weill, *Mes Romans*, vol. 1 (Paris, 1886), pp. 373–4. On Weill see Joe Friedemann, *Alexandre Weill Ecrivain Contestaire et Historien Engagé (1811–1899)* (Strasburg and Paris, 1980).

31 Ludwig Kalisch, *Bilder aus meiner Knabenzeit* (Leipzig, 1872). His work was also serialized in the weekly Leipzig journal *Gartenlaube*. On the *Gartenlaube* and topics related to the present discussion see Henry

Wasserman, *Jews, Burgertum and Bürgerliche Gesellschaft in a Liberal Era* (*1840–1880*), unpublished doctoral dissertation, Hebrew University (n.d.) (Hebrew), esp. pp. 115–18, 131–6.

32 Kalisch, *Bilder*, pp. 63, 221. For a detailed list of other German-Jewish writers who dealt with such themes, see Walter Jacob, 'A Bibliography of Novels and Short Stories by German-Jewish Authors 1880–1914', *Studies in Bibliography and Booklore* 6 (1963), 75–92.

33 As he wrote in *Le Matricide*:
   The hatred of the Jews is Christian in origin
   One impresses it on the child, it is in the doctrine
   The best of Christians is full of prejudices
   When it comes to a Jew. And we are judged
   Condemned, from the smallest human error.
   See *Agathina ma Femme! Mes Grandes Juives de l'Histoire* (Paris, 1879), pp. 102–3. This does not reflect a constant tension between Jews and gentiles in Weill's stories. As in 'Kella', friendships develop on an intimate level to the point that Jewish characters (like Kalman) risk their lives for gentiles (like Tony).

34 See Auerbach's fascinating letter to Karl E. Französ, as published in Margarita Pazi, 'Berthold Auerbach and Moritz Hartmann. Two Jewish Writers of the Nineteenth Century', *Leo Baeck Institute Yearbook* 18 (1973), 204.

35 Sorkin, *Transformation*, pp. 152–5. On this genre in general see Wilhelm Stoffers, *Juden und Ghetto in der deutschen Literatur bis zum Ausgang des Weltkriegs* (Graz, 1939).

36 Quoted in Jacob Shatzky, 'Jewish Ideologies in Austria During the Revolution of 1848', in S. W. Baron, E. Negel and K.S. Pinson (eds.), *Freedom and Reason. Studies in Philosophy and Jewish Culture in Memory of Morris Raphael Cohen* (Glencoe, Ill. 1951), p. 434.

37 The attraction of his work among 'assimilated' Jews is characterized by the Czech translations undertaken by a circle of Czech-Jewish academicians for their *Kalendář česko-židovský*, 1881–2, edited by August Stein. On the animus of this group see Hillel J. Kieval, *The Making of Czech Jewry. National Conflict and Jewish Society in Bohemia, 1870–1918* (New York and Oxford, 1988), pp. 27–35.

38 At the end of 'Rander's Children', Kompert places in the mouth of the vagabond the remarks that after all that has transpired Jerusalem must be rebuilt. Throughout the story he had dismissed the feasibility of any such project due to the inherent difficulty of the Jews creating a state of their own – a problem compounded by their unbalanced occupational structure.

39 See Shmuel Ettinger and Israel Bartal, 'The First Aliyah: Ideological Roots and Practical Accomplishments', *The Jerusalem Cathedra*, vol. II, ed. Lee I. Levine (Jerusalem and Detroit, 1982), pp. 197–210. It would

appear to me that the eccentric novels of Benjamin Disraeli that glorified Judaism and illuminated its Eastern roots contributed to this mode. Not incidentally, he too, from the vantage-point of an English conservative who identified with the landed aristocracy, castigated the attributes that marked the 'modern' Jew – cosmopolitanism, atheism and assimilation.

40 L. A. Frankl, *Libanon. Ein poetisches Familienbuch*, 3rd edn (Vienna, 1864); see also *Nach der Zerstörung. Hebräische Elegien* (Vienna, 1856); *Ahnenbilder* (Vienna, 1866); *Rachel. Romantischen Gedichte* (Vienna, 1842).

41 Israel Bartal, ' "Old Yishuv" and "New Yishuv": Image and Reality', *The Jerusalem Cathedra*, vol. 1, ed. Lee I. Levine (Jerusalem, 1981), pp. 216–18.

42 Pierre Mercier, *Louis Wihl* (Paris, 1860), p. 25.

43 On Wihl's association with Hess see S. Schwarzfuchs, 'Introduction', M. Hess, *Rome et Jerusalem* (Paris, 1981), pp. 22, 29. On his turbulent relationship with Heine see Antonin Vallentin, *Poet In Exile. The Life of Heinrich Heine*, reissue (New York, 1970), pp. 272–4; Prawer, *Heine's Jewish Comedy*, p. 728; Jeffrey L. Sammons, *Heinrich Heine. A Modern Biography* (Princeton, 1979), *passim*.

44 Originally published in *Archives Israélites* (1852); reprinted in Stauben, *Scènes de la Vie Juive*, p. 271. The responses to Wihl's poetry were mixed as can be seen from the review in *Der Orient*, see Salo W. Baron, 'The Impact of the Revolution of 1848 on Jewish Emancipation', *Jewish Social Studies* 11 (1949), 248, n.78. Stauben both translated and annotated a collection of Kompert's stories. Cf. also the strong anti-Christian poem of A. Léon-Velle, *Le Juif* (Paris, 1860).

45 Cf. the less sympathetic but still positive portrayal in L. Herzberg-Frankel, *Polnischen Juden. Geschichten und Bilder* (Vienna, 1867) which evolves around similar themes with a different emphasis. There the poignant portrait of the 'Meshumed' points to the havoc wrought within the traditional family by the rising tide of Christianity. See also L. Hollaenders, *Moschek, Moeurs Polonaises* (Paris, 1859). For a different perspective on the implications of this literature see Steven E. Aschheim, *Brothers and Strangers. The East European Jew in German and German Jewish Consciousness, 1800–1923* (Madison and London, 1982), pp. 3–31.

46 Stauben, *Scènes de la Vie Juive*, p. 194. In *La Verité Israélite* (1861), Stauben contributed tales of this nature. It is noteworthy in this context to point out that a literary work which became compulsory for Jewish children in parochial Jewish schools, Isaac Lévy, *Isaïe ou le Travail* (Paris, 1862) utilized the village genre for didactic purposes.

47 For visual and literary references to the Golem, see Emily D. Bilski, *Golem! Danger, Deliverance and Art* (New York, 1988).

48 For the historical context in which the romantic historic novels were written see Bernard Lewis, *History. Remembered, Recovered, Invented* (New York, 1975), ch. 1; on the German-Jewish newspapers in the nineteenth

century as a vehicle for the dissemination of Jewish literature, see Itta Shedletzky, *Literaturdiskussion und Belletristik in den jüdischen Zeitschriften in Deutschland 1837–1918*, unpublished doctoral dissertation, The Hebrew University, Jerusalem, 1986.

49 For example, one writer who has not been discussed, Karl Emil Französ, wrote over twenty articles on Heine. See Alexander Malycky, 'A Note on the Writings of Karl Emil Französ on Heinrich Heine', *Studies in Bibliography and Booklore* 6 (1962–3), 73–4 and bibliographical references mentioned, esp. n.7. Alexandre Weill wrote a long memoir on Heine, whose reliability is now questioned. See Sammons, *Heinrich Heine*, p. 251, and on his relationship with Heine see Valentin, *Poet in Exile*, pp. 272, 299; Prawer, *Heine's Jewish Comedy, passim*; Sammons, *Heinrich Heine*, p. 344.

50 It would appear that the zealousness with which Central and Western European Jews adapted the Moorish style in architecture in the middle of the nineteenth century is also related in part to the phenomenon described in this article. See H. Hammer-Schenk, *Sygagogen in Deutschland: Geschichte einer Baugattung im 19. und 20. Jahrhundert (1780–1933)*, 2 vols. (Hamburg, 1981); Hannelore Künzl, *Islamische Stilelemente im Synagogenbau des 19. und Frühen 20. Jahrhunderts* (Frankfurt-am-Main, Berne, New York and Nancy, 1984); Carol Herselle Krinsky, *Synagogues of Europe: Architecture, History, Meaning*, second printing (Cambridge, Mass. and London, 1985).

Jewry in the modern period: the role of the 'rising class' in the politicization of Jews in Europe

MICHAEL GRAETZ

Today it is a historical commonplace to refer to the mutual interaction between economy and politics, the fact that economic power can lead to political influence and vice versa. The modern economic elite, which first began to demand its share in political decision-making in the mercantilist-preindustrial phase, did so increasingly after the advent of the industrial revolution. Jews were represented in this elite and, like their non-Jewish counterparts, they too attempted to translate economic influence into political power. The beginnings of such a process can already be discerned in efforts undertaken by court Jews during the seventeenth and eighteenth centuries; that tendency gained added momentum in the nineteenth century among bankers, large merchants and industrial entrepreneurs. Court Jews such as Samuel Oppenheimer, Samson Wertheimer, Leffmann Behrens, Behrend Lehmann, Joseph Süss Oppenheimer and others not only proved themselves to be outstanding financiers, merchants and army purveyors, but diplomats and politicians as well.

Joseph Süss Oppenheimer (1699–1738), born in Heidelberg, was appointed by Karl Alexander of Württemberg as his court financier and private banker.[1] During the reign of Karl Alexander, in the years 1733–7, Süss rose rapidly in the administrative ranks from financial counsellor to head of the mint, leaseholder of taxes and administrator of the domain, finally advancing to a position of power tantamount to being the uncrowned ruler of Württemberg. He placed his full range of talents and inventiveness at the service of his sovereign, and gave unconditional support to Karl Alexander's policies of enlightened absolutism. Those policies aimed to transform a backward region, dominated by a medieval, estate-based, dualistic form of rule, into a state governed along strict centralist lines.

The case of Joseph Süss Oppenheimer was perhaps the best known but by no means the only instance where court Jews became involved in politics. Isachar Behrend Lehmann (1661–1730), resident of Halberstadt, served the Elector Frederich August I (August the Strong) as Polish resident and Electoral-Saxon court financier. Lehmann played a key role in the dramatic events which made it possible for August to gain the Polish royal crown in 1697. In one of the contemporary documents, the following judgement is to be found: 'The Jew performed quite excellent services in this matter.'[2]

In the nineteenth century, there was an increasing number of such examples of mutual interaction between individuals holding positions of power in the economic and political elites.[3] During the vehement discussions between Bismarck and Thiers at Versailles in 1871 following the Franco-Prussian war, on the questions of reparations and new borders, two Jews were also present: Alphonse de Rothschild and Gerson Bleichröder. Both were descendants of court Jews and stood at the head of private banks – Rothschild in Paris and Bleichröder in Berlin. In their capacity as 'state bankers', they had worked their way up to a position of power and were in a favourable situation to help facilitate a peace agreement between the two former belligerents. Both bankers endeavoured valiantly to defend the interests of their respective countries. Rothschild especially under-scored his loyalty to France by insisting on speaking French, which provoked Bismarck's anger.

These peace negotiations in the aftermath of the Franco-Prussian war were not the first, and certainly not the last, occasion on which the Jewish economic elite played an outstanding role. The Roths-childs undoubtedly enjoyed a particular influence, at least during the first half of the nineteenth century, by dint of their leading role in trading with government bonds in Europe. Although their principal interest focused on financial transactions, they were not chary of involvement in politics and diplomacy, as long as these affairs were conducted behind closed doors. They did their utmost in an attempt to preserve the peace in Europe as bankers of the 'Holy Alliance' – James de Rothschild at the side of King Louis Philippe in Paris, and Solomon de Rothschild with Metternich in Vienna in the years 1839–40.[4]

In addition to the Rothschilds, there were also the so-called *Kaiserjuden* (Imperial Jews), as they were termed by Chaim Weiz-mann, who held prominent positions in the Empire of Wilhelm II: individuals such as Max Warburg, James Simon, Walter Rathenau and Albert Ballin, who all had close ties with the Emperor. Ballin took

over as general director of the shipping line 'Hamburg-Amerika' in
1886, and within a decade had transformed it into the world's leading
shipping firm.[5]

He was not afraid to get involved in political action whenever he
deemed it necessary. Thus, after Admiral von Tirpitz's decision to
construct a first-class war fleet had brought about a deepening
deterioration in British–German relations, Ballin seized the initiative
and helped arrange negotiations on arms limitations. From 1908 until
the outbreak of the First World War on 4 August 1914, he undertook
a series of indefatigable trips in shuttle diplomacy between Berlin and
London in an attempt to salvage the peace by means of an accord
between the two states. His partner in the negotiations on the British
side was none other than Sir Ernest Cassel, one of the most important
bankers in the City of London. Although, like Ballin, of German
origin, Cassel had worked his way up into the top echelons of British
society and was a member of the Jewish circle of friends around
Edward VII.

One final example can serve to illustrate the close link between
economy and politics, and the particular role played by Jews in this
connection.[6] In November 1875, the Rothschilds in London arranged
a credit of four million pounds for the Prime Minister Disraeli,
allowing him to purchase 45 per cent of the shares of the Suez Canal
Company, which the bankrupt ruler of Egypt had been forced to sell.
Thus, it was thanks to the efforts of Jewish bankers that England was
able decisively to strengthen its position in Egypt, a country of
strategic importance astride the passage to India.

However, such cases, which illustrate the influence exercised by
members of the Jewish bourgeois class in the modern political sphere,
do not provide an adequate answer here to the question of
politicization of that class *per se*, since in none of these cases were
policies pursued to further interests that were specifically Jewish. It
may perhaps flatter Jewish self-identity to note that Jews have
become centrally involved in the great game of politics in modern
states, often achieving an undeniable degree of success. Yet even if
Jews rose to ministerial posts in the nineteenth century, as in the case
in 1848 of Crémieux and Goudchaux in the Second Republic in
France, or Disraeli in Great Britain, the question still remains
whether the position of the Jews – as a collective in their Diaspora
history – was characterized by passivity and political powerlessness.

Any attempt to link court Jews and the politicization of Jewish
society naturally runs up against resistance, because many observers
– both Zionist and non-Zionist, and as diametrically opposed in

orientation as Hannah Arendt and David Ben-Gurion – regard the existence of Diaspora Jewry as being marked by a salient negative feature: the distinctive lack of *political* power. They contend that from the destruction of the Second Temple until well into the present century, Jews remained completely devoid of any tradition of political thought and aspiration. In their view, Jewish history over nearly two millennia has been the history of political powerlessness, impotence and incapacity for decision-making in this sphere. 'Jewish history' writes Hannah Arendt,

> offers the extraordinary spectacle of a people, unique in this respect, which began its history with a well-defined concept of history and an almost conscious resolution to achieve a well-circumscribed plan on earth and then, without giving up this concept, avoided all political action for two thousand years.[7]

In January 1944, at a time when the extent of the destruction of European Jewry was already known, Ben-Gurion commented on what he considered to be the lack of political aspiration among Diaspora Jews:

> There have been a number of great revolutions . . . but the Jewish revolution is fundamentally of a different order and its task is, therefore, all the harder. All other revolts, both past and future, were uprisings against a *system*, against a political, social or economic structure. Our revolution is directed not only against a system, but against *destiny*, against the unique destiny of a unique people.[8]

Even before Hannah Arendt and David Ben-Gurion, the initial ideologues of Zionism had pondered similar ideas. Leon Pinsker, for example, could state the following in his pamphlet *AutoEmancipation* of 1882:

> Among the living nations of the earth, the Jews occupy the position of a nation long since dead. With the loss of their fatherland, the Jews lost their independence and fell into a state of decay. . . . This ghostlike apparition [was] of a people without unity or organization, without land or other bond of union, no longer alive, and yet moving about among the living.[9]

Representatives of political Zionism since the time of Herzl have in large part adopted this negative judgement on the lack of Jewish ambition in the political sphere. To quote Ben-Gurion again:

> What, therefore, is the meaning of our contemporary Jewish revolution . . . Our entire history in the Galut [Exile] has represented a resistance of fate – what, therefore, is new in the content of our

contemporary revolution? There is one fundamental difference: in the
Galut, the Jewish people knew the courage of *non-surrender* . . . even, as
in our day, in the face of being burned alive by tens of thousands . . .
Resisting fate is not enough. *We must master our fate; we must take our
destiny into our own hands!* This is the doctrine of the Jewish revolution –
not non-surrender to the Galut but making an end of it.[10]

In antithesis to this concept of political impotence is the view which
sees the heart and centre of Jewish history in the distinctive autonomy
enjoyed by the Jewish community in the period between the loss of
sovereignty in antiquity and the modern national renaissance. That
autonomous community, supported by privileges and under the
protective power of a non-Jewish sovereign, constituted a political
body which was far from passive: it was no mere object tossed about
by the waves of external political forces. A tradition of leadership and
political consciousness made possible not only the development of a
set of internal policies, but also the option of external policy, of
political action in dealing with the non-Jewish environment, especially in periods of distress.

These two diametrically opposed notions – the one emphasizing a
long-term continuity in Jewish politics and policy; the other, Jewish
political powerlessness – can be complemented by a third, a
mediating view: the thesis that from the time of Jewish state
sovereignty in antiquity down until renewed modern sovereignty in
the twentieth century, the Jews never completely abandoned political
thought and action. However, continuity does not imply that a
transformation was not necessary in the transition to the modern
period. Because the Jews had been without a sovereign state since the
time of the destruction of the Second Temple, thus lacking their own
territory and monarch, it was not easy for them to develop a collective
will and pursue resolutely the realization of a political plan.

The Messianic concept of salvation proved to be an obstacle to
modern politics, since traditional Judaism rejected any attempt to
speed the coming of the Messiah by mass exodus to the Holy Land.
This view sought textual support in the Talmudic *Midrash Shir
Hashirim Rabba* in its interpretation of chapter 2, verse 7 of the 'Song of
Songs': 'That ye awaken not, nor stir up love, Until it please.'[11]
According to this interpretation, Jews should be encouraged to
endure the Diaspora and to wait, biding their time in political
passivity until divine deliverance.

None the less, an alternative line of thought hinted at the possibility
of a 'restorative' or so-called 'realistic' Messianism,[12] and drew

encouragement from the saying of Rabbi Samuel (180–250 CE): 'It is only the subjugation to foreign power which separates the present from the Messianic period.'[13] The twelfth-century sage Maimonides interpreted this dictum in his work *Mishneh Torah* as a reference to the political continuity linking the communal autonomy of the Middle Ages to the Jewish sovereignty which would be restored in the Messianic age:

> The Messiah will arise and restore the kingdom of David to its former might. He will rebuild the sanctuary and gather the dispersed of Israel. All the laws will be reinstituted in his days as of old. Sacrifices will be offered and the Sabbatical and Jubilee years will be observed exactly in accordance with the commandments of the Torah . . . Do not think that the Messiah needs to perform signs and miracles, bring about a new state of things in the world . . . Rather it is the case in these matters that the statutes of our Torah are valid forever and eternally. Nothing can be added to them or taken away from them. And if there arise a king from the House of David who mediates on the Torah and practises its commandments like his ancestor David in accordance with the Written and Oral Law, prevails upon all Israel to walk in the ways of the Torah and to repair its breaches . . . then one may properly assume that he is the Messiah.[14]

All variants of Messianic hope for salvation – whether quietistic, activistic or even apocalyptic – are characterized by the theocentric world-view. This is the case despite the fact that in contrast to the restorative interpretation by Maimonides of the Messianic idea, we can also note an antinomian variant which, negating the quietistic attitude, found its most extreme expression in the Messianic movement led by Sabbetai Zvi – a movement informed by a vision of a Jewish kingdom on earth and moved by a frenzied thirst for redemption and political power. In such instances, too, though, theocentricity means that the course of earthly events is ultimately and essentially dependent on divine intervention. Quite naturally, such a theocentric view is diametrically opposed to an anthropocentric conception which places the human being – as initiator of action – at the centre of the political stage.

It follows from this theocentricity that the only option for protest open to a traditionally oriented leader of a Jewish community in times of crisis was a call, binding on all Jews in the country, to pray and fast. Thus, for example, Rabbi Yehoshua Heshil of Apta, the leader of a Hasidic community, ordered a weekly day of fasting and prayer for all Jews in Tsarist Russia after Alexander I had issued a decree on 11

April 1823 that Jews should be expelled from all villages in the Empire. The rabbi hoped by this means to prevent the expulsion by calling in divine assistance and intervention.[15]

However, it was not only the theocentrism of normative rabbinical Judaism which presented an obstacle to politicization. The Enlightenment (Haskalah) and the efforts for emancipation undertaken by the rising bourgeois stratum likewise partially impeded that process, paradoxical as this may sound. After all, ever since the appearance of Moses Mendelssohn's *Jerusalem*, the principle of the strict separation of church and state had also begun to take hold and spread among Jews. Such strict separation acted as a brake on Jewish politicization. That notion was formulated by Mendelssohn's followers, the so-called *maskilim* and their associates, as follows: the Jewish community had to forgo any and every exercise of political or state power – even the use of a rabbinical ban. 'Since the destruction of the Second Temple, the Jews have ceased to be a political-national entity',[16] as the Chief Rabbi of the Vienna Jewish Community, Moritz Gudemann, stated on the occasion of the publication of Herzl's *Der Judenstaat*.

The principal obstacles which had to be surmounted on the path leading to Jewish political activity in the modern period lay in the dominance of traditionalism. A change in consciousness only emerged with the rise of a new leadership elite to take the place of the traditionally oriented community leaders of the past. The secular and rabbinical leaders, with their medieval political conception of an autonomous Jewish community, were unable to bring about the necessary shift in perspective and action, since they were still too strongly bound to traditional structures and patterns of thought. Only those individuals who had freed themselves in part or fully from such structures – namely members of the rising Jewish bourgeois stratum – were in a position to provide Jewish politics with a new and decisive impetus. This statement, too, may at first sound somewhat paradoxical, because Jewish politics, viewed historically, constituted the prerequisite for a national-Jewish renaissance. However, the representatives of the Jewish bourgeois class repeatedly expressed their aversion to national-Jewish tendencies – as, for example, in the statement issued by the Sanhedrin and Assembly of Notables in the years 1806–7, in the manifesto of the Alliance Israélite Universelle (1860) and in the ideological statement issued by the 'Centralverein' (1893) in Germany.[17]

De Tocqueville's classic analysis of the *ancien régime* in France and the revolutionary transformation there at the end of the eighteenth century provides a possible explanatory framework for this contradictory behaviour.[18] De Tocqueville was occupied by the question of what factor had motivated specifically the bourgeois class to take over the leadership of political transformation. It is a well-known tenet of Tocquevillean analysis that he viewed the 'politicization' of the bourgeois class as the expression of a discrepancy between economic power and political impotence. Rooted in the frustration of the rising bourgeoisie which, despite its growing economic importance, had, in contrast with the nobility, no power to effect political decisions, there arose a determination to engage in the political struggle against the privileged strata of society.

The politicization of the Jews and the role played in this process by the Jewish bourgeois stratum was, to a certain extent, rooted in an analogous and similarly frustrating situation. Here too, there was a discrepancy between economic power and political powerlessness. However, in the Jewish case, that discrepancy was unable to lead to revolution, since the bourgeoisie involved here was that of an ethnic–religious minority – a bourgeoisie, moreover, which rejected violent change. In place of the storming of the Bastille and the deposing of the king, this minority demanded only equality in respect to civil rights, and fought against discrimination.

The Jewish bourgeoisie, the privileged court Jews and their descendants in the nineteenth century – the bankers, large merchants, university graduates and intellectuals – formed the elite which overcame the obstacles blocking the path to a modern form of politics. The struggle they embarked upon was not a short-term process. Rather, the struggle confronting them involved various stages extending over many years; indeed, it entailed a long-term development that was to stretch over a span of more than a century. It will be sketched here paradigmatically in terms of its three decisive phases: first, the efforts to prevent the expulsion of Jews from Prague, Bohemia and Moravia during the years 1744–5; second, the struggle for emancipation in France and in the German states between 1788 and 1815; and, finally, the campaign to emancipate the Jews in the Balkan states on the occasion of the Berlin Congress in 1878.

On 22 December 1744, a courier of Empress Maria Theresa arrived in Prague carrying an order for the expulsion of all Jews in the city; the final date for their departure was stipulated as the end of January 1745 at the latest. The immediate cause of this expulsion order appears to have been the suspicion that the Jews had betrayed the Habsburg Empire to the Prussians when the latter conquered Prague. Although this groundless allegation had been disproved, that did not prevent Maria Theresa from insisting on the expulsion decree. Indeed, she even added a supplementary decree ordering the expulsion, too, of all Jews resident in the two crown lands, Bohemia and Moravia.[19]

Complaints voiced by the Christian population about the economic competition posed by the Jews and their growing numbers had, for many years, been a source of worry to the Habsburg rulers, and they had been waiting for an opportunity to remove this 'noxious' element from their midst. Undoubtedly, the Jesuit education of Maria Theresa had also played a role in her harsh decision in favour of expulsion.

The Jews reacted in two different ways to the decreed expulsion. As always in times of crisis, some turned their eyes to the heavens and hoped to effect divine intervention by means of fasting and prayer, in this way warding off disaster and bringing about the deserved punishment of the enemies of the House of Israel.

However, along with that traditional, theocentric reaction, a comprehensive political campaign was also initiated for the first time. At its centre stood the representatives of the Jewish economic elite of the time, the court Jews. In an urgent appeal directed to the most important communities in the German Nation of the Holy Roman Empire, the current situation was sketched in brief, and six Jewish communities, including Amsterdam and London, immediately attempted to intercede with their governments.

At the centre of this political action stood the court Jew Wolf Wertheimer, the son of the great Samson Wertheimer, who was at the time the most important creditor of the Vienna court, and had cultivated extensive relations with rulers throughout the German Empire. Samson Wertheimer had bequeathed to his son both financial power and privileges, as well as a ramified network of connections. Wolf Wertheimer, resident as a court Jew in Augsburg, proceeded to utilize those relations to their full extent after having received the appeal for help from Prague via the Jewish community in Vienna at the end of December 1744. His personal acquaintanceship with the King of Saxony (who was also King of Poland) and with the Elector of Bavaria, among others, was of great assistance, and made it possible for Wertheimer to conduct direct correspondence with various rulers. At the same time, by dint of his paramount position as a court financier of the House of Habsburg, he was able to make a key request of his 'colleagues' at court, namely the other court Jews throughout the Empire: that they intercede with their respective sovereigns on behalf of the Jews in Prague.

None the less, this large-scale campaign failed to alter the fate of the Prague Jews, and the heads of the Prague community were obliged to turn over the keys to the ghetto to the municipal authorities there at the end of March 1745. In the severe cold of a harsh winter, sick, impoverished Jews streamed by the hundred to Saxony and Prussia, a river of refugees that continued to flood on until the month of May. In contrast, efforts to intercede bore welcome fruit for the Jews in Bohemia and Moravia, and a decree by Maria Theresa issued on 15 May 1745 postponed the threatened expulsion there indefinitely.

This first phase in Jewish political action in the modern period did not result in any ideological innovation, nor was there any specific, permanent organization on the scene ready to pursue Jewish political aims. The only new factor had been the emergence on to the stage of a group of Jews who had accumulated unanticipated material wealth and power in the new economic system of mercantilism, and had gone on to utilize their power to further a number of specifically Jewish political aims. This then was a first step down the path to politicization.

The second phase brought about a major shift – not just because the elite of the rising Jewish bourgeoisie had grown in numerical strength, but also because that elite had developed a sense of identity, acquiring a clear concept of the need to struggle in order to defend Jewish interests and to achieve Jewish emancipation.

This type of politicization can be seen first as a phenomenon emergent among the Jews in France at the time of the Revolution. It is true that the Jews there prior to 1789 had not been distinguished by any revolutionary spirit, nor had they played any role in the genesis of revolutionary ideology. They likewise had remained aloof from the great political actions of the time: the revolt of the nobility, for example, or the proclamation of the National Assembly by the Third Estate, or the uprising in July 1789 led by the rural populace.

None the less, French Jews very quickly accommodated to the new circumstances, learning the language and postulates of the Revolution. They employed methods which evolved in the wake of the new political circumstances, and thus dispatched deputations and memoranda to the National Assembly or Assembly of Estates in Paris, seeking out and finding eloquent indefatigable proponents of the Jewish cause among the deputies. Figures such as Abbé Gregoire, Clermont-Tonnerre, Mirabau, Duport and others struggled, despite all obstacles and impediments, for equal civil rights – until a successful conclusion was reached on 27 September 1791.

In this struggle for emancipation, the Jews made their first acquaintance with the rules of modern parliamentary politics, and with the importance of public opinion promoted by freedom of the press. In this connection, co-operation between Jewish representatives and the Commune, the municipal government of Paris, was of especial significance. Therein one could see just how profound was the impact exerted by the ideological message of the Revolution on Jews and non-Jews alike. From that point on, the emancipation of the Jews was bound up inseparably with the principles of the rights of man.[20]

In the wake of the Revolution and under its impact, the attitude of the Jewish elite altered: in contrast to earlier periods, it did not request pity, mercy and forbearance when it came to the Jews, but rather raised demands for equality in the name of 'eternal unalterable human rights'. Accordingly, the Jews were not shown mercy or granted any special favour when they, like other groups in French society, were accorded civil rights – rather, one acted in terms of rational-universal basic principles, the common heritage of all men. 'How is it possible', wrote the Jewish delegates to the National Assembly on 28 January 1790,

> to think that the legislator, whose basic principles today are nourished at the eternally flowing spring of Reason and Justice, might, when it comes to the case of equal civil rights for Jews, deviate from these principles? . . . Such a deviation from rational-universal principles would be harmful to the French nation itself.[21]

The representatives of the Jews, both Sephardic and Ashkenazic – individuals such as Furtado, Gradis, Lopes Dubec on the one side, and Cerfberr, Berr Isaac Berr and Rabbi David Sintzheim on the other – all contributed towards introducing new modes of political behaviour. These were norms they had adopted from the outside, from the rising French bourgeoisie, the Third Estate, and which they now had put to use in their struggle to promote Jewish interests. Hence, they no longer requested privileges based on a special, particularistic relationship between a sovereign and the Jewish community, but rather referred solely and exclusively to rules which applied to all those belonging to the same social group, irrespective of whether they were Jews, Catholics or Protestants.

The link between membership of the bourgeois class and political activity with regard to Jewish affairs became more evident during the revolutionary period in France. The Sephardic and Ashkenazic representatives can be included among this social stratum by dint not only of their economic position, but also of their consciousness – which was no longer identical with that of the majority of French Jewry, then still faithful to tradition. The elite in the Bordeaux Jewish community in particular strongly identified itself with the non-Jewish bourgeois stratum in French society.

Abraham Furtado, the most outstanding representative of the revolutionary period, was not only familiar with the writings of the encyclopedists, but had assimilated and internalized their way of thought; thus he worked intensively together with certain bourgeois circles, namely the future Girondists, supporting their struggle for a new political order, a constitutional monarchy.[22] Furtado and his Jewish associates wished to be in attendance at meetings of the Third Estate, and were also the first to struggle for active and passive voting rights in the Estates Assembly in Bordeaux. They likewise insisted on contributing to the drafting of the *cahiers de doléances*. Their initiative enjoyed enormous success, and they thus proved capable of combining general politics with specifically Jewish political concerns in this revolutionary period.

What was the situation then among the rising Jewish bourgeois class on the eastern side of the Rhine? The mere fact that there had been no revolution in the German states proved a decisive factor in shaping a differential chain of development. Fully two decades were to elapse after 1789 before Jewish petitions to German rulers (especially in Prussia) also began to include a demand for full emancipation.

When the Jews did raise an express demand for equal civil rights in Prussia in 1808, it was a sign of the growing influence exerted by the legacy of the revolutionary ideas set in motion during the turbulence of 1789. When, in the wake of the Napoleonic victories, the Kingdom of Westphalia was subsequently established, it granted Jews the same rights as the Christian citizenry. In Prussia, Hardenberg and Stein pushed ahead with the implementation of a series of sweeping reforms, which, among other things, granted protected Jews municipal civil rights. Thus, as early as 1809, David Friedländer was elected by the Berlin Municipal Parliament to the unsalaried position of town councillor, as its first Jewish member. These developments inspired the representatives of the Jewish bourgeois classes to make the demand for equal civil rights the central point in their petitions to the rulers and their ministers.

As earlier in France, this radical shift became unmistakably evident in the petitions from Berlin, Königsberg or Breslau: rights are no longer beseeched, but rather demanded. No longer is any reference made to a special relationship posited as existing between the Jewish corporate body and its sovereign; rather, rational-universal principles are invoked, the eternal and natural rights of man. As Jacobson wrote to Hardenberg, no 'residue of prejudice, religious fanaticism, misunderstanding of governmental weakness' should in future constitute an impediment on the path to 'freedom and acceptance among the rest of the citizenry'.[23]

The matter at stake now was a total, 'revolutionary' change in legal status – in contrast to the various attempts at reform undertaken in German states during 1790; they had been based only on the expectation of partial improvements, the abolition of one or another restriction, such as group liability or the limitations on freedom of movement and choice of profession. It was no longer a struggle for the rights of a private individual – rather, what was demanded now were the equal civil rights owed to the citizen of the state. The granting of civil rights to the Jews was to precede their assimilation into the majority society and culture. Moreover, in this view, religious autonomy and ceremonial and ritual laws could not, under any circumstances, be utilized as a reason to deny fully equal status.

The actions of Jewish delegates in Vienna at the time of the Congress in 1814–15 indicate just how deeply these arguments regarding basic principles had penetrated into the consciousness of the elite. When the defence of the civil rights already acquired in the German states was on the agenda, representatives of the community in Frankfurt-am-Main wrote to Freiherr von Stein as follows:

> We must refer resolutely for support to this principle and fact: that, by the granting of civil rights to us, we have only received that which is due to all members of the state in accordance with sacred natural law and the basic principles of political union.[24]

There can be no doubt that the rising Jewish bourgeoisie had internalized the principle of emancipation. However, it is possible to discern certain differences. The representatives of Jewish communities in Prussia, Frankfurt-am-Main and the Hanse cities demanded full equality under state law. In contrast, the leading families in Vienna tended to demand little more than a partial improvement in their legal situation. On 11 April 1815, five key figures in the Vienna elite – Arnstein, Eskeles, Herz, Lamel and Auspitz – wrote the following to the Habsburg Emperor:

> We would consider ourselves fortunate enough if only the exalted promise were finally fulfilled, if only the general principle of granting Israelites equal status with members of all other religions in respect to rights of acquisition, trade and property were to be proclaimed by Your Majesty as law.

At issue here was only the matter of economic equality, while the political aspect was passed over in silence.

The dimension of collective consciousness was likewise as yet not strongly articulated – there was little willingness to speak for all the Jews in Germany rather than merely in the name of a single community. A number of the representatives of the Jews during the Vienna Congress had clearly not yet advanced to a full, modern level of political consciousness – a consciousness based on the political solidarity of all Jews, independent of geographical location, and defined solely by their situation as an ethnic–religious minority.

None the less, there can be little doubt that the principles which had been clearly expressed in France at the time of the Revolution in 1789 were gradually also assimilated and internalized by the Jewish leadership in the German states as the operative ideological basis for a Jewish politics. Here too, a close mutual interaction is discernible between the spheres of economy and politics, between an elite position in one sphere and an ability to exercise influence in the other.

The leaders of the various key communities – men such as Friedländer, Jacobson and Gomperz in Prussia: Rothschild, Baruch, Gumprecht and Uffenheimer in Frankfurt-am-Main; Arnstein, Eskeles, Herz, Lamel and Auspitz in Vienna – were all economically prominent and successful as court Jews or the descendants of court Jews, as bankers and large merchants. Now, in the struggle for equal rights, they were able to translate economic into political power.

Israel Jacobson (1768–1828), for example, began his career at the age of twenty-six as a finance agent of Duke Karl Wilhelm Ferdinand of Braunschweig. Within a decade, he had risen to be one of the most wealthy bankers of his time, serving several rulers simultaneously: he was in the service of the Landgrave of Hessen-Darmstadt as commercial counsellor, the Margrave of Baden as a court agent and the Duke of Mecklenburg-Schwerin as financial privy councillor. During the period of the military occupation by the French and of the Kingdom of Westfalia, he was active in arranging loans and floating bonds, working together with Jerome, the brother of Napoleon Bonaparte.

Jacobson missed no opportunity to utilize his influential position, acquired by his success in the field of government bonds and credits, in the political struggle to attain equal rights for Jews.[25] He had already proved the existence of a close link between his eminence in a pre-industrial economy and his ability to engage in political activity on behalf of the ethnic–religious minority to which he belonged in connection with the abolition of the *Leibzoll* (Jews' toll) in Braunschweig (1803) and Baden (1804), followed by efforts to gain equal civil rights in Westfalia (1808) and Prussia (1812).

Jacobson can be regarded as one of the representatives of the rising bourgeoisie who familiarized the Jewish public with a new ideology and mentality. He was fully cognizant of his financial power, which opened various doors into the ruling circles of society, and he knew very well just how to remind Hardenberg of the past services he had rendered the state. None the less, the arguments which he used were based on fundamental principles and reflected the values of that social stratum which aspired to the status of being enlightened, rational and liberal in outlook.

Thus Jacobson wrote to Hardenberg that the rulers of the Prussian state, who wished to see themselves as bearers of the torch of Enlightenment, light and wisdom, could not fall behind when it came to the regeneration of the Jews, and were thus obliged to grant them civil rights.

In the period between the second and third phases, a great shift took place, and there was a noticeable change in both general and Jewish politics. As a result of the progressive legal equality granted in Europe, and thanks to the Industrial Revolution, society increasingly opened its portals to the Jews. The Jewish bourgeoisie grew in numerical strength, and came to include groups based on propertied wealth and on a university education (*Besitzburgertum* and *Bildungsburgertum*)[26] as well as representatives of the upper and the middle strata. The members of this class internalized the culture, mentality, values and norms of the non-Jewish bourgeoisie, a process which also influenced their political aspirations and activity. It was thus no accident that an initial highpoint in politicization was reached during the third phase even before the advent of the Jewish national movement.

The Berlin Congress, the largest gathering of statesmen in Europe since the Vienna Congress, had, of course, not been convened by Bismarck in order to promote Jewish emancipation, but rather to attain a new international settlement in the Balkans and to salvage political stability in Europe. Bismarck was elected its president, and among those present were such statesmen as Disraeli, Salisbury, Gorchakov, Shuvalov, Waddington and Andrassy. Among the decisions taken was that to recognize Romanian independence and regulate it by an international treaty.

This action was finalized on 1 July 1878 after a lengthy debate which had led, *inter alia*, to the acceptance of Article 44:

> In Romania the distinction of religion, creed or confession cannot be brought up against anyone as a motive of exclusion and incapacity, as regards the enjoyment of civil and political rights, admission to public employment and honours, or exercise of different professions or industry. The freedom and open practice of all religions shall be assured to all citizens of the Romanian state, and also to foreigners.[27]

In this way, the international recognition of Romanian independence had been inseparably linked with equal rights for all inhabitants, regardless of their ethnic–religious affiliation.

What political pressure had induced someone like Bismarck, who had never revealed any particularly pro-Jewish proclivities, to include such an article in the treaties with Romania and other Balkan countries? The Jewish bourgeoisie, which had rapidly learned the rules of the game of modern political struggle, had succeeded in pushing through this passage. In view of the deplorable situation of the approximately 250,000 Romanian Jews, and thanks to the co-operation of powerful bankers with *ad hoc* committees of politicians and intellectuals, as well as with the newly established international Jewish organizations – such as the Alliance Israélite Universelle (1860) and the Anglo-Jewish Association (1871) – a 'European concert' was constituted, and systematic endeavours undertaken to put an end to the antisemitic excesses and to the discrimination to which the Jews in Romania were victim.

Both the propertied and educated segments of the bourgeoisie were equally involved in this issue. Writers such as Berthold Auerbach and

Ignatz Kuranda, the philosopher Moritz Lazarus and politicians such as Adolphe Crémieux, Eduard Lasker and Bernhard Oppenheim co-ordinated the actions they undertook with bankers such as the Rothschilds in London and Paris, and Baron Hirsch.

At the head of this group was Gerson von Bleichröder (1822–93), grandson of Gerson Jacob from Bleicherode in Harz, who had played an integral role in the mercantilist system as an army purveyor and court perfumist. Gerson von Bleichröder attained a leading position in the transaction of government bonds, and he had been selected by Bismarck as his financial adviser and banker. Indeed, there were many who dubbed Bleichröder the 'last of the court Jews'. Not only did he try to give the Chancellor the best possible advice regarding his private investments, he also left no stone unturned in efforts to provide Bismarck with the necessary credit to finance his expansionist policies. With great skill, Bleichröder had defused the Romanian railway crisis (1871–2), salvaged the large investments made by German Junkers and spared Bismarck a political scandal, even though he himself lost a substantial sum of money as a result.

At the end of 1877, he was thus able to approach the Chancellor with a quiet conscience: 'For twenty-two years I have served Your Majesty faithfully, without any compensation. Now the time has come to request such a compensation. What I ask is equality for the Jews of Romania.'[28] With the writing of this letter, the Jewish banker of the Chancellor had sent a key signal. He had initiated a course of political action which would culminate at the Berlin Congress. Down to the moment of decision, Bleichröder co-ordinated all steps in that direction from his business offices located on Behrenstrasse in Berlin.

At the beginning of January 1878, he received a letter from Alphonse de Rothschild in Paris:

> Let me beg you to use all your powerful influence with your government so that the situation of the Jews [in the East] be regulated in a separate article in the peace treaty; otherwise, given the present anti-Jewish sentiment which clearly exists in Romania, the worst can be expected as regards the fate of the Jews after the war. On the other hand, you can confidently point to the fact that in all those countries which granted Jews equality and a dignified human existence, our co-religionists have been loyal supporters of their government. Considering the tolerant view of Prince Bismarck, it should be easy for you to proceed in the indicated way, and I anticipate with great eagerness the receipt of your reports on a matter which interests me greatly.[29]

Even without this request from Rothschild, Bleichröder would most probably have directed his appeal to the Jewish communities in Germany in any case, asking them to request Bismarck 'that German diplomacy intervene on behalf of equal rights for Jews in the new Romania now under discussion'.[30] He also undertook energetic efforts directed at von Bülow and the Jewish parliamentarians during the debate on the ratification of the trade agreement in the Reichstag. Under his influence, Eduard Lasker stipulated the condition that the trade agreement should contain a clause on the inviolability of civil rights, and should rule out all forms of discrimination.

Despite the pivotal position of powerful individuals in the struggle for equal rights, it is necessary to bear in mind the decisive importance of another salient development: the emergence on the scene of the international Jewish organizations. The Alliance Israélite Universelle, for example, based itself on a broadly scattered network of committees in all parts of Europe in order to maintain a permanent programme of political–diplomatic activity. It initiated conferences,[31] such as that held in Brussels in 1872: at this two-day conference, under the chairmanship of Crémieux, representatives of the educated Jewish bourgeoisie from France, Germany, England, Holland, Belgium, Austria, the United States and Romania gathered together to discuss the situation faced by the Romanian Jews and to debate the necessary political action to be taken.

Thanks to the well-organized network of the Alliance and the so-called 'Committees for Romanian Jews', it proved possible to keep up constant political and economic pressure. Jews in the West were warned against any involvement with Romanian government bonds, and great efforts were made to prevent ratification of the various trade agreements between Romania and Germany, France, England or Italy. Special assistance was expected to be forthcoming from Jewish parliamentarians in this regard.

In January 1877, representatives of the Alliance, after prior consultation among their delegates in Paris, presented a memorandum to the conference of ambassadors in Constantinople convened by the Great Powers after the Russo-Turkish War (1877–8). This document demanded full civil, political and religious equality for all residents of the Turkish provinces who were not followers of Islam. Charles Netter, as a special envoy of the Alliance, undertook to distribute the memorandum at the conference.

In 1878, when efforts were focused on the approaching Berlin Congress, the Alliance called on all segments of the European Jewish bourgeoisie to join in a common struggle to attain international support for equal rights in the new states of Eastern Europe.

The Alliance Israélite Universelle thus brought the politicization of Jews in the nineteenth century to its first highpoint by attempting to utilize all the means available in a modern, liberal, parliamentary system to defend a common Jewish cause.

In conclusion, it should be noted that there were indeed numerous shortcomings in the attitude of the court Jews and their descendants, the merchants, bankers and educated bourgeoisie, who had been designated as 'privileged' Jews. On the other hand, it is clear that without the rising bourgeoisie it would have been impossible to remove the obstacles impeding the effective politicization of Jews in the modern period.

Thanks to the presence of a Jewish economic elite in the nineteenth century, a certain power was available to Jews to pursue and promote collective, political aims, although Jews, as an ethnic–religious minority, lacked the basic requisite attributes of sovereignty, such as a national territory and government. This bourgeoisie opened up Jewish society to outside influences and facilitated the penetration of new ideological concepts. It cannot be denied, of course, that the resulting politicization was initially the undertaking of only a small elite.

None the less it was in this manner that the foundations were gradually laid and preconditions created for the entry of the masses, middle-class and proletariat, into Jewish politics. This fundamental development occurred even before the rise of the Jewish national movement and the Jewish labour parties, which later drew the broad strata of the population into the political arena.

Notes

Translated by William Templer, Institute for German History, Tel Aviv University.

1 S. Stern, *The Court Jew* (Philadelphia, 1950), pp. 115–36.
2 H. Schnee, *Die Hoffinanz und der moderne Staat* (Berlin, 1953), vol. III, pp. 172–81.
3 F. Stern, *Gold and Iron: Bismarck, Bleichröder and the Building of the German Empire* (London, 1977), pp. 6–7, 148–55.
4 E. Corti, *Die Rothschilds* (Frankfurt-am-Main, 1971), pp. 196–227.
5 L. Cecil, *Albert Ballin, Business and Politics in Imperial Germany, 1888–1918* (Princeton, 1967), pp. 167–261.

6 R. Davis, *The English Rothschilds* (London, 1983), pp. 178–200.
7 H. Arendt, *The Origins of Totalitarianism* (New York, 1958), p. 8.
8 David Ben-Gurion, 'The Imperatives of the Jewish Revolution (1944)', in A. Hertzberg, *The Zionist Idea* (New York, 1959), p. 607 (italics in original).
9 L. Pinsker, 'Auto-Emancipation', in Hertzberg, *The Zionist Idea*, p. 184.
10 David Ben-Gurion, 'The Imperatives of the Jewish Revolution', ibid., p. 609 (italics in original).
11 See *Babylonian Talmud*, Tractate *Ketubot*, 111a; and D. Biale, *Power and Powerlessness in Jewish History* (New York, 1986), pp. 3–9, 54–117, 123–7, 136–41, 206–10.
12 G. Scholem, *The Messianic Idea in Judaism* (New York, 1972), pp. 14–15, 24–33; and A. Funkenstein, 'The Political Theory of Jewish Emancipation', *Deutsche Aufklarung und Judenemanzipation*, supp. 3, *Jahrbuch*, Institut fur Deutsche Geschichte (Tel Aviv, 1980).
13 *Babylonian Talmud*, Tractate *Sanhedrin*, 99a.
14 Maimonides, *Mishne Torah* (Laws concerning the installation of Kings, pars. 11–12).
15 I. Halperin, *Yahadut mizrah eiropah* (Jerusalem, 1968), pp. 348–54.
16 M. Gudemann, *Nationaljudentum* (Vienna, 1897).
17 M. Graetz, *Les Juifs en France au XIXe siècle* (Paris, 1989), pp. 11–31.
18 A. de Tocqueville, *L'Ancien Régime et la Révolution* (Paris, 1967), (1st edn: 1856), pp. 57–84.
19 B. Mevorah, 'Maaseh hahishtadlut beeiropah lemniat gerusham shel yehudei bohemiah vemoraviah, 1744–1745,' *Zion* 28 (1963), 125–64; B. Mevorah, 'The Imperial Court-Jew Wolf Wertheimer as Diplomatic Mediator (During the War of the Austrian Succession)', in *Scripta Hierosolymitana* (Jerusalem, 1972), pp. 184–213.
20 D. Feuerwerker, *L'Emancipation de Juifs en France* (Paris, 1976), pp. 239–399.
21 'Petition de Juifs Etablis en France, Adressée à l'Assemblée Nationale, le 28 janvier 1790', in *La Révolution Française et l'Emancipation des Juifs* (Paris, 1968), pp. 6–7.
22 F. Malino, *The Sephardic Jews of Bordeaux: Assimilation and Emancipation in Revolutionary and Napoleonic France* (Alabama, 1978), pp. 57–73.
23 I. Freund, *Die Emanzipation der Juden in Preussen* (Berlin, 1912), vol. II, pp. 91–6, 399–452.
24 S. Baron, *Die Judenfrage auf dem Wiener Kongress* (Vienna, 1920), pp. 146–93.
25 H. Schnee, *Die Hoffinanz und der moderne Staat* (Berlin, 1954), vol. II, pp. 109–54.
26 H.-U. Wehler, *Deutsche Gesellschaftsgeschichte, 1815–1849* (Munich, 1987), vol. II, pp. 174–240; W. E. Mosse, *Jews in the German Economy, 1820–1935* (Oxford, 1987), pp. 1–95.

27 Quoted in Stern, *Gold and Iron*, p. 378.
28 N. M. Gelber, 'Sheelat hayehudim lifnei hakongres haberlinai beshnat 1878', *Zion* 8 (1942), 35–50.
29 Quoted in Stern, *Gold and Iron*, p. 373.
30 Gelber, 'Sheelat hayehudim'.
31 N. M. Gelber, 'The Intervention of German Jews at the Berlin Congress, 1878', in *Leo Baeck Year Book* 5 (1960) 221–48.

The impact of emancipation on German Jewry: a reconsideration

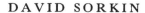

DAVID SORKIN

It has become one of the axioms of Modern European Jewish history that emancipation begot assimilation. The removal of civic and political disabilities is thought to have propelled the Jews into a confrontation with an irresistibly attractive secular culture and society that obliterated the ideological coherence and destroyed the social cohesion of the pre-emancipation autonomous community. As for so much else in European Jewish history, German Jewry has provided the paradigm for this view. Anyone who has even a passing acquaintance with the last two centuries of Jewish history can cite the apostasy of Mendelssohn's children or Heinrich Heine, and anyone conversant with the classic literature of Zionism knows that the malaise of Western European, but especially German, Jewry was an assimilatory national self-denial. When one thinks of assimilation in European Jewish history, indeed in the modern Jewish experience, one thinks of German Jewry.

I would like to question the validity of this axiom by offering a different reading of German Jewry's experience in the age of emancipation. I think German Jewry in fact provides an example of a process very different from assimilation. While the encounter with German culture and society did result in the loss of one form of Jewish identity and community, as well as some members (whether through conversion or indifference), it also resulted in the creation of a viable, if complex and generally misunderstood alternative. Against the background of embourgeoisement, the Jews' emancipation and encounter with German culture and society produced a new kind of Jew, the 'German Jew', who lived in a new kind of Jewish community, a primarily voluntary one.[1]

To understand this identity and the community which supported it we must be willing to replace the categories inherited from the more recent past with ones appropriate to the period. The view that the encounter with secular culture and society entailed assimilation presupposed one of two views of Jewish identity: either the 'Jew' is opposed to the 'German', in which case assimilation meant denationalization – Jews claimed to be Germans and thus denied their nationality and the political and social structures that supported it; or the 'Jew' is opposed to the 'Christian', in which case assimilation meant Christianization – Jews attempted to enter German society and thus denied their own religion by making it conform to Christian standards or by renouncing it altogether. These categories are inappropriate since they are both static and anachronistic, imposing norms derived from twentieth-century ideologies – Judaism as either a national or a religious phenomenon – onto the nineteenth century. They thus preclude the possibility of recognizing an interplay of factors – secular and religious, political and social, external and internal – in the creation of Jewish identity in the nineteenth century.

Instead I would propose the category of a subculture. We can define a subculture, preliminarily, to denote a minority group use of the majority culture which has two characteristics. First, while it is in large measure composed of elements of the majority culture, it is nevertheless identifiably distinct and functions as a self-contained system of ideas and symbols. The boundaries between it and the majority culture are shifting and permeable, yet there are boundaries. It means that there was a creative element in the Jews' encounter with German culture – the transmutation of the German into the German-Jewish. It is in this process that we will find a new form of ideological coherence. What replaced rabbinic Judaism was not any one interpretation of Judaism, but an ideology of emancipation that determined cultural preferences and political assumptions.

Second, because the Jews' use of the majority culture was rooted in its social structure and political position it served to turn the group into a cohesive community. A set of new institutions legitimated by the Jews' peculiar use of the majority culture, its system of ideas and symbols, helped turn their common attributes into the common bonds of a community. While its members had multiple affiliations, ties with both the majority and minority groups, it was the minority group which formed the primary community. Here, then, was a new form of social cohesion that took the place of the autonomous community. Bonds of a different sort now linked Jew to Jew.[2]

To understand the formation of German Jewry's subculture we

must begin with the complex and multifaceted transformation which German Jews underwent in the age of emancipation (*circa* 1780–1870). In the eighteenth century German Jewry had been an impoverished, geographically dispersed and socially differentiated community; by the middle of the nineteenth century it was increasingly an affluent, urbanized and homogeneous bourgeoisie.

German Jewry's economic structure changed radically in the seventeenth and early eighteenth centuries. Whereas for centuries the Jews had earned their livelihood primarily from usury, they now gradually shifted to commerce, not only because of mercantilist policies that encouraged them to do so, but also because usury had become largely inviable as the result of a legislated reduction in the permissible rates of interest and a general inflation caused by the influx of gold and silver from South America.[3] Of the 272 heads of Jewish households in Frankfurt in 1694, for example, 163 were engaged in retailing, especially textiles, while only 109 still lent money and dealt in old clothes.[4] The last complaints about Jews engaged in usury were heard in the Duchy of Kleve in northwest Germany in 1737.[5] The impact of this shift was an increase in social differentiation: it enriched a few at the expense of the rest. On the basis of tax and community records, one historian has estimated that of the 60,000 to 70,000 Jews in Germany in 1750 nearly 50 per cent were marginally employed or destitute; perhaps 2 per cent were rich; somewhere between 7 and 20 per cent were propertied and secure; and some 16 to 27 per cent were at the level of the guild burghers. Hence the indigence of the majority, and the accumulation of great wealth by a miniscule minority, was perhaps the most conspicuous characteristic of the Jews' economic life in the eighteenth century.[6]

In a little over a century, German Jewry's economic structure had changed radically once again: tax records show that by 1870 fully 80 per cent of the community were bourgeois, and 60 per cent were in upper income brackets.[7] Hamburg Jewry conveniently illustrates the change: whereas in 1816 only 38.3 per cent of the Jews paid taxes, by 1832 the number had risen to 65 per cent and by 1848 to 93.2 per cent.[8] This process of economic ascent took place largely through the commercial expansion that accompanied the Industrial Revolution. German Jews for the most part did not participate in industrialization itself but in the 'tertiary' activities of trade and commerce that complemented it.[9] In 1848–9, 44.7 per cent of Prussian Jews were employed in commerce and credit, whereas in Württemberg the number reached 52.2 per cent and in Bavaria 51.2 per cent.[10] By 1861 the percentage of Prussian Jews engaged in commerce had risen to 58, whereas only 2 per cent of the Christian population were similarly employed.[11] Yet ironically it was the ignominious occupations of itinerant peddling, used-clothes dealing and small-scale usury, the mark of the Jews' indigence in the eighteenth century, that had prepared the ground for this change. In the words of one German historian, the Jews' familiarity with trade and credit from their earlier occupations made them both 'predestined and qualified' to benefit from the expansion of commerce.[12] By the last third of the nineteenth century the Jews were no longer at the extremes of the economic scale as they had been a century before, but were now firmly in the middle.

Changing residential and demographic patterns were also part of German Jewry's embourgeoisement. In the eighteenth century German Jews had been dispersed throughout the countryside, small towns and some of the larger cities. This dispersion resulted from the Thirty Years War: the invading Swedish and Habsburg armies allowed Jews to enter areas they had been expelled from in the preceding 150 years, or where they had never before resided. After the war the Jews were allowed to remain where the Princes defied the Estates in the name of *raison d'état* (e.g., Minden, Herford, Halberstadt, Cleves and Landsberg, Heidelberg and Mannheim; Dessau).[13] In the course of the nineteenth century, German Jewry reconcentrated in the cities and towns. In the period from 1816 to 1871 the number of urban Jews quadrupled. Urbanization went hand in hand with commercialization and family life. Merchants often moved to the cities to be closer to their markets (new possibilities were being opened up by the railways), as well as to provide their children with a better education.[14] By 1871 the 470,000 Jews in the unified Reich (excluding Alsace-Lorraine) were a largely urban population. Moreover, the German-Jewish population had significantly increased, some 74 per cent in the period from 1820 to 1871 (as against the Christian 63 per cent). In 1816 Jews constituted 1.2 per cent of the Prussian population, in 1861 they accounted for 1.4 per cent.[15]

By the middle of the nineteenth century, then, German Jewry's profile had been substantially transformed. A new set of what must be seen as pre-eminently bourgeois attributes distinguished it from without and unified it within. Men married later, waiting until they were economically established; couples had fewer children, a higher proportion of whom survived; families tended to settle in towns and cities which offered better educational and economic opportunities; and there they clustered in the same neighbourhoods.[16] The Jews exhibited these bourgeois characteristics to so high a degree that their transformation preceded by at least a generation that of the general German populace.

The same attributes contributed to unity within the community as well. The Jews' occupational concentration tied them to other Jews. There was little of the divisive internal competition that plagued Jews in Eastern Europe.[17] The 'equalizing distribution of wealth', the fact that most Jews became part of the middle or upper bourgeoisie, with few actually reaching the top, reinforced the community's solidarity. Most of the Jews who had been at the bottom of the economic scale in the eighteenth century either achieved prosperity or emigrated.[18]

Defection from this urban and homogeneous bourgeois community was insufficient to endanger either its solidarity or its continued existence. The annual rate of apostasy for the entire period from 1800 to 1870 has been estimated to be no more than six or seven in 10,000, with an absolute total of 11,000 conversions from 1800 to 1870. Conversion and intermarriage were marginal phenomena. They were visible because they occurred among the economic and cultural elites in the major urban areas (e.g., Mendelssohn's children or Heine and Börne). Or because they occurred in waves – with the abrogation of emancipation after 1815, or during the height of political reaction in the 1820s – and thus seemed more important than their actual numbers.[19]

What was the role of secular culture in this transformation or embourgeoisement? Secular culture played a conspicuous role because of the process of political and civic emancipation. That process not only coincided with German Jewry's embourgeoisement; contemporaries understood the transformation to be a direct result of emancipation. German Jews attributed their embourgeoisement to the rights which allowed them, with significant exceptions, to live, work and study where they pleased. With historical hindsight we can assert that the embourgeoisement of German Jewry was powered by Germany's own rapid development: its transformation from multiple states whose corporate societies were based on agrarian, guild and mercantilist economies to a new unified German state which was a bourgeois society experiencing unprecedented industrialization, urbanization and commercialization. Yet German Jews in the nineteenth century saw the changes in their political status as both representative and determinant. The political process of emancipation had provided them with a set of terms in which they understood themselves and the world around them.

The emancipation process could provide German Jewry with such a set of terms because it was conceived as a quid pro quo in which rights were predicated upon regeneration. Emancipation explicitly presupposed a radical transformation of German Jewry. For liberal advocates of emancipation from Dohm onwards, 'civic amelioration' (*bürgerliche Verbesserung*), was a *double entendre* meaning both an improvement of the Jews' political status and an improvement of the Jews as men. Dohm stated this himself when he proclaimed the purpose of his tract to be an examination of the question, 'if and by what means the Jews can become morally and politically better than they are now'.[20] The Jews' moral status was consequently a public political issue throughout the period of their transformation. Thus in the intragovernmental debate preceding the 1812 Prussian Edict of Emancipation, the issue of moral regeneration was central. The Minister of Justice, Kircheizen, perhaps the major adversary of emancipation, contended that political freedom would not lead to moral improvement, even though, following Dohm, he recognized that the Jews' present faults had been produced by their civic disabilities:

> The Jew who today is base, having had a corrupt education and knowing through example and habit no other criterion for his actions than profit, will not simply be improved tomorrow and give up all of his national defects when the law is promulgated.[21]

From Dohm onwards the Jews were to achieve moral regeneration through a variegated reform of their lives. They were to abandon morally debilitating occupations, such as petty commerce, for artisanry and farming; to devise new forms of education that would contribute to the creation of 'moral and political character'; and to revise their religion so that it, too, would contribute to their moral betterment. This view of the Jews' amelioration was in keeping with its advocates' motives; Dohm took up the issue of the Jews' emancipation because it provided the ultimate testing-ground for his Enlightenment ideals. Like other Enlightenment thinkers, he believed that the Jews constituted the most persecuted, despised and degenerate portion of European society. If they could be perfected, then surely the Enlightenment ideals of progress and the perfection of society were attainable goals. Thus emancipation became an issue of education or re-education. And this conception carried over into the actual process of emancipation. Where emancipation was implemented, particularly in the southwestern states in the *Vormärz* era (1815–48), the state enacted legislation affecting the Jews' education, occupations and communal structure.[22] Emancipation thus became an incremental process of education under the supervision of the tutelary state.

The liberal advocates of the Jews' emancipation understood the re-education they prescribed in very specific terms: they used their own very highly developed ideal of man. The states' policies of mercantilism and administrative centralization had led them to create a bureaucracy which soon emerged as a distinct social group, a 'bourgeoisie of education'. This group no longer fitted the estate structure: it stood in contradiction to a society based on birth in so far as it included both commoners and aristocrats by making individual merit and achievement its criterion of admission. From the 1770s the 'bourgeoisie of education' increasingly came to be known as the *Gebildeten* from their educational ideal of *Bildung*.

Best translated as 'self-formation', *Bildung* was a new ideal of individualism. It promised a form of secular salvation through the perfection of the whole man. Reason was to be applied to the creation of character, which was understood in aesthetic terms – the categories used to analyse the unity of a work of art were transferred to the understanding of personality – and thus the ideal represented a form of aesthetic individualism. Unity or harmony of personality, rather than ethics, was the primary consideration. The *Gebildeten* enunciated this ideal in a new public sphere of journals, sermons and literature, and institutionalized their independent standing as a new social group emerging from a corporate order disintegrating under the diverse pressures of political centralization and economic change in a new public social world of associations.[23]

The ideal of *Bildung* played an important role in the ideological battle over the Jews' status, as it increasingly came to be synonymous with emancipation. The 1809 emancipation edict of Baden provides a convenient illustration:

> We, Carl Friedrich, by God's grace Duke of Baden, Duke of Zähringen, have granted the Jews of our state equality in civic relations in our sixth constitutional edict.
>
> This legal equality can become fully operative only when you [the Jews] in general exert yourselves to match it in your political and moral formation [*politische und sittliche Bildung*]. In order that we may be certain of this effort, and that in the meantime your legal equality does not redound to the disadvantage of the other citizens, we legislate in this regard the following . . . [24]

The edict lists the various reforms – of occupations, education and community structure – which would engender the Jews' 'political and

moral formation'. *Bildung* thus came to represent the multiple aspects
of regeneration which Dohm had suggested and which were endlessly
repeated and discussed for the next ninety years. The salience of
Bildung as the symbol of regeneration can also be seen in the tracts of
the two foremost advocates of emancipation in the public debate
following the Congress of Vienna's recision of rights. Johann Ludwig
Ewald (1747–1822), a pastor and senior civil servant in Baden,
structured his defence of emancipation around *Bildung*: the first part is
entitled 'education' (*Bildung*), the second half 'rights'. He argued that
the two were inseparable and concomitant elements of the emancipation process: 'Education [*Bildung*] must keep pace with rights; rights
must inspire the courage for education; education must create
competence for purposeful use of rights.'[25] Alexander Lips, professor
of philosophy at Erlangen, summed up his defence of emancipation
saying, 'We have excluded him because he is uneducated [*nicht
gebildet*], and we leave him uneducated [*ungebildet*] because he is
excluded.'[26]

The fact that emancipation remained incomplete, stagnating,
retreating and intermittently progressing for some ninety years, gave
German Jews ample opportunity to internalize its terms. Yet they
were also predisposed to accept the ideal of *Bildung*. The ideal of man
that had served the autonomous community for generations, the
talmid hakham, lost its ability to retain the loyalty of increasing
numbers of intellectuals. What induced this decline were the same
factors that had produced the *Gebildeten* and changed German Jewry's
economic and social structure, as well as a range of internal Jewish
factors.

State consolidation and mercantilism brought about the decline of
the autonomous communities. The interrelated processes of geographical dispersion and social differentiation robbed the autonomous communities of their social basis, while the states' usurpation of
civic functions and juridical jurisdiction deprived the communities
and rabbis of their power. In the Duchy of Kleve, for example, the
authorities began to superintend the Jewish community's tax collecting and expenditure with increasing regularity from the 1720s.[27] In
Berlin in 1698 the state first asserted its right to regulate the election of
community leaders and then, after investing them with greater
authority over the administration of supporting the poor and taxes,
required their close supervision by the state bureaucracy.[28]

The rabbinate, the embodiment of the ideal of the *talmid hakham*,
was caught at the centre of this change. First, its social basis was

rapidly eroded. Rabbis lost their financial independence: because the communities undergoing social differentiation and geographical dispersion were unable to provide salaries, rabbis often became dependent upon wealthy individuals, in many cases court Jews. Aviezer Selig Margalioth, for example, a rabbi who was active in Halberstadt at the end of the seventeenth century, complained about rabbis who resided with their wealthy patrons: 'The scholars denigrate and defame each other, especially those who are maintained by the wealthy in their homes with their wives and families. They are full of selfishness and self-interest.'[29] Rabbis also had recourse to the obsolete practice of accepting fees for rendering civil decisions. Glückel of Hameln told the tale of a stepfather and stepson, both with the surname 'Gans' (the German for goose) who wrangled in the courts over the son's inheritance from his deceased father. Third parties summoned rabbis from elsewhere because they were thought to be neutral. 'The Rabbis and authorities came, they pondered the case at due length, but they accomplished nothing – except to depart with fat fees. One of these rabbinical judges . . . made off with enough to build himself a handsome studyroom; and he had painted on its wall three or four rabbis in their clerical hats, plucking the feathers from a goose.'[30] The same Aviezer Margalioth suggested that the only way to keep civil adjudication just was for rabbis to refuse fees and beyond that to 'have a wagon waiting before the door'. Only if they were willing to abandon their positions at a moment's notice would they be free from the pressures wielded by their wealthy patrons, whose interests were often at stake.

Second, between the failure of Sabbateanism and the spread of the new casuistry, *pilpul*, the traditional rabbinic elite found itself in a spiritual vacuum. *Pilpul* tended to make the entire prescriptive tradition equivocal: because the casuist pitted his individual interpretation against the authority of tradition, he tended to blur the distinction between truth and falsehood, good and evil, the permissible and the impermissible. The failure of Sabbateanism had discredited mysticism as an intellectual pursuit. The famous controversy in which Rabbi Jacob Emden (1697–1776) accused Rabbi Jonathan Eybeschütz (1695–1764) of the heresy of mysticism demonstrated that mystical speculation was no longer publicly tenable.[31]

The combined loss of social basis, power and intellectual self-confidence led to a growing belief that there was an enormous discrepancy between the reality of the rabbinate and the ideal of the *talmid hakham*, that morality and learning were no longer identical.

The elites therefore subjected the educational system that produced the *talmid hakham*, as well as the ideal itself, to increasingly searching criticism. The criticisms that Judah Loew of Prague (1525–1609) had levelled against the *heder* and *yeshiva* almost two centuries before, which had then been idiosyncratic, now became a commonplace.[32]

The Haskalah resulted from the collision of this internal criticism with the Enlightenment. The Haskalah was thus the culmination of a prolonged internal development, a radicalization of ideas and impulses present in Jewish society for over a century. The Enlightenment allowed these ideas to be systematized by providing the rubric of a new ideal of man. Wessely's *Words of Peace and Truth* (1781), often seen as the manifesto of the Haskalah, in fact merely organized the sorts of criticism that had been aired by three generations through a new ideal of universal man and the corresponding distinction between divine and human knowledge (*torat ha-shem* and *torat ha-adam*). When the *maskilim* attempted, in the words of one historian, to 'restore the Jews to the world of reality', it meant that in one form or another they accepted the fundamental criticism that the Jews needed regeneration.[33] The Haskalah did not emerge merely through contact with German culture and society: it had autochthonic roots. Moreover, the men who propagated it, the *maskilim*, emerged out of the specific conditions of autonomous communities in decline. A product of processes under way among German Jews since 1648, the *maskilim* were in many ways analogous to the *Gebildeten*: a new social group emerging from a decaying corporate order; its position in society dependent upon education; and its vision for the transformation of society formed, as it were, by its educational views writ large.

When emancipation became an imminent prospect with the Napoleonic Wars, the *maskilim* and their successors, the ideologues of emancipation, adopted the ideal of *Bildung* and the programme of regeneration with boundless enthusiasm. The introduction to the first journal which Jews published in German, the *Sulamith* (from 1806), proclaimed its task to be 'the development of the Jews' intensive educational ability [*Bildungsfähigkeit*]'.[34] The ideologues came to see their role in emancipation as prodding their fellow Jews to uphold the quid pro quo in order to prove that they were 'worthy' of rights. 'Worthiness' thus became a code word. In the same journal a co-editor admonished his readers: 'Show that you are worthy of the name citizen and subject.'[35] From the Napoleonic period onwards, the ideologues also agreed that the state should play a supervisory role in this process. As a sermon delivered in 1831 (in Mainz) put it: it was the sovereign's role, 'to raise his people to the highest level of well-being, morality and culture of which they are capable'.[36]

The ideologues of emancipation thought the required regeneration to be as all encompassing as had the advocates of their emancipation: it included occupational restructuring, educational reform, and even the reform of religious education and prayer. The ultimate goal of that regeneration was the Jews' integration into state and society. For that integration to succeed, the Jews also had to show that they did not have conflicting political loyalties. They had to demonstrate, as did their brethren in France at Napoleon's Sanhedrin, that to be a Jew was to be different in religion alone. Thus the introductory article to the *Sulamith* proclaimed that Judaism 'is not in the least harmful to the individual or bourgeois society'.[37] One of the co-editors proclaimed: 'We no longer constitute a distinct [political] entity; but rather as citizens are merely individual members of the state. We belong to no guild and therefore must consider our brother as neither Jew nor Christian but merely as a fellow citizen.'[38] Here, in a nutshell, was an ideology of emancipation. It was a liberal credo in a country in which liberalism was linked to the state, a form of politics intimately tied to culture.

In keeping with their understanding of emancipation, the ideologues saw whatever changes that occurred among German Jews in relationship to the emancipation process. They saw their overall transformation, then, as part of their struggle for rights. Thus, for example, they viewed occupational restructuring in terms of their programme of regeneration. They encouraged their fellow Jews to become artisans and farmers, since these were considered to be the productive and morally beneficial professions, despite the fact that such a shift bore little relationship to the realities of economic life in the German states.

That the ideology of emancipation was a sufficiently potent instrument to be able to make German Jews understand the realities of their lives in a particular way is no minor point. One of the central contentions of the axiom that emancipation led to an ineluctable assimilation was that the migration out of the autonomous community entailed a loss of community because German Jewry no longer had a unifying ideology. Once rabbinic Judaism lost its authority to govern and legitimate a distinctly Jewish way of life because of the attractions of secular culture and society, once the community had lost its constitutive ideology, nothing took its place. In this view, once religious belief divided German Jews, no ideology of equivalent power could unite them, the result being a loss of ideological coherence and social cohesion that ended in apostasy, self-denial and self-hatred.

In point of fact, the ideology of emancipation lent unity to German Jewry by supplying a new form of ideological coherence. It provided a fundamentally secular ideology which the emerging German-Jewish bourgeoisie used to transform their common economic, social and demographic attributes into common bonds. It did this by offering a coherent system of ideas and symbols.

We have already surveyed a number of the ideology's basic ideas. First, emancipation was essentially a pedagogical issue, a question of the Jews' regeneration. Second, it required unquestioned loyalty to the tutelary state, for the state made regeneration possible. Third, it assumed a view of history and historical change. Salo Baron has called this the 'lachrymose theory of pre-revolutionary woe.'[39] The ideologues thought that the Enlightenment's cultural revolution was responsible for emancipation, since until its ideals of universal mankind and toleration had been propagated, the Jews had been subjected to persecution and discrimination. These three ideas taken together – a notion of emancipation, a view of the state and a concept of historical change – explained why emancipation was a quid pro quo and thus delineated a programme of action. Emancipation was a question of regeneration because the Jews had to measure up to the Enlightenment ideals that made it possible. The tutelary state presided over the realization of those ideals; thus the Jews had merely to avail themselves of the opportunities the state provided by undergoing the prescribed regeneration. *Bildung* symbolized that regeneration. It represented the whole ensemble of Enlightenment ideals that made emancipation possible and to which the Jews were to respond reciprocally. Occupational restructuring, and the reform of education, religion and manners would lead to *Bildung*. For the ideology of emancipation, *Bildung* was synonymous with citizenship.

A number of symbols supported this notion of *Bildung*. Moses Mendelssohn was its mythic hero. According to the ideology he was the progenitor of regeneration because he had introduced the Jews to the Enlightenment. He was German Jewry's Horatio Alger, the self-made man of culture. Jews to the East and West served as positive and negative stereotypes. The *Ostjuden* were the antithesis of *Bildung*, representing all the negative characteristics of a Jewry that had not yet benefited from the Enlightenment. The Sephardim, in contrast, stood for *Bildung* at its best. They had an exemplary educational system that integrated secular and religious subjects; a streamlined liturgy free of the excrescences of persecution (e.g., *piyutim*), and saw themselves as members of a European cultural community whose languages they commanded.[40]

The ideology of emancipation thus offered a distinct political outlook (the tutelary state), a view of history (lachrymose theory), a notion of German Jewry as a community (a religious confession), as well as a mythic hero (Mendelssohn) and both positive and negative stereotypes (Sephardim and *Ostjuden*). While the ideology borrowed many of its key elements from the culture of the German middle classes – its ideas of history, politics and general adherence to the Enlightenment – as a cultural system it was distinct, constituting a minority group variation on the majority culture. It not only contained specifically Jewish elements (e.g., the figure of Mendelssohn, stereotypes of Jews to the East and West), but also endowed majority culture symbols with minority group meanings. For instance, it gave *Bildung* a compensatory meaning in representing a programme of regeneration which it lacked in the majority culture.

Yet no matter how distinct or coherent an ideology may be, to have an impact it must have a social and institutional basis. The ideology of emancipation engendered institutions of three sorts, all similar to those of the *Gebildeten*, which enabled it to permeate the increasingly affluent and homogeneous German-Jewish bourgeoisie.

First, the ideology came to expression and was propagated in a new German-language public sphere. Journals, sermons and books that proclaimed one or another aspect of the ideology proliferated in the first four decades of the nineteenth century. German Jewry's public sphere emerged because of the ideology and not vice versa. Editors, preachers and authors openly proclaimed that they created new media to further the progress of emancipation. A co-editor of the *Sulamith* asserted that its audience comprised Jewish readers fluent in the 'German mother tongue' who desired 'systematic education' (*Bildung*) but also all 'educated men' (*Gebildeten*) who could be enlisted for the causes of emancipation and regeneration. He called the journal a forum 'for every friend of mankind, be he of whatever religion he may'.[41] A contributor to the *Sulamith* argued that the sermon was the only institution that could reach the new Jewish *Mittelklasse* and provide it with the education and ideas necessary for emancipation.[42] This new public sphere, similar to that which the *Gebildeten* had created in the last third of the eighteenth century, made the ideology readily available to anyone who picked up a journal, listened to a sermon, read a volume of sermons or skimmed a pamphlet or book.

Second, the ideology helped shape the school featuring a dual secular and religious curriculum as well as the temple. Although the *maskilim* in Berlin succeeded in founding a school that reflected their educational views in 1778 (the Free School), they did not manage to establish others until the Napoleonic era, when the states enlisted education in the struggle against France. These schools (Breslau, 1791; Hanover, 1798; Dessau, 1799; Sessen, 1801; Frankfurt, 1804; Wolfenbüttel, 1807; Mainz, 1814) attempted to provide their students with the education emancipation demanded: a sound occupation that would make them productive, and the religious training that would make them moral. Because the schools found it difficult to locate artisans and farmers willing to take Jewish apprentices, they quickly abandoned trying to train students for the occupations the ideology stipulated, giving them solid commercial training (mathematics, bookkeeping, modern languages) instead. In the effort to teach the students religion, the ideologues who staffed the schools produced textbooks and catechisms of Judaism and replaced the bar mitzvah (which they thought demonstrated mere rote skills) with the confirmation service (which they thought demonstrated a knowledge of moral precepts). These schools served as one institutional basis for religious reform, in some cases introducing modified services to a community. While these schools, with the exception of Dessau, never gained the attendance of more than 20 per cent of eligible Jewish students, and by and large served the poor, they did offer a model for the elementary schools which proliferated in anticipation of, and because of, compulsory school laws: eleven in Württemberg by 1825; thirty-five in Baden in 1835; and forty-five in Posen in 1847.[43] The temples introduced the German-language sermon as well as liturgical reforms. The sermon was a major medium for the propagation of the ideology. Introduced in Dessau during the first decade of the century, it became a fixed feature in most urban centres and many town communities by 1840. Its success was abetted by some states which made it a legislated requirement as part of their tutelary politics (Kurhessen, 1823, Württemberg, 1828).[44]

Third, the ideology suffused a new public social world of associations. From their very origins the Enlightenment and the ideal of *Bildung* had been linked with associations, or *Vereine*. Those associations played a key role in the transition from an Estate society based on birth and closed corporations to a bourgeois society based on merit understood as the formation of personality. In the nineteenth century, Germany's bourgeois society was constituted in associations.[45] As the new German-Jewish bourgeoisie emerged in the course of the nineteenth century they also established associations. They did this first by restructuring the older associational life of the autonomous community. The *hevra* that had been dedicated to the fulfilment of a particular commandment became a *Verein* devoted to the realization of some aspect of the *Bildung* that made German Jews merit emancipation. The *Hevrah Kadishah* of Breslau, for example, was founded in 1725 and then renamed the 'Israelite Sick-Care and Burial-Society'. The traditional commandments of visiting the sick, benefaction and burial were subsumed under, and legitimated by, the secular notion of philanthropy which the Jews' political situation made prominent. As the society's historian put it in 1841: 'auspicious political relations contributed to the creation of that well-being and general development [*Bildung*] which makes true beneficence possible'.[46] The ideology of emancipation and the ideal of *Bildung* served to legitimate the activities of a society which in 1840 was sufficiently affluent and bourgeois to build a sixty-room hospital with the latest equipment.

In the second place the German-Jewish bourgeoisie founded new associations whose purposes derived directly from the ideology: associations for mutual aid; insurance; occupational restructuring; hiring proxies for military service; aiding Jewish university students; and reading societies. All of these were understood to contribute to the *Bildung* that qualified Jews to be citizens. The Berlin Society of Friends, for example, one of the most famous associations of the late eighteenth and early nineteenth centuries, began as a secularized welfare society for men on the periphery of the Jewish community. Joseph Mendelssohn explained the association's purpose explicitly in terms of the ideology of emancipation:

> The light of the Enlightenment – which in our century has spread throughout Europe – has shown its beneficent effect on our nation for more than thirty years. Among us as well (as among Christians), the number of those who separate the kernel from the husk of religion grows daily . . . We would hope that none who takes the welfare of our nation to heart, which depends solely upon its greater Enlightenment, will refuse to join this society.[47]

These societies not only sought to promote the programme of regeneration that emancipation required, but also aimed to develop a new kind of sociability in keeping with citizenship. The new Jewish bourgeoisie was to socialize on the basis of its *Bildung*. The founding statutes of the 'Association of Frankfurt-am-Main for the Promotion of Artisanry among its Israelite Brethren' asserted that it aimed to create 'useful members of society' but also to promote the 'civic virtues' necessary for free men.[48]

Sociability became an independent value because it contributed to *Bildung*. At the twenty-fifth anniversary celebration of the Berlin 'Association of Brothers', a welfare and social organization established in 1815, the director spoke of friendship's 'moral worth': 'the association . . . aspires to be a unifying bond of love for its numerous members'. The director also called the association a 'point of gathering for intelligence, education [*Bildung*] and well-being'.[49] In other words, the associations had subsumed if not supplanted the divine commandments that had governed the traditional *hevrah* with the effort to achieve *Bildung* and meet the demands of citizenship. The associations accordingly produced the sorts of songs, speeches and poems which, manifesting a command of high German and manipulation of cultural conventions, were integral to bourgeois associational life in Germany.[50] A playfully satirical poem written for the twenty-fifth anniversary (1846) of the 'Society of Friends' in Breslau highlights the centrality of sociability and jocularly points to the specifically minority-group nature of the association, while also giving hints of the politicization of the 1840s:[51]

> The world is poisoned with association mania,
> Associations are founded every day.
> In the state, in the church, for fun and from need.
> But before they can be named, they have already passed away.
>
> Then every association totters while in diapers.
> Yes, today in particular with political tricks.
> And everywhere one immediately suspects politics,
> And without further ado the baby expires.
>
> There will soon be more associations in the world
> Than people who can live on this earth,
> For rejoicing, for fasting, for monetary speculation
> For speechifying and even for emancipation.
>
> The hard liquors swear destruction,
> The others the death of any spiritual direction.
> Though whatever one does in associations,
> The chief thing remains the banquet.

But the banquet which we now enjoy,
Must vex all new associations.
We can joyously assemble in song,
And need not anxiously barricade the door!

By 1900 there were approximately 5,000 associations in Germany. Whereas only 6 per cent of these had been founded before 1800, 18 per cent were founded between 1800 and 1850. German-Jewry's public social world took shape in the Vormärz era.[52] By the middle of the century at least thirty-nine associations devoted to occupational restructuring existed throughout Germany. Of these only three (Kassel, Berlin, Anhalt-Dessau) had been founded before 1820; sixteen were founded in the 1820s; twelve in the 1830s; and eight in the 1840s. To take one prominent example: for a Jewish population of 9,000 in 1840, Hamburg had sixty associations. Of fifteen benevolent associations, eleven were founded after 1800. Of twelve private philanthropic associations, ten were founded after 1800. Just as the ideology gave German Jewry a coherent standpoint, so the new public social world imbued with that ideology made it a cohesive community.[53]

Let us now redefine the subculture using the details of our analysis. First, German Jewry created a distinct cultural system of ideas and symbols in response to the emancipation process by transforming the culture it appropriated, fashioning a minority group variation on the middle classes' culture of liberalism. Thus the appropriation of German culture did not lead to the loss of the 'Jewish' but to the creation of the 'German-Jewish'. At the very moment that religious belief and practice divided the Jews, their adherence to the ideology of emancipation and the ideal of *Bildung* bound them together. Thus, for example, the new movements in Judaism that appeared during the period – Reform, Conservative, neo-Orthodox as well as the academic study of Judaism, *Wissenschaft des Judentums* – while separated by their conflicting interpretations of Judaism, were united by a common adherence to *Bildung* and the ideology of emancipation. They should be seen as the diverse creations of a subculture which offered a spectrum of viable cultural–religious attitudes ranging from secularism to Orthodoxy.

Second, that cultural system legitimated a set of institutions which made the new German-Jewish bourgeoisie into a community. German Jews had a set of ideological and social institutions that paralleled those of the German bourgeoisie. Those institutions allowed that new bourgeoisie to conduct a properly bourgeois way of life within the confines of the Jewish community. At the very moment that the obligatory community, the *Gemeinde*, became the locus of conflict for religious practice and belief, the public social world of associations provided a new form of cohesion.

The case of German Jewry patently does not substantiate the axiom that emancipation, which paved the way for the ensuing encounter with secular culture and society, led to the loss of Jewish identity through either the attenuation of Judaism or the Jews' dissolution as a group. German Jewry's transformation resulted in the ideological coherence and social cohesion of a subculture. That subculture emerged from a specific set of conditions that prevailed in Germany: on the one side a highly ideological integration of the absolutist state, in which culture and specifically the ideal of *Bildung* had a central role; and the deterioration of the autonomous community through social differentiation, with the Jews in turn becoming homogeneously middle-class during a prolonged process of political emancipation on the other. Since neither these conditions nor their consequences obtained in either Western (France, England) or Eastern (Russia) Europe, German Jewry's subculture was singular, and this singularity in large part accounts for its having been generally misunderstood and misrepresented. If by acknowledging its singularity we have come closer to recognizing the precise historical nature of the German-Jewish community in the nineteenth century, then we shall be obliged to relinquish the venerable practice of making it the paradigm of Jewish assimilation in modern Europe.

Notes

An earlier version of this chapter was presented at the Center for European Studies, Harvard University.

1 For an eloquent restatement of the traditional view of assimilation see David Vital, *The Origins of Zionism* (Oxford, 1975), pp. 23–48; 201–32. The concept of 'assimilation', albeit central to the study of European Jewish history, has not received much scholarly attention. See Jacob Toury, 'Emantsipatsiyah veasimilitsiyah: musagim utnayim', *Yalkut moreshet* no. 2 (April, 1964); and David Sorkin, 'Emancipation and Assimilation: Two Concepts and Their Application to the Study of German Jewish History', *Leo Baeck Institute Yearbook* 35 (1990), pp. 17–33. Many American scholars of European Jewry have relied on the definition of assimilation supplied by Milton Gordon in his *Assimilation in American Life* (New York, 1964).

2 The following discussion is based on David Sorkin, *The Transformation of*

German Jewry (New York, 1987), chs. 2–5. Although the concept of a 'subculture' has been widely used in the social sciences since the 1950s in the United States and England, in my discussion I follow its application in the study of German history, which began with Guenther Roth's description of the socialists in his *The Social Democrats in Imperial Germany: A Study in Working-Class Isolation and National Integration* (Totawa, N.J., 1963). M. Rainer Lepsius has tried to understand Germany's entire socio-political structure in the Imperial and Weimar periods through the notion of 'subcultures' or 'socio-cultural milieux'. See his influential 'Parteiensystem und Sozialstruktur: zum Problem der Demokratisierung der deutschen Gesellschaft', in Gerhard A. Ritter (ed.), *Deutsche Parteien vor 1918* (Cologne, 1973) pp. 56–80. For a recent and more satisfactory use of the term than Roth's, see Vernon Lidtke, *The Alternative Culture: Socialist Labor in Imperial Germany* (New York, 1985).

3 On interest rates see Max Neumann, *Geschichte des Wuchers in Deutschland bis zur Begründung der heutigen Zinsengesetzes* (Halle, 1865), pp. 292–347, 539–44. On inflation see Bernard D. Weinryb, 'Prolegomena to an Economic History of the Jews in Germany in Modern Times', *Leo Baeck Institute Yearbook* 1 (1956), 299–301.

4 I. Kracauer, *Geschichte der Juden in Frankfurt a.M. (1150–1824)* 2 vols. (Frankfurt, 1925–7), vol. II, pp. 108–13; and Gerald Lyman Soliday, *A Community in Conflict: Frankfurt Society in the Seventeenth and Early Eighteenth Centuries* (Hanover, N.H., 1974), pp. 180–1.

5 Fritz Baer, *Das Protokollbuch der Landjudenschaft des Herzogtums Kleve* (Berlin, 1922), p. 67.

6 For the overall statistics see Jacob Toury, 'Der Eintritt der Juden ins deutsche Bürgertum', in *Das Judentum in der deutschen Umwelt, 1800–1850*, ed. Hans Liebeschütz and Arnold Paucker (Tübingen, 1977), pp. 139ff. For specific cases of differentiation and destitution see Baer, *Das Protokollbuch*, pp. 65–78; Kracauer, *Geschichte der Juden in Frankfurt*, vol. II, pp. 31–33, 145; and Karl E. Demandt, *Bevölkerungs- und Sozialgeschichte der jüdischen Gemeinde Niedenstein, 1653–1866* (Wiesbaden, 1980), pp. 43–5. For the poor themselves see Rudolf Glanz, *Geschichte des niederen jüdischen Volkes in Deutschland* (New York, 1968). For impoverished immigrants see Moses A. Shulvass, *From East to West: The Westward Migration of Jews from Eastern Europe During the Seventeenth and Eighteenth Centuries* (Detroit, 1971), pp. 13, 67–74, 108–10.

7 Jacob Toury, *Soziale und politische Geschichte der Juden in Deutschland, 1847–71* (Dusseldorf, 1977), pp. 114, 277.

8 See Helga Krohn, *Die Juden in Hamburg, 1880–1850* (Frankfurt, 1967), pp. 49–50.

9 Avraham Barkai, 'German Jews at the Start of Industrialization', in Werner E. Mosse, Arnold Paucker and Reinhard Rürup (eds.), *Revolution and Evolution: 1848 in German-Jewish History* (Tübingen, 1981), p. 135.

10 Toury, 'Der Eintritt', p. 232.

11 Monika Richarz, *Jüdisches Leben in Deutschland: Selbstzeugnisse zur Sozial-geschichte, 1780–1871* (Nördlingen, 1976), p. 37.

12 Hans Mommsen, 'Zur Frage des Einflusses der Juden auf die Wirtschaft', in *Gutachten des Instituts für Zeitgeschichte*, vol. II, (Stuttgart, 1966), p. 353, quoted in Barkai, 'German Jews at the Start of Industrialization', p. 135.

13 Jonathan I. Israel, 'Central European Jewry during the Thirty Years War', *Central European History* 16, no. 1 (1983), 3–30. For individual cases, see Bernhard Brilling, *Geschichte der Juden in Breslau von 1454 bis 1702* (Stuttgart, 1960), pp. 70–1; L. Donath, *Geschichte der Juden in Mecklenburg von der ältesten Zeiten bis auf die Gegenwart* (Leipzig, 1874), pp. 83–6; and Arnd Müller, *Geschichte der Juden in Nürnberg, 1146–1945* (Nuremberg, 1968), pp. 95–7. For the role of Eastern immigrants see Shulvass, *From East to West*, pp. 23–4.

14 Richarz, *Jüdisches Leben in Deutschland*, pp. 30–1, 137, 245, 290.

15 Henry Wasserman, 'Jews, Bürgertum and "Bürgerliche Gesellschaft" in a Liberal Era in Germany, 1840–1880', unpublished dissertation, Hebrew University, 1979, pp. 10–14.

16 Lawrence Schofer, 'Emancipation and Population Change', in Mosse, Paucker and Rürup, *Revolution and Evolution*, pp. 63–89; Barkai, 'German Jews at the Start of Industrialization', *passim*; and Steven M. Lowenstein, 'The Rural Community and the Urbanization of German Jewry', *Central European History* 13 (1980), 218–36, and Steven M. Lowenstein, 'Jewish Residential Concentration in Post-Emancipation Germany', *Leo Baeck Institute Yearbook* 28 (1983) 471–95.

17 Barkai, 'German Jews at the Start of Industrialization', p. 138.

18 Toury, *Soziale und politische Geschichte*, pp. 112–14.

19 Ibid., pp. 53, 60.

20 *Uber die bürgerliche Verbesserung der Juden*, 2 vols. (Berlin and Stettin, 1781–83), vol. II, p. 152.

21 Quoted in Ismar Freund, *Die Emanzipation der Juden in Preussen*, 2 vols. (Berlin, 1912), vol. II, p. 341.

22 Paul Tänzer, *Die Rechtsgeschichte der Juden in Württemberg, 1806–1828* (Berlin, 1922); Reinhard Rürup, 'Die Emanzipation der Juden in Baden', in *Emanzipation und Antisemitismus* (Göttingen, 1975), pp. 48–9.

23 Rudolf Vierhaus, *Deutschland im Zeitalter des Absolutismus* (Göttingen, 1978) and Rudolf Vierhaus, 'Bildung', in *Geschichtlicher Grundbegriffe*, ed. Otto Brunner, 4 vols (Stuttgart, 1972), vol. I, pp. 508–23; Jürgen Habermas, *Strukturwandel der Offentlichkeit* (Darmstadt, 1962); Fritz Ringer, *The Decline of the German Mandarins* (Cambridge, Mass., 1969), pp. 14–61; and Hans Weill, *Die Entstehung der deutschen Bildungsprinzip* (Bonn, 1930).

24 *Sulamith*, 2, no. 3, (1809), 152.

25 *Ideen über die nöthige Organisation der Israeliten in Christlichen Staaten* (Karlsruhe, 1816), p. 83.

26 *Uber die künftige Stellung der Juden in den deutschen Bundesstaaten* (Erlangen, 1819), p. 60.

27 Baer, *Das Protokollbuch*, p. 101.

28 Selma Stern, *Der preussische Staat und das Judentum*, 4 vols (Tübingen, 1962), vol. 1, pp. 110–12.

29 *Hiburei Likutim* (Venice, 1815), quoted in Moritz Güdemann (ed.), *Quellenschriften zur Geschichte des Unterrichts und der Erziehung bei den deutschen Juden* (Berlin, 1891), p. 190.

30 *The Memoirs of Glückel of Hameln* (New York, 1977), pp. 29–30.

31 Chimen Abramsky, 'The Crisis of Authority within European Jewry in the Eighteenth Century', in *Studies in Jewish Intellectual and Religious History*, ed. Siegfried Stein and Raphael Loewe (Tuscalousa, Ala., 1979), pp. 13–28.

32 *Kitvei Maharal mi-Prag*, ed. Avraham Kariv, 2 vols. (Jerusalem, 1982) vol. II, pp. 321–8; A. F. Kleinberger, *Hamaḥshavah hapedgogit shel hamaharal miprag* (Jerusalem, 1962); Isidore Fishman, *The History of Jewish Education in Central Europe from the End of the Sixteenth to the End of the Eighteenth Century* (London, 1944); and Sorkin, *The Transformation*, pp. 41–62.

33 Isaac Barzilay, 'The Ideology of the Berlin Haskalah', *Proceedings of the American Academy of Jewish Research* 25 (1956), 1–6.

34 *Sulamith*, 1, no. 1 (1806), 9.

35 Ibid. no. 6 (1807), 377.

36 *Predigt gehalten in der Synagoge zu Mainz* (Mainz, 1832), pp. 17–23.

37 *Sulamith* 1, no. 1 (1806), 8.

38 David Fränkel, 'Die Lage der Juden alter und neuer Zeiten', *Sulamith* 1, no. 6 (1807), 382.

39 'Ghetto and Emancipation', *The Menorah Journal* 14 (1928), 515–26.

40 Sorkin, *The Transformation*, pp. 51, 54–7, 76–7, 89; Steve Aschheim, *Brothers and Strangers: The East European Jew in German and German Jewish Consciousness, 1800–1923* (Madison, Wis., 1982).

41 *Sulamith* 1, no. 1 (1806), 28.

42 Ibid., 4, no. 2 (1815), 248.

43 On the schools, see Mordekhai Eliav, *Haḥinukh hayehudi bigermanyah* (Jerusalem, 1960); and Sorkin, *The Transformation*, pp. 125–30.

44 Alexander Altmann, 'The New Style of Preaching in Nineteenth-Century German Jewry', *Studies in Nineteenth-Century Jewish Intellectual History*, ed. Alexander Altmann (Cambridge, Mass, 1964); A. Kober, 'Jewish Preaching and Preachers', *Historia Judaica* 7 (1945), 103–34.

45 Thomas Nipperdey, 'Verein als soziale Struktur in Deutschland im späten 18. und frühen 19. Jahrhundert', in *Geschichtswissenschaft und Vereinswesen im 19. Jahrhundert* (Göttingen, 1972); Wolfgang Hardtwig, 'Strukturmerkmale und Entwicklungstendenzen des Vereinswesens in Deutschland, 1789–1848', *Vereinswesen und bürgerliche Gesellschaft in Deutschland*, ed. Otto Dann, Historische Zeitschrift Beiheft 9, n.s. (1984), 11–50.

46 Jonas Graetzer, *Geschichte der israelitischen Kranken-Verpflegungs-Anstalt und Beerdigungs-Gesselschaft zu Breslau* (Breslau, 1841), pp. 38–9.

47 Quoted in Ludwig Lesser, *Chronik der Gesellschaft der Freunde in Berlin zur Feier ihres funfzigjährigen Jubiläums* (Berlin, 1842), pp. 9–10.

48 *Bericht über die Entstehung und den Fortgang des Vereins in Frankfurt a.M. zur Beförderung der Handwerke unter den israelitischen Glaubensgenossen* (Frankfurt, 1825), p. 10 and (Frankfurt, 1827), p. 1.

49 *Festrede zur fünf und zwanzigjährigen Jubelfeier des BrüderVereins zu Berlin, gehalten in der General-Versammlung am 19. Januar 1840 vom Director des Vereins, Dr. J. L. Auerbach* (Berlin, 1840), pp. 4–7.

50 Herbert Freudenthal, *Vereine in Hamburg* (Hamburg, 1968), pp. 514–47.

51 *Fest-Gesänge zum 25sten Stiftungsfeste der Gesellschaft der Freunde am 11. Januar, 1846* (Breslau, 1846). Leo Baeck Institute Archive, New York. File, Ludwig Cohn.

52 Jakob Thon, *Die jüdischen Gemeinden und Vereine in Deutschland* (Berlin, 1906, esp. pp. 60–1.

53 For a general discussion of the *Vereine* see Sorkin, *The Transformation*, pp. 113–23.

Gender and Jewish history in Imperial Germany

MARION A. KAPLAN

Every Friday evening, after she lit the candles, mother blessed us. She laid her hands on our heads and said words in Hebrew . . . a warm kiss ended this small, solemn ceremony . . . [Afterwards] . . . we had dinner. A beautifully set table, with the sabbath candles burning. . . . [on Saturdays] . . . our parents always had lots of company . . . cousins and friends even came to us children . . . We . . . played . . . read, and if there were enough of us . . . we read from the classics dividing up the roles [for] *Don Carlos*, the *Maiden of Orleans, Iphigenie* or another. (1880s)[1]

We kept a kosher home. Every Friday evening we went to the synagogue . . . Then on Saturdays again we went to the synagogue, and in the evenings my parents would go out to the B'nai B'rith lodge . . . Our circle was really all Jewish. We had lots of relatives and we didn't mix much with other people. Family life was very strong . . . We all had music lessons at home. That was the done thing . . . I was the fourth [daughter] and . . . learned the cello . . . and the piano . . . Then in 1914 the war came. We had the biggest black, white and red flag in the whole street. When Germany had a victory on the battlefield everybody hung out flags . . . and ours was perhaps three stories high! (Pre-war era)[2]

Mother . . . came from a religious background, though she rebelled against it . . . Father had been devoted to the Kaiser, and he used to take me . . . to see the Kaiser and his entourage drive past . . . I was absolutely smitten with the royal family . . . But in the revolution [1918] . . . when I was thirteen, I remember looking at the portraits of the Kaiser and Queen Luise in the drawing room, hanging over the sofa, and saying to Mother, 'What are they doing here? They are ridiculous. They ought to go.' Mother simply said, 'What a shame. They are so nicely *framed*.'[3]

The sabbath and German classics, synagogue and piano lessons, *kashrut* and carefully crafted picture frames, Jewish friends and German nationalism are the separate threads which composed the fabric of Jewish life in Imperial Germany. In approaching these elements of the Jewish experience, this chapter will discuss the generally unexamined ground of women's and family history. It explores Jewish identity, bourgeois class formation and gender roles,[4] while questioning and revising some favourite themes of German-Jewish history (the extent of 'assimilation' of German Jews and the concept of *Bildung* in particular). Women's history allows us to look beyond formal political emancipation and even beyond *Bildung* in our attempt to understand the composition of Jewish identity. It alerts us to the significance of the Jewish family and community in the overall picture of Jewish self-awareness and acculturation. Moreover, it offers a concrete picture and a locus for studying how seemingly contradictory tendencies – the maintenance of Jewish identity and the drive toward acculturation – happened and were understood at the grass-roots level.

Historians of modern German Jewry have focused on the public efforts of Jews to achieve equality. They have documented the struggle for political rights and obligations, for economic and professional opportunities. From this perspective, they have observed the relatively elevated status of Jews in economic and cultural spheres, and have noted German Jewry's deeply held identification with German culture and the German national state. They concluded that German Jews had 'assimilated' – successfully according to some, disastrously according to others. But this is only half the picture. In mistakenly assuming that the majority of the Jewish population, women, were subsumed in their category of 'Jews', historians have neglected their powerful and sustained influence on German-Jewish identity. As a result, they have frequently over-estimated the extent to which Jews 'assimilated' into German society. They have used 'assimilation' to mean fusion with the majority. This usage also carried with it the connotation that Jews wanted to give up their 'Jewishness', that were it not for antisemitism, Jews would not have remained Jews. The word is not subtle enough. It seeks to explain external, public conduct and, by implication, personal behaviour and feelings. Yet, it ignores important emotional and behavioural factors, particularly in the private sphere. It becomes even more problematic when we study Jewish women. For, when concentrating on them we can see both the attempt to become like other Germans and the resistance to homogenization especially within the family and the Jewish community.

Jews flaunted their Germanness as they privatized their Jewishness. But they were unwilling or unable to surrender entirely their identity as Jews.[5] To paraphrase Yehuda Leib Gordon, an advocate of the Enlightenment in Eastern Europe, they were men and women on the street and Jews at home. They continued to share with other Jews values, memories, sentiments, ambivalence and intellectual–existential or religious symbols. A collective consciousness and self-consciousness prevented them from fusing with the dominant society. They 'acculturated' by accepting the external, objective behaviour and standards of the dominant culture. Adapting to styles of dress and manners of speech,[6] moving out of predominantly Jewish neighbourhoods into newer ones (often forming new 'enclaves'), and accommodating to contemporary middle-class attitudes towards work and achievement, they saw no contradiction between their *Deutschtum* and their *Judentum.* They shared a deep loyalty to the fatherland with other German citizens. Yet their sentiments and their perceptions often separated them from the rest of the population. Their career patterns, their marking of holidays and life-cycle events, and their attitudes toward conversion and intermarriage also distinguished them. Their social contacts, too, isolated them from other Germans. Not only were they often excluded from gentile circles, but they 'had an emotional affinity with each other, which drew them together and tended to exclude gentiles'.[7]

A study of women in their private and public communal roles suggests that we must modify our previous historical interpretations which stress the one-way road of assimilation.[8] Jewish women, paradoxically, served as agents of modernization and tradition, of acculturation and apartness. On the one hand, they saw that their families, and especially their children, acculturated, adapting to the manners, mores, speech, clothing and education of the German bourgeoisie. Many joined with progressive forces to demand women's rights; helped to initiate the field of modern social work in Germany; were pioneers in women's higher education and in the professions. They urged their Jewish communities to keep up with changing German attitudes towards women's place in the home and society. Still others demonstrated their feeling of Jewish solidarity and of Jewish self-consciousness by insisting on traditional rituals and roles at home, by maintaining familial and Jewish communal networks, or by organizing exclusively Jewish women's societies. Often, individuals could be found exhibiting all of these tendencies at the same time. Although painfully aware of their position in a society increasingly intolerant of heterogeneity, most Jewish women saw no conflict between being German while retaining their religious or cultural legacy. They mixed their Jewish heritage and contemporary German bourgeois practice, to create a form of social life – of ethnic culture – which was not a way-station *en route* to homogenization but a balance between integration and identity.[9]

Further, expanding Jewish (male) history to include women offers a more complete, if more complex image of what we mean by Jewish identity. George Mosse has emphasized the central importance of the ideal of *Bildung* in German-Jewish consciousness.[10] The concept of *Bildung* combines the English word 'education', the belief in the primacy of culture and in the potential of humanity, with notions of character formation and moral education. The German bourgeoisie, in its climb to recognition and power, had legitimized itself compared to those above and below it through its *Bildung*. Nineteenth-century bourgeois liberals urged Jews, too, to develop intellectually as a way of integrating into class and nation, and Jews eagerly adapted.[11] Jews then, and historians since, have given profound weight to the 'education' element in *Bildung*. It meant developing one's own intellectual potential, self-cultivation, attainable through schooling and the university, a doctrine of aesthetic individualism – available to men only.

Although it enticed them, this *Bildung* left women out. Much as they had been overlooked by nineteenth-century liberals, with the extraordinary exceptions of a John Stuart Mill or a Theodor von Hippel, governments and educators ignored their intellectual needs, excluding them from the universities (with some exceptions), until 1908. Serious self-cultivation, too, was a perilous path, offensive to a society which expected a smattering of intelligence and polish – but not more – from its women. The ideal of *Bildung*, of seminal importance to our understanding of Jewish integration and identity, represented, according to David Sorkin (1987), the 'integral self-development by which the whole *man* [my italics] would develop his inherent form by transforming all of his faculties, mind and body, into a harmonious unit'. Even George Mosse's original and profound contribution to our understanding of Jewish identity does not include, because nineteenth-century liberals did not consider, women in the notion of the individual. He writes that:

Wilhelm von Humboldt provided the model for German citizenship for newly emancipated Jews: through fostering the growth of reason and aesthetic taste, each *man* [my italics] would cultivate his own personality until he became an autonomous, harmonious individual. This was a process of education and character building in which everyone could join regardless of religion or background: only the individual mattered.

Obviously only the male individual had a chance to do this. 'Everyone' could not join the process of education and character building since the former was impossible for women and the latter was based on a male model.[12]

Women's history encourages us to look beyond *Bildung* as education and beyond the German Enlightenment tradition. It shifts our examination to the implications of character formation and moral education – the relatively neglected sides of *Bildung*. This variant of *Bildung* encompasses the importance of the private sphere, the role and meaning of family – a family of *Bildung*, to be sure. Placing greater emphasis on character formation and moral education, the concept of *Bildung* becomes a broader one, more applicable to a greater number of Jews, especially women. *Bildung* then becomes not only the never-ending cultivation and education of the male personality; it implies, as we shall see, the formation of the cultured, disciplined and harmonious bourgeois family and the socialization of well-bred children. Bourgeois Germans insisted on family life and *Bildung*: as in the European and American bourgeoisies, 'family and breeding [became] the stigmata of authentic respectability'.[13] Symbolically, the familial aspect of *Bildung* was as important as an advanced education to bourgeois Germans of all faiths and of greater importance to the majority of German Jews. The latter could not all achieve the academic and professional heights open to a small, though growing, number of Jewish men, yet their social and cultural education proceeded apace within the family. Their own cultured, respectable, tranquil and steady families announced they were at one with other Germans. Their *Bildung* included the idea of proper bourgeois comportment and morality, of middle-class respectability, of what George Mosse has called a 'bourgeois utopia'.[14] The family was the concrete embodiment of this bourgeois morality, the cornerstone of middle-class respectability. It was a major agent in the spread of this side of *Bildung*. When German Jews noted that 'quotations from Goethe were part of every meal', they were pointing not only to the value placed upon Goethe, but equally importantly to the family and the meal, the context in which cultural transmission took place.[15]

Bildung served not only as their entrée into cultured German society. It became for many Jews 'synonymous with their Jewishness'.[16] To be a cultivated middle-class family was an essential part of their Jewish identity. It was often an extension of their religious life and, increasingly, a substitute for it. Among Jews, images of intimate and extended family preceded the making of the German bourgeoisie but also complemented it. It was the image of a comfortable family life that became not only a class emblem for Jews and an important vehicle towards integration, but an important element of ethnic identity. Like the German middle class, Jews moulded their dual identities as Jews and Germans around domestic values and private family life.

This essay hypothesizes that women, for reasons beyond their control, helped shape modern German-Jewish identity by constructing the German-Jewish bourgeois family. They became the mediators of *Bildung* within home and family while remaining the guardians of tradition as well. By focusing on women we begin to recognize the more traditional attitudes and institutions that persisted in dynamic tension with the forces of secularization. Finally, by analysing women's role in the family and community, one can argue that the definitions of 'Jewishness' and 'Germanness' must be expanded to include the bourgeois family itself.

Creating the bourgeois family

The period between 1870 and 1918 was, for the great majority of German Jews, one of upward economic mobility. The changes produced by an industrializing society affected family life and women's role in it. Women's work within the home and family, from bearing and raising children to doing or managing housework and consumption functions, was transformed as modern institutions, technology and the economic successes and aspirations of the Jewish petty and upper bourgeoisies altered traditional roles and expectations. The perception of what was women's 'proper' sphere shifted along with economic and social transformations. From the position of helpmate, where house and business often flowed together, woman's place was consigned to the home and to the role of 'leisured' lady, an indication of and an accoutrement to her husband's status.[17] Still, women clung, often tenaciously, to old roles and values in an effort to maintain the family in the face of the instabilities of the era and to sustain and enhance their respected role in it. Only the definition of women's work changed, from the physically tedious and gruelling and the economically useful to the cultural and social, from helpmate and housewife to cultural connoisseur and mother-*par-excellence*.

As cultural administrators, women played a role in designing the tone and style, the way of life and identity of the bourgeoisie. While husbands continued to work outside the home, albeit in a more professional capacity, it was in the household and family that the most visible *embourgeoisement* took place. The bourgeoisie set itself apart from other classes by designing and propagating a culture of domesticity, one which was dominated by women and contrasted to the market-place, the habitat of men. The household is therefore a key location for exploring issues of class formation, ethnic identity and gender relations.

For Jews, in particular, the household was the juncture at which gender, class and ethnic identity encountered each other. The home was where Jews absorbed the impact of their economic success and prepared to achieve the social status commensurate with it. It was where they experienced the 'approach–avoidance' conflicts inherent in assimilation – the desire both to maintain their family, Jewish community and heritage and move toward an integrated social and cultural life with their gentile neighbours. The walls around Jewish homes became highly permeable, allowing German bourgeois modes to penetrate intimate familial relationships as well as the décor and atmosphere of their interiors and permitting the display of Jewish acculturation to flow to the exterior. Jews were intent upon acculturation. Outwardly, they tried to look, speak and act like other Germans. Inwardly, they accepted middle-class mores for their family and made them their own. In a society in which proper behaviour, public and private, differed according to class, it was the task of the mother and housewife to act as cultural mediator (*Kulturträger*) between the intimate sphere of the family and society at large. She had to raise children according to proper bourgeois criteria. Mothers were responsible for the behavioural and cultural attainment of the family, for its *Bildung*, for the way it presented itself to the outside world. As Jewishness became more and more privatized, something one spoke about, felt or acted upon only inside the family, mothers' tasks as cultural mediators became more central and more complicated. Their role was to help the family acculturate to a bourgeois Protestant culture, to prepare them for the world, to maintain a sense of family and tradition, and to provide the salve for the pain of an alienatingly conformist, ruthlessly competitive, frequently hostile environment. Contradictory and in constant flux, mothers had to raise proper German children, present a family in the appropriate light to a society intolerant of differences, maintain some of those differences and create a refuge for a minority to come home to.

In an era in which German industrial progress tempted Jews to endeavour to attain the economic and social mobility which was permitted to them by legal emancipation women served an important economic function which reached beyond the home. In consolidating their middle-class status, they had to mediate between the lures of the market-place and the needs of the family, between outer display and inner frugality: they had to consume enough while economizing and managing. Their consumer functions have often been trivialized in comparison to earlier producer functions. Yet, guidebooks to good housewifery stressed careful consumption as a form of income conservation. Thrift contributed to the family's welfare and was taken as seriously as the husband's earnings. Thrift could cushion the instabilities of the period, compensate for an uneven economy and moderate the results of fluctuating business profits.[18] Thrift and hard work, virtues of necessity in the early Imperial era, became ends in themselves later on.

Like the modest strata of German civil servants and the *Bildungsbürgertum*, Jews measured their respectability more and more in terms of their consumption patterns and their private lives. Not only manners, exemplary family lives, literate conversations, but cleanliness and orderliness were paramount virtues. The ideal of housewifery, of a spotless home run by a *tuechtig* (efficient and capable) home manager who carefully instructed and regulated her servants, came to replace women's former productive work. These model homemakers decorated, polished and ordered their homes incessantly.

Jewish women, caught in the midst of rapid economic and geographic mobility, may have sought domestic order to compensate for the changes in their lives, but they also had other duties to fulfil in their endless campaign against dirt and disorder. According to one Jewish newspaper, the industrious management of the household not only provided for the family, but for the economy, the society and the state.[19] Furthermore, Jewish women were the shapers and guardians of bourgeois respectability in a group striving to be accepted by the gentile bourgeoisie. This implied not only imitating them, but creating a huge distance between themselves and their more 'backward' Eastern European co-religionists. Antisemites as well as many German Jews noted the filth in which East European Jews ostensibly lived. Antisemites complained of a 'Jewish garlic smell'. It is no wonder, then, that German-Jewish housewives exhibited a true horror of garlic and scrubbed and polished their 'Jewishness' away. Both gentiles and Jews believed that dirt could lead to decadence, but for German Jews it could also lead to the feared identification with their proletarian, Eastern, non-assimilated brothers and sisters living in the ghettos of Berlin and other major cities.[20]

Increasingly, as production and business enterprise left the home, it became the location for the social and cultural education of people ('die Erziehung des Menschen zu einem sozialkulturellen Wesen').[21] For bourgeois mothers, with fewer children and less work outside the home, this meant greater maternal attention. While the physical work of mothering eased, the cultural job expanded. Mothers were to produce well-behaved children, intelligent, decorous and mannerly, products of a good upbringing (*gute Kinderstube*), the synonym for 'class-specified good breeding'.[22]

It was thought to be the job and pride of Jewish mothers to be arbiters of German culture, to train their own children in the ways and manners of the male and female bourgeoisie: in fact, to create a Jewish bourgeoisie as gendered and as stylized as its gentile counterpart. They were uniquely equipped to do so. Traditionally kept from religious learning, women had acquainted themselves with secular culture even before the ghetto walls came down. They preserved their cultural presence in the family, enhancing it with very high attendance in advanced secular schools. They were capable of imparting both high culture as well as the ideas and customs of the social classes they emulated (and were part of). Their education, and the appreciation of German culture which they shared with their offspring, enhanced their family's status as much as their heavy furniture, fancy salons and decorative accessories. Further, the Jewish middle class, dependent on intellectual rather than manual skills, inculcated values of responsibility, dependability and trustworthiness in its children. These children would in all likelihood live by their wits and temperament. Therefore, character formation and moral education were essential goals of good parenting (as well as – as we have mentioned – signs of *Bildung*). Like the middle class in general, Jews were more dependent on individual traits of character than other classes. This occurred not only at work, but in the *Guten Ton* which

Jews used to display a bourgeois life-style and to distinguish
themselves from lower social classes.

Jews also had special issues to confront on their climb into the
bourgeoisie. They were convinced that their emancipation had been
earned by their *Bildung* (defined in the broadest sense); their
appreciation of German language, literature and etiquette. For them,
Bildung implied not only 'education', but a rational, cultured, well-
bred personality, a person of refined manners, aesthetic appreciation,
a person who would be accepted by similar Germans. Because they
continued to link the improvement of their status to their own self-
betterment, it was essential to them to exhibit these ideas and
behaviours in the family. Gentility, associated with quiet comportment, was a must. One daughter commented on her mother's
example: her mother had 'unlearned an audible laugh . . . smiling in
her quiet way . . . With mother everything was as quiet and
unobtrusive as possible, her appearance, her dress, the way she acted
and spoke. She could have passed for the wife of a Christian
minister.'[23] Gentility signified class to bourgeois Germans. To Jews,
gentility denoted class *and* Germanness – since they were one and the
same thing to them.

Bourgeois Jewish women encouraged their children to enjoy the
attributes of a cultured life. In the cities, mothers spent more
structured time with their children than in the countryside where
children played outdoors and indoors and where time and space
flowed more casually. Walks were important activities for children,
who seemed especially to enjoy accompanying their mothers to the
markets. Some have less favourable memories of walks. They were
constantly reminded of their posture and demeanour. Of such walks,
one writer despaired:

> naturally one expected that we children would behave ourselves like
> the offspring of a well-behaved middle-class family. What torture these
> Saturday or Sunday walks . . . We were all dressed very carefully and
> were expected to return as neatly as when we left. What a chain [*Fessel*]
> for a lively child![24]

These criticisms remind us of the silent, internal costs of class
formation and acculturation. Parents demanded bourgeois respectability of themselves and their offspring and acculturating Jewish
parents insisted on even greater public decorum in order to gain
acceptance for their families.

Walks were only one aspect of children's general physical education. Mothers saw to it that children took part in sporting and other activities from hiking to swimming, ice skating and gymnastics. Even daughters participated in the more strenuous exercises, remarking on the newness of these physical ventures for girls and on the role of chaperones at some of them. Well-mannered young ladies had to be accompanied, even on ice-skating excursions, where their mothers sat around fires, 'turning themselves as if on a spit'. Bike-riding was the one sport that mothers could not chaperone.[25] Jews also tried to harden their children to the elements, much like other Germans. Children complained of their rigorous encounters with the German climate. One mother made her daughter walk to school every day (1912) 'by rain or shine, ice or snow, which for a six-year-old, took about an hour each way. I suffered. But – perhaps it was good training for difficult times to come . . . '[26] Jewish families may have been influenced by a general, growing emphasis on health (the *Lebensreform* movement) and nationalism. Both of these caused Germans to place great value on physical upbringing, on the bearing, fortitude and sports abilities of young people. Although it is difficult to distinguish Jewish patterns from general ones, we can detect an urgency among Jews to appear robust and 'German' in contrast to the pale, unhealthy ghetto image which German antisemites foisted upon them. The Jewish stereotype was one of agedness, the epithet 'old' was used to contrast them to the vigorous young Germans.[27] In Wilhelmine Germany, where health was equated with patriotism, Jews strove to achieve standards set by their society. Whereas Goethe had commented earlier on the pale, sickly ghetto Jews of Frankfurt, one generation after Emancipation, German Jews strained every muscle to distance themselves from that stereotype.

Mothers took charge of educating healthy minds as well as bodies. In their gender-specific tasks of putting children to bed or entertaining them, for example, women transmitted German (and other European) folk and fairy-tales and literature. According to one woman, it was her mother who loved *Hermann und Dorothea*, Walter Scott, Dickens and Heine.[28] Jacob Picard recalled that while he was learning his first Hebrew bedtime prayer, his grandmother read Grimm's fairy-tales to him.[29] Another favourite form of entertainment before the advent of the gramophone or radio was reading aloud. Many read the German classics aloud or took roles in German classical plays. Henriette Hirsch recalled taking part in *Don Carlos*, *The Maiden of Orleans*, and *Iphigenia*. This was a common and popular pastime in many families which adopted Schiller, Goethe and Lessing for their general renown, and because, as symbols of an Enlightenment tradition and *Bildung*, Jews could read progressive messages in their works.[30] Jews also enjoyed Theodor Fontane (a particular favourite of theirs) and 'lighter' authors.[31] Further, while boys had to concentrate on the ancient classics as part of their Gymnasium education, girls could indulge in popular romances (the 'Backfisch' Romane) and the 'low-brow' literature of their day.[32] Although her brother admonished her for reading 'junk', one woman recalled her enjoyment and noted that this was also a way to learn about social customs.[33] This was certainly the case for Fontane novels as well. His depiction of the bourgeois milieu, its habits and foibles, was probably read as much for information and careful emulation as for entertainment.

Women also subscribed to newspapers and periodicals, probably as much for the fashion and style they endorsed as for the news they conveyed. Many memoir writers recalled that their mothers were the eager newspaper consumers.[34] The *Gartenlaube* gave advice to housewives regarding style and culture as well as, for example, information on the newest vogue in domestics' uniforms.[35] Jacob Picard wrote that his mother subscribed to the *Gartenlaube*, which 'typified the cultural and social level of bourgeois society at the end of the 19th century'.[36] While his father read the local news and his grandfather subscribed to the Orthodox *Israelit*, it was his mother's reading matter which facilitated his introduction to the German bourgeois world and its cultural manifestations.

Mothers with some musical talent introduced music lessons to their children. One woman recalled: 'When we were two years old, we had a daily music lesson. With great care, she [the mother] taught us the story and the music of . . . *Hansel and Gretel*, before she took us to see it. I was four . . . '[37] To play an instrument – usually piano for girls – and to have an appreciation of music in general was an essential attribute of a bourgeois child's education, one for which the mother was not only responsible, but often an active contributor.

Mothers bought the toys, subscribed to the children's journals, and supervised childhood play. Most Jewish children enjoyed the games and toys that absorbed gentile children except during the period of Hanukkah and Purim when they played special games.[38] Dolls, dolls'-houses and miniature kitchens occupied girls and drums, guns, toy horses and trains entertained boys.[39] Children's journals were also segregated by sex: boys read *Der gute Kamerad*; girls read, *Das Junge*

Mädchen and very small children read *Herzblättchen's Zeitvertreib*.[40] Jewish journals promoted themes similar to German journals. Children learned that 'the highest praise that one can give a child is to call it an obedient child'.[41] 'More mature female youth' learned that 'to help others and to do good, gives every loving woman's soul a boundless treasure of satisfaction'.[42]

Patriotism played a key role in an Imperial bourgeois childhood. Mothers dressed their children in patriotic garb and decorated the children's room (*Kinderstube*) with favourite toys and, often, with historical pictures and portraits. Reading material also followed patriotic themes. The *Israelitischer Jugendfreund*, for example, combined Old Testament stories, poetry, riddles, book reviews and biographical sketches (of male historical figures) with adoration of the Kaiser and large doses of patriotism. To be sure, patriotism was not uniquely Jewish, but Jewish children received an extra message: that Jews in particular had reason to be grateful to the Kaiser for an all-encompassing love. The *Israelitischer Jugendfreund* informed children that 'we will never let ourselves be outdone in our love of Kaiser and Reich. Not despite, but because we are Jews, we are faithful and upright Germans . . . '[43]

Although physical and educational activities dominated children's time, manners and obedience, bourgeois respectability in its feminine and masculine varieties, were omnipresent requirements. These 'cultural measures of gentility' were the work of housewives.[44] Rowdiness was anathema. Children had to be polite at all times. This included curtsies from girls and bows from boys. When company arrived, children were to be seen briefly, but not heard. And, like adults, their behaviour was to be decorous. Mothers had to restrain their children from behaviour attributed to Jewish children by antisemites. The latter depicted Eastern European Jewish children, but by implication all Jewish children, as noisy, dirty, undisciplined, and unmannerly – *ungebildet*, in other words. Antisemites castigated 'Jewish' national or cultural attributes. They were quick to hurl the epithets 'Wie in einer Judenschule' or 'Jüdischer Hast' in their disdain for disorder; and Jews were eager to show by their calm and mannerly bearing that these slurs had no semblance of reality. Gentility in family life and individual comportment followed from a general desire to fit in. It is no wonder that in asserting their claim to German culture, Jews enforced 'a modulation of tone, a lowering of the decibel level' upon themselves and their children.[45]

Traditions maintained

As busily as women moulded the bourgeois home and family, they also shaped the milieu in which traditional sentiments were reinforced. Jewish observance, more than that of other religions, took place in the home, in a familial setting. Family life, the observance of the sabbath and holidays (whether religiously or secularly marked), and dietary laws were most clearly within women's sphere of influence. Thus, in attempting to measure 'Jewishness' or the retention by Jews of shared religious, cultural, or existential symbols and feelings, it is crucial to examine women's relationship to their religion or their ethnic heritage within the home, the extent of their specific ritual practices and sentimental associations, and their social contact with family and other Jews.

Women impressed their offspring as much with their feelings about their religion and heritage as with their observance of religious forms. Memoir writers often seem more affected by their mothers' attitudes to their religion as it was revealed in the home (whether positive or negative) than by their fathers' attendance at synagogues or their own religious instruction or synagogue participation.[46] The *in*formal transmission of Jewish practice – affective, 'ethnic', private and personal, including foods, family, and hearth – was women's domain.

Especially in rural areas, but also in the cities, Jews – and particularly women – were conscious of the Jewish calendar and the tradition of particular rituals and foods on these days. Urban residents may have reduced the number of holidays and their religious content in comparison to rural Jews. This was especially the case among second-generation city dwellers. Yet, in all but a minority of families, there was an awareness of and an attempt to commemorate the major holidays, if only by a family reunion and traditional meal. In fact, for many Jews, *religion and family were one totality*. For them, family provided the meaning that religion once had. The family became the cornerstone of a more secular version of Judaism, visible testimony to the 'embourgeoisement of Jewish piety'.[47] And, even as the family functioned to maintain religious tradition, religion functioned to affirm family connectedness. One woman wrote of the 1880s in Berlin: 'Besides the ceremony of Friday nights there was a strict rule of family togetherness . . . This was not always easy, but proved itself to be the right thing to do.' When it was impossible for all of her siblings to appear on the sabbath, the blessing over bread was made for those children present and for those who were absent.[48] The holidays and sabbath were occasions to reaffirm the family.

Whether such rituals were observed as a result of real spirituality or simply family traditions, communal custom, or a 'semi-conscious feeling of solidarity with the rest of Jewry'[49] is difficult to determine. While it is impossible to enter the hearts and minds of bygone generations,[50] and while there is no doubt that Orthodox religious observance declined in the period under study, we have no conclusive evidence that people *felt* less 'Jewish', simply because they practised a streamlined and modernized form of their religion. Their participation in the updated rituals of their parents is indicative of their Jewish group identity.

Furthermore, for women, it was in some ways easier to consider oneself religious than for men. They experienced less dissonance between religious practice and their daily routine. Moreover, since women were excluded from many Jewish rituals to begin with, they had fewer positive commandments to fulfil, therefore their actions had less relationship to religious sentiment than those of men. For example, the daughter of the Orthodox leader Esriel Hildesheimer wrote that while the men and boys prayed at sunset, the women and girls read short stories and fairy-tales to each other while finishing their mending.[51] When men began to neglect these observances, it indicated waning religiosity. Women, for whom religion was less formalized and more internalized, could continue their forms of religious participation without a break in their previous patterns or feelings. Fritz Stern has reminded us that 'a good deal of religious consciousness and sentiment can live on without necessarily finding expression in socially observable conduct'.[52] This was especially so for Jewish women.

Even among the most assimilated urban bourgeois Jew, who no longer observed dietary rules or the sabbath and whose religious behaviour was often a conglomerate of Christian and Jewish forms (Christmas trees and bar mitzvah in the same family were not uncommon in the late Imperial era), it was frequently the women in the family who left memories of Judaism with their children. Born in 1876, the wealthy scion of a Berlin Jewish family wrote that he had no religious schooling or training, but 'it is true that in my early childhood, my mother accustomed me to pray every night.' And, while his parents were 'religiously indifferent', his grandmother, who lived with him, left him with memories of carefully observed religious practice and daily morning prayers.[53] Another young man (born 1876) noted the totally unreligious behaviour of his parents. His father was willing to attend *Gemeinde* meetings, but not synagogue. As if hardly cognizant of the import of his words, the son added, 'the religious holidays remained mere concepts to me, and I knew when Christmas, but not when Hanukkah, occurred. Yet, every Friday night, I saw my mother praying conscientiously and softly, standing at the prescribed passages . . .'[54] Charlotte Wolff, who described the excitement of Christmas, the 'festive meal of goose, red cabbage and a heavy Christmas pudding', also wrote of a 'special day of the week to look forward to – the Sabbath . . . On Friday evenings my mother put two silver candlesticks on the dinner table; food was special . . . and, we had a small glass of port wine afterwards.'[55] Toni Ehrlich (born 1880, Breslau) recalled that her family, who were among the 'better situated social circles', together with most of their Jewish acquaintances, had Christmas trees and enjoyed sugar Easter eggs. While her parents seem to have observed only Yom Kippur, she remembered her mother, remarkably, praying at home every Saturday morning.[56] Memoirs typically skirt over women's private prayers. Thus the historian knows far more about the perceived inferiority of women's private rituals than about their actual neglect of them.

Even when women abandoned certain rituals, there seems to have been a time lag between when husbands and wives gave them up. One daughter (born 1862, Posen) noted that while her mother fasted and prayed on Yom Kippur, for her father 'it was easier to fast after a hearty breakfast'.[57] Another woman recalled that her father ate pork with no compunction while her mother prayed fervently that her daughters would not neglect their religion when they grew up.[58] Furthermore, even when a couple gave up certain practices at the same time, it seems as if women were more troubled by it. Freud, for example, persuaded his wife to drop all religious practice. She did so, but to the end of their days husband and wife were still bickering because Martha wished to light candles on the sabbath.[59] These and many more examples suggest that women resisted the complete abandonment of their religious heritage – not always successfully – in the only acceptable manner of female opposition: quietly, within the shelter of the home. Such gender-specific private observance was probably perceived as less important by both women and men, since men defined status and prestige in terms of public observance.

Women's initiation of life-cycle ceremonies, such as those surrounding birth, indicated their determination to participate in a public, communal, yet separate sphere. In the case of birth rituals, neighbours and friends would sew and hang amulets around the room where the baby was to be delivered. They believed these would ward off evil spirits which could hurt mother and child. Rituals often ran parallel to the public ceremonies which took place in the synagogue. A mother's return to the synagogue and baby naming, for example, were elaborate ceremonies. On a sabbath, approximately four weeks after the birth, when her state of 'impurity' (post-natal bleeding) had drawn to a close, the mother could re-enter the synagogue. Her female friends accompanied her on this day, guarding her from any danger while she was still 'impure'. Once she was blessed in the synagogue, she was as safe as any 'pure' woman and was reintegrated into the community. On the same day, her daughter or son (who would already have been circumcised) was then welcomed into the community through the baby-naming ceremony, *Holekrash*.[60] The mother invited every child of the locality to her home. The children surrounded and lifted the cradle, calling 'Holekrash, what should the child be named?' They then shouted its secular (as opposed to Hebrew) name, repeating this ceremony three times. They were rewarded with fruit or candy. To bring these rituals into line with official religion, the cantor or Jewish teacher was requested to read biblical verses during the event. Elements of *Holekrash* appear in rabbinical literature as early as 1100, but anthropologists dispute whether the ceremony was essentially a Jewish one or one that Jews picked up from pagan and Christian sources. In terms of women's history, however, the important point is to recognize women's agency in defining and enacting religious family rituals and to acknowledge their initiation of communal rites of passage. A community of women believed it was fulfilling religious prescripts by guarding mother and infant and welcoming them into Jewish society.

Obviously, there were women who gradually dropped the observance of most ritual, particularly second generation urbanites. Toni Ehrlich, for example, would later eat pork, something her mother had forbidden (despite their Christmas tree). And, there were women who, for social or other reasons, encouraged their families to move away from the practice of their religion. Nevertheless, the predominant role of the Jewish woman as housewife provided both a richer sphere of activity and a more constricting boundary for women than for men, inhibiting the former more than the latter in assimilatory behaviour. Women were psychologically and socially more committed to the family, and their extra-familial opportunities were more limited. While there were certainly social climbers among them who assumed that the denial of their Jewishness would improve their position in German society, these were the minority. Intermarriage statistics consistently show Jewish males to have been the group far more prone to cut all ties with Judaism. (In 1907, 12 per cent of Jewish men and 9 per cent of Jewish women intermarried. These figures jumped between 1911 and 1915 to 22.4 per cent of Jewish men and 13.6 per cent of women.)[61] Female conversion, too, was less than that of males and usually necessitated by serious economic need.[62] Between 1873 and 1906 women were one-quarter of all converts. By 1912 their share increased to 40 per cent, probably as a result of their entry into paid employment and the growth of antisemitism in the job market.[63]

Despite increasing rates of conversion and intermarriage, most Jewish women remained enclosed in a small circle of Jewish friends and family. They were responsible for family networks; for the care of grandparents and orphans; in short, for the moral and material support, the continuity and organization, of an often geographically dispersed family system. Frequently this was left to the oldest woman in the family until she was unable to fulfil the responsibilities. When her grandmother died, Eva Ehrenburg (born 1891, Frankfurt) recalled her mother assuming responsibility for the family network 'so that the connection would be maintained'.[64] The aged were seen as family responsibilities. Grandparents frequently lived within walking distance of their grandchildren in towns and big cities alike. They often moved in with their children when they became widowed. Single women also lived with an ageing mother or father, often giving up their own marriage possibilities to care for their parent.[65] Jewish women participated in cousins' clubs, initiated vacations or a *Kur* with other family members, and planned regular family gatherings. Frequently such meetings led to discussions of possible marriage partners, with women considering the likelihood of two people being suited and men talking over the financial prerequisites. Naturally, it was easier to maintain intimate family connections in the towns. Yet, even when heightened mobility tore these ties asunder, women, in particular, travelled to visit relatives. Girls and young women were sent to care for sick relatives, to help sisters who had just given birth, to spend vacation time with distant cousins, to meet prospective marriage partners, to learn how to run a household with an aunt or cousin, or to enjoy 'the big city' while visiting a relative. Whereas boys left home for an apprenticeship or the university, girls left, temporarily, in order to maintain family connections.

It has been suggested that the family was particularly important to Jews, an itinerant people, forced to move from country to country with no history of permanence or belonging. Placed in a foreign culture, amidst different religions, the Jewish family provided roots and security. Even Jewish feminists, who would seek the emancipation of the individual from traditional socio-cultural constraints, clung to the notion of the family as the cornerstone of Judaism.[66] Did the Jewish family, in fact, provide stronger human ties and support than other families of similar class and place? Was this the result of religion, economic necessity (we know, for example, that there was among many Jews a close connection between business life and family life), strong group identity, or the pressure of a hostile environment? Further, if the family was no stronger than others, what role did the *idea* of the closely knit Jewish family play? More research must be done in this area before we begin to exhaust the questions, let alone the answers. Still, it appears undeniable that the family was an extremely important centre of activity for Jewish women, and, it may be hypothesized, that this focus impeded women's assimilationism. The family circle provided a buffer between Jews and an often unfriendly society as well as an extra level of communality and sociability. As such, it provided insulation against complete assimilation.

The predominant role of women in the home and family – that is, their relegation to the private, rather than public sphere – meant that Jewish women had less access to gentile environments and less opportunity to meet non-Jews than Jewish men. Men spent more of their time in non-Jewish surroundings, making the acquaintance of a wider circle of gentiles, and were often unable to fulfil religious duties during their travels or as a result of business considerations. While class, geographical location, the bonds and vitality of the *Gemeinde*, and male attitudes played their parts in shaping women's religious and ethnic identification in each era, it may be suggested that society reinforced women's familial preoccupations, giving them the unique potential to combine Jewishness with acculturation to the German majority.

Women's familial focus, although primary, did not preclude their participation in Jewish public activities. Even as Emancipation abolished the ghetto and its strictures, practical necessity and religious tradition encouraged the continuation of a charitable network among Jews. Jewish women were crucial in maintaining traditional charitable societies. Men rigidly excluded them from the management of communal affairs, but allowed them to extend their

practical housekeeping to the community at large. Women donated
their spare time to benevolent societies, including those that engaged
in poor relief, aid to sick and pregnant women, and the preparation of
female corpses (*Chevra Kadisha*). During the nineteenth century,
growing numbers of Jewish women's groups began to broaden their
welfare activities, paralleling the growth of German women's associations. Some concentrated on the education of poor girls, others
continued an old tradition of gathering dowries for needy brides, still
others cared for the travelling indigent, needy children or adolescent
girls. Their ministrations were well-meaning and basic and there was
personal contact between donors and recipients. Women's societies
continued to grow and modernize in the late nineteenth century,
expanding their interests, particularly in the area of girls' education
and child welfare and creating impressive social and economic
enterprises. The expenditures and incomes of some of these groups
were on a scale that rivalled the work of many male-owned businesses
(for example, some owned old-age homes, vacation homes, girls'
clubs). Further, in 1904, Bertha Pappenheim, a leader in Jewish
welfare work in Frankfurt-am-Main, organized the Jüdischer
Frauenbund, a national women's organization which eventually
grew to 50,000 members. The strong sense of Jewish identity among
Frauenbund members, whose feminist goals mingled with its attempt
'to strengthen Jewish communal consciousness',[67] indicated the
vigour and continuity of tradition and community in the face of rapid
social change at the turn of the century.

Although German-Jewish women were prominent in the work of
the non-sectarian German women's movement and in the advancement of social work, the majority of organized Jewish women
remained within Jewish local or national organizations. Even among
those Jewish women most active in broader social welfare or feminist
activities, many donated their efforts to specifically Jewish endeavours as well.[68] Removed from the centres of power and decision
making, women contributed continuity and organization to the
national, local, cultural, educational and social welfare aspects of
Jewish communal life. Jewishness, the modernized practice of their
religion within the family as well as a strong sense of solidarity with
other Jews, defined their identity more than has been recognized by
historians and more than they themselves may have realized.
Although they were excluded from synagogue rituals, seated in a
women's gallery and restricted in their access to a Jewish education
equal to that of their brothers, their second-class citizenship did not

extend to their participation in the Jewish community. This is where they found work, demonstrated competence and built self-esteem. And this is also where they continued their work of maintaining Jewish structures and traditions.

Conclusion

In this period of upward economic and social mobility the role of women was essential to the creation of a German-Jewish bourgeoisie. Women transformed the home into the model German bourgeois household, contributing to the social position of Jews and to their sense of class and, hence, 'Germanness'. Women who did not work outside the home and who focused on the creation of domesticity were the *de facto* symbols of having 'made it' into the bourgeoisie. A good *Haushalt* equalled a good 'house' and, more importantly, a respectable middle-class family. Also, women's role was crucial to the process of acculturation. Women not only brought German culture into the home in the form of domesticity or even high culture or *Kultur* (this children also learned at school); they made children respectable, clean, orderly and mannerly. They passed on that side of *Bildung*, centred on character formation and moral education, which German Jews integrated – along with education – into their understanding of the spirit of their 'Germanness' *and* their 'Jewishness'.

Women coupled faith with domesticity. They helped their families look, act and feel like Germans by promoting a culture of domesticity recognizable to other bourgeois Germans. All the while, many continued to perform rituals, cook special Jewish dishes, and think and act in terms of Jewish life-cycles, family and community networks and the Jewish calendar. Still, Jewish religious customs and German accoutrements were not perceived as, nor were they, contradictory. The goal and achievement of domesticity were to help the family adjust to its German environment, to 'look' German, while it remained Jewish. As time went on, it was the cultured family and the community – including extended kin and friendship networks as well as Jewish charity and cultural associations – rather than the strict observance of religious customs which provided vehicles for Jewish identity in Germany. In the midst of their successful push towards acculturation, theirs was a holding action, as much to maintain tradition as to hold the family and community together.

Notes

1 Henriette Hirsch, 'Erinnerungen an meine Jugend' (born 1884, Berlin),
   memoir collection of the Leo Baeck Institute, New York (hereafter:
   memoirs, LBI), pp. 1–4.
2 Betty Lipton, 'At Home in Berlin' from John Foster (ed.), *Community of
   Fate: Memoirs of German Jews in Melbourne* (Sydney, London and Boston,
   1986), pp. 23–5.
3 Gertrud Catts, 'A Portable Career', in Foster, *Community*, pp. 36–7.
4 'Gender' is a socially imposed division of the sexes. It is the cultural
   definition of behaviour defined as appropriate to the sexes in a given
   society at a given time. As a cultural product – rather than a biological
   given – it changes over time and under varying circumstances. The
   gender system includes relations of production, reproduction and the
   family, as well as the enculturation of gender roles in childhood and their
   perpetuation in adult life. See, for example Gayle Rubin, 'The Traffic in
   Women: Notes on the "Political Economy" of Sex', in Rayna Reiter
   (ed.), *Toward an Anthropology of Women* (New York, 1975), p. 179.
5 The *Centralverein deutscher Staatsbürger jüdischen Glaubens* is an interesting
   case in point. Its activities parted from the assimilationism of the late
   1870s, but its vocabulary did not adapt. Thus 'assimilation' which once
   meant fusion to most Germans – Jewish and gentile – continued to be used
   as a descriptive label for what was really something else. See Ismar
   Schorsch, *Jewish Reactions to German Anti-Semitism, 1870–1914* (New York,
   1972); Peter Pulzer, 'Why was there a "Jewish Question" in Imperial
   Germany?', in *Leo Baeck Institute Year Book* 25 (1980), 142.
6 Jews were careful to speak proper German, but many maintained a
   language loyalty to Judaeo-German as well. See Werner Weinberg, *Die
   Reste des Jüdisch-deutschen* (Stuttgart, 1969), esp. pp. 11–12, 14–15, 19.
7 Charlotte Wolff, *Hindsight. An Autobiography* (London, 1980), p. 6. This
   extended to Austrian Jews as well: 'In one way we all remained Jewish',
   wrote Freud's son. 'We moved in Jewish circles, our friends were Jews,
   our doctor, our lawyer were Jews.' Quoted by Egon Schwarz, in
   'Melting Pot or Witches' Cauldron? Jews and Anti-Semites in Vienna at
   the Turn of the Century', in David Bronson (ed.), *Jews and Germans from
   1860-1933. The Problematic Symbiosis* (Heidelberg, 1979), pp. 276–7.
8 For a longer discussion of the terms 'assimilation', 'acculturation' and
   'integration', see my article 'Tradition and Transition: The Acculturation, Assimilation and Integration of Jews in Imperial Germany: A
   Gender Analysis', *Leo Baeck Institute Year Book* 27 (1982), 3–35.
9 Uriel Tal, *Christians and Jews in Germany: Religion, Politics, and Ideology in the
   Second Reich, 1870–1914* (Ithaca, N.Y., 1975), p. 290.
10 George L. Mosse, *German Jews beyond Judaism* (Bloomington, Ill. 1985).
11 Ibid., pp. 11, 14. See also George L. Mosse, 'German Jews and Liberalism

in Retrospect', in Introduction, *Leo Baeck Institute Year Book* 32 (1987), xiii-xxv.

12 David Sorkin, 'The Genesis of the Ideology of Emancipation, 1806–1840', *Leo Baeck Institute Year Book* 32 (1987), 19. Mosse quoted from 'German Jews and Liberalism', p. xiii.

13 See, for example, Wilhelm H. Riehl, *Die Familie* (Stuttgart, 1889). The quote is from Peter Gay who described Mabel Loomis's attitudes, particularly 'because money was not abundant' in her home, as insistent on these characteristics: *The Bourgeois Experience: Education of the Senses* (New York, 1984), p. 74.

14 George L. Mosse, 'The Secularization of Jewish Theology', in *Masses and Man. Nationalist and Fascist Perceptions of Reality*, ed. George L. Mosse (New York, 1980), p. 258. For penetrating dicussions of bourgeois culture and the bourgeoisie, which include issues of gender and family, see: Jürgen Kocka, 'Bürgertum und bürgerliche Gesellschaft im 19. Jahrhundert: Europäische Entwicklungen und deutsche Eigenarten', in *Bürgertum im 19. Jahrhundert: Deutschland im europäischen Vergleich*, vol. 1, ed. by Jürgen Kocka (Munich, 1988), pp. 11–76; Ute Frevert (ed.), *Bürgerinnen und Bürger* (Göttingen, 1988).

15 Mosse, *German Jews*, p. 14. Peter Gay suggests that 'the claim to cultivation is probably more characteristic of more bourgeois than any other of their cultural habits'. This cultivation included totems in the home; 'pictures on the wall, music in the parlor, classics in the glassed-in bookcase'. Girls had to play the piano; family and breeding were absolutely essential: Peter Gay, *The Bourgeois Experience*, p. 28.

16 Mosse, *German Jews*, p. 4.

17 Ute Frevert, *Frauen-Geschichte: Zwischen Bürgerlicher Verbesserung und Neuer Weiblichkeit* (Frankfurt-am-Main, 1986), pp. 104–27.

18 *Deutsche Hausfrauenzeitung*, 1 October 1886, p. 1.

19 *General Anzeiger; Illustriertes Unterhaltungsblatt*, 1 February 1904, vol. IV, no. 5, p. 37.

20 See, for example, Steven E. Aschheim, *Brothers and Strangers: The East European Jew in German and German Jewish Consciousness, 1800–1923* (Wisconsin, 1982); Jack Wertheimer, *Unwelcome Strangers: East European Jews in Imperial Germany* (New York, 1987).

21 Ingeborg Weber-Kellermann, *Die deutsche Familie: Versuch einer Sozialgeschichte* (Frankfurt-am-Main, 1978), p. 107.

22 Ibid., p. 108. For women's role as mothers and wives, see also Barbara Beuys, *Familienleben in Deutschland* (Hamburg, 1980), pp. 422–42.

23 Johanna Meyer-Loevinson, memoirs, LBI, pp. 4, 28.

24 Anna Kronthal, *Posner Mürbekuchen, Jugend-Erinnerungen einer Posnerin* (Munich, 1932), p. 17; Toni Sender, *Autobiographie einer deutschen Rebellin*, ed. Gisela Brinker-Gabler (Frankfurt-am-Main, 1981), first publ. as *Autobiography of a German Rebel*, New York, 1939), p. 31; Henriette Hirsch,

memoirs, LBI, p. 48. The quotation is from Toni Sender, *Autobiographie*, p. 31.

25 Chaperone quote from Clara Sander, memoirs, LBI, p. 51. See also, Johanna Meyer-Loevinson, memoirs, LBI, p. 17; Kronthal, *Posner*, p. 23; Alice Ottenheimer, memoirs, LBI, p. 5.

26 Marianne Berel, memoirs, LBI, p. 51. (We are told elsewhere that 'chilly doses of fresh air' was the British answer to child care as well: Ellen Ross, paper delivered to the Women and Society Seminar, Columbia University, Jan. 1987, p. 9.)

27 George L. Mosse, 'The Jews and the German War Experience', in *Masses and Man*, pp. 280–1.

28 Clara Geismar, memoirs, LBI, p. 57.

29 Utz Jeggle, *Judendörfer in Württemberg* (Tübingen, 1969), p. 275.

30 Interview with Ilse Blumenthal-Weiss, born 1900, lived in Berlin. New York, 1981. See also Julie Braun Vogelstein, *Was niemals stirbt. Gestalten und Erinnerungen* (Stuttgart, 1966), p. 184.

31 Peter Gay, *Freud, Jews and other Germans* (New York, 1978), p. 111; Joachim Remak, *The Gentle Critic: Theodore Fontane and German Politics, 1848-1898* (Syracuse, 1964), pp. 32, 90, n.11. Interview with Ilse Blumenthal-Weiss. See also Johanna Meyer-Loevinson, memoirs, LBI, p. 39.

32 Toni Ehrlich, memoirs, LBI, p. 24.

33 Interview with Ilse Blumenthal-Weiss.

34 Geismar, memoirs, LBI, p. 57; Jacob Picard, 'Childhood in the Village', *Leo Baeck Institute Year Book* (1959), p. 285.

35 *Dienstbare Geister: Leben und Arbeitswelt städtischer Dienstboten* (Berlin, 1981), p. 130 (fashions of 1902 and 1905). Sender discovered cartons of the *Gartenlaube* in her attic, p. 32; see also Hirsch on the *Gartenlaube*, p. 2.

36 Picard, 'Childhood', p. 285. See also Jeggle, *Judendörfer*, p. 164.

37 Berel, memoirs, LBI, p. 50.

38 Elfie Labsch-Benz, *Die jüdische Gemeinde Nonnenweier* (Baden-Württemberg, 1980), p. 30.

39 Weber-Kellermann, *Die deutsche Familie*, p. 112; Ottenheimer, memoirs, LBI, p. 4; Bertha Katz, memoirs, LBI, p. 13.

40 Hirsch, memoirs, LBI, p. 2.

41 *Israelitischer Jugendfreund*, vol. I(1895), p. 294.

42 Ibid., p. 171.

43 Ibid.; also vol. IV (1898), p. 18.

44 Mary Ryan uses this formulation in her book *Cradle of the Middle Class* (New York 1981), p. 161.

45 Aschheim, *Brothers*, p. 9. See also John M. Cuddihy, *The Oredeal of Civility: Freud, Marx, Lévi-Strauss, and the Jewish Struggle with Modernity* (New York, 1974).

46 Men's relationship to their religion would be measured by synagogue attendance, observance outside the home (like not working on the

sabbath), and only lastly by ritual in the home. An example of a mother's negative attitudes is illustrative: Julius Bleichroeder felt closer to his faith than his wife. 'As tied as Julius felt to Judaism he failed to pass this on to even one of his children': Charlotte Hamburger-Liepmann, memoirs, LBI, p. 67.

47 George Mosse, 'The Secularization of Jewish Theology', p. 258.
48 Johanna Meyer-Loevinson, memoirs, LBI, p. 23.
49 Gershom Scholem, 'On the Social Psychology of the Jews in Germany, 1900–1933', in David Bronsen (ed.), *Jews and Germans from 1860–1933. The Problematic Symbiosis* (Heidelberg, 1979), p. 18.
50 Phillipine Landau, born 1869, Worms, wrote: 'nothing was maintained as a result of deep feelings, but for tradition or a result of habit'. In Monika Richarz (ed.), *Jüdisches Leben in Deutschland. Selbstzeugnisse zur Sozialgeschichte im Kaiserreich* (Stuttgart, 1979), p. 343.
51 Esther Calvary, memoirs, LBI, p. 19.
52 'Comments on the Papers of Ismar Schorsch, Vernon Lidtke and Geoffrey G. Field', *Leo Baeck Institute Year Book* 25 (1980), 73.
53 Richarz, *Jüdisches Leben*, pp. 298–9.
54 Ibid., p. 362.
55 Wolff, *Hindsight*, pp. 6, 21.
56 Toni Ehrlich, memoirs, LBI, pp. 6, 9–10, 61.
57 Kronthal, *Posner*, p. 27.
58 Antoinette Kahler, archives of LBI no. 2141/1, p. 53.
59 Quoted by David Aberbach, 'Freud's Jewish Problem', *Commentary*, June 1980, p. 37.
60 For further information on Holekrash, see Max Weinreich, 'Holekrash: A Jewish Rite of Passage', in *Folklore International, Essays in Traditional Literature, Belief, and Custom in Honour of Wayland Debs Hand*, ed. D. Wilgus (Pennsylvania, 1967), pp. 243–53.
61 *Zeitschrift für Demographie und Statistik der Juden* (hereafter: *ZDSJ*), Berlin, February 1910, p. 29; January–February 1924, p. 25; October 1930, p. 54. The differences are even more pronounced in the cities. In 1904 in Berlin and Hamburg respectively 19 per cent of men and 13 per cent of women and 8 per cent of men and 5 per cent of women married out of the Jewish faith: *ZDSJ*, January 1905, p. 11 and March 1906, p. 47.
62 *ZDSJ*, January 1908, p. 13.
63 Toury suggests that in all of Germany, approximately 11,000 Jews converted between 1800 and 1870. Thereafter, between 1870 and 1900 another 11,500 conversions took place: Jacob Toury, *Soziale und politische Geschichte der Juden in Deutschland, 1847–1871* (Duesseldorf, 1977), p. 60. See also *Im deutschen Reich*, August 1913, pp. 339, 342.
64 Eva Ehrenberg, *Sehnsucht–mein geliebtes Kind* (Frankfurt-am-Main, 1963), p. 24.
65 Henriette Hirsch, memoirs, LBI, p. 65. This was a very common phenomenon, mentioned in many memoirs.

66 Rahel Straus, 'Ehe und Mutterschaft', in *Vom jüdischen Geiste: Ein Aufsatzreihe*, ed. Der Jeudische Frauenbund (Berlin, 1934), p. 21.

67 Marion A. Kaplan, *The Jewish Feminist Movement in Germany: The Campaigns of the Jüdischer Frauenbund, 1904–1938* (Conn., 1979), p. 86.

68 See, for example, the activities of Henriette Goldschmidt, Rosa Vogelstein and Henriette Fürth. The first two women were wives of rabbis.

Jewish assimilation in Habsburg Vienna

MARSHA L. ROZENBLIT

The Jews of Central Europe were not legally emancipated until the last third of the nineteenth century. But, long before, they had correctly perceived that the societies in which they lived desired, even expected, them to abandon traditional Jewish life-styles and behaviour patterns in order to become Europeans. Either as a precondition for legal rights, or in gratitude for having received those rights, Jews felt pressed to alter their occupational structure, learn to speak the vernacular, adopt European culture and reform their religion, thus changing what it meant to be Jewish.[1]

Most Jews in Central Europe accepted the challenge and embraced modernity. They took advantage of the social and economic opportunities open to them even before complete emancipation, and they embarked on an admittedly slow but nevertheless very real process of transformation. Learning German, adopting German names, obtaining secular education, becoming respectable businessmen and modern-style commercial employees (rather than petty traders and pedlars), reforming Judaism and asserting their patriotism, Jews declared that they had become members of Central European society. Although the transformation did not affect most German Jews until the third quarter of the nineteenth century, the process nevertheless ultimately engulfed them all.[2]

Despite the preconception of some radicals, Jewish modernization did not precipitate total assimilation, the disintegration of Jewish group identity. Jews certainly acculturated – adopting the outward cultural forms of European society – but they did not disappear. Instead, Jews generally associated primarily with other Jews, inhabiting a Jewish social universe and maintaining Jewish cohesiveness. Moreover, Jewish leaders constructed new ideologies which would justify continued Jewish distinctiveness. Jewish integration, therefore, generated a new kind of Jew, but it did not herald the demise of the Jewish people. Hostility to the Jews played an important role in continued Jewish identity, but surely the urge to remain Jewish equally helped to preserve the Jews as a distinct group.

Habsburg Vienna provides a significant case of Central European Jewish acculturation. The patterns of settlement and the demographic composition of the community meant that integration followed a different timetable than in other cities. The size and nature of the Jewish population facilitated rapid acculturation in the early nineteenth century and impeded the process of assimilation in the second half of the century. Although the impetus to acculturate encouraged Jews throughout the century to abandon traditional Jewish behaviour patterns and to adopt a modern urban life-style, the realities of late Habsburg Vienna generated an especially vigorous reassertion of Jewish identity, thus guaranteeing continued group cohesiveness.

Until the revolution of 1848, Austrian law prohibited Jewish settlement in Vienna and prevented the establishment of an organized community in the Austrian capital. The authorities did, however, permit a few wealthy Jewish merchants the privilege of residing and doing business in Vienna. These 'tolerated' Jews, their families, employees and retainers, as well as some illegal residents, together made up Viennese Jewry, which numbered, according to very approximate estimates, some 300 souls in 1800, 900 in 1820, 2,000 by 1840, and almost 4,000 by 1848.[3] Only after the revolution and the lifting of residency restrictions did Jews stream into Vienna from the Austrian provinces. By 1869, when the first accurate statistics became available, the Jewish community had grown ten times, and over 40,000 Jews resided in the Austrian capital; by 1880 their numbers had nearly doubled again, now to 73,222. By the turn of the century 146,926 Jews were living in Vienna. On the eve of the First World War Vienna's Jews numbered 175,318.[4] Vienna as a whole experienced rapid population growth in this period as well, growing from approximately half a million people in 1857 to over two million by 1910. Thus, despite their demographic growth the Jews continued to form about 9 per cent of the total urban population in the final decades of the Monarchy.[5]

In the first half of the nineteenth century, the tiny Jewish community of Vienna went far in adopting the German culture around them. It is true that despite Joseph II's Edict of Toleration in 1782 and despite their privileges, the Jewish merchants in Vienna endured endless restrictions, oppressive taxes and a profoundly precarious legal status. Moreover, the authorities refused to allow them to organize an official community. Nevertheless, most Viennese Jews in this period possessed great wealth – they could not reside in the city without it – and many of them sought entrée into Austrian high society. The Arnstein and Eskeles families, for example, entertained European diplomats during the Congress of Vienna in 1815, and Fanny Arnstein and other wealthy Jewish women ran literary salons where they mixed with the intellectual elite of Austria. Religious observance in this group probably declined considerably in the early decades of the century.[6]

However, it is impossible to measure exactly the degree to which the Viennese Jews in the 1820s or 1830s assimilated. What can be stated with certainty is that the very nature of the community certainly precluded a traditional Jewish occupational distribution and life-style. Many of the tolerated Jews were large-scale business-men, trading in silk, wool or jewels, while others were bankers, and some were manufacturers (of textiles and chocolate, for example). Several had received imperial patents of nobility for their services to the crown.[7] Moreover, the absence of a traditional Jewish commun-ity, a *kehillah*, to enforce normative Jewish religious and social behaviour certainly facilitated both growing Jewish religious indif-ference and the adoption of European culture. Those Jews who sought integration could pursue their goals without fear of ex-communication, ostracism or organized opposition to their new life-styles.

The fact that Viennese Jews were among the earliest in Europe to reform religious worship provides clear evidence that as early as the 1820s most of them had internalized the cultural values of European society. In 1819, a group of tolerated Jews led by the wealthy merchant Michael Lazar Biedermann petitioned the government to allow them to introduce an organ, a German-language sermon and some German prayers in the services in the synagogue first permitted to the Jews in 1811. Seeking reforms along the lines of those advocated in Berlin and Hamburg, these Jews articulated a desire to 'abolish the abuses' of Jewish worship. They wanted to make religious services relevant to their modern sensibilities, and 'to promote true religiosity, inculcate pure moral teaching and ennoble the heart'.[8] Although the authorites refused permission to introduce these reforms, in 1826 they did allow the Jews to hire a modern rabbi and renovate the synagogue, creating a dignified setting for prayer.

Isak Noah Mannheimer, the 'religious teacher' hired by Viennese Jews, belonged to the first generation of European reform rabbis. Born in Copenhagen in 1793, Mannheimer possessed a secular education and impressive oratorical abilities. Firmly instructed by the government not to introduce any innovations not sanctioned by Jewish religious tradition, he constructed a form of synagogue worship for Vienna – the Vienna Rite – that satisfied the prevailing demand for dignity and worthiness in Judaism.[9]

In the 1829 statutes that he crafted for the *Stadttempel*, the newly renovated synagogue of Vienna, Mannheimer announced that Viennese Jews would use the traditional Jewish liturgy, but they would do so in an atmosphere designed to stimulate devotion and religious elevation. Order and decorum would reign supreme. The statutes stipulated that Jews must take their seats silently, not walk about during services and remain quiet at all times. Congregants should not pray aloud, except during periods of communal singing, and even mourners had to intone the *kaddish* softly so as not to interfere with the cantor's rendition of the mourner's prayer. The statutes also abolished the public sale of synagogue honours. Above all, the *Synagogenordnungen* of 1829 called for a musically exquisite cantor to lead services and for a 'religious teacher' (later called preacher) to serve as pastor and spiritual leader for the Jews. Clearly emulating modernized Christian forms of worship, Viennese Jews wanted a rabbi with a secular education to give edifying sermons, and they expected these sermons to form the focal point of the synagogue service. Such concerns resembled those of modernizing Jewish communities in other German states in this period, but their zeal for a new-style rabbi placed Viennese Jews at the forefront of early religious change in Central Europe – although it should be stressed that the emphasis here was on the aesthetic rather than the liturgical aspects of reform.[10]

The synagogue which the Viennese Jews rebuilt in 1826, the *Stadttempel*, certainly provided the wealthy with a setting for prayer that corresponded to their self-image as men of status and prestige. Austrian authorities prevented them from constructing a synagogue that could be identified as such from the street, but inside the shell of an ordinary building on Seitenstettengasse in the Inner City, Vienna's Jewish notables built an impressive place of worship, which conformed to the demands of Jewish religious tradition, except for the fact that the reader's desk, or *bimah*, was placed at the front of the congregation.[11] Moreover, the cantor hired by the Viennese Jews in 1826, Salomon Sulzer, not only sang magnificently, but also composed music for the *Stadttempel* which added immeasurably to the beauty of the liturgy.[12] Viennese Jews could now feel that Jewish worship compared favourably with that in any church. They had successfully modernized the service so that its style reflected wealthy European taste.

Despite their eagerness for aestheticizing Jewish worship, Viennese Jews never did reform the content of Jewish liturgy. In the 1820s a combination of government opposition and traditionalist pressure precluded radical religious innovation. The Vienna Rite, first composed in 1826, and published in Mannheimer's 1840 prayerbook, remained a traditional service conducted entirely in Hebrew. Only the sermon and some prayers for the government were in German. While Mannheimer did excise a few prayers which offended reform sensibilities – a few *piyyutim*, some vengeful prayers, and some Talmud passages – he did not remove any of the prayers of central concern to the ideologues of Reform. Thus Jews in Vienna continued to pray for a Jewish return to Zion, and for the restitution there of the Davidic dynasty and the sacrificial system of worship.[13] Moreover, despite their initial efforts, the Viennese Jews never installed an organ, that symbol of the Reform movement, in their beautiful, modern synagogue.[14]

Viennese Jews in the 1820s successfully reformed their services and created a modern synagogue style consonant with European taste without any of the communal conflict so typical of religious reform in Europe. They could do so because most Jews in the Austrian capital were wealthy merchants who had managed to adopt European tastes, and because Viennese-Jewish traditionalists possessed no institutional structures from which to attack the modernists. The utter precariousness of the Jewish legal position which dictated that only wealthy Jews could live in Vienna, and the consequent tiny size and institutional weakness of the unofficial community made both acculturation and religious modernization possible and painless.

In the 1840s the situation began to change. The government did not permit the formation of an organized, legally constituted Jewish community until 1849, and the system of permitting only wealthy Jews the privilege of toleration persisted until the revolution of 1848. Nevertheless, the Jewish population of Vienna grew significantly in the 1840s probably because the government then ignored the presence of many Jews residing illegally in the capital.

Although no information is available about the economic standing of these Jews, most were, in all likelihood, poorer and more traditional in life-style than the great 'tolerated' merchants. Many of them rejected the modern style of services at the *Seitenstettengassentempel*. Despite official Jewish attempts to eliminate private synagogues, the number of small, informal prayer groups (*minyanim*) which adhered to a more traditional style of worship grew in the two decades before 1848.[15] And this development probably acted as a further brake on the reform of the Viennese liturgy.

In the 1840s, removing the prayers for Zion became a central issue in the Reform movement in the states which would later constitute the German Empire. But Viennese Jews did not even consider tampering in this way with the content of the services they had instituted in the *Stadttempel*. The growth in the number of more traditional Jews, governmental opposition to substantive reform and a semi-feudal state structure which did not yet demand modern national identification, all combined to create a situation in which Jews must have felt that prayers for Zion in no way called their political loyalties into question. Moreover, Viennese Jewish spokesmen, like Isak Noah Mannheimer himself, understood Jewish attachments to Zion in wholly symbolic terms and viewed Jewish peoplehood as a religious concept, thus rendering prayers for Zion uncontroversial in the Austrian context.[16]

Only when the government lifted Jewish residency restrictions in 1848 did Jews migrate to the Austrian capital in large numbers. This migration transformed a small, relatively well-to-do community into one with huge numbers of poor, traditional Jews. Indeed, in 1869, only one-third of the 40,000 Jews in the city possessed sufficient means to pay taxes to the *Israelitische Kultusgemeinde*, the organized Jewish community, and this proportion held good until the First World War.[17] Different groups of Jews migrated to Vienna, each with its own level of wealth and modernization. In the initial phase of the migration, from 1848 until 1880, Jewish migrants to Vienna came from Bohemia and Moravia, and to an even greater extent from Hungary, especially from western Hungary and western Slovakia. Thus, about 20 per cent of the fathers of Jewish children born in Vienna in 1860 had themselves been born in Czech lands, and 40 per cent in Hungary. By 1880, the figures were 26 per cent and 45 per cent respectively.[18]

On the other hand, during this period few Jews migrated to Vienna from Galicia. In 1860, only 7 per cent of the fathers and in 1880 only

15 per cent were born in Galicia or Bukovina. It was not until the turn of the twentieth century that large numbers of Galician Jews, fleeing acute problems at home, flooded into the Austrian capital, transforming the very nature of Viennese Jewish life. Thus, by 1910, only 14 per cent of new Jewish fathers came from Bohemia and Moravia; 19 per cent from Hungary; and over one-third (35 per cent) from Galicia.[19]

Bohemian Jews were the richest of all these immigrants, or at least the most successful of all the immigrant groups once they had established themselves in the city. In 1860, 5 per cent of the fathers of Jewish children born in Vienna had themselves been born in Bohemia, but 8 per cent of the new entrants to the *Israelitische Kultusgemeinde*'s tax rolls in the period between 1855 and 1867 were of Bohemian origin. Moravian Jews were able to pay their Jewish communal taxes in proportion to their share of the Jewish population. The Hungarians, however, were by far the poorest of all the early Jewish immigrants to the capital. In 1869, 42 per cent of the fathers of Jewish children born in Vienna in that year were Hungarian, but in the period from 1855 to 1867 only 22 per cent of all new taxpayers had been born in Hungary. Although the early Galician Jews in Vienna appear to have been prosperous, those arriving in large numbers at the turn of the century were destitute. In the 1860s and 1870s Galician Jews paid a proportional share of *Gemeinde* taxes. By 1910, when 35 per cent of the new fathers came from Galicia, only 5 per cent of the new taxpayers had been born in that part of the Habsburg Empire.[20]

It is impossible to measure the extent to which the Jews who migrated to Vienna had already Europeanized. Some of the Jews (including those from small towns) who migrated from Bohemia, Moravia, Hungary and even Galicia had adopted the German language and modern culture before their arrival. Their urbanization therefore only augmented modernization and economic enterprise already initiated. Joseph Wechsberg's memoirs, for example, reveal that the German-speaking, prosperous Jews of Ostrau, Moravia, translated their yearning for further advance into migration to Vienna.[21] In Germany as well, urbanization often followed economic modernization and acculturation.[22] Of course many Jews who migrated to Vienna came from Prague, Budapest, Lemberg and Cracow, and many of them had already encountered modern European culture in those metropolitan centres. Among the Jews from Galicia, the prosperous immigrants of the 1850s, 1860s and 1870s mostly came from Lemberg and Cracow, and, predictably, these Jews sent their sons to state high schools (the gymnasiums) in numbers corresponding to their percentage of the Jewish population.

The masses of poor, traditional, small-town Jews who migrated to Vienna from Galicia at the turn of the century, on the other hand, did not send their sons to gymnasiums in significant numbers, not only because of their poverty but also because they then still remained at a distance from secular culture.[23] Although it would be unwise to advance a theory of geographical determinism, there is some evidence to suggest that the Moravian and Bohemian Jews in Vienna had already modernized to some extent prior to their migration, but that the Hungarian (and later the Galician) Jews constituted reservoirs of traditional Jews in the capital. Of course, most Jews who moved to Vienna did so because freedom of movement enabled them to escape the economic backwardness of the provinces. Some of these people welcomed Viennese opportunities to modernize, acculturate and even assimilate; others did not desire to change; and most had no time to worry about such issues.

The religious history of Viennese Jewry offers an interesting insight into the level of acculturation of the immigrants to the city. In 1858, in response to the growing size of the Jewish community, Jewish leaders opened a second communal synagogue, this time in the Leopoldstadt, Vienna's second district. The men who supervised religious affairs insisted that the services in the new temple should replicate exactly the services in the *Stadttempel*. They hired as rabbi Adolf Jellinek, a well-known modern rabbi and scholar, who lobbied for the institution of an organ in the new synagogue, an effort successfully blocked by Mannheimer.[24] Thus Jewish leaders assumed that the new immigrants either wanted modern-style services or would come to accept such services as a natural part of life in the big city. On the other hand, realizing that most Jews who attended the new temple, an elegant Moorish-style building, might behave in a more traditional (that is, noisy) style, they issued an extremely strict and detailed list of synagogue rules to ensure proper order and decorum, and they printed these rules in Hebrew characters to make sure that everyone could read them.[25]

The new immigrants proved to be somewhat more traditional than the Jewish leaders of Vienna had expected. When Mannheimer died in 1865 and Jellinek replaced him at the *Stadttempel*, the community hired Moritz Güdemann, a graduate of the Breslau Seminary and a conservative modern rabbi, to preach at the Leopoldstadt temple.[26] Moreover, after 1868, the leaders of the official community (the

Israelitische Kultusgemeinde) allowed the proliferation of private and internally autonomous synagogues. They must have reasoned that it would be better to let traditionalist Jews pray by themselves than act as a pressure group on communal services.

More important, efforts by the already modernized and acculturated Jews in Vienna to implement ideological reforms in 1871 met with such stiff opposition that the innovators had to retreat into a face-saving set of 'modifications' of the Vienna Rite. In the wake of emancipation in 1867, some Viennese Jews sought to remove prayers for Zion from the communal liturgy, arguing that such prayers represented a 'lie' for emancipated Jewry. They also sought finally to install an organ, that symbol of the Reform movement. After the *Israelitische Kultusgemeinde* voted to institute these reforms, controversy raged in the Viennese Jewish community for over a year and a half. Opponents of reform included modernized Jews who preferred to pray in the traditional manner. By far the most vocal contingent in the anti-Reform camp, however, were the members and supporters of the *Schiffschul*, a traditional private synagogue, most of whose members came from Hungary. Even when the *Gemeinde* backed down in 1872, deciding to forgo an organ and merely to relegate the prayers for Zion to silent devotion, members of the *Schiffschul* persisted in their campaign. They denounced the leaders of the *Gemeinde* as heretics and called for the creation of a separate Orthodox community in Vienna.[27] The secession campaign went on until the Austrian authorities finally insisted that it had to stop.

What prompted the Viennese Jewish leaders to abandon their drive for ideological reform was not primarily the opposition of one traditional *minyan*. Leaders of the *Gemeinde* undoubtedly feared that the rabbi of the *Schiffschul*, Salomon Spitzer, the son-in-law of the famous anti-modernist Hungarian rabbi, Moses Sofer, could mobilize the masses of traditionalist Hungarian Jews in Vienna to secede from the *Gemeinde* itself. The presence of so many Hungarian Jews in the city, and the fact that so many of them still pursued a traditional, religious life-style, acted to inhibit further religious reform. Most Hungarian Jews in Vienna came from bastions of religious Orthodoxy in western Hungary. Many came from the area around Pressburg, where the *yeshiva* provided important leadership for the struggle against religious change in Hungary. Others came from the Burgenland, where the Jewish communities persisted in their allegiance to Orthodoxy until their dissolution in 1938.[28] Naturally, not all the Hungarian Jews in Vienna were still attached to

Jewish tradition, but in the early 1870s they remained traditional in sufficient numbers to pose a threat to the organized
community.[29]

In the second half of the nineteenth century, then, and especially in
the decades after the emancipation of 1867, Viennese Jewry experienced two simultaneous processes: the modernization and acculturation of the Jews who had settled in the capital and the constant
infusion of new immigrants, a large proportion of whom pursued
traditional life-styles at the time of their arrival. By the end of the
century, many Viennese Jews had indeed acculturated. They spoke
High German and had adopted German names. They also dressed
and acted like other Austrians, obtained a secular education and
identified with German culture, while simultaneously largely abandoning much of Jewish ritual observance. They prided themselves on
being loyal Austrian citizens.[30] Some became leading figures in
Austro-German culture and leaders of the literary and musical avant-
garde. Indeed, the existence of people like Arthur Schnitzler, Stefan
Zweig, Gustav Mahler and Sigmund Freud has led many to assume
that Viennese Jewry was well on the way to total assimilation. The
frequency of conversion to Christianity among the Jewish upper
classes has reinforced the notion of a rapidly assimilating Jewish
population. Nevertheless, because migration was constant, and
growing from decade to decade, Vienna always contained a large
percentage of traditional Jews.

More significant, perhaps, than this constant influx of newcomers
from the east was the fact that even when Jews in Vienna
acculturated, they did not, for the most part, sever their ties with
Jewish life. The urban environment encouraged Jews to abandon
traditional Jewish life-styles, but Jews in Vienna created new forms of
behaviour that continued to mark them as Jews, both to themselves
and to the gentiles in whose midst they lived. Jews continued to
concentrate in certain sectors of the economy, they tended to live in
Jewish neighbourhoods, to associate with, befriend and marry other
Jews and to inhabit a Jewish social universe. They also developed new
ideologies which asserted the legitimacy of continued Jewish distinctiveness in the modern world.

The economic transformation of the Jews provides an important
illustration of how Jews did not assimilate into the society around
them. In Austria Jews traditionally had concentrated largely in petty
trade. Jews who migrated to Vienna, and especially their Viennese-
born children, tended to forsake this type of livelihood in order to

pursue careers as middle-class businessmen, as clerks, salesmen and managers, or as professionals. In the late nineteenth century, about two-fifths of Jews in the work-force were merchants, one-quarter pursued clerical, managerial and sales positions in private enterprise, 12 per cent were professionals, 4 per cent were industrialists, 3 per cent civil servants, 12 per cent artisans and 4 per cent workers.[31] Although only 3 per cent of all Jewish men marrying in 1870 worked as 'business employees', by 1910 35 per cent of Jewish bridegrooms pursued careers as clerks, salesmen and managers. This new economic concentration certainly reflected the acculturation of Viennese Jews. These clerks and managers spoke German well, dressed like other Viennese burghers and probably had to violate the sabbath to pursue their new careers.

However, despite acculturation, the Jews tended to remain distinct from the rest of the Viennese work-force. Most Viennese concentrated in the industrial sector of the economy and worked in the factories and workshops of the city. A much smaller percentage of gentiles than of Jews worked as merchants. Although many Viennese worked as clerks, they did so for the imperial or municipal civil service, and much less frequently for private businesses. In 1910, only 12.5 per cent of all Catholics in Vienna held clerical, sales or managerial positions in industry or commerce, but 30.8 per cent of all Jews did so.[32] Thus, the Jews retained a distinct position in the Viennese economy. Given the traditional concentration of the Jews in trade, it would have been surprising if modernization had taken a different course, simply eliminating ethnic divergences.

Jews in Vienna also asserted their distinctiveness by clustering in certain neighbourhoods. In 1880, almost half of Vienna's 73,000 Jews lived in the Leopoldstadt (District II), 17 per cent in the Inner City (District I) and 10 per cent in the Alsergrund (District IX);[33] and by the end of the century the Leopoldstadt had become the Jewish ghetto in the popular imagination. Sigmund Mayer, a wealthy Jewish businessman, noted in his memoirs that the influx of traditional Jews into the Leopoldstadt gave it a noticeably Jewish atmosphere: stores were closed on Saturday and people scurried through the streets on Friday carrying large pots of *cholent*, the traditional sabbath dish.[34] The Leopoldstadt (with the Brigittenau, Vienna's District XX), a large island in the Danube Canal, came to be called *Die Mazzesinsel*, the island of matzah, because of the large number of Jews it contained.[35]

Jews tended to live with Jews rather than with other people of their own social class. Although within areas of Jewish concentration rich and poor did not necessarily live side by side, both categories did reside in the same districts, especially in the Leopoldstadt and the Alsergrund. An examination of a cross-sectional sample of Viennese Jewry, of *Gemeinde* taxpayers and community charity recipients reveals striking similarities in the residential concentration of prosperous and poverty-stricken Jews. True, rich Jews tended to favour residences in the fashionable Inner City where poor Jews almost never lived. The Jewish lower class was most likely to live in the Leopoldstadt, but that area none the less continued to attract large numbers of prosperous Jews. About a quarter of all *Gemeinde* taxpayers (and about 15 per cent of the richest taxpayers) lived there.[36]

Jewish immigrants also tended to take up residence among other Jews rather than with gentiles who came from the same part of the monarchy. Thus, for example, Jews from Bohemia and Moravia lived with Hungarian Jews rather than with Czech gentiles, most of whom lived in Favoriten (District X). Of course class differences are important here: most Czechs in Vienna were working class and few Jews worked in Vienna's factories. Nevertheless, Bohemian and Moravian Jews also avoided middle-class Czech neighbourhoods in Landstrasse (District III) and elsewhere, undoubtedly because of linguistic, cultural, religious and ethnic barriers.[37]

Jews in Vienna also erected a rich network of organizations within which they could mix with other Jews, work for good causes, receive recognition and assert Jewish identity. Alongside the legally mandated *Israelitische Kultusgemeinde*, which handled religious matters, there existed literally hundreds of charitable, humanitarian, social, cultural and political organizations. Some of these organizations met the desire of the wealthy to help poor Jews. Others provided opportunities for recent immigrants to associate with people from their home territory and offer each other mutual sustenance. Still others enabled adults or the youth to gather and work for political causes. Singing clubs, gymnastic associations, reading groups, women's societies and political organizations may have had different agendas, but they all served to create a social world in which Jews associated to a large extent with each other.[38]

Jews tended to befriend and marry each other. No statistical evidence exists about Jewish friendship patterns. The memoir literature, however, indicates that even men and women who were almost totally assimilated mainly mixed with other Jews. Stefan

Zweig, for example, wrote that nine-tenths of his friends were other bourgeois Jews. Arthur Schnitzler moved 'in the solid Jewish bourgeois circles', and Sigmund Freud's disciples, friends and associates tended to be other Jews.[39] The Jewish boys who attended gymnasiums surely adopted German culture in those elite institutions, but secondary education did not provide Viennese Jews with many opportunities to make friends with gentiles. Indeed, most Jewish boys in gymnasiums attended the schools in the first, second and ninth districts which contained an overwhelming proportion of Jewish pupils. Of the high-school boys in the Leopoldstadt, four-fifths were Jewish; in the ninth district, two-thirds; and in the Inner City, two-fifths. In such an environment, Jews experienced acculturation in the company of other Jews.[40] And if such highly acculturated Jews had mostly Jewish friends, then surely ordinary Jewish men and women tended to make their friends among fellow Jews as well.[41]

Intermarriage – that is Jewish–gentile marriage – was probably also relatively rare in Vienna. According to the official statistics, in 1895 only about 4 per cent of the Jews who married did so with non-Jews. In fact, however, the number was higher. Austrian law prohibited civil intermarriage, and thus one of the partners in a mixed marriage had to convert to the religion of the other, or to a neutral category, *konfessionslos* (without religion), prior to the marriage. The 4 per cent statistic only includes those Jews who married *konfessionslos* partners. It is thus impossible to gauge the true number of mixed marriages.[42] Conversion to Christianity, on the other hand, did occur relatively frequently in the Habsburg capital. In 1868 only seven Jews converted, but in 1880 110 converted to Christianity or *Konfessionslosigkeit*, and in 1900 599 did so.[43] Vienna's conversion rate was the highest in late nineteenth-century Europe. Not all of Vienna's Jewish converts accepted baptism to enhance their careers or to assimilate totally. Many converted simply to marry. With the notable exception of such famous converts as the composer Gustav Mahler, the satirist Karl Kraus or the socialist Victor Adler, most converts, or at least their offspring, probably did assimilate fully into Viennese society, even if that was not their original intention. Nevertheless, although Vienna's conversion rate was high by contemporary standards, it did not pose a threat to the vitality of Jewish life in Vienna.[44]

In addition to erecting structural barriers to assimilation, Jews articulated ideological justifications for separate Jewish identity. In the early and middle years of the nineteenth century they conceived this identity in religious terms. Rabbis like Isak Noah Mannheimer, Adolf Jellinek and Moritz Güdemann all propounded the notion that the Jews constituted a people with a religious mission to spread the word of God in the world. None of these rabbis reduced the notion of Jewishness, however, to an abstract set of theological principles. They all asserted an identity for the Jews that was not only religious but also carried ethnic overtones.

Mannheimer, for example, reiterated that Judaism was not a set of philosophical doctrines but 'a historically transmitted . . . interconnected whole, made holy through divine revelation, established through paternal tradition and filial piety and through a sense of belonging'. What united the Jews in this view, was in large part their sense of belonging together.[45] Mannheimer liberally used the word *Volk* (people) to refer to the Jews, although he conceived the Jewish people as a religious community, receiving spiritual sustenance from the Torah, working for the victory of God in the world.[46]

Similarly, Adolf Jellinek always used words like *Stamm* (tribe) and *Volk* to refer to the Jewish people, although he too saw the Jews as a people endowed with the duty to spread the values of the Torah: freedom, loyalty, love, justice, morality and especially monotheism in the world. The Jewish people – loyal to the countries in which they resided – possessed no political or national aspirations; on the contrary, their genius lay precisely in that they functioned solely as a religious community spreading the word of God.[47]

Moritz Güdemann, more conservative in religious matters than either Mannheimer or Jellinek, espoused identical views to his more reform-minded colleagues. Although he defended the retention of prayers for Zion in the liturgy, he based his defence on the symbolic significance of Zion in Judaism. Prayers for Zion, he insisted in a sermon of 1871, only served to express the longing for God's redemption of all mankind.[48] The Jews were a religious community, a people bound together by belief in God, fulfilling a religious mission: spreading the prophetic message and helping the other nations to recognize God and thus facilitate redemption. For Güdemann, Jewish ethnic consciousness was identical to the Jewish belief in God.[49] All of these men emphasized the universal dimensions of Judaism even as they acknowledged the distinctiveness of the Jewish people.

Naturally not all Viennese Jews thought in such lofty terms in the middle of the nineteenth century, yet most would probably have agreed with their rabbis. Assimilating Jews all over Europe defined

Jewishness in religious terms in that period. The sermons and writings of the Viennese rabbis, however, reveal that such a religious definition transcended the mere confessional and included an ethnic aspect as well. These Jews may not have thought in secular national terms, but their sense of Jewish identity did include the emotional, familial bonds that unite all Jews. Acculturating Jews did not abandon the national component of Jewish identity as the Zionists later charged. They merely understood the national or ethnic dimension of Jewishness in religious terms because such an under-standing facilitated the integration into European society which they desired. Despite the religious rhetoric, most Jews still felt that they belonged to the Jewish people. In a sense, therefore, they understood Jewish identity in a traditionally Jewish way: as an interrelated web of religion and peoplehood. Modernization for them did not mean a radical re-definition of what it meant to be a Jew, but merely the continuation of normative Jewish views. Whether such views were unique to Vienna or dominated modern Jewish communities remains to be seen. If Viennese Jews had a stronger sense of Jewish ethnic identity than did other acculturated Jews in this period it is because of the multinational nature of Austria and the more traditional composition of the Viennese Jewish community.[50]

This strong sense of Jewish peoplehood enabled Viennese Jews to respond forcefully to the threat of antisemitism in the 1870s and 1880s. In 1886 they organized a defence organization, the *Österreichisch-Israelitische Union*. This organization not only took the antisemites to court, it also vigorously asserted Jewish pride and Jewish folk-consciousness. Emphasizing the Austrian patriotism of its large membership, the Union firmly declared the legitimacy of preserving Jewish consciousness.[51] In the twentieth century Zionism and other forms of Jewish nationalism also attracted many Viennese Jews.

The patterns of Jewish acculturation and assimilation in Vienna both resembled and differed from those unfolding elsewhere in Central and Western Europe, and the differences derived from the demographic composition of the Viennese Jewish community itself. At the beginning of the nineteenth century, the tiny size and wealthy composition of the community generated one of the most assimilated Jewish communities in Europe. Viennese Jewry – unlike the Jewish communities of French or German cities – became more socially and culturally distinct with the passage of time. Of course, assimilated

Jews rarely reverted to the traditional way of life. Rather, the influx of traditional Jews from the 1840s onwards created a large, constantly renewable reservoir of non-acculturated or partially acculturated Jews.

Urbanization in Germany did not necessarily create similar reservoirs in Berlin or Frankfurt, since Jews in the small towns of the hinterlands had largely modernized before their move to the cities. The fact that Vienna's immigration arrived primarily from bastions of Jewish traditionalism in Hungary and Galicia, areas of dense Jewish concentration and staunch Jewish loyalty, meant that in the second half of the nineteenth century Vienna became the home of large numbers of non-modern Jews. Of course many of these Jews successfully acculturated and some disappeared totally into the majority population. Nevertheless, the deep-rooted urge of Jews to remain Jewish, combined with the simultaneous influx of new immigrants and the potency of Viennese antisemitism, guaranteed the group's distinctiveness in the Habsburg capital. Whether because of the will to survive or as an expression of pride in the face of hostility, Viennese Jews continued to assert their own identity and cohesion in the nineteenth century.

Notes

1 Jacob Katz, *Out of the Ghetto: The Social Background of Jewish Emancipation, 1770–1870* (Cambridge, Mass., 1973), pp. 57–79.
2 For an excellent discussion of the process of Jewish modernization in Germany – and the slow pace of that process – see Steven M. Lowenstein, 'The Pace of Modernisation of German Jewry in the Nineteenth Century', *Leo Baeck Institute Yearbook* 21 (1976), 41–56.
3 Akos Löw, 'Die soziale Zusammensetzung der Wiener Juden nach den Trauungs- und Geburtsmatrikeln, 1784–1848', unpublished Ph.D. dissertation, University of Vienna, 1952, pp. 161–3; Israel Jeiteles, *Die Kultusgemende der Israeliten in Wien mit Benützung des statistischen Volkszählungsoperatus vom Jahre 1869* (Vienna, 1873), pp. 40–3.
4 K.-k. Statistische Central-Commission, *Bevölkerung und Viehstand von Böhmen etc. nach der Zählung vom 31. Dezember 1869* (Vienna, 1871), vol. XI, 'Nieder-Oesterreich', pp. 2–13; K.-k. Statistische Central-Commission, *Österreichische Statistik* 1:2, pp. 2–3; 63:1, pp. 48–9; *Statistisches Jahrbuch der Stadt Wien* (1910), p. 25.
5 For a fuller discussion see Marsha L. Rozenblit, *The Jews of Vienna, 1867–1914: Assimilation and Identity* (Albany, 1983), pp. 16–18. On general Viennese population see *Bevölkerung und Viehstand . . . 1869*, vol. XI, pp. 2–13 and *Österreichische Statistik*, n.s., 2:1, p. 33*.

6 Max Grunwald, *Vienna* (Philadelphia, 1936), pp. 155–213; Sigmund Mayer, *Die Wiener Juden 1700–1900: Kommerz, Kultur, Politik* (Vienna and Berlin, 1917), pp. 273–300.

7 For biographical sketches of all the tolerated Jews in Vienna in 1829, see Bernard Wachstein, 'Das Statut für das Bethaus der Israeliten in Wien: Seine Urheber und Gutheisser', in *Die ersten Statuten des Bethauses in der Inneren Stadt aus Anlass der Jahrhundertfeier (2. Nissan 5686/17. März 1926)* (Vienna, 1926), pp. 9–36.

8 Sigmund Husserl, *Gründungsgeschichte des Stadt-Tempels der Israel. Kultusgemeinde Wien* (Vienna and Leipzig, 1906), esp. pp. 66–113; Gerson Wolf, *Vom ersten bis zum zweiten Tempel: Geschichte der Israelitischen Cultusgemeinde in Wien (1820–1860)* (Vienna, 1861), pp. 14–17. For general overviews of religious reform in Vienna in the 1820s see Hans Tietze, *Die Juden Wiens: Geschichte-Wirtschaft-Kultur* (Leipzig and Vienna, 1933), pp. 150–7 and most recently Michael A. Meyer, *Response to Modernity: A History of the Reform Movement in Judaism* (New York and Oxford, 1988), pp. 146–51.

9 Moses Rosenmann, *Isak Noa Mannheimer: Sein Leben und Wirken* (Vienna and Berlin, 1922), pp. 21–7, 36, 54, 57, 62, 66. On Mannheimer's oratorical abilities, see Alexander Altmann, 'The New Style of Preaching in Nineteenth-Century German Jewry', in Alexander Altmann (ed.), *Studies in Nineteenth-Century Jewish Intellectual History* (Cambridge, Mass., 1964), pp. 71–2, 79, 100.

10 'Statuten für das Bethaus der Israeliten in Wien', Central Archives for the History of the Jewish People (hereafter: CAHJP), AW 1271. For comparison with German *Synagogenordnungen*, see Steven M. Lowenstein, 'The 1840s and the Creation of the German-Jewish Religious Reform Movement', in *Revolution and Evolution: 1848 in German-Jewish History*, edited by Werner E. Mosse, Arnold Paucker and Reinhard Rürup (Tübingen, 1981), pp. 255–97; and Jakob J. Petuchowski, *Prayerbook Reform in Europe: The Liturgy of Liberal and Reform Judaism* (New York, 1968), pp. 105–22. On the rise of the modern, pastoral rabbi see Ismar Schorsch, 'Emancipation and the Crisis of Religious Authority – The Emergence of the Modern Rabbinate', in *Revolution and Evolution*, pp. 205–47.

11 Max Eisler, 'Die Seitenstetten Tempel', in '100 Jahre Wiener Stadt-Tempel. Jubiläumsausgabe 5586-5686, 1826–1926', *Menorah* (March 1926), pp. 154–5, 157 in CAHJP, AW 1271; Meyer, *Response to Modernity*, pp. 147–9.

12 Hanoch Avenary (ed.), *Kantor Salomon Sulzer und seine Zeit: Eine Documentation* (Sigmaringen, 1985); Salomon Sulzer, *Schir Zion: Gesänge für den israelitischen Gottesdienst* (1838; rev. edn, ed. Joseph Sulzer, Leipzig, 1905).

13 Letter of Mannheimer to Leopold Zunz, 31 October 1826, in M. Brann and M. Rosenmann, 'Der Briefwechsel zwischen Isak Noa Mannheimer

und Leopold Zunz', *Monatsschrift für Geschichte und Wissenschaft des Judenthums*, n.s., 25 (1917), 299–300; letters of Mannheimer to Dr Wolff, rabbi in Copenhagen, 22 July 1829 and 4 July 1830, in 'Zwei interessante Briefe Mannheimer's', in ibid., 20 (1871), 280–2, 334–5; I. N. Mannheimer, *Tefilat Israel; Gebete der Israeliten*, 4th rev. edn (Vienna, 1851). Mannheimer's prayerbook remained unchanged through scores of reprintings down to the present.

14 Letter of Mannheimer to Wolff, 4 July 1830, 'Zwei interessante Briefe', pp. 334–5; Rosenmann, *Mannheimer*, pp. 93–4.

15 The only private synagogue which Jewish leaders permitted was the so-called Polish synagogue. See *Bethaus Verwaltung Protocolle 1832–35*, 20 October 1832, in CAHJP, AW 1258/3. On suppression of private *minyanim* see, for example, 2 May 1833, 8 October 1833, 31 August 1835 in ibid.; 21 May 1840 in *Bethaus Verwaltung Protocolle 1835–42*, AW 1258/4.

16 On Mannheimer's positive defence of prayers for Zion see his 1841 opinion on the new Hamburg Temple Prayerbook, printed in *Theologische Gutachten über das Gebetbuch nach dem Gebrauche des neuen Israelitischen Tempelvereins in Hamburg* (Hamburg, 1842), p. 97. On his understanding of Jewish peoplehood in religious terms see his *Gottesdienstliche Vorträge gehalten im israelitischen Bethause in Wien* (Vienna, 1876), especially vol. 1, pp. 48–66; vol. 11, pp. 20–37 and 78–100.

17 In 1869, about 2,000 Jewish men paid taxes to the *Gemeinde*. Multiplying that number by six to account for wives, children and other dependants, only 12,000 of Vienna's 40,000 Jews could pay their taxes. For a list of Jewish taxpayers see *Verzeichniss der Mitglieder der israelitischen Kultusgemeinde in Wien 1869* in CAHJP, AW 46. In 1857 approximately 1,000 Jews paid taxes to the *Gemeinde* – see the list for 1857 in CAHJP, AW 34 – but since the Austrian census did not enumerate actual residents in that year, it is impossible to determine the percentage of all Jews able to pay taxes. For similar lists of voters in 1880, 1890, 1900 and 1910, see CAHJP, AW 3086, 3096, 50/10 and 55/1. Performing similar arithmetic with these lists as in 1869 reveals that two-thirds of all Jews were poor, incapable of paying 10 gulden or 20 Kronen (the minimum tax – worth about $5 in America at that time) to support the Jewish community.

18 Figures for the period after 1850 are based on my computer-assisted analysis of 947 Jewish brides and grooms from 1870, 1880, 1890, 1900 and 1910; 1,387 mothers and fathers of Jewish newborns in 1869, 1880, 1890, 1900, and 1910; and 177 mothers and fathers in 1860. The birth and marriage registers are located at the present offices of the *Israelitische Kultusgemeinde* in Vienna. For a fuller discussion of the migration of Jews to Vienna and the demographic composition of the Jewish community see my *Jews of Vienna*, pp. 13–45. For information on the 1840s see Löw, 'Die soziale Zusammensetzung', pp. 152–4.

19 Marsha L. Rozenblit, 'A Note on Galician Jewish Migration to Vienna', *Austrian History Yearbook*, 19–20 (1983–4, pt. 1, 145–52).

20 These figures are based on a computer-assisted analysis of the tax files of 2,609 members of the *Israelitische Kultusgemeinde* between 1855 and 1914, CAHJP, AW 805/1–25.

21 Joseph Wechsberg, *The Vienna I Knew: Memories of a European Childhood* (Garden City, N.Y., 1979), p. 137.

22 Steven M. Lowenstein, 'The Rural Community and the Urbanization of German Jewry', *Central European History* 13, no. 3 (1980), 218–36.

23 Rozenblit, *Jews of Vienna*, pp. 36–7, 40–1, 115–16.

24 17 June 1858, 24 June 1858, *Bethaus-Vorstand Protokolle 1858*, CAHJP, AW 1259/4; letter from IKG to Bethaus-Vorstand, 18 June 1858, Akten des Bethausvorstandes, 1851–81, AW 1264/2; Rosenmann, *Mannheimer*, pp. 93–4; Moses Rosenmann, *Dr. Adolf Jellinek; Sein Leben und Schaffen* (Vienna, 1931).

25 'Verwaltungsregeln und Verordnungen', 1864, CAHJP, AW 1760/1.

26 Moritz Güdemann, *Aus meinem Leben*, unpublished memoir, Leo Baeck Institute, 1899–1918; Ismar Schorsch, 'Moritz Güdemann – Rabbi, Historian and Apologist', *Leo Baeck Institute Yearbook* 11 (1966), 42–66.

27 CAHJP, AW 1257, 'Liturgie 1872'; AW 1224/1, *I. Sections-Protokolle 1868–75. Die Neuzeit*, Vienna's liberal Jewish newspaper closely covered the reform controversy and regularly denounced Viennese traditionalists. For the Orthdox side see *Rabbinische Gutachten betreffs der vom Vorstande der isr. Cultus-Gemeinde in Wien, am 21. Jänner J. gefassten und zur Ausführung gebrachten Reformbeschlüsse* (Vienna, 1872).

28 Hugo Gold, *Die Juden und die Judengemeinde Bratislava in Vergangenheit und Gegenwart* (Brünn, 1932); Hugo Gold, *Gedenkbuch der untergegangenen Judengemeinden des Burgenlandes* (Tel Aviv, 1970); Josef Klampfer, *Das Eisenstädter Ghetto*, Burgenländische Forschungen 51 (1966).

29 Certainly *Die Neuzeit* blamed Hungarians, especially those from Pressburg, for the fact that Vienna did not introduce ideological Reform in that period. See, for example, 3 February 1871, pp. 52–3; 10 February 1871, p. 62; 10 March 1871, pp. 110–11; 17 March 1871, pp. 121–3; 9 February 1872, pp. 61–4; 23 February 1872, pp. 85–7; 12 April 1872, pp. 172–3; 3 May 1872, pp. 203–5; 26 July 1872, pp. 337–8; 6 September 1872, pp. 399–402. For a full discussion of the reform problem in Vienna see Marsha L. Rozenblit, 'The Struggle over Religious Reform in Nineteenth-Century Vienna', *AJS Review* 14, no. 2 (1989), 179–221.

30 For a recent treatment of the loyalty of Viennese Jews to German culture see Robert S. Wistrich, 'The Modernization of Viennese Jewry: The Impact of German Culture in a Multi-Ethnic State', in Jacob Katz (ed.), *Toward Modernity: The European Jewish Model* (New Brunswick, N.J. and Oxford, 1987), pp. 43–70.

31 Rozenblit, *Jews of Vienna*, p. 50. For a full discussion of the occupational transformation of Vienna Jews, see pp. 47–70.

32 *Österreichische Statistik*, 33:1, p. viii; 66:1, p. xvi; 66:2, pp. 7–37, 49, 60–4; n.s., 3:1, p. 13*; 3:2, pp. 44–5, 132; *Statistisches Jahrbuch der Stadt Wien* (1901), pp. 67–8, 73–94.

33 Stephan Sedlaczek, *Die k.-k. Reichshaupt- und Residenzstadt Wien*: *Ergebnisse der Volkszählung vom 31. December 1880* (Vienna, 1887), pt 2, pp. 24, 126–7; *Statistisches Jahrbuch der Stadt Wien* (1901), pp. 50–1.

34 Sigmund Mayer, *Ein jüdischer Kaufmann 1831 bis 1911: Lebenserinnerungen* (Leipzig, 1911), p. 463.

35 For an evocative description of its Jews in the interwar period see Ruth Beckermann (ed.), *Die Mazzesinsel: Juden in der Wiener Leopoldstadt 1918–1938* (Vienna and Munich, 1984).

36 Information on residential distribution of *Gemeinde* taxpayers from tax files, CAHJP, AW 805/1–25; information on those receiving communal charity from AW 1890, 1897 and 1899. Data from a cross-sectional sample of all Viennese Jews derives from the birth and marriage records (see note 18). For a full discussion of Jewish residence see Rozenblit, *Jews of Vienna*, pp. 71–98.

37 Rozenblit, *Jews of Vienna*, pp. 94–6.

38 For a fuller discussion, see Rozenblit, *Jews of Vienna*, pp. 147–54. For a list of such organizations, see pp. 199–207.

39 Stefan Zweig, *The World of Yesterday* (New York, 1943), p. 116; Arthur Schnitzler, *My Youth in Vienna*, trans. Catherine Hutter (New York, 1970), p. 146; Martin Freud, 'Who Was Freud?', in Josef Fraenkel (ed.), *The Jews of Austria*: *Essays in Their Life, History and Destruction* (London, 1967), pp. 204, 207; Ernest Jones, *The Life and Work of Sigmund Freud*, edited and abridged by Lionel Trilling and Steven Marcus (Harmondsworth, 1961), pp. 287, 422.

40 *Österreichisches statistisches Jahrbuch* v (1875), 32–43; *Österreichische Statistik*, 3:2, pp. 32–3, 40–1; 35:4, pp. 30–1, 38–9; 70:3, pp. 32–3; n.s., 8:2, pp. 40–3; Rozenblit, *Jews of Vienna*, pp. 99–125.

41 For parallels in Germany see Gershom Scholem, 'On the Social Psychology of the Jews in Germany: 1900–1933', in David Bronsen (ed.), *The Jews in Germany from 1860–1933: The Problematic Symbiosis* (Heidelberg, 1979), pp. 9–32; and Marion A. Kaplan, 'Tradition and Transition – The Acculturation, Assimilation and Integration of Jews in Imperial Germany – A Gender Analysis', *Leo Baeck Institute Yearbook* 27 (1982), 3–35.

42 *Statistisches Jahrbuch der Stadt Wien* (1896), pp. 34–5; Rozenblit, *Jews of Vienna*, pp. 128–31.

43 Jakob Thon, *Die Juden in Österreich* (Berlin, 1908), p. 70.

44 See Rozenblit, *Jews of Vienna*, pp. 132–46.

45 'Gutachten des Herrn Predigers Dr. Mannheimer in Wien', in Salomon Abraham Trier (ed.), *Rabbinische Gutachten über die Beschneidung* (Frankfurt-am-Main, 1844), pp. 89–104.

46 Isak Noah Mannheimer, *Gottesdienstliche Vorträge gehalten im israelitischen Bethause in Wien*, ed. S. Hammerschlag (Vienna, 1876), 2 vols.

47 These views infuse all of Jellinek's writings. See especially *Bezêlem Elohim: Fünf Reden über die israelitische Menschenlehre und Weltanschauung* (Vienna,

1871); *Zwei Kanzel-Vorträge in der Synagoge zu Ungarisch-Brod* (Leipzig, 1847); *Ein neuer Morgen*; *Rede für das Neujahrsfest 5654* (Vienna, 1893); *Zeitstimmen*, vol. I (Vienna, 1870), pp. 73–84; vol. II (Vienna, 1871), pp. 41–54; *Predigten* (Vienna, 1862), vol. I, pp. 117–25; and *Der jüdische Stamm: Ethnographische Studien* (Vienna, 1869).

48 Moritz Güdemann, *Jerusalem, Die Opfer und Die Orgel*; *Predigt, am Sabbath, 25. Adar 5631 (18. März 1871)* (Vienna, 1871).

49 See for example, Moritz Güdemann, *Sechs Predigten im Leopoldstädter Tempel zu Wien* (Vienna, 1867), pp. 11–18; *Nationaljudenthum* (Leipzig and Vienna, 1897); *Jüdische Apologetik* (Glogau, 1906) and *Das Judenthum in seinen Grundzügen und nach seinen geschichtlichen Grundlagen dargestellt*, 2nd edn (Vienna, 1902).

50 Wistrich, 'The Modernization of Viennese Jewry', p. 59, argues that Viennese Jews had a greater sense of Jewish ethnic identity than Jews in German cities. Such a statement is impossible to prove, but if it is true it is due to the multinational nature of Austria and the more traditional composition of the Viennese Jewish community.

51 Rozenblit, *Jews of Vienna*, pp. 155–9; and Jacob Toury, 'Troubled Beginnings: The Emergence of the Österreichisch-Israelitische Union', *Leo Baeck Institute Yearbook* 30 (1985), 457–75. Wistrich, 'The Modernization of Viennese Jewry', pp. 60–3, goes too far when he argues that Josef Samuel Bloch, the founder of the Union, was a Jewish nationalist. The Union espoused Jewish ethnic pride and Austrian patriotism, not Jewish nationalism.

The social vision of Bohemian Jews: intellectuals and community in the 1840s

HILLEL J. KIEVAL

For the Jews of the Habsburg monarchy, political emancipation and social integration were often frustratingly difficult processes. The problem derived in part from the conservative, hierarchical nature of 'Austrian' society, compounded by the government's inability – or unwillingness – to match the wide-ranging transformations that it encouraged in the cultural sphere with commensurate political reforms. Thus, while Jews in Bohemia, Hungary and lower Austria by and large accepted the educational and occupational reforms of Joseph II and his successors – constructing state-supervised primary schools along the model of the German *Normalschule*; placing their sons in gymnasiums and eventually universities; patterning behaviour, dress and language on middle-class, urban models; establishing many of the early textile plants in the monarchy – tangible improvements in their legal and political status lagged far behind. Only with the advent of the revolution of 1848 did marriage and residence restrictions disappear. The last barriers to free economic activity were not demolished until 1859 and full legal emancipation was achieved only with the creation of the dual Monarchy in 1867.[1]

The relative weakness of the Habsburg state and the disintegrative effects of competing social and political forces contributed further impediments to Jewish integration. The Habsburg monarchy lacked both effective, centralized state institutions and a strong political culture. Its territories comprised a multitude of distinct societies defined by language and ethnicity, whose traditional structure and complexion, by the middle of the nineteenth century, were in the process of breaking down under the challenge of modern nationalism. The emerging national movements, meanwhile, competed with the state for power while offering alternative visions of society and in so doing complicated Jewish efforts for mobility, status and security.[2]

The combination of these factors – lagging reform, weak political culture, the emergence of middle-class, national movements and a relatively high rate of Jewish acculturation – produced what might be called an episode of uncertainty among Habsburg Jewry. The decade of the 1840s offered no clear vision of social integration, no obvious programme of political emancipation, no determined cultural path. These were years of experimentation in both politics and the arts, and the as yet undelineated boundaries of ethnic affiliation created extensive opportunities for the testing of cultural possibilities. How was political emancipation in the end to be achieved? In what kind of society would the Jews find acceptance? What were the linguistic and cultural boundaries of such a society likely to be? Given that both the assimilation to non-Jewish cultural patterns and integration to the larger social environment were commonly held goals of Habsburg Jewry, what was unclear to many were which cultural patterns and which larger community offered the best prospects for fulfilment.

The present chapter focuses on six Bohemian Jews, born between 1815 and 1822: Moritz Hartmann (1821–72), Siegfried Kapper (1821–79), Isidor Heller (1816–79), Simon Hock (1815–87), David Kuh (1818–79) and Leopold Kompert (1822–86). With the exception of Simon Hock, all were recipients of a gymnasium education during the 1830s and studied at universities at the start of the 1840s; hence they had mastered the 'high culture' of the Habsburg state. All pursued writing – including both journalism and *belles-lettres* – as a vocation, but typically had to subordinate this passion to a career in one of the liberal professions. To varying degrees, they all looked to politics as the arena in which both personal designs for advancement and more universal visions of progress might be achieved. Because of their status as acculturated Jews, deprived to a large extent of the fruits of their intellectual training, they fit what Paul Mendes-Flohr has suggested are the main attributes of the modern intellectual: they were 'cognitive insiders' while at the same time 'axionormative dissenters'.[3]

This 'generation of the 1840s' was the first in the history of Bohemian Jewry to pursue gymnasium and university education in a sustained fashion; the first also to pass through the revived and expanded system of German-Jewish primary schools dominated by committed *maskilim*, including Peter Beer, Herz Homberg and, later, Wolfgang Wessely.[4] Its quest for social integration took place in an atmosphere in which nationalism was tied to political liberalism and democratic reform, and at a time when promoting the claims of the various nationalities within the Habsburg Monarchy appeared to be perfectly compatible with the struggle for Jewish emancipation. The cultural, linguistic and political identity of this generation was sufficiently fluid as to allow for wide-ranging experimentation and 'border-crossing'. Not only did the writers in question comfortably combine German and Czech loyalties, but they also were involved in the national revivals of other Habsburg populations, most notably the Hungarians and the South Slavs.

The concept of 'community' existed as a problematic ideal for Jewish intellectuals who stood midway between alienation from traditional Jewish society and comfortable inclusion in a non-Jewish environment. Yet it is also the number and variety of 'communities' offered up by this compact group of writers that is interesting and that calls out for explanation. What did the large number of possibilities mean in terms of Jewish mobility and integration in the middle of the nineteenth century? Did their visions of community indicate a break from, or continuity with, the 'classical assimilationism' of the post-Haskalah? Lastly, how did the political experiences of this generation during the 1840s affect its notions of community, on the one hand, and real prospects for integration, on the other?

Family culture and high culture

Nearly all the biographical descriptions of the six individuals under consideration comment on the fact that they were born to 'middle-class' Jewish families.[5] That term, of course, is of limited descriptive value for the early nineteenth century, since it could encompass almost any occupation from artisan to rabbi, from the proprietor of a stall in the flea market to the owner of a factory in one of the suburbs of Prague. One needs to look for more precise measures in order to locate these families within their contemporary Jewish social settings. One criterion might be the attitude of the family towards primary and secondary education, as well as its means of providing such education. Although I am forced to rely on incomplete biographical data, the families in question did seem to be distinguishable in at least two ways: they did not, by and large, belong to the wealthiest stratum of the community, for whom it was fashionable to substitute private tutoring in the home for primary schools; on the other hand, they almost all sent their sons to classical secondary schools (gymnasiums), which did cost money, and for which the families underwent considerable material sacrifices.[6]

I have no specific information on the schools attended by David Kuh, other than the fact that they were in Prague and included a classical gymnasium. Similarly one can only assume that Leopold Kompert was educated in the German-Jewish school in Mnichovo Hradiště (Münchengrätz) before being sent by his father, a wool merchant, to the Piarist gymnasium in nearby Mladá Boleslav (Jungbunzlau).[7] Isidor Heller, who was born in Mladá Boleslav, was apparently groomed to become a talmudic scholar and studied simultaneously in the gymnasium and the *yeshivah*. We do not have precise information concerning his earlier education, however, and so cannot determine whether he only attended the traditional *heder* or the *Normalschule* as well.[8]

Moritz Hartmann appears to have made a number of starts and false turns before ending up – like Kompert, as well as Heller before him – in the Piarist gymnasium in Mladá Boleslav. Born in the Czech village of Daleké Dušniky, he spent short periods of time at a (presumably Jewish) *Normalschule* in Březnice, the *Hauptschule* in Neukollin and the Altstädter gymnasium in Prague; he also received home tutoring at times. Finally, in 1833 Hartmann travelled the long distance from his home to Mladá Boleslav where his maternal grandfather, Isaac Spitz, was rabbi. Boarding at his grandfather's house, Hartmann attended the Piarist gymnasium for the next five years.[9]

Siegfried (born Salomon Israel) Kapper grew up in Smíchov on the outskirts of Prague. The eldest of nine children, he received his earliest education, at the age of five, from his father in the spirit of the Haskalah. The father taught from the Hebrew Bible, using the text as a springboard to secular learning: the creation story led to a presentation of the rudiments of astronomy, geography and natural science; from the story of the Pharoahs the boy was introduced to world history.[10] In the Kapper household Enlightenment rationality appears to have coexisted happily with folk cultures of various forms, ranging from the Jewish stories of a mendicant musician, who was a frequent guest in the home, to the Czech folktales and songs of the street. Kapper's biographer, Oskar Donath, has shown that he received his first formal schooling at a two-form Czech *Volksschule* in Smíchov (which was in reality 'utraquist', i.e., bilingual); for the next two years he went to a Jewish school that met at the 'Klaus' Synagogue in Prague. What is unclear is whether Kapper attended only *heder* or the *Normalschule* as well. But since Donath describes the school as a place where Kapper learned Hebrew and 'perfected his German', the answer is probably the second.[11]

Simon Hock's early life and education offer an important contrast to those of his five contemporaries. Probably as a result of his mother's piety, Hock attended neither a *Normalschule* nor a gymnasium. Instead, he followed a fully traditional educational course: *heder* until the age of ten, followed by study at the *yeshivah* of Rabbi Judah Loeb Schlesinger, the last of its kind in Prague by the middle of the century. Whatever Western education he received he acquired on his own, risking parental opposition along the way. Hock's father apparently was the more open of the two parents to secular education. Following his mother's death, which occurred when he was fourteen, Hock undertook an intensive campaign of self-education, serving at the same time as tutor to his younger siblings.[12]

The quest for 'secular' knowledge on Hock's part took place within the limits of acceptable religious behaviour. He did not break with his family over this issue; he never took part in a regular course of study at a non-Jewish secondary or high school; and he appears to have remained loyal to normative religious practice for his whole lifetime. While other Jewish youth of similar economic backgrounds entered the gymnasium world of high culture, Hock laboured in the world of commerce, at first with a maternal aunt and later with his father. Though committed to scholarship and writing, he pursued these ends as an avocation and not as a profession.[13] Hock's enlightenment occurred outside the main institutions of acculturation that linked the Jew to the state and its high culture. Perhaps as a result of this, he never experienced the estrangement from Jewish tradition that so marked the careers of his five compatriots. In many respects he serves as an instructive contrast to them, their personal dilemmas and their imaginative resolutions to the problem of community.

For Kuh, Kapper, Hartmann and company, the road from the local Jewish community to the larger society led through a five- or six-year course of study at a gymnasium and invariably brought in its wake a break with the traditional culture of their childhood surroundings. One of the more striking examples of this emerges from the early career of Moritz Hartmann. Hartmann, it seems, was sent to the gymnasium in Mladá Boleslav precisely because his grandfather, Isaac Spitz, was the rabbi there, and he continued to live with his grandfather throughout his gymnasium years. Otto Wittner claims, perhaps rightly, that Hartmann cherished the memory of those years in his grandfather's house, and that the grandfather served as a model for sympathetic characters in later works of fiction.[14] The fact remains, however, that Hartmann broke with Judaism during the time that he lived with his grandfather. According to the version recounted by Hartmann himself, when he was thirteen years old he went for a walk in the woods and ostentatiously tossed his phylacteries (*tefilin*) – used by Jewish men in morning prayer – into the trees.[15]

In the case of Siegfried Kapper, it was the father who had already moved far beyond the confines of the traditional Jewish community, both literally and figuratively. Joseph Kapper was listed in official registers as a pedlar (*Hausierer*), but Siegfreid Kapper reveals in his unpublished 'Selbstbiographie' that his father's career was considerably more interesting than might otherwise be suspected. For if Joseph Kapper was a pedlar, he was also, at various points in his life, an artisan, a soldier in the French army and a teacher at various Swiss institutions (under the name of Fischer).[16] In the autumn of 1830 – hence after one year of lessons with his father, two years at the Czech *Volksschule* in Smíchov, and two years at the Prague Jewish School – Siegfried Kapper entered the Piarist gymnasium on Prague's Malá Strana (Kleinseite). Kapper's six years at the gymnasium proved to be the formative intellectual experience of his life. During his final two years he studied with the writer and poet Johannes Zimmermann. It so happened that the Malá Strana gymnasium during this time played a key role in the elaboration of romantically inspired Czech cultural nationalism. Václav Svoboda was one of its most influential teachers – though he probably did not teach Kapper; in 1817 he had almost certainly aided the ethnologist Václav Hanka in the preparation of the controversial literary forgeries known as the Králové dvůr and Zelená hora manuscripts, which purported to consist of fragments of ancient Czech poems. It was not until the 1880s that the manuscripts were proved beyond doubt to have been nineteenth-century fabrications. In the meantime Kapper could take comfort, together with other young Czech intellectuals, from the idea that the early Czechs had also possessed a rich literary past.[17]

To say that the gymnasium and university years represented the crucial cultural experience for Jewish intellectuals of the 1840s is not to imply that this experience was unambiguously positive or free of conflict. First, most accounts of life at the Piarist gymnasium in Bohemia indicate that the teachers were uninspiring, the educational atmosphere stifling and the main pedagogical technique, memorizing.[18] Jewish students, moreover, found that they had to overcome considerable hostility on the part of both teachers and fellow students if they were to succeed in their studies. One of Moritz Hartmann's teachers, a former Jesuit, was fond of remarking to his class that Jews ought to be studying *Schacher* (haggling) rather than Latin.[19] Moritz, the main character in Leopold Kompert's novella

Die Kinder des Randars (written in 1847), which bears strong autobiographical features, is also subjected to religiously inspired humiliations at the Bunzlau (Mladá Boleslav) gymnasium. When he arrives to register at the school the rector pointedly asks the mother whether she wishes the boy to be addressed as 'Moses' or 'Moritz'. On the fourth day of school Moritz is ordered to kneel before the teacher's desk as punishment for arriving late for class. When the boy protests that he must not kneel, the teacher threatens to 'lock him up'. Moritz in the end kneels.[20]

Despite these antagonisms and the tedium of the classical curriculum, the gymnasium provided Jewish students with their first prolonged exposure to the literary culture of Central Europe as well as to local patriotism. It was at Mladá Boleslav that Hartmann and Kompert were first introduced to Goethe, Heine and the German romantic poets; at the gymnasiums of Prague that Siegfried Kapper and David Kuh first learned to appreciate the role of the Czech literary revival in the evolution of Bohemian cultural life. It was during their years at the gymnasium that Jewish students first mastered the high culture that promised an avenue of social mobility, faced the prospect of literature (especially poetry) as a vocation, made the first lasting friendships with non-Jews and conceived the possibility of entering into common political cause with non-Jewish society. By the time they began their university careers, they were firmly committed to a life of letters, to which their actual courses of study and subsequent professions might have related only tangentially.[21]

The university and the wider world

During the years 1837 to 1840 most of this circle of Bohemian-Jewish intellectuals made their way to Prague to embark upon university study. Siegfried Kapper entered the philosophy faculty in the autumn of 1837. Moritz Hartmann arrived in the city in the winter of 1838, took classes at the Neustädter Gymnasium in order to complete the sixth and final form (the second *humanistische Klasse*) and entered the university in the autumn of the same year, where he was joined for a short while by his gymnasium classmate Leopold Kompert.[22] By this time Isidor Heller, recently returned from France, was back in Prague for his second try at university study. I do not know where David Kuh began his university career – very likely Prague as well – but by 1840 he was a student in Vienna.[23]

If the tedium of classroom instruction in the gymnasium could not deter students such as Hartmann, Kapper and Kompert from gaining an education and entering the world of literature, the walls of the university were unable to contain them once they had arrived in Prague. Numerous facets of intellectual life, including literary creativity, took place outside the confines of the university, especially in nearby cafés. One of these in particular, the 'Roter Turm', served as a meeting place for a group of writers and poets – influenced by Byron, Heine, Lenau and the German romantics – that adopted for itself the name Young Bohemia. Among the more active members of this group were Heller, Hartmann and Kapper; but also Alfred Meissner, the son of a German-speaking physician from Teplice and later Karlový Vary (Karlsbad), Friedrich Hirschl, a Hungarian who later Magyarized his name to Szarvady, and the physician Friedrich Bach. Of these, only Meissner was not Jewish.[24]

The poets of Young Bohemia took from the German romantics their love of lyrical poetry and their appreciation of the inter-connectedness of language, landscape and heroic striving. Heine and Börne in particular served as models for the application of literature and cultural criticism to political and social ends. At the same time, Rudolf Glaser – described by Otto Wittner as 'the librarian of one of Prague's largest institutes and a writer of no apparent importance' – provided Young Bohemia with its first literary opportunity.[25] His journal *Ost und West*, which appeared between 1837 and 1848, offered the Young Bohemia group an important public forum, publishing hundreds of their poems, essays and literary translations.

Ost und West was committed to a unique political programme, which came to be regarded as emblematic of the liberal, bi-ethnic, 'Bohemian' consensus of the decade that preceded the revolution of 1848. It expressed a political and cultural mode of aesthetics that cultivated original lyrical creations as well as the 'folk' literature of the peoples of East Central Europe and combined this with liberal politics in the service of constitutionalism and reform. The name of the journal itself, which may have derived from Goethe's remark, 'Orient und Occident sind nicht mehr zu trennen' (the East and the West will no longer be divided), suggested a mediating mission for Austria, and particularly Bohemia, in both realms.[26]

In addition to Kapper, Heller and Hartmann, the Jewish contributors to *Ost und West* included L. A. Frankl, Friedrich Bach, Ignaz Kuranda, Gustav Karpeles, David Mendl and Wolfgang Wessely. Kapper in particular immersed himself in the role of *Vermittler* (mediator), translating more than forty pieces of the 'national poetry' of the Czechs, Slovaks and Moravians (whose literature occupied a distinct category in the journal). As a purveyor of Czech and Slovak literature to the German reading public of Europe, Kapper occupied a position second only to the poet Karel Sabina.[27] Meanwhile, Kapper, Heller, Hartmann and Mendl used the pages of *Ost und West* to publish their own original work, which bore such titles as: 'Öst-Westlicher Divan', 'Concordia', 'Der Utraquist' and 'Chorgesang der Wiener Studenten-Legion'. Wessely, a teacher at the Prague *Normalschule*, offered in the spirit of Herder an anthology of rabbinic aphorisms.[28] *Ost und West*, it seems, provided the young Jewish poets of Bohemia with more than a literary forum. It served as a 'society of letters', whose middle-class constituents shared with the Jews not only common educational and social backgrounds but also a political vision of Central Europe as ethnically pluralistic and democratic at the same time.

None of the Jewish students examined in this essay managed to complete his university studies in Prague. Financial pressures forced most to seek outside employment as private tutors – at times interrupting their studies for longer or shorter periods – but the main reason appears to have been dissatisfaction: dissatisfaction with the university, impatience with Prague as a provincial city.[29] Indeed, next to poetry, *Wanderlust* and quest constituted the main themes of the 1840s, both during and after the university years. Moritz Hartmann might have left Prague altogether in 1838 in favour of Leipzig, where censorship laws were much less severe, but for the fact that he could not obtain a residence permit. He did ultimately go to Vienna in 1840 where he attended university, shared a room for a while with David Kuh, continued to write for *Ost und West*, as well as for L. A. Frankl's *Sontagsblätter*. In 1842 he began a trip that took him to Trieste, Venice, Switzerland, Munich and ultimately back to Vienna. For two years he managed to hold the position of tutor (*Hofmeister*) in the house of Prince Schwarzenberg. He eventually gave this up as well in order to make his way back to Leipzig in search of a publisher for his by now considerable poetic opus. From there he went to Brussels, where he oversaw the publication (in Leipzig) of his first book of poems, *Kelch und Schwert*; on to Paris and Germany, where he spent some time; and back to Bohemia in 1847, where the following year he was put on trial because of some political writings just as the revolution broke.[30]

The peregrinations of Hartmann's colleagues were no less daunting. Isidor Heller only returned to Prague in 1838 after his application for membership of the French Foreign Legion was turned down by the commander in Nancy. He later lived in Vienna as a teacher; edited a literary journal, *Der Ungar*, in Pest; left Pest in 1847 after an unhappy romance; converted quietly to Protestantism; moved to Leipzig, where he wrote short stories and political articles and returned to Pest at the end of March 1848 to edit a new political journal, *Der Morgenröthe.*[31]

Siegfried Kapper completed the two years of 'philosophical studies' in the summer of 1839 and proceeded to enrol in the medical faculty, upon the urging of his father. But by now he had reached a dead end in Prague, forced to devote all of his time to private tutoring. His luck was no better the next year even though he managed to inherit Hartmann's teaching position with the wealthy Mauthner family. And so, in the autumn of 1841, we find Kapper, too, in Vienna, where he made a valiant effort to resume his medical studies.[32] From this point until he received his medical degree in 1847, Kapper lived a relatively sedentary existence in Vienna. But after 1848 he will have left the confines of both liberal Vienna and nationalist Bohemia for years of work and travel in the South Slavic lands of Serbia, Croatia and the Banat.[33]

Leopold Kompert put up with university life in Prague for less than a year – in 1838 – before escaping to Vienna. He soon found a position as *Hofmeister* to a wealthy merchant with five children, a job which made it impossible for him to continue his formal studies, but did improve his material circumstances and gave him some time to devote to poetry and fiction. He began his *Wanderjahre* in 1840, taking off by ship up the Danube, living for a while in the villages of the Hungarian plain and eventually making his way to Pressburg (Pozsony, Bratislava) where he befriended the publisher of the *Pressburger Zeitung*, Adolf Neustadt. While publishing his first stories in the *Pressburger Zeitung* and the *Sontagsblätter*, Kompert also signed on as *Hofmeister* for the family of Count Andrássy. Only in 1847, after learning of the death of his mother, did he decide to resume university study.[34]

Significantly, the one person not to travel at this time was Simon Hock. His quest for Western enlightenment, for a broadening of cultural horizons, took place not only in the context of the established Jewish community but also within the confines of the city of his birth. Hock joined forces in 1835 with other Jews – traditional in religious practice but 'enlightened' in outlook – to create an association that would promote 'a united stylistic form' together with 'the scientific progress of the age'. His collaborators included Koppelmann Lieben; Daniel Ehrmann, who later served as rabbi of numerous Bohemian communities; the future physician, Moritz Kuh; Guttmann Klemperer, later rabbi in Tábor; and Josef Schack.[35] They called their new association 'Aurora', to suggest the dawning of a new age. Yet it was essentially conservative in its attachment to Jewish culture and Mendelssohnian in tone even half a century after the master's death.

Simultaneously, Jewish *Wissenschaft* exerted a growing influence on Hock and his friends. In 1835 Leopold Zunz came to Prague to serve as preacher of the recently dedicated reformed synagogue. Though he stayed for only one year, he was replaced by Michael Sachs, a conservative reformer and scholar who had a major impact on Jewish life in Prague before leaving for Berlin in 1844.[36] Hock attached himself to Zunz, Sachs and later to Solomon Judah Rapoport (who became chief rabbi of Prague in 1840), and became an ardent *dévoté* of mid-century *Wissenschaft*. He began to write journalistic pieces in the 1840s for the *Allgemeine Zeitung des Judentums* and *Der Orient* dealing alternatively with the conditions of Jewish life in Prague and the Reform movement in Germany, which he opposed. It was during this time also that Hock conceived his plan to produce a massive history of the Jews of his city. Though he did write an important study based on tombstone inscriptions in the ancient Jewish cemetery, he never completed the larger project and the manuscript that he was working on ultimately was lost.[37]

It is tempting to view the impressive amount of travel undertaken by young Jewish intellectuals in the 1840s as an indication of a broader cultural restlessness. Removed from the villages of their parents or ancestors, alienated as well from the entrenched Jewish community of Prague, filled with social and intellectual ambitions but as yet unemancipated and unintegrated into the non-Jewish environment, the Jewish students expressed their loss of roots symbolically by wandering. In contrast, Hock's sedentary existence reflected a sense of comfort and satisfaction with his identity both as Jew and as European. He apparently had achieved in his own life a happy synthesis of traditional Jewish culture and European science and rationalism, represented by his dual interest in German stylistics and *Wissenschaft des Judentums*. Though implicitly loyal to the Habsburg state, Hock was also a Jewish patriot committed to preserving the history of the community in Prague, transmitting knowledge of the Jewish past and assuring the cultural health of the community in the future.

But if this picture is correct in its rough outline, it fails to account for two important points. First, the wanderings reflected the existence of a hopeful world and expanding opportunities. Kompert, Kuh and Heller might have felt stifled by the immobility of Prague, but they could take advantage of Hungary's occupational opportunities, relative political freedom and national experimentation. Siegfried Kapper could sample the folk cultures of Bohemia, Moravia and Slovakia before going on to those of the South Slavs, because he felt that they were promising fields in which both Jews and non-Jews could participate.[38] The second point is that the travels were not aimless; they invariably led to (sometimes back to) Vienna. Students and intellectuals of all nationalities gravitated to Vienna in the years preceding 1848. This university city and imperial capital offered – for a few heady years, at least – a place of opportunity *par excellence*, where politics and culture could be wed and untold visions of community born.

Community and ethnic strife

It was in Vienna, too, that the cross-cultural ventures of *Ost und West* bore interesting fruit. In 1843 Václav Bolemír Nebeský (1818–82), who may already have struck up an acquaintance with Bohemian-Jewish students in Prague, arrived in Vienna to study medicine.[39] Here he formed a close relationship with Siegfried Kapper and David Kuh and with them embarked on a project that combined elements of political liberalism, incipient Czech nationalism and the struggle for Jewish emancipation.

Nebeský's early life paralleled that of his Jewish colleagues in some telling ways. Born to a Czech father and a German mother, he attended mainly German schools – including the gymnasium in Litoměřice (Leitmeritz) – although the family spoke Czech at home. He was exposed to German and classical literature at the gymnasium and later took up Greek and German philosophy in Prague. Before arriving in Prague in 1836 he apparently knew very little Czech history and literature; these he acquired as part of his extra-curricular intellectual formation in the university environments of Prague and Vienna.[40] Nebeský belonged to a group of Byronist Czech poets, which included Karel Sabina and K. H. Mácha, that had joined literary romanticism to political activism and that also showed an interest in Jewish cultural themes. At some point, perhaps after reading Herder, Nebeský became convinced that the Czech nation could reap enormous benefits if it were to succeed in recruiting the potential talent of Central European Jewry. He appears to have been struck, in particular, by the role that Heinrich Heine and Ludwig Börne played in the cultural politics of Germany. In any event, he, together with Kapper and Kuh, hit upon the idea of launching a newspaper campaign designed to elicit the support of Bohemian and Moravian Jews for the Czech national movement.[41]

Before the end of 1843 Nebeský was able to report to a friend that the first article in the campaign was ready to appear in print:

> A good article, excellently written; it will work terrifically. One can already sense this a little among the Jews of Vienna. I am going to continue to work in this direction. We could get a lot of help [*gute Kräfte*] from the Jews; they are an excellent, wonderful people, full of spirit and action. They have already helped the Germans a lot. Would that they would help us, too![42]

One cannot say with certainty what article Nebeský was referring to: possibly the three-part series by David Kuh that ultimately appeared in the *Allgemeine Zeitung des Judentums* in April 1844; possibly the anonymous 'Berichte' from Prague that began to appear in *Der Orient* in February.[43] But the February report, probably written by Kuh, does appear to have inaugurated the official campaign.

The dispatch from Prague opened with the words: 'The position of the Jews in a country in which the nationality struggle is taking place, and with it the language struggle, is a difficult one.' Neutrality in such a situation was impossible, and the Jews must choose a side to support, 'something which they ought not to do and yet must'.[44] Choosing sides, the writer admitted, was accomplished more easily in Hungary, where the Magyars clearly had the upper hand, where the government – despite itself – tended to support the supremacy of the Magyar language; where the landed aristocracy was independent and not merely a shadow of the regime. In such a situation, Jews benefited from Magyarization. 'The Magyar values and loves anyone who speaks Hungarian well.'[45]

But for the Jews of Bohemia, where the government represses the 'Slavic element', and where the local elites have only just begun to cherish their language and local culture, the situation is different. Here the regime rules, in the full sense of the word; the aristocracy has no real political power; its *Landtag* is but a silent monument to an ancient freedom. What political strategy is open to Jews who live in this type of context 'between Scylla and Charybdis'? The reporter's advice was to ignore discretion: 'Not [to be] petty, cowardly, or self-interested, but to be true sons of your fatherland!'[46] In this instance, 'fatherland' referred not to the Empire as a whole but to the smaller Czech 'state' within it. This political community stood at an undetermined distance between the ghetto and the emancipating central state. And the Jew owed loyalty to this intermediate body in the name of his own geographic origins, the linguistic culture of his early environment, and, above all, the new flag of nationalism. 'The Jews should help to set in motion the machinery of nationality – language; attach themselves to those people who are occupied with scholarly research into the Czech language in order to appear as Czechs to their (unfortunately one cannot as yet say fellow-) citizens.' The report closed by singling out the efforts of Siegfried Kapper 'and a few other Jews', who involved themselves in Czech language and literature, thus serving as a model to be followed by others.[47]

In *Der Orient* of 14 May 1944, the same reporter wrote of efforts on the part of some within the Prague Jewish community to establish a teaching position in Czech language in the city's *Normalschule*:

> If these words are actually put into practice, then this is very welcome news, and this step promises much good for Bohemian Jewry generally. Common research efforts in language and literature will lead to an intellectual *rapprochement* between Jews and Christians, and the intellectual interaction will also make the social bond stronger.[48]

He ridiculed the 'feeble-minded' (*Schwachköpfe*) within the Jewish community who opposed the teaching of Czech in Jewish schools on the grounds that it would antagonize the government authorities. 'I need only refer these "timid sirs" to our own beloved provincial governor [*Landeschef*], who himself has given many indications of how highly he values the language of his subjects.'[49]

The major thrust of the newspaper campaign consisted of two parallel series of articles: David Kuh's 'Ein Wort an Juden und Slaven', which appeared in the *Allgemeine Zeitung des Judentums* on 1 April, 8 April and 15 April, and Nebeský's 'Něco o poměru Slovanů a židů' ('Concerning the Relations between Slavs and Jews'), which came out in the Czech-language newspaper *Květy*. Kuh's argument for a new involvement of Jews in the national movement of the Czechs derived from both a principle – that nationality is a culturally determined phenomenon – and an observation – that the German national movement had gained much strength through the participation of 'foreigners' in its cultural life.

> That which has made the Germans so great intellectually, which has positioned them as the most educated and thoughtful of people on the earth, is that they, for the most part, have never neglected the

spirit. [. . .] Frenchmen and Jews, Danes and Slavs, have vied
with one another to carry the stones for the building of the German
temple of glory.

But who, Kuh asked, had bothered to help the Slavs?[50]

No one, of course. But here Kuh added a rhetorical touch which
revealed an optimism that would elude him in the future. He
identified himself with that Czech nation that stood isolated from the
rest of Europe: 'What we are and what we shall become we are and
shall become only through ourselves.'

> Among our heroes and wisemen, our poets and artists, there is not even
> one from a foreign tribe [*Stamm*]. But nations are not to be divided into
> full- and half-blood races, and it is the highest triumph of a particular
> cultural direction when foreign geniuses and foreign powers subordi-
> nate themselves to it and serve it with joy.[51]

Kuh placed much of the blame for the lack of participation of
outsiders in Czech cultural life on the Czechs themselves. They simply
were not interested. And yet the potential for Jewish–Slavic co-
operation in East Central Europe was so great – Kuh mentions that
the vast majority of Europe's Jews lived in Slavic lands – that neither
side should miss the opportunity of joining forces. 'Take hammer and
trowel in hand and eagerly and ceaselessly cultivate the education of
the nation, the [building] of common bonds, and the reconciliation of
hearts.'[52]

In the second instalment of the series Kuh shifted his focus to
questions of prejudice and persecution and adopted a dramatically
different tone. If his first article had been marked by hope and
optimism, the second was marked by bitterness and disappointment.
Kuh admitted to being frustrated at the lack of improvement in the
political, economic and social condition of the 300,000 Jews (his
count) living in the German Confederation. And he spoke with
stubborn pride of this people, who had withstood a millennium of
Christian persecution only to wake up to new strength and vitality;
certainly they must possess unusual qualities.[53]

It is curious, given the ultimate purpose of the articles, that Kuh's
next remarks, addressed to Czech intellectuals, were laced with scorn
and anger:

> If only a single one of you, Slavic intellectuals [*Gelehrten*], would admit
> to this; if only one of you would step ahead of the crude masses and
> emancipate himself from Jew hatred; this one person would make a
> beneficial, eternal impact not only on the Jews, not only on his own
> people, but indirectly on the whole world.

You kill so much proud hope, so much budding talent, you West Slavs, through the stifling swamp air of your stupid hatred and your contempt. Do you think you are only killing the Jews? No, you are robbing yourselves, you are suppressing the spiritual blossoms that were to have borne fruit for you.[54]

Almost three times as many Jews lived among the Slavs as among the Germans, Kuh argued. They might some day form a mighty and powerful middle class that could be of service to the young Czech nation. Why should one deliberately alienate them, reject their services? If the Czechs should close their doors to Jewish participation, if they should waste the opportunity at hand, they could not lay the blame at the door of the Jews

> who have had to fight the greatest, heaviest and most adverse impediments in order not to doubt humanity; who have had to struggle . . . not to lose faith in themselves and in their inner freedom. [. . .] Do you want to accept the fact that [the Jew] rightly turns his back on you in disgust . . . and allies with the German nationality and German culture?[55]

In the end, the Jews were not asking so much from the Slavs: not relief from burdensome taxation, not civil equality, not political emancipation – the Czechs were not in a position to grant any of these things. All that the Jews asked for was a measure of love and esteem, 'which man has the sacred right to demand from his fellow man, his own likeness'.[56] It is difficult not to be both moved and puzzled by the stridency of Kuh's remarks. The articles were intended for a Jewish audience: why was it necessary to direct so much pent-up emotion at the Slavs, whom, after all, one wanted to court? And why remind the Jewish readers of the *Allgemeine Zeitung des Judentums* of the centuries of hatred and persecution that the Jews had suffered at the hands of their hosts?

In fact, the final article in the series did much to 'balance the score'. Kuh directed his attention this time to the Jews, and lashed out at them, one could say, with equal fury:

> You, West Slavic Jews, who are so proud of your cleverness and your intellect, who are so proud of the sciences, who even tend exotic plants . . . I ask you whether you have sunk so low through oppression that you must wait until someone raises you up and draws close to you?[57]

Kuh seems to have subscribed to a variation on the 'mission theory' of Judaism, arguing that the Jews were called upon 'to realize the highest and most noble ideals', but also – together with the Western

Slavs – to serve as spiritual intermediaries between Eastern and
Western Europe. He called upon the Jews to abandon old cultural
forms in the name of a new, better order for all Central Europeans:
'You must become actively involved, sacrifice much, tear down much
in order to achieve even more, in order to build more grandly.' And a
prime symbol of the revolution in Jewish culture would be the
attempt on the part of some within the Prague Jewish community to
cultivate the Czech language and to teach it in their schools. 'Then
the time will surely come when you will no longer have to go begging
to your brethren in Germany in order to quench your thirst for
European learning and culture, which rages in you still so
vehemently.'[58]

Kuh's articles in the *Allgemeine Zeitung des Judentums* have frequently
been cited – together with Siegfried Kapper's *České listy* (1846) and
Moritz Hartmann's *Kelch und Schwert* (1845) – as having marked the
high point of Czech-Jewish cultural collaboration before 1848. The
subsequent defections of Hartmann and Kuh from the Czech camp,
accordingly, are typically understood as representing a sudden
about-face, explained partly by the anti-Jewish violence that erupted
in 1844 and again in 1848 and partly by the inhospitable reception of
Kapper's work on the part of Czech intellectuals such as Karel
Havlíček Borovský.[59] Doubtless, the events of 1844 and 1848, as well
as the critical reviews of Kapper's Czech writings, did cause much
disappointment. But the entire Kuh–Kapper–Nebeský venture was
shot through with ambivalence and mistrust from the beginning.
Kuh used the pronoun 'we' only once when referring to the Czech
nation, at the very beginning of the first essay. In the second part,
while analysing Czech attitudes toward Jews, he steered clear of the
first-person voice altogether. And in the concluding part, ostensibly a
criticism of Jewish behaviour, the 'we' that bound the writer to his
subject was certainly implicit. One might add that the angry,
accusatory tone of Kuh's second article overwhelmed the series as a
whole. He never really shook himself loose from it, even as he tried to
'even the score' in the last segment. What was to have been a criticism
of Jewish cultural behaviour and an exhortation to change ended
with yet another denunciation of the anti-Jewish behaviour of
European Christian society, especially in the Slavic lands. Kuh held
out the hope of an eventual reconciliation between Jews and Slavs,
but he did so in the manner of an Abraham bickering with God over
the fate of Sodom and Gomorrah.

I am convinced that the well-intentioned and appropriate words of a single one among the Slavic intellectuals will travel like lightning among your [the Jewish] masses, will rouse them and win them over to a great European nation, and, in so doing, provide salutary reconciliation to both parties.[60]

Perhaps Nebeský was to have been that single Slavic intellectual ready to receive the Jews of Central Europe. Even his overture, however, was more cautious than warm. Responding to Kuh in *Květy*, Nebeský found himself essentially repeating Kuh's criticism of the Jews, reproaching them for never having shared the national aspirations of the Slavs. On the contrary, he added, the Jews' attachment to 'foreign elements' had undermined the Czech 'national element'. This 'tragic isolation', as Nebeský put it, which was harmful to both sides, ought to stop.[61] That Nesbeský desired and valued Jewish participation in Czech culture was nevertheless clear. Jewish–Czech co-operation, he wrote, would be 'a nice development for humanity':

> It was no nation of mean spirit that played such a role in the history of mankind, in whose language the Bible, the book of books, was written; a nation that withstood the wildest storms of the most tragic centuries while maintaining its character, its religion – the oldest in the world.[62]

It was one of fate's cruelties that industrial riots should have broken out in Prague and other parts of Bohemia so soon after the start of the Czech–Jewish courtship. The riots were carried out primarily by textile workers protesting at the introduction of mechanization in the cotton-printing industry and the nearly simultaneous drop in real wages. Jews had played a conspicuous role in the development of textile production – particularly in cotton printing – throughout the Habsburg monarchy. One of the largest firms in Bohemia, the Porges family's cotton-printing plant in Smíchov, just outside Prague, employed 569 workers in 1835; by 1843 it employed 700. In 1835 there were 117 cotton-processing plants in Bohemia, of which fifteen of the largest were located in Prague and owned by Jews. By the 1840s the Epstein and Porges families alone produced more than 10 per cent of the entire Austrian output in printed cotton fabric. The Porges brothers were also the first to introduce steam engines into the printing process and were granted titles of nobility for their trouble.[63]

A string of bad harvests in the early 1840s had resulted in a general rise in prices. At the same time factory owners responded to a crisis in the industry by holding down wages. But the immediate background to the events of June 1844 involved the introduction of machines – the so-called *perrotin* – into the cotton-printing factories. When the Porges brothers introduced the *perrotin* to their plant in Smíchov, they also lowered wages. Venting their anger at the predominantly Jewish factory owners, the Prague textile workers went on the rampage and destroyed machinery in plants owned by the Porges, Dormitzer, Brandeis, Schick and Epstein families.[64] Soon the riots expanded beyond the bounds of industrial protest and spilled over into acts of violence against Jews generally. On 21 June a mass meeting of cotton workers, at which anti-Jewish speeches were made, was broken up by the police. But it quickly re-formed as a mob that streamed into the Jewish quarter destroying market stalls and shops and attacking individual Jews. Eventually the military and the police intervened to restore order. Riots erupted several days later as well, this time led by some 2,000 railway workers.[65]

To complete the isolation of Prague Jewry, the commercial and lower middle classes sided whole-heartedly with the rioting workers in the aftermath of the June storm. Non-Jewish merchants and shopkeepers presented a petition to the government in Vienna urging that it enforce existing restrictive legislation on Jews and also limit their economic activity. The petition signalled the start of an anti-Jewish movement among Prague's *Kleinbürgertum*, which lasted at least until 1848 and which reached its peak in 1847 in a campaign that involved 1,800 masters from virtually every guild in the city.[66]

Following closely on the heels of the Kuh–Kapper–Nebeský initiative, the riots of 1844 transformed the cautious scepticism of some Jewish intellectuals to outright disillusionment. Dispatches from Prague that reached the offices of *Der Orient* in Leipzig seethed with bitterness at the actions of the Czech mobs. The reports were written by two different individuals, each anonymous. The tone and style of the first set of reports, however, closely resembled Kuh's series in the *Allgemeine Zeitung des Judentums* and at one point were appended with the initials 'D.K.' Another set of dispatches, more conservative in tone but equally critical of Czech actions, carried the signature '24'. I cannot be certain about the authorship of the articles, but there are good reasons to believe that the first set – reports dated 23 and 24 June and 10 and 22 July – was written by David Kuh, and the second – particularly the long report of 26 June – by Simon Hock.[67]

A pained sarcasm dripped from the opening lines of Kuh's dispatches and was retained throughout the series. It derived from what he saw as the complicity of the educated middle class in the anti-Jewish excesses: 'The blessed Libussa and yet another queen will be shedding tears of joy in their graves', he wrote, 'that their loyal subjects have maintained the ancient Jew-hatred [*Judenhass*] down to the year 1844. If the wandering Jew [*der ewige Jude*] is a fable, eternal Jew-hatred is certainly no myth.'

> Textile workers rise up against their bosses, who happen to belong to the Jewish ethnic group [*Volksklasse*], cause damage and destruction to factories, and our dear cultivated and educated Czechs know of nothing better to do than to exhibit openly their own crude and crass Jew-hatred, accusing all Jews, as a single body, of fraud.[. . .] Oh Czechs, you call for freedom and independence at a time when you have dehumanized yourselves [*da Ihr Euch entmenscht*], when you have sunk to the level of beasts of prey.[68]

Kuh laid the blame for the anti-Jewish riots – which he labelled 'the crude acts of crude men' at the doorstep of national and religious fanaticism. He lashed out in particular at Professor Svoboda of the Malá Strana gymnasium who, it will be recalled, was not only a fervent nationalist but also had a role in promoting, and perhaps producing, Václav Hanka's 'medieval' Czech manuscripts of Zelená Hora and Králové dvůr.[69] He accused Svoboda of fomenting anti-Jewish sentiment, of humiliating Jewish students in front of their Christian colleagues and, in the end of 'preaching a Crusade against the Jews'. Foreshadowing his subsequent attack on the authenticity of the manuscripts – while hinting at a political rationale for his stand – Kuh sarcastically suggested: 'the creature SV—a, by the way, is an expert in the Czech language. Perhaps he is preparing the Prague scene for a Bohemian epic, wherein he and his beloved Czechs can shine in glory.'[70]

Ultimately Kuh understood the riots of 1844 to be a by-product of the absence of emancipation, both Jewish and Christian. When the 'birth pangs' of Czech nationalism first began to be heard, he wrote, after the dust had settled and the troops had left, the Jews thought to themselves that real freedom might be coming to Bohemia.

> It was as though we could already see the Jews sitting in the newly built city hall; in uniform, marching along with their fellow citizens; occupying numerous chairs at the university. We didn't think at all about the little things – like living in the Christian [parts of the] city, opening shops in the market-place, and the like. That was then, but no longer. We've [since] lived through the dark Middle Ages.[71]

The initial shock came from the fury of the mob. But if the mob knew only to vent its anger at the Jews, one ultimately had to deplore the type of state that did not teach its subjects any differently, that capitalized on social and political inequality to pit one disadvantaged group against another. The educated classes, moreover, with their 'refined Jew-hatred', chose cynically to encourage and manipulate the discontented masses. Yet it was the 'patriarchal' state, which distributed privileges like sweets to favourite children and under which groups measured their well-being not in objective terms but in relation to that of other social groups, that endangered the security of the Jews the most. Only complete Jewish and Christian emancipation could end the cycles of violence against Jews.[72]

Simon Hock's reporting from Prague contained neither the political radicalism nor the cynicism of David Kuh's. To be sure, Hock also railed against the violence and deplored the 'retreat to the Middle Ages'. What he was witnessing was 'once again a war of might against right, of force against humanity [*Menschlichkeit*], of blind hate against reason'. The order of the day was no longer progress, but reaction. In the past, governments had withheld civic rights from the Jews; now 'the people' scoffed at their human rights.[73] But the overall tone of Hock's reporting was conservative and even pious. He thanked 'the eternal Guardian of Israel, who has never abandoned us', and also the 'watchful and wise authorities' for intervening to restore order, thus preventing the riots from causing more harm than they did. In fact the flowery, exaggerated language with which he expressed his thanks to the government causes one to wonder if the remarks were not intended as irony.[74]

Also unlike that of Kuh, Hock's dispatch of 26 June contained an internal critique of recent events based on a strong sense of Jewish ethnic solidarity. His target was Prague's wealthy Jewish families who, in the past, pursuing status and mobility, had turned their backs on the rest of the community. These people now found themselves under attack by the very Gentiles whom they had tried to court.

> At the hour of need the Christian friend – who before had only a handshake and a smile for you – now had ready a kick and a sneer. Your poor co-religionists, however, whom you had kept at a distance, unfortunately were beaten up on your behalf.[75]

Perhaps in the future, Hock wrote, Jewish notables would not look down contemptuously on their Jewish brothers from an isolated and 'half-Christian perch'. Rather, as their forefathers had done, wealthy Jews would attach themselves ever more forcefully to the Jewish community; 'tie the knot that binds them to their co-religionist ever more tightly; make the interests of the community their own; strive for its well-being as for their own; and base their own pride and worth on the realization of this obligation.'[76]

Narrowing of vision: the retreat to German culture

In the weeks and months that followed the June riots the voices that only recently had called for a common Czech-Jewish political front fell silent. Doubt-ridden and inconsistent from the beginning, the vision of a new community based on common Jewish and Czech interests could not be sustained in the face of popular violence combined with the tacit collusion of Czech elites. One of the few individuals who continued to urge Czech–Jewish unity during the second half of 1844 and throughout 1845 was the little-known Ignác Schulhof. Writing in *Der Orient* in September and October 1844, Schulhof maintained that the promise of Jewish integration into Czech society was not dead (one anti-Jewish professor did not an entire society make), and insisted on the immersion of Bohemian Jews in the Czech language and culture.[77] Siegfried Kapper also refused to lose faith, at least for the moment. He busied himself with the writing of poetry, and in 1846 published the first collection of poems in the Czech language to be written by a Jew, *České listy* (Czech leaves, or letters). Kapper's poetry explored the themes of Jewish longing and hope, to which he added an imaginative identification of the Jewish and Czech nations, matching tragedy for historical tragedy and offering the vision of a common future.[78]

Whatever hope Kapper may have had, however, of a positive reception of *České listy* by the educated Czech public was quickly crushed by the leading Czech journalist of the day, Karel Havlíček Borovský (1821–56). Havlíček reviewed Kapper's book in *Česká včela* – which he edited – in November 1846. In the review he criticized Kapper, not for his poetry, but for the idea that Jews could regard themselves as Czechs:

> The Jews who live in Bohemia frequently count themselves among our nation, they frequently call themselves Czechs. This is a completely false point of view. With regard to Jews one should bear in mind not only their creed and religous confession . . . but primary consideration should be given to their origin and nationality [*národnost*].
>
> How can Israelites [*Israelité*] belong to the Czech nation when they are of semitic origin? [. . .] Thus one cannot claim that the Jews living in Bohemia and Moravia are Czechs of the Mosaic religion; rather one must consider them to be a separate, Semitic nation, which simply

happens to live among us and sometimes understands or speaks our
language. [. . .] Undoubtedly all Jews – whatever country or part of
the world they may live in – consider themselves as a nation, as
brethren, and not solely as co-religionists. And this bond that ties them
together is stronger by far than the bond to the country in which they
live. We hope that there is no need to prove the point that it is
impossible to belong simultaneously to two fatherlands and two
nations, or to serve two masters. Therefore anyone who wants to be a
Czech must cease to be a Jew.[79]

Though laced with an undertone of resentment toward the Jews of
Bohemia-Moravia, Havlíček's piece in *Česká včela* also contained
remarkable perceptions on the nature of Jewish cultural life in his
country. His rejection of Jewish assimilation into the Czech community was based, not on religious prejudice, but on a Herderian idea of
the sacredness of distinct, national cultures. Nor did his lack of
interest in a Czech–Jewish alliance mean that he opposed the
granting of political rights to the Jews. In fact, he came out in favour
of Jewish emancipation in the 1850s.[80] But the Jews, in Havlíček's
view, constituted a distinct nation bound together by ancestry,
history, language and religion. And of Kapper's putative Czech
patriotism he wrote: 'With one eye he looks at Jerusalem – the Land of
Promise – with the other, at the Czech fields which he claims to love.
However, his poems clearly reveal that he loves still more what is truly
his own – which is only natural and praiseworthy.'[81]

Havlíček – unlike other, more sympathetic, reviewers – appreciated the role of traditional Jewish themes in Kapper's writing,
including the power of Jewish yearnings for redemption. Poems with
titles such as 'For Ever Eastward' (*K východu*), 'Ben-Oni' (Son of
Sorrow) and 'The Ninth of Ab' (*Na devátý ab*) lent poignancy to the
rest of the volume and its call for Czech–Jewish union. Kapper sought
to harness and redirect the age-old longing for Zion that had been the
expression of Jewish hope for many centuries:

> New cities rise from the ruins of ancient lore,
> New nations come and others pass unnamed
> Old gods must will their reign to gods unknown before,
> And forests whisper now, where once thundered seas untamed.[82]

But the old longing remains potent, even as the poet searches for a
new haven. As long as the Jew – the boy with coal-black, wavy hair in
the poem 'Ben-Oni' – is rebuffed by the world around him, he cannot
help but remember the distant 'Star of Zion':

I do not ask of You to end my woeful bane,
To guide my steps, to aid me to return
To the distant shrine for which I long in vain,
Where the Star of Zion ne'er again shall burn.
For the Rose of Sharon I no longer pine,
Nor for the fruits from a sloping Jordan hill,
Its milk and honey I gladly will decline,
Its pleasant days and nights so cool and still.
My plaintive prayer is free from all regret,
For wasted joys and sweetness spent in vain,
If but for once in life I could forget
The bitter drops of my fellow-men's disdain.[83]

The juxtaposition of Zion and Europe, of the landscape of Palestine and Bohemia's Czech countryside, also surfaces in Leopold Kompert's novella, *Die Kinder des Randars*. The itinerant beggar (and prophet?) Mendl Wilna is a favourite guest of the innkeeper Rebb Schmul. For hours Mendl Wilna regales the family with his 'holy error' (*heiliger Irrtum*): stories of Jerusalem and of its imminent rebuilding. On sabbaths the beggar takes Rebb Schmul's son to the fields surrounding his village and there – standing in the midst of the Czech countryside – speaks at length of his 'distant fatherland': '[He] described to him the lands that he had just travelled through [in his imagination] or entertained him with fables and sacred tales. He never spoke a word about his own home [Heimat].'[84] In a chapter entitled 'Wo ist des Juden Vaterland', Kompert portrays the inner conflict of divided loyalties and cultural affinities in Moritz as a young gymnasium student. Cultural conflicts born of the classroom itself engender in Moritz a longing for Mendl Wilna's Jerusalem, on the one hand, and a desire to merge with the Hussites – the national heroes of his Czech friend Honza – on the other.

> Moritz also read history, but he was struck by a different spirit. As a Jew he did not understand the nature of the religious struggles of Bohemia; it was all the same to him if one took communion in one or both kinds. [. . .] But the political significance seized him mightily. Here he saw a battle for good and freedom and independence; here his own feelings could join in. Jerusalem and Bohemia! The same spirit of the night enveloped the two giant corpses with the silence of the grave.[85]

As Havlíček would have it, the longing for Zion, the positioning towards the East, represented more than a pious memory (or a 'holy error'). It was a living reality that helped to define the ethnic distinctiveness of Jews. And he reproached those Jews who wanted to abandon their culture, including their 'natural' language, Hebrew. To those who had already thrown Hebrew overboard, he offered the advice that they take up German, as it had apparently become the second mother tongue of European Jewry.[86]

Havlíček's reply to Siegfried Kapper did close the door on the brief experiment in Czech–Jewish literary and cultural co-operation. The fact that it was sandwiched between anti-Jewish riots in 1844 and 1848 seemed to emphasize the finality of the rejection. Equally significant, however, was the fact – often overlooked – that Havlíček had been Václav Bolemír Nebeský's closest collaborator and confidant throughout the 1840s. Nearly all of Nebeský's early pronouncements on Czech–Jewish co-operation had appeared in Havlíček's paper *Česká včela*; Nebeský himself took over the editorship of the paper in 1847. One must conclude, then, that Havlíček had given his tacit approval to the Nebeský–Kapper–Kuh initiative in 1843 and 1844 and that he, himself, decided to put a stop to it by attacking the work of Nebeský's closest Jewish ally in the same organ that had started it all.[87]

Havlíček's contention that the Jews of the Czech lands constituted their own nation did not find much of an echo among the Jews themselves. Jewish political efforts, social ambitions and sense of identity throughout the middle decades of the nineteenth century were predicated on the opposite notion, that a separate Jewish nationality did not exist in Central and Western Europe. Intellectuals, industrialists and tradesmen alike desired political rights, economic opportunity and social advancement above all. The order of the day simply did not leave room for Jewish cultural nationalism. If Jews did seem to take to heart one piece of advice, it was to complete their embrace of German language and culture, well under way since the first efforts at Jewish 'modernization' in the 1780s. With the elaborate network of German–Jewish primary schools in place, secondary and higher education squarely within the German orbit and a state apparatus that offered clear advantages to German speakers (west of Hungary, at least), there was little to hold Jews back from complete German acculturation. Nor, in the face of Czech popular antagonism, did there appear to be any alternative.

In the summer of 1844 Moritz Hartmann wrote to Alfred Meissner in Prague expressing the outrage that was by now common among Bohemian Jewish intellectuals. He also unwittingly offered an apt metaphor for the shrinking cultural horizon of his fellow Jews. In an allusion to his already completed book of poems, *Kelch und Schwert* (part of which glorified the democratic and social ideals of the Hussites), Hartmann wrote: 'When one hears about a revolution of the kind made by your fellow Praguers [i.e. the anti-Jewish riots – H.K.], the best thing for a person to do is to become a loyal citizen and make his volume of poetry smaller by half.'[88]

> Pfui; what a miserable pack of hounds! There is no idea of national consciousness there, of proletarian sentiment, of historical memory, or of a view to the future. Miserable, pitiful, petty materialism. The fleamarket their Bastille, the ghetto their St Denis . . . if it were to come down to it, I would be the first volunteer for Austria, in other words for Germany. [. . .] My friend, the time has come for us in Bohemia to stand as Germans; that will be our post in the future.[89]

Gradually, between 1844 and 1850, the Jewish intellectuals of Bohemia did make up their minds to 'stand as Germans', combining an adherence to German culture with an ongoing commitment to democratic politics. Only Siegfried Kapper, David Mendl and Ignác Schulhof retained their pro-Czech sympathies to varying degrees. Kapper, in fact, did not respond directly to Havlíček's devastating review of his work. He simply stopped writing original prose and poetry in Czech, devoting himself instead to the more-appreciated calling of translation. Kapper took his medical degree in 1847, participated in the revolution in Vienna in March 1848, became a doctor of surgery in 1851 and practised for a number of years in Croatia, Serbia and the Banat before returning to his native land in 1854. His literary output after 1847 consisted of translations from Czech and from Serbian, travel accounts (*Südslavische Wanderungen*, 2 vols., 1853), and fiction in German. He, like Kompert, now chose Jewish themes for his fiction, seeking to recapture the quality of life in the towns and villages of Bohemia both before and in the face of the disappearance of traditional Jewish society. He published, among other things, ghetto stories, a *Bildungsroman* based on Jewish gymnasium life in *Vormärz* Bohemia, and a novel about a Jewish family in the Bohemian countryside.[90]

During the 1848 revolution in Prague, Moritz Hartmann made good his promise to promote German progressivism. He attended the Frankfurt Pre-parliament (*Vorparlament*) as a trustee and was then elected to the National Assembly from Leitmeritz (Litoměřice), where he sat on the far left. When Austria recalled its delegation from the Assembly in Frankfurt, Hartmann sought refuge in Stuttgart; when this city was occupied by Prussian troops, he began a prolonged period of travel, pausing for a number of years in Switzerland and in Paris, but visiting England, Scotland and Ireland as well, serving as a war correspondent on the Crimean front, then on to Germany once more, France, Switzerland and Italy. The democrat and lover of German culture, Hartmann's true *patria* was Europe; his feet, however, rarely found rest.[91]

Isidor Heller was back in Pest in March 1848, where he edited the political journal *Die Morgenröthe*. But his second stay in Hungary also ended abruptly. By the end of May he was forced to abandon both Pest and the paper as the result of articles that he had written against the government of Louis Kossuth, articles that protested against Hungarian policies towards its national minorities. Returning to Vienna in June 1848, Heller wrote leading articles under his real name for *Der Freimütige*. As a political moderate he was able to remain safely in Vienna until December, at which point he made his way to Frankfurt, and from there to Berlin. Heller finally managed to get himself into trouble in 1852, by publishing a brochure entitled *Sendschreiben eines österreichers an die deutsche Nation*, in which he accused Prussia of being a hindrance to German unity. The Prussian authorities reacted by giving Heller twenty-four hours to leave Berlin. Ensconced once more in Vienna, Heller found a receptive audience in Austrian government circles; served as private secretary to Baron Bruck (in Constantinople!); wrote on foreign affairs for the *Österreichische Zeitung* and eventually edited the paper *Der Fortschritt*. In his political writings Heller argued for freedom of religion, equality and autonomy for the nationalities of the monarchy, but against the 'overreaching' of the nationalities beyond the reasonable bounds of autonomy.[92]

Simon Hock lived through the revolution of 1848 in Prague apparently uninvolved in revolutionary activity *per se*. He contributed articles to the *Österreichisches Central-Organ für Glaubensfreiheit*, criticizing the Jewish community for failing to respond to the events of 1848 by democratizing its own structure. But he himself did not lead a revolt against the communal authorities. Rather, after marrying in 1849, he became involved in the day-to-day affairs of the Prague community, helping to write its new statutes in 1850, and settled down to his life-long vocation of investigating and writing the history of the Jews of Prague. In 1856 he collaborated with Koppelmann Lieben to bring out a collection of 170 gravestone inscriptions from the Prague Jewish cemetery together with accompanying biographies. Though he never fulfilled his ambition of publishing a complete history of Prague Jewry, he remained committed to the writing of local history throughout his remaining years.[93]

Interestingly, David Kuh rebounded from his disillusionment with Czech nationalism by trying his hand as an actor with a German theatre troupe travelling through Moravia. Tiring of this, he began a career in journalism and found himself in 1848 in Pest trumpeting the cause of Hungarian independence in the pages of an obscure German paper. He soon started his own (German) paper in the Hungarian town of Pécs (Fünfkirchen), where he supported Kossuth's politics and agitated against Hungary's Slavic populations. When the Hungarian revolution collapsed, Kuh was sentenced to six years in prison, but was released in 1850 following the proclamation of a general amnesty.[94]

At this point Kuh returned to his native city of Prague, founded first the *Prager Zeitschrift für Literatur* and then the more successful *Tagesbote aus Böhmen*, achieved respectability, co-founded the German Independent Party, served in the Bohemian Diet (1862–73) and finally in the Austrian Reichsrat (1872–3).[95] In the autumn of 1858 Kuh's paper, the *Tagesbote*, published an anonymous attack on the authenticity of the Králové dvůr manuscript, which, it will be recalled, had been 'discovered' in 1817 and purported to represent an early example of Czech national literature. The charge elicited a storm of protest from the Czech middle class. František Palacký himself launched a public campaign against Kuh, asking sarcastically how his 'Börsen-Blatt' (clearly implying *Judenblatt*) suddenly became interested in literary issues. Czech nationalists pressured the by now elderly Hanka to initiate a libel suit against Kuh. The sensational trial took place in the summer of 1859 and coincided with the rebirth of political life in Bohemia following the collapse of neo-absolutism. Kuh, it seems, was indeed found guilty of libel, though he was ultimately vindicated. In the 1880s Tomáš Masaryk would be attacked by loyal Czech nationalists for publishing the very same claim about the manuscripts in his journal *Athenäum*. By Masaryk's time, however, the charge of forgery proved incontrovertible.[96]

Christoph Stölzl wonders openly why Kuh, who apparently remained on friendly terms with Nebeský and other Czechs in the 1850s, should have taken it upon himself to launch an attack on the famous 'Czech manuscripts'. Surely the answer to this question is not hard to find. It lies in the anti-Jewish uprisings of the 1840s and in

Kuh's reading of both the origins and the shortcomings of middle-class nationalism. The modern Czech movement, he noted, had been born and nurtured in the gymnasiums and universities, the very places where he and his generation had come to love the 'other' language and culture of Bohemia. There they had created their own vision of an alternative society, an open, meritocratic community whose benefits were to be enjoyed fully by both Czechs and Jews. Cultural nationalism, however, was itself the by-product of an uneasy tension that existed between the Enlightenment rationalist tradition and the romanticism of the nineteenth century. It always carried the danger that myth and fanaticism would replace reason and tolerance in the effort to further the national cause. Siegfried Kapper's Malá Strana gymnasium had been the setting for the Hanka forgery of 1817, aided and abetted by the influential Professor Václav Svoboda. Perhaps inevitably, it was the same Svoboda who incited his students to violence against Jews during the riots of 1844. His was a *trahison des clercs* that ultimately alienated Kuh and most of his fellow Jewish intellectuals from the Czech cause as a whole.

Kuh sought the ultimate revenge in 1858. His charge that the Czech manuscripts were fakes implicitly discredited the romantic-intellectual stream of the Czech national movement. He was also able to punish Václav Svoboda and all other Czech intellectuals who had either supported or condoned the violence of the 1840s. Stölzl, I think, correctly points to the significance of the fact that the person who launched the attack on the sacred icons of Czech national renewal was the same one who fourteen years earlier had tried ('with . . . an almost religious idealism') to bring Jews and Czechs together.[97] With the campaign in the *Tagesbote*, Kuh symbolically closed the chapter on a brief experiment in the modern history of Czech Jews. But he also did more. As Moritz Hartmann had suggested in 1844, Kuh was making the book 'smaller by half', signalling the retreat of educated Jews and intellectuals from Czech concerns.

The retreat was not to be permanent, however. Beginning in the last third of the century, demographic and social factors would prove to be more important in determining cultural affiliation than the political experiences of the monied and educated elite. The removal of family and occupational restrictions in the 1840s and 1850s had been followed by a steady growth in the rural and small-town Jewish population of Bohemia. By the 1870s and 1880s tens of thousands of Jews – provincial in origin and conversant in Czech language and culture – flocked to the larger cities and towns of the Crown lands, there to find work in industry, banking and commerce and to feed their children through the expanded networks of secondary and higher education. The first Czech-Jewish student association was founded in Prague in 1876; the first Czech-Jewish religious association five years later; the first political organization of Jewish Czech nationalists emerged in 1893 and with it came a Czech-language Jewish newspaper. While Jews from the Czech provinces were overwhelming the traditional community in Prague and other urban centres, the Czech national movement itself was usurping the power of German elites in virtually all public spheres.[98]

Consequently, the socio-political context in which Jewish life was carried out, in which cultural choices and alliances were made, bore only the remotest resemblance to that of the 1840s. The popular violence and political insults of that decade were largely forgotten, but not because the Czech populace no longer vented its fury on the Jews nor because the political relationship was now free of tension. If anything, the 1890s witnessed a great deal more violence against Jewish life and property and much greater political pressure directed by Czech nationalists toward Jews. But in the 1840s both the German elites and the Habsburg house held sway in Bohemia. Until at least the 1870s the Jews of Bohemia could afford to follow a 'narrow' vision of community – one that essentially excluded both the Czech nation and Jewish ethnic nationalism – because the German Habsburg option was still alive. By the twentieth century the social vision of Czech Jews was compelled to widen as the former options were closed.

Notes

1 Other stepping-stones towards legal emancipation included the lifting of the prohibition on Jewish ownership of landed property (1841), and Franz Josef's Constitutional Edict of 1849, which granted Jews equality with Christians under law. On Jewish emancipation in the Habsburg monarchy, see Wolfgang Häusler, 'Toleranz, Emanzipation und Antisemitismus: Das österreichische Judentum des Bürgerlichen Zeitalters (1782–1918)', in Nikolaus Vielmetti (ed.), *Das österreichische Judentum: Voraussetzungen und Geschichte* (Vienna and Munich, 1974); Wolfdieter Bihl, 'Die Juden', in Adam Wandruszka and Peter Urbanitsch (eds.), *Die Habsburgermonarchie, 1848–1918*, vol. III: *Die Völker des Reichs* (Vienna, 1980), pp. 890–6; and the following chapters in Jacob Katz (ed.), *Toward Modernity: The European Jewish Model* (New Brunswick and Oxford, 1987): Hillel J. Kieval, 'Caution's Progress: The Modernization of

Jewish Life in Prague, 1780–1830', pp. 71–105; Michael Silber, 'The Historical Experience of German Jewry: Its Impact on the Haskalah and Reform in Hungary', pp. 107–57; and Lois C. Dubin, 'The Italian Role in the Cultural Politics of the Haskalah', pp. 184–224.

2 On the politics of nationalism in the Habsburg Monarchy, see generally Adam Wandruszka and Peter Urbanitsch (eds.), *Die Habsburgermonarchie, 1848–1918*, vol. III: *Die Völker des Reichs* (Vienna, 1980); Robert A. Kann, *The Multinational Empire, 1848–1918*, 2 vols. (New York, 1950) and *Austrian History Yearbook*, 3 (1967).

3 See Paul Mendes-Flohr, 'The Study of the Jewish Intellectual: Some Methodological Proposals', in Frances Malino and Phyllis Cohen Albert (eds.), *Essays in Modern Jewish History* (Rutherford, N.J., 1982), pp. 142–72; also Georg Simmel, 'The Stranger', in Kurt H. Wolff (trans. and ed.), *The Sociology of Georg Simmel* (New York, 1950), pp. 403–8; and J. P. Nettl, 'Ideas, Intellectuals, and Structures of Dissent', in Philip Rieff (ed.), *On Intellectuals, Theoretical Studies: Case Studies* (Garden City, N.Y., 1969).

4 On the system of German–Jewish primary schools after 1815, see Johann Wanniczek, *Geschichte der Prager Haupt- Trivial- und Mädchenschule der Israeliten, deren Verfassung und merkwürdigen Vorfälle von ihrer Grundung bis auf gegenwärtige Zeiten* (Prague, 1832); also Ruth Kestenberg-Gladstein, *Neuere Geschichte der Juden in den böhmischen Ländern. Erster Teil: Das Zeitalter der Aufklärung, 1780–1830* (Tübingen, 1969); and Kieval, 'Caution's Progress'.

5 The main biographical sources consulted were the following. For Hartmann: Constant von Wurzbach, *Biographisches Lexikon des Kaiserthums Österreich*, 60 vols. (Vienna, 1856–91), vol. VIII, pp. 4–11; Heribert Sturm (ed.), *Biographisches Lexikon zur Geschichte der böhmischen Länder*, 3 vols. (A–M) (Vienna, 1975–84), vol. I, p. 544; S. Wininger, *Grosse jüdische Nationalbiographie*, 7 vols. (Czernowitz, 1925–36), vol. III, pp. 8–10; and Otto Wittner, *Moritz Hartmanns Jugend* (Vienna, 1903). For Heller: Wurzbach, *Lexicon*, vol. VIII, pp. 272–5; Sturm, *Lexicon*, vol. I, p. 589. For Hock: David Kaufmann, Introduction to Simon Hock, *Die Familien Prags nach den Epitaphien des alten jüdischen Friedhofs in Prag* (Pressburg, 1892), pp. 1–36; and Guido Kisch, *In Search of Freedom: A History of American Jews from Czechoslovakia* (London, 1949), pp. 43, 270–1, 272–3. For Kapper: Oskar Donath, *Siegfried Kappers Leben und Wirken* (Berlin, 1909; offprint from *Archiv für slavische Philologie*, 30); Donath, 'Siegfried Kapper', *Jahrbuch der Gesellschaft für Geschichte der Juden in der Čechoslovakischen Republik* 6 (1934), 323–442; Wurzbach, *Lexicon*, vol. X, pp. 451–2; and Sturm, *Lexicon*, vol. II, p. 102.

For Kompert: Stefan Hock, 'Komperts Leben und Schaffen', in Leopold Kompert, *Sämtliche Werke*, vol. I (Leipzig, 1906), pp. v–lviii; Wilma Iggers, 'Leopold Kompert, Romancier of the Bohemian Ghetto',

Modern Austrian Literature 6 (1973), 117–38; Wurzbach, *Lexicon*, vol. XII, pp. 404–10; Wininger, *Nationalbiographie*, vol. III, pp. 506–7; and Sturm, *Lexicon*, vol. II, p. 238. For Kuh: Wurzbach, *Lexicon*, vol. XIII, p. 340; *Allgemeine Zeitung des Judentums*, 11 February 1879; and Christoph Stölzl, 'Zur Geschichte der böhmischen Juden in der Epoche des modernen Nationalismus', part 1, *Bohemia* 14 (1973), 200–3; part 2, *Bohemia* 15 (1974), 138–42.

6 Johann Wanniczek, who served as director of the *Normalschule* in Prague from 1827 to 1838, railed in writing against the tendency of many Jewish families to circumvent the state school in favour of private tutoring. The government sought to curb the practice after 1815 by clamping down on the many private tutors (*Bocherim*) who plied their trade in Prague with measures that included the expulsion of many of them. An ordinance of 1819, moreover, required all *Hauslehrer* to receive instruction in the teaching methods of *Bne Zion* – since 1812 the required textbook of Jewish morality – from the author himself, Herz Homberg. Previous ordinances had made an examination in this text obligatory for all prospective Jewish brides and grooms as well as for all Jewish students who chose not to attend the community school.

The year 1815 appears to have marked an important upswing in the fortunes of the Prague *Normalschule* for other reasons as well. It was at this point that the hours of instruction in the winter were finally extended from only two hours per day (5 p.m. to 7 p.m.) to two hours in the morning (8 a.m. to 10 a.m.) plus two in the afternoon (2 p.m. and 4 p.m.). It was also in 1815 that Anton Raaz, formerly director of the non-Jewish *Hauptschule* in Kutná Hora, was appointed director of the Prague Jewish school, providing it apparently for the first time with both the organization and the direction that it had lacked up to this time. Lastly, following a period of critically low attendance during the Napoleonic wars (only 144 pupils in 1809; less than 400 in 1814), the figures began to shoot up dramatically after 1815 and soon reached an annual average of between 700 and 800 students. (See Wanniczek, *Geschichte*, esp. pp. 32–3, 36–7, 39, 42–3, 46, 52–3, and 55–6).

7 For Kuh, see Wurzbach, *Lexicon*, vol. XIII, p. 340; for Kompert, Wurzbach, *Lexicon*, vol. XII, pp. 404–10; Wininger, *Nationalbiographie*, vol. III, pp. 506–7; and Hock, 'Komperts Leben und Schaffen'.

8 Wurzbach, *Lexicon*, vol. VIII, pp. 272–5.

9 Wittner, *Moritz Hartmanns Jugend*, pp. 9–11; Wurzbach, *Lexicon*, vol. VIII, pp. 5. In 1832 the young Hartmann presented himself at the *Hauptschule* in Neukollin, where an aunt of his lived, and took an examination that apparently was required of students who sought to circumvent the primary schools. He passed the examination and the following year, chaperoned by his father, moved to Prague, where he attended the first class of the Altstädter gymnasium. For reasons that are unclear – perhaps

because the father's business required him to return home – this
arrangement did not work out. It was at this point that Hartmann set out
for his grandfather's home in Mladá Boleslav.

10 Donath, 'Siegfried Kapper', pp. 325–6; and Siegfried Kapper, 'Autobiographie I', in Donath, 'Siegfried Kapper', p. 396.

11 Donath, 'Siegfried Kapper', p. 326; Donath, *Siegfried Kappers Leben und
Wirken*, pp. 404–5; and Kapper, 'Autobiographie II', in Donath,
'Siegfried Kapper', p. 398.

12 Kaufmann, Introduction to *Die Familien Prags*, pp. 5–8. Hock once
recounted to the writer Salomon Kohn that the same man who warmed
cholent for the sabbath afternoon meals of Prague Jews also ran a lending
library of secular works consisting largely of German fiction. For a
nominal fee, he lent books out on Friday afternoon, when servants or
other household members would bring their pots of food for warming
over the sabbath. Hock shocked his mother when, as a nine- or ten-year-
old boy, he asked her for the few kreutzer that it cost to borrow books
from this makeshift library. In panic, she offered to pay him ten times the
amount he was seeking if he agreed to refrain from reading such works.

13 Kaufmann, Introduction, pp. 9–12.

14 Wittner describes Isaac Spitz as 'pious, without clinging to dogma,
himself a poet with a clear knowledge of the world and of man' (*Moritz
Hartmanns Jugend*, p. 11).

15 Wittner, ibid., pp. 20–1.

16 The elder Kapper, though a native of Smíchov, had apparently spent the
years 1810 to 1816 abroad in activities that ranged from fighting for the
French to teaching for the Swiss. According to Siegfried Kapper, the
father learned the craft of glassmaking upon his return to Bohemia in
order to be exempted from the provisions of the *Familiantengesetze* and
thus be allowed to marry ('Autobiographie I', p. 396).

17 Donath, 'Siegfried Kapper', pp. 327–8; Donath, *Siegfried Kappers Leben
und Wirken*, pp. 405–8. On the Králové dvůr and Zelená hora manuscripts, see Hanuš Jelínek, *Histoire de la littérature tchèque. Des origines à 1850*.
2nd edn. (Paris, 1930), pp. 275–84. Jelínek explains the cultural
significance of the forgeries as follows: 'La nation tchèque, qui réclamait
sa place parmi ses soeurs, et qui, elle aussi, avait une histoire si glorieuse,
serait-elle seule condamnée à ne point posseder de chants digne de ce
passé? Prouver par des vestiges littéraires l'existence d'une antique
civilisation slave indépendente de l'Occident latin et germanique, tel
était le rêve des partiotes' (p. 278).

18 Moritz Hartmann complained in retrospect of his 'wasted' gymnasium
years to Alfred Meissner: 'Wie würden wir im Vormärz um unsere Jugend
betrongen! Sechs Jahre sassen wir auf den Bänken des Gymnasiums, um
nichts zu tun, als die schönste, früchtsbarste Zeit des Lebens zu verlieren,
also um die Jahre vorübergehen zu lassen, welche in anderen Ländern die

Säemonate des Lebens sind, und brach liegen zu bleiben. Sechs Jahre lernten wir wörtlich lateinishce Regeln auswendig, ohne je einen ordentlichen lateinischen Autor lesen zu dürfen; vier Jahre lernten wir Grieshisch, um an Ende nicht zwei Verse Homers übersetzen zu können, und noch lernten wir Lateinisch und Griechisch besser also unsere Muttersprache' (quoted in Wittner, *Moritz Hartmanns Jugend*, p. 10).

19 Wittner, ibid., p. 11.
20 Leopold Kompert, *Sämtliche Werke*, vol. 1(Leipzig, 1906–7), pp. 116–18.
21 Donath relates that Kapper 'schon am Gymnasium als "Poet" fühlte'. When he arrived in Prague in the autumn 1837 he quickly gravitated toward the circle of aspiring poets known as 'Young Bohemia' (Donath, 'Siegfried Kapper', p. 329).
22 Ibid., Wittner, *Moritz Hartmanns Jugend*, pp. 14, 17–20; Wurzbach, *Lexicon*, vol. XII, pp. 405–6.
23 Wurzbach, *Lexicon*, vol. VIII, p. 273; vol. XIII, p. 340.
24 Donath, 'Siegfried Kapper', pp. 328–9; Wittner, *Moritz Hartmanns Jugend*, pp. 17–20.
25 Ibid., p. 23.
26 See Wittner, *Moritz Hartmanns Jugend*, pp. 23–4. Glaser sketched out his ambition for the journal in its June 1837 announcement: 'The interests of the cultured nations are becoming more and more similar; more and more the spatial and spiritual distance between them is disappearing; and everything that furthers this goal will be taken up with great favour. May this new literary undertaking also serve in part . . . as a literary mediation between the Slavic East and Germany, and thereby contribute to the world literature, which is still taking shape. What country would be more appropriate [to this endeavour] than Bohemia, with its half Slavic, half German, population; Bohemia, the border between the European East and West; a country rich in writers who are familiar with all of the Slavic dialects' (reproduced in Alois Hoffman, *Die Prager Zeitschrift 'Ost und West': Ein Beitrag zu Geschichte der deutsch-slawischen Verständigung im Vormärz* [Berlin, 1957], table 1, and p. 27).
27 Hoffman, *Die Prager Zeitschrift 'Ost und West'*, pp. 316 ff.
28 Ibid.; W. Wessely, 'Zur Anthologie der Rabbinen', *Ost und West*, 7 February 1845. Wessely introduced his brief anthology with the remark: 'Der Sagenschatz und Mythenkreis der alten Hebräer, so wie ihr grosser Gnomenreichthum ist trotz des vielen Schönen, das Herder in seiner Blumenlese zur Kenntniss brachte, und trotz der merhrfachen Bearbeitung, die sie, namentlich die Gnomeologie in neuerer Zeit gefunden hat, noch immer viel zu wenig bekannt und gewürdigt worden.'
29 See, for example, Kapper's *Selbstbiographie*, p. 397: 'So blieb mir nur die Nacht zum Studieren und der Weg vom Hause zum Clementinum und zurück zum Versemachen. An Sonn- und Ferialtagen schrieb ich Dramen.'

30 Wittner, *Moritz Hartmanns Jugend*, pp. 23–4, 38; Wurzbach, *Lexicon*, vol. VIII, p. 6.

31 Wurzbach, *Lexicon*, vol. VIII, p. 273.

32 Donath, 'Siegfried Kapper', p. 331–2.

33 Ibid., pp. 352–63.

34 Wurzbach, *Lexicon*, vol. XII, pp. 406–7.

35 David Kaufmann, Introduction to Hock, *Die Familien Prags*, pp. 9–10.

36 In Kaufmann's words, 'Wohl ging die Wirksamkeit Zunzens in Prag wie ein schneller Traum vorüber, aber schon 1836 trat die glänzende Erscheinung Michael Sachsens an seine Stelle, durch die macht seines Wortes, durch den Zauber seiner Rede wie durch ein hoheitsvolles Wesen mit sich fortreissend und emportragend. In solcher Sprache waren die Lehren und Gedanken des Judenthums noch nicht verkündet worden; es war dies die Erfüllung einer ungestillten Sehnsucht, die Verwirklichung eines Ideals, der Bund judischen Geistes und deutscher Cultur, die goldenen Früchte des Judenthums in den silbernen Schalen der klassischen Bildung' (*Die Familien Prags*, p. 11). On the careers of Sachs and Rapoport in Prague, see David Rosin, 'Erinnerungen an S. L. Rapoport', in *Das Centenarium S.J.L. Rapoport's. Festgabe des "Österreichischen Wochenschrift"* (Vienna, 1890), pp. 400–3.

37 Kaufmann, Introduction, pp. 11–12.

38 Kapper first began to study Serbian language, literature and folk culture in Prague under the influence of the writings of Jakob Grimm. Later, while in Vienna, he became a friend of the writer Vuk Stefanović Karadžić and continued his studies in South Slavic culture (Donath, 'Siegfried Kapper', p. 333).

39 For a biographical sketch of Nebeský, see Wurzbach, *Lexicon*, vol XX, pp. 109–12, and Sturm, *Lexicon*, vol. III, p. 13.

40 See Wurzbach, *Lexicon*, vol. XX, p. 110.

41 Donath, 'Siegfried Kapper', pp. 333–4; and Donath, *Leben und Wirken*, p. 427.

42 Quoted in Donath, 'Siegfried Kapper', p. 334, and Donath, *Leben und Wirken*, p. 427. Donath does not indicate who the recipient of the letter was.

43 Articles in *Der Orient*, particularly those that originated from the Habsburg monarchy, were often published anonymously or with the author's initials only. This may have been done to bypass Austrian censorship laws and to evade the scrutiny of the secret police (though the newspaper in question was published in Leipzig). The censorship laws were not lifted until March 1848, during the early phase of the revolution, and the *Österreichsiches Centralorgan* – the voice of liberal, Austrian-Jewish opinion in 1848 – stands out for the prominent bylines that it attached to its articles. Nevertheless, Kuh's series in the *Allgemeine Zeitung des Judentums* ('Ein Wort an Juden und Slaven', 1 April, 8 April

and 15 April 1844) did appear under his full name. The report from Prague in *Der Orient* of 1 February 1844, which inaugurated the Nebeský–Kuh–Kapper newspaper campaign, resembles the series in the *Allgemeine Zeitung des Judentums* in tone, style and language.

44 *Der Orient*, 13 February 1844.
45 Ibid.
46 Ibid.
47 Ibid.
48 *Der Orient*, 14 May 1844; see also the follow-up report of David Kuh to the *Allgemeine Zeitung des Judentums*, 'Aus Böhmen', 6 May 1844.
49 *Der Orient*, 14 May 1844.
50 Kuh, 'Juden und Slaven', 1 April 1844.
51 Ibid.
52 Ibid.
53 Ibid., 8 April 1844.
54 Ibid.
55 Ibid.
56 Ibid.
57 Ibid., 15 April 1844.
58 Ibid.
59 See, for example, Stölzl, "Zur Geschichte," pt. 1, pp. 200–21; Kisch, *In Search of Freedom*, pp. 33–44; and Donath, *Leben und Wirken*, pp. 426–35. In contrast, Michael Riff argues that Hartmann's *Kelch und Schwert* was never intended to be a pro-Czech statement and, moreover, that Hartmann accepted the notion of German–Jewish acculturation 'without any question'. My own view is that this conclusion is true only after 1844. Cf. Michael Riff, 'Jüdische Schriftsteller und das Dilemma der Assimilation im böhmischen Vormärz', in Walter Grab and Julius H. Schoeps (eds.), *Juden im Vormärz und in der Revolution von 1848* (Stuttgart and Bonn, 1983), pp. 58–82.
60 Kuh, 'Juden und Slaven', 15 April 1844.
61 Nebeský, 'Opět něco o poměru Slovanů a Židů', *Kvety* (July 1844), quoted in Donath, *Leben und Wirken*, p. 431.
62 Ibid., pp. 431–2. Kuh followed up his series in the *Allgemeine Zeitung des Judentums* with a progress report in the 6 May 1844 issue. He remarked that the *rapprochement* of Jews and Slavs had taken a small, though not unimportant, step forward. A number of Jewish notables, including Leopold Edler von Lämmel and Forchheimer had donated money to the *Matice česká* (Foundation for Czech National Culture). Kuh reported on Nebeský's piece in *Květy*, adding that he was the first Slav writing for a Slavic newspaper who presented the Jews in an appreciative and unprejudiced light. Finally, Kuh remarked that many among Prague's Jews expressed the desire to see the establishment of a chair in Czech language at the German–Jewish *Normalschule* ('Aus Böhmen', *Allgemeine Zeitung des Judentums*, 6 May 1844.)

63 Stölzl, 'Zur Geschichte', pt. 1, p. 188; William O. McCagg, *A History of Habsburg Jews 1670–1918* (Bloomington, 1989), pp. 75–6.

64 Stölzl, 'Zur Geschichte', pt. 1, p. 204; McCagg, *Habsburg Jews*, pp. 77–8.

65 Riff, 'Judische Schriftsteller', p. 69; see also the reports of Prague correspondents to *Der Orient* in the 9, 23 and 30 July 1844 issues.

66 Stölzl, 'Zur Geschichte', pt. 1, p. 205; also the report in *Des Orient*, 22 October 1844, pp. 333–4.

67 The dispatches of 23 and 24 June appeared in *Der Orient* on 9 July 1844; the report dated 10 July appeared on 23 July 1844; and the 22 July report appeared in the 30 July 1844 issue of the paper. The dispatch dated 26 June, and signed '24', was published in *Der Orient* on 23 July 1844.

68 *Der Orient*, 9 July, 1844.

69 See p. 251 above.

70 *Der Orient*, 23 July 1844 (dispatch dated 10 July); also *Der Orient*, 9 July 1844.

71 *Der Orient*, 30 July 1844.

72 Ibid.

73 *Der Orient*, 23 July 1844, report of 26 June.

74 For example: '[Die Behörden] die in der Stunde der Gefahr, uns mit väterlicher Sorgfalt bedacht, mit bewunderungswürdiger Gewandheit Strenge und Milde zu paaren, und die gehörigen Mittel zu ergreifen gewusst, um den Aufruhr im Keime zu ersticken, und das Schiff der Ordnung durch die gefährlichen Klippen, sicher in den hafen des Friedens zu steuern.' (*Der Orient*, 23 July 1844).

75 *Der Orient*, 23 July 1844.

76 Ibid.

77 See Schulhof's contributions to *Der Orient* of 3 September, 15 October and 22 October 1844; and of 3 September, 10 September and 12 November 1845. I have not been able to obtain any biographical information on him, but cannot help but wonder whether he was not perhaps the father or uncle of the early twentieth-century Czech-Jewish writer and activist, Stanislav Schulhof.

78 For Kapper's *České listy* see Donath, 'Siegfried Kapper', pp. 338–41; and Kisch, *In Search of Freedom*, pp. 34–6, 202–12.

79 Partial texts of Havlíček's review are printed in Kisch, *In Search of Freedom*, pp. 213–44 (in Czech, with an English translation on pp. 36–8), and in Donath, *Leben und Wirken*, p. 434 (in German). My translation is based upon both sources.

80 Havlíček, 'Emancipace židů', *Slovan*, 12 October 1850; repr. in his *Politické Spisy*, ed. Z. Tobolka, vol. III (Prague, 1902), pp. 402–8.

81 Kisch, *In Search of Freedom*, p. 37.

82 Kapper, 'The Ninth of Ab' (*Na devátý ab*); reprinted and translated in Kisch, *In Search of Freedom*, pp. 210–12.

83 Kapper, 'Ben-Oni' (Son of Sorrow), in Kisch, *In Search of Freedom*, p. 208.

84 Kompert, *Aus dem Ghetto* (Leipzig, 1906), vol. I, p. 84.

85 Ibid., pp. 141–2.

86 'If the Jews want to know our personal opinion, we would advise them, if they insist on throwing overboard their language and literature, to attach themselves to the Germans and German literature, since the German language has become the second mother tongue of the Jews.' (In Kisch, *In Search of Freedom*, p. 38.)

87 See, again, the entries on Nebeský in Wurzbach, *Lexicon*, vol. XX, pp. 109–12; and Sturm, *Lexicon*, vol. III, p. 13.

88 Hartmann to Meissner, in O. Wittner (ed.), *Briefe aus dem Vormärz: Eine Sammlung aus dem Nachlass Moritz Hartmanns* (Prague, 1911), pp. 255–6. *Kelch und Schwert* did eventually appear (Leipzig, 1845), not reduced by half, but complete.

89 Ibid.

90 The works in question are 'Die Kohlen', which appeared in *Libussa* in 1849; *Herzel und seine Freunde: Federzeichnungen aus dem böhmischen Schulleben* (Leipzig, 1853); and *Falk: Eine Erzählung* (Dessau, 1853). On Kapper's later years, see: Donath 'Siegfried Kapper', pp. 345–87; Wurzbach, *Lexicon*, vol. X, pp. 451–52; and Riff, 'Jüdische Schriftsteller', pp. 71–9.

91 Wurzbach, *Lexicon*, vol. VIII, p. 6; Sturm, *Lexicon*, vol. I, p. 544; and Wininger, *Nationalbiographie*, vol. III, pp. 8–10.

92 Wurzbach, *Lexicon*, vol. VIII, pp. 272–5.

93 David Kaufmann, Introduction, pp. 19–27; Hock published regular reports from Prague in the *Österreichisches Central-Organ* as well as other articles, among them: 'Etudes aux deux crayons: über jüdische Zustände in Prag'; 'Die Prager Judengemeinde im Jahre 48' and 'Im Namen der verfolgten Juden in Böhmen, an ihre verfolgten Brüder in Ungarn'.

94 Wurzbach, *Lexicon*, vol. XIII, p. 340; *Allgemeine Zeitung des Judentums*, 11 February 1879 (obituary reprinted from the *Neue Freie Presse* of Vienna).

95 Sturm, *Lexicon*, vol. II, p. 340.

96 On David Kuh and the Králové dvůr manuscript see Stölzl, 'Zur Geschichte', pt. 2, *Bohemia* 15 (1974), 138–42; also Wurzbach, *Lexicon*, vol. XIII, p. 340; and *Allgemeine Zeitung des Judentums*, 11 February 1879.

97 Stölzl, 'Zur Geschichte', pt. 2, p. 139.

98 On the modern transformation of Czech Jewry, see Hillel J. Kieval, *The Making of Czech Jewry: National Conflict and Jewish Society in Bohemia, 1870–1918* (New York, 1988).

The entrance of Jews into Hungarian society in *Vormärz*: the case of the 'Casinos'

MICHAEL K. SILBER

In the last twenty years, the theme of Jewish social integration has been the focus of several social histories on the Jews of Germany and Western Europe.[1] The most thorough has been Jacob Katz's pioneering study on the complex relations between Jews and Freemasons from the inception of the first masonic lodges in the eighteenth century down to Hitler's Germany. Katz based his account on a wealth of material, the most important being previously inaccessible masonic archives. In this case-study of the 'neutral society', a concept he introduced elsewhere, Katz chronicled in depth the shifting fortunes of Jews in their quest for social acceptance in Western Europe and in particular in Germany.[2]

Was the social integration of the Jews in the different European countries more or less a uniform process or was it influenced by the varying structures and values of the host societies? Hungary is an interesting testing ground, for while Hungarian Jewry shared many of the features of German Jewry, the two host societies were quite different from each other. It would have been convenient to compare Jewish social integration in the two countries had there been masonic lodges in Hungary; the Freemasons, however, were banned in the Habsburg realms throughout most of the nineteenth century.[3] There did exist, however, an analogous 'neutral society' in Hungary whose history may provide the answers we seek – the social clubs, the so-called 'casinos'. There is enough *prima facie* evidence that Jews were indeed received into the casinos as early as the pre-1848 period to warrant a more detailed investigation.[4]

There are several methodological problems in researching the entrance of Jews into the casinos. Unlike the masonic lodges, the casinos were not centrally organized and therefore never generated the documentation that the Freemasons did, nor did they succeed in preserving more than a fraction of their archives.[5] Therefore, our historical reconstruction of the social integration of Jews into Hungarian society will of necessity be patchy; nevertheless, the broad contours of the process seem to be clear.

Although the focus of this paper will be the *Vormärz* period, that is, the generation before the 1848 revolutions, it will prove nevertheless instructive first to cast a glance at the state of Hungarian Jewry at the turn of the nineteenth century. The received wisdom about the nature and extent of Jewish assimilation in Hungary has been largely fashioned by the history of the *fin de siècle*, a fact which has unfortunately exercised an undue influence upon the assessment of other periods. A brief survey of the turn of the century can serve as a convenient yardstick against which to measure the history of Jewish integration in *Vormärz*.

Assimilation in *fin-de-siècle* Hungary

Located on the periphery of Central Europe, Hungarian Jewry was a latecomer to modernization. Nevertheless, by the First World War, the Jews of Hungary and especially of Budapest had earned a reputation as one of the most assimilated Jewries on the continent. During the previous fifty years, they had enthusiastically adopted the Magyar language – most impressively, even broad segments of Orthodox Jewry were now speaking Magyar – and the Magyarization of family and personal names was fashionable. Many had passionately embraced Hungarian nationalism, while conversely only a handful subscribed to the Zionist ideology preached by the Budapest-born Herzl.

But what did this assimilation entail? In the last three decades our conceptions of the process have become increasingly refined; different elements of assimilation have been analytically identified and some have been shown to be largely independent of the others. Thus, while recognizing that the majority of Jews in the modern period opted to discard traditional Jewish culture and have undergone extensive acculturation, Jewish historians have also argued that acculturation did not necessarily lead to more advanced stages of assimilation (although these advanced stages were clearly predicated upon acculturation).[6] Acculturation of many European Jewries was seldom accompanied or followed by 'structural assimilation', that is by some form of social intercourse which transcended the formal and segmented nature of traditional Jewish–gentile relations. On the other hand, in those rare instances where Jews were received into non-Jewish society, it was assumed that their primary allegiance would be transferred to the new reference group, that this was a 'zero-sum' process where social integration could only take place at the expense of loyalty to the Jewish community.

The state of Hungarian Jewry at the turn of the century bears out these distinctions. Acculturation by then was an accomplished fact: Jews were disproportionately represented in the secondary schools, in the universities, in the learned professions, in journalism and the arts. On the other hand, they seem to have made little progress in the social sphere. A foreign observer who could glowingly state that 'nowhere in the world were Jews better treated' than in Hungary, nevertheless was surprised that in this land 'there exists a social chasm between Jews and Christians which is matched by few other countries' including Germany.[7] Budapest rowing teams were divided along confessional lines; at the universities, student life was marked by growing antagonism between Jewish and non-Jewish students. On the shores of Lake Balaton, Jews tended to take their holidays at Siófok, while Christians went to bathe at Balaton-Földvár. The liberal Count Miklós Zay who was troubled by the growing social isolation of Hungarian Jewry, published an article 'Jews in Society' in 1904 where he recounted his own unhappy experience with prejudice.

> In 1897, I was the president of the great evening ball in the capital. When the time came to issue invitations, I was embarrassed to hear that Jewish families did not at all appear on the roster. For a while I protested, but the members of the organizing committee insisted that if Jews were to be invited, those who usually attend the ball will keep away. I personally became convinced of the truth of this allegation.[8]

Social segregation was most noticeable in the area of associational life. As one Zionist critic asserted bitterly, without exception in every large town in Hungary there exists 'at least one social club which is *Judenrein*'.[9] The worst offender was the Budapest *Országos Kaszinó*, the Country Casino, which was notorious for not accepting Jews 'on principle'. It was the worst, because this most influential casino was presided over by the 'shining, talented leader of the liberal party', the darling of the liberal press, Dr Sándor Wekerle, a man who was to serve three times as prime minister.[10] Although the statutes explicitly stated that membership was open to all, in practice Jews were all but excluded from its very inception in 1883. On the eve of the First

World War, to be sure, one could find twenty or so mostly ennobled men of Jewish origin in the casino, but significantly they were all or almost all converts to Christianity. 'Only one road is open to the wealthy and prominent Jew in his rise in society', wrote Count Zay, 'to abandon his father's faith and convert.'[11] Most observers were even less sanguine. In his insightful survey of Hungarian history, Paul Ignotus noted that at the turn of the century even converted Jews were almost entirely excluded from the upper reaches of Hungarian society.

> You could be the richest, the best educated, even officially the highest-ranking man in the kingdom, but if you had Jewish blood you could not hope to play *chemin de fer* in the premises reserved for the upper-middle-class gentry in the centre of Budapest. I knew a converted Jew, gentleman farmer, and ex-member of Parliament, titled and dandified, who could out-duel, out-ride, out-serenade all the Hungarian gentry of his circle; and he married a dowerless, most attractive girl of the ancient lesser nobility, 'the belle of the county ball' and of gentry parties in Budapest. After their wedding, she was still invited to the county balls, but they received a tactful warning that *he* had better plead public duties on that occasion. And he – and she – agreed; after all, she must not lose her old friends and there was no way of getting round such limitations.[12]

If walls of prejudice separated Jews from Hungarian society, they seemed to have been particularly insurmountable when it came to relations with the gentry. It was accepted wisdom that the company of the titled aristocracy was more accessible to Jews than the gentry's Country Casino in Budapest where high government officials congregated. It was also agreed that however bad social relations may have been in the capital, they were far worse in the provinces. 'The part of Hungarian society which harbours perhaps the least sympathy for Jews', wrote Zay, 'is the provincial gentry.'[13]

Surprisingly, as recent studies have shown, the ranks of the gentry were not hermetically closed and a considerable number born as commoners, as well as members of the minority nationalities were absorbed into what at first glance appeared to be a monolithic class of Magyar noblemen. The best example of this upward social mobility was Sándor Wekerle himself, a man of German middle-class stock. This openness, however, was of little benefit to Jews. As one observer noted, the factor which by the end of the century held these disparate elements together and helped crystallize their class identity was antisemitism.[14]

Anti-liberal attitudes began to gain currency among the gentry only in the late seventies and early eighties. Commenting in 1884 on the social decline of the gentry as a result of recent economic and political developments, the distinguished Albert Berzeviczy noted with alarm its growing tendency to embrace an alien, Junker-type politics, stamped by an agrarian and anticapitalist spirit. The gentry, once the mainstay of liberalism, now sought to make the sophistic distinction between the liberal views of their fathers and the present-day 'stock-exchange liberalism' or 'Jewish-liberalism'. 'It is undeniable', Berzeviczy lamented, 'that antisemitism has become widespread among the gentry.' The present course would only lead to disaster, he warned. He urged the gentry to return to the glorious ideals of the previous generations, to abandon the spirit of exclusiveness and to strive to amalgamate with the middle-class.[15]

Indeed, in the pre-1848 period, the theme of social amalgamation had often been voiced by liberal gentry. Recognizing that the national survival of Hungary demanded its economic modernization, men like Louis Kossuth actively worked towards the bourgeois transformation of Hungarian society. A change of mentality and habits was demanded of both the nobility and the traditional non-Magyar urban elements. Kossuth envisaged the 'bourgeoisfication' of the former and the 'nationalization' of the latter. Ideally, the two constituents, now transformed, would merge to form a Western type 'second estate'. 'Without an independent, enfranchised second estate', he argued, '. . . there is no hope for our nation.'[16]

Although Kossuth's utopia was never realized, there was indeed a brief period during the so-called 'Era of Reforms' (1825–48) when Hungarian liberals spoke of the need to achieve a sort of social *rapprochement* between the various classes. But did these high-sounding ideals remain empty words or was there a conscious effort to translate them into reality? Perhaps nothing proved a better litmus test of the sincerity of these intentions than the question of receiving Jews into Hungarian society. As elsewhere, the Jewish question soon became the touchstone of liberal ideals.

Hungarian society in *Vormärz*

Probably the most noticeable feature of Hungarian society in the first quarter of the nineteenth century was its static character. Impervious to those developments which had transformed the contours of society throughout Western and even Central Europe, Hungarian society appeared to be unchanged and unchanging. Society was rigidly stratified along quasi-feudal lines; an unbridgeable divide seemed to separate one segment from the other.

Hungary was first and foremost an agrarian society. At the bottom of the social and political pyramid were the peasants who constituted more than four-fifths of the Hungarian population. Although their lot had gradually improved in the last half century as a result of reforms initiated by Maria Theresa and Joseph II, they were still un-emancipated serfs bound by feudal obligations to their noble lords. Typical of the region, Hungary had a very weak middle class; only 5 per cent of the Christian population lived in urban centres. Whatever urban life there may have been was characterized by a pre-modern economy, mainly handicrafts and some trade organized in medieval guilds. Trade and industry in the modern sense were rudimentary: of the urban dwellers less than a fifth actually engaged in these activities. Some fifty cities, the so-called royal free or privileged cities, enjoyed a measure of municipal autonomy and were controlled by a small, tight-knit patriciate, mostly of German origin. Until 1840, most of these cities possessed the right not to tolerate Jews within their city walls and the burghers, fearing the growing economic strength of the Jews, fought tooth and nail to prevent their settlement. As a result, most of Hungary's estimated 300,000 Jews lived in noble-owned villages and unincorporated market towns. Even after legislation in 1840 permitted Jews to dwell in the privileged cities, many of them continued to campaign to have the law rescinded. In mentality and style of living, this was an embattled, backward-looking estate of burghers, not a French-style bourgeoisie – not even a German *Bürgerthum*. On political and economic issues, it sided consistently with the conservative Habsburg court against the liberal Magyar nation-alist movement.

Indeed, the main champions of liberal nationalism in Hungary were not members of the urban middle class as elsewhere in Central and Western Europe, but instead a segment of the rather numerous nobility. In Europe, Hungary's noble estates ranked second in size only to Poland's, constituting about 5 per cent of the population. In terms of preserving its *corporative* political power, it was unrivalled on the continent. The nobles owned the land and exercised judicial and political authority over the serfs living on their estates. They formed the 'political nation', controlling the local county administration and the national Diet in Pressburg where the cities were accorded no more than token representation. Moreover, not only the political, but most often the economic and cultural life of the country lay largely in their hands.

The nobility itself was greatly stratified. Although, in theory, all its members were politically on equal footing, they diverged greatly in wealth, power and outlook. At the apex of the noble estate stood the magnates, the titled aristocracy of barons, counts and princes. Some of these families, such as the legendary Esterházys, were immensely wealthy; most, however, led more modest lives. Of these several hundred aristocratic families, a minority was to provide a significant segment of the leadership of the liberal nationalist movement. Most of them, however, were cosmopolitans who wanted nothing to do with either Magyar nationalism or Magyar culture. Politically conservative, they too allied themselves with the Habsburg court against the liberal nationalism of the lower and middle nobility.

The remaining noble families, perhaps 130,000 in all, were again sharply divided. Most belonged to the so-called 'sandalled nobility' who were often no better off economically than the peasants. It was only the middle nobility, who formed about one-fifth of the noble population, that actually exercised considerable political power. The 'gentry' as they came to be known in contemporary parlance, led comfortable lives on their country estates. They were provincial patriots, often narrowly parochial, who were very different from the sophisticated aristocrats in outlook. Politically, they were the most important group in Hungary. Most of the county assemblies were under their control, as was the Lower House of the Diet which was growing increasingly powerful at the expense of the aristocratic upper chamber.

As a group, they were almost all Magyars. They perceived themselves as the true defenders of Hungarian liberties against the machinations of both the Habsburg court and its aristocratic allies. It was mainly from their ranks that the supporters of liberalism were drawn. Many Magyar nationalists found in the new liberal ideology affinities with the age-old struggle of the Hungarian estates to preserve their political liberties against absolutist Vienna.[17]

This sharp stratification of Hungarian society was paralleled by rigid divisions in day-to-day social life. The memoirs of an influential nineteenth century liberal, Ferenc Pulszky, provide a vivid description of these divisions, as well as of the changes which began to sweep Hungarian society in the third and fourth decades of the nineteenth century. Until the 1830s, he recalled, marriage between members of the noble and burgher estates was almost unknown and viewed as a social disaster. Such sentiments were not directed at the burghers alone: 'the gentry shut itself off not only from below, but from above, as well'. A noble who spent too much time in the company of his aristocratic betters was as likely to become the object of ridicule as his fellow who married beneath himself. 'In other words', wrote Pulszky, 'society was sharply divided into different classes which may have come into contact with each other, but never totally amalgamated [*összeolvadni*] with each other. It was to Count Stephen Széchenyi's credit that he attempted this fusion through the establishment of the Pest Casino.'[18]

The Pest National Casino

Indeed, it was with the widespread emergence in the late 1820s and early 1830s of the so-called casinos, societies modelled along the lines of the English club and condemned by Metternich as 'institutions for the diffusion of modern Liberalism',[19] that the first steps towards social *rapprochement* between the various classes in Hungary were attempted. And surely it is no coincidence, that one of the first demands for Jewish emancipation was to issue from just such a club, the *Jurátus-Kaszinó* at Pressburg, the meeting place in the mid 1830s of the law students who traditionally attended the Diet as observers.[20]

When the first Hungarian casino was inaugurated in Pest in 1827, its promoter, the liberal Count Stephen Széchenyi, declared that the purpose of the club was to create a framework in which people 'of any social standing' would be able to meet and spend their leisure moments chatting in a friendly atmosphere or reading journals of their choice. It followed that membership in the club of Pest was, at least theoretically, open to 'any person of integrity behaving like a gentleman'.[21]

In the summer of 1829, soon after the casino was established, Széchenyi proposed that Jews, too, should be eligible for membership. Since one of the objectives of the club was to encourage the trade of domestic agricultural produce, it was clear that Jewish participation in the casino would further this aim. Although the argument was blatantly pragmatic, it is all the more revealing of just how far men like Széchenyi were willing to follow through the imperatives of their liberal ideology. In the interest of creating a vigorous new nation, Széchenyi insisted that traditional social prejudices be transcended or at least set aside. It is quite remarkable that an aristocrat like

Széchenyi who harboured little sympathy towards Jews, was nevertheless willing to suppress his almost visceral aversion and include them in his vision of a newly constituted Hungarian society.

His proposal, however, met with vehement opposition. 'A heated debate on the pros and cons of Jewish membership in the club is taking place', the Count confided to his diary.[22] An agent of the secret police reported that Count George Károlyi, Széchenyi's liberal partner in founding the casino, would not countenance the idea and threatened to hand in his resignation. When it came to the vote, only Baron Nicholas Wesselényi, the leader of the liberal opposition at the Diet, and four other members supported Széchenyi's proposal; more than fifty opposed it.[23]

Almost a decade was to go by before the question of admitting Jews arose once again. 'Wodianer wishes to become a member of the casino', recorded Széchenyi in his diary in October 1837.[24] Samuel Wodianer, the richest merchant in Hungary at the time, was apparently the first practising Jew to apply for club membership. Perhaps he should have anticipated his rejection, for five years before even his converted relative Moritz Ullmann had been rebuffed. If Wodianer was the richest merchant in Hungary, Ullmann was rapidly making a name for himself as the country's most daring entrepreneur. From the thirties on, he had his finger in every major investment scheme in Hungary; his most notable achievements were the establishing of the country's first bank and its first railway. Again it is to Széchenyi that we owe the record of his thwarted social ambition. The Count, whose many projects brought him into frequent and not altogether pleasant contact with this hard-nosed businessman, noted (perhaps with some satisfaction), that 'Ullmann seems disgusted that he was denied membership of the casino'.[25] The Wodianers and the Ullmanns were to be frustrated in their social aspirations for almost another generation. It was not until the 1850s that several Wodianers and Ullmanns – the first 'Jews' to be admitted to the Pest National Casino – began to appear on the membership rosters and that was many years after their ennoblement and conversion to Christianity.[26]

But it should come as no surprise that the Pest National Casino refused to accept Jewish businessmen, since nearly all Christian burghers were also barred. Indeed, the clinching argument during the 1829 debate over Jewish membership had been that 'it would be impossible for us to merge with the Jews, since experience has shown that magnates do not wish to associate even with the gentry or the burghers'.[27] Only partial success could be attributed to the Pest National Casino in pursuit of its aim to encourage the social amalgamation of the various classes of Hungarian society. True, it did provide a new framework in which the different strata of the nobility were brought closer together. Here for the first time the gentry mingled on a daily basis with the high aristocracy. However, as Pulszky noted, 'even the well-established wholesale merchants of Pest were ill at ease in their company and went on to establish a separate casino, while as to the petit bourgeois [*Spiessbürger*], even the richest among them could not overcome their reservations about either group, and continued to frequent their coffee-houses for social recreation'.[28] From 1830 onward both clubs resided jointly in the stock exchange building: the National Casino, or as it was popularly known, the 'magnate casino' occupied the first floor, while the 'merchant casino' was located on the second floor – 'completely separated from one another', as one foreign observer noted.[29] We can be certain that no Jew was admitted to the Pest Merchant Casino, certainly not before 1846. Until then, Christian and Jewish merchants not only did not mix socially with each other, they also maintained separate trade associations. Only in 1846, when the Pest Wholesalers Corporation was established by forty-eight men of both confessions, did the barriers of segregation begin to come down in the business world.[30] Even this step affected only the wealthiest wholesale merchants; at the lower levels of the burgher class, hostility continued to simmer for a long time to come.

The first steps into the provincial casinos

The Pest National Casino was the most important in Hungary and served as a model for similar establishments throughout the country. Its regulations and practices were assiduously copied by other casinos which began to spring up in large numbers throughout the provinces. In 1831, there were only three such clubs outside Pest; in 1833, there were already twenty-three in Hungary and five in Transylvania.[31] By the end of the decade, casinos could be found in practically every major Hungarian town.

Many casinos tried to adhere to Széchenyi's programme of social amalgamation. A conscious attempt was made to tone down class differences. When a member of the Budavár Casino insisted that he be addressed as 'sir' [*úr*], he was greeted with hoots of derision and roundly condemned for what was deemed inappropriate 'caste mentality'.[32] Nevertheless, the very success of the casino movement was at odds with this trend to toleration. Once the casino began to expand, perhaps it was natural for the members to cluster into smaller circles and cliques. If at first this would take place within the given club, it was not unusual for a discontented group to secede and form a new casino, often along class lines. Hence, in one locale often there would be two casinos – that of the gentry (*úri kaszinó*) and that of the burghers (*polgári kaszinó*). Such was the case, in towns like Kaposvár, Székesfehérvár, Szekszárd and Pécs; in Baja there were three: that of the nobility, that of the 'non-noblemen' (probably the *honoratiori*) and that of the burghers.[33] There is no denying that this repeated fission worked at cross-purposes to Széchenyi's vision. A typical example was the Debrecen Casino founded in 1833. It was initially a mixed casino, but as the years passed, the burgher element began to bridle at the nobility's domination of the society. Finally, in 1841, the disgruntled burghers left to establish their own *polgári kaszinó*, and typically, the original society now became known as the club of the noblemen, the *úri kazinó*.[34] However, it would be rash to conclude that social homogeneity was the rule. On the contrary, many casinos, even those designated as *polgári* or *úri*, were not always strict about the social background of the candidate and one could find numerous members of other classes. In Szombathely, for example, although there were two casinos, neither one was based on class distinctions. In the 'casino of the gentry' most of the administrative positions were filled by burghers.[35]

Jews did not benefit even where the first indications of social flexibility began to appear. The mixed casino of Szombathely had turned down the application in the late 1830s of a doctor, reported Kossuth's liberal *Pesti Hírlap*, for no other reason 'I am ashamed to say, but that he was a Jew'.[36] Interestingly, the very application of the Jewish doctor seems to indicate that despite the *de facto* policy of exclusion, the power of liberal norms was such that there was no explicit statute barring Jews. In this they may have been following the lead of the Pest National Casino where such a statute was never formally introduced.

There were clubs in the provinces, however, which did specifically exclude Jews. The regulations of the casino of Gyöngyös were copied almost verbatim from those of its parent club in Pest. The first paragraph stated the objective of the organization and expressed the ambition to eliminate class distinctions within the walls of the club:

> The casino is an establishment which sets itself the goal of developing good taste, cultivated behaviour, striving for the benefit of the public,

to further intellect and mutual understanding. This pleasing place, dedicated to social activity, belongs to society as a whole, and one sector may not demand from another extra or exceptional privileges.[37]

New regulations, which were instituted in November 1839, specified quite liberal procedures for accepting new members. However, a qualifying phrase – 'that is with the exception, in general, of Israelites'[38] – made it clear that these were not applicable to Jews. Not only was membership closed to them, but the balls sponsored by the casino and usually open to the general public, barred them as well. 'Jews and servants are not to be admitted', concluded the paragraph on dances.[39] This was a clear departure from the Pest model. The relatively few casino regulations which have survived do not allow for any conclusive generalizations, but it would seem that Gyöngyös was one of few casinos with such explicit by-laws. The burghers and the high aristocrats eventually left the casino in 1842 to found their own clubs. Three years later, a suggestion was made at the Gyöngös Casino that Jews with 'diplomas' should be considered, but this was quickly defeated. (The reference was to university-trained professionals – before the emancipation of 1867, only medicine, not law, could be practised by Jews.) It was not until 1858 that the first two Jewish members were admitted into a once again united casino.[40]

In Komárom and Eger, the first a royal privileged city, the second the seat of the local diocese, a similar situation prevailed. When a Jewish merchant applied in 1834 to the casino of Eger (located in Heves county not far from Gyöngyös), it was resolved that 'No Israelites will be accepted with the exception of the diplomaed and these only after a secret ballot.' It was only some time around the mid forties that the first Jew, typically a doctor, Agoston Rosenthal, was accepted into the club.[41] In Komárom, the issue of Jewish admission was first raised on 4 November 1837, soon after deliberations on the admission of army officers. Although the statutes explicitly stated that membership was open to all regardless of rank or religion, it was argued that members had to be patriotic citizens (*hazafiak*) and Jews certainly did not fit this category. The assembly finally resolved that 'an Israelite can become a member of the casino only if he is elected by unanimous vote of the entire assembly. Therefore, should even one vote be cast against him, he cannot become a member.'[42]

This bleak picture should not make us blind to the considerable changes which were taking place even in the most recalcitrant casinos. True, Jews in general were still being excluded. But perhaps this was to be expected since, as we have seen, royal privileged cities such as Komárom or the seats of bishoprics such as Szombathely or Eger (where 'Jews were hardly allowed to sleep over'),[43] fought bitterly to keep Jews out of their precincts. It is all the more remarkable that the issue of Jewish membership should have been raised at all before 1840. Even these tales of frustrated social acceptance implicitly indicated a turn for the better. The Jewish doctor in Szombathely probably would not have applied for membership had he not been encouraged by the casino's socially mixed membership, by the increasingly overall liberal climate of opinion – witness the indignation of the *Pesti Hirlap* – and by some of the more liberal members of the club itself who probably sponsored his application. In most of these examples and in those which will follow, there seems to have been at least a minority of members who prodded their societies to adopt a more liberal policy towards Jews. It is also noteworthy that Szombathely, Komárom, Gyöngyös and Eger were located in counties (Vas, Komárom and Heves) which were among the most liberal in Hungary.[44] Although the cities were often autonomous pockets of conservatism, nevertheless the impact of the liberal surroundings could not be entirely ignored.

The initial step, therefore, was to suggest that the Jewish equivalents of the *honoratiori* – commoners who belonged to the intelligentsia and learned professions such as law or medicine – could apply for membership. This was a logical step, for the *honoratiori* occupied a special position in Hungarian society, often serving as a bridge between commoners and nobles. Even when commoners were not welcomed into some of the more exclusive noble casinos, it was almost a universal rule that these restrictions did not apply to the *honoratiori*.[45] Therefore, it should come as no surprise that when Jews stormed the casinos in the 1830s, Jewish doctors were in the vanguard. Their limited success should not blind us to the growing deference shown to liberal ideas. If the walls did not yet come tumbling down, nevertheless, by the mid 1830s the cracks were beginning to show even in the more conservative strongholds.

Balls, duels and grand tours

During the mid 1830s there were many reports of growing social contact between Jews and non-Jews, as well as of new behavioural modes among Jewish youth. The appearance of Jews at local casino dances was the first sign of this phenomenon. In 1838, at the inauguration of the casino in Palánka (in the southern county of Bács), a ball was held in which 'the more cultured local Jews also participated'. The editor of *Jelenkor*, a newspaper with a conservative–liberal affiliation under the auspices of Széchenyi, lauded this as a 'positive step towards progress which deserves to be emulated'.[46]

However, even when public opinion took a turn for the better from the later 1830s, the social absorption of Jews was still far from being a complete success. Early in 1841, the Hungarian press played up an incident at the annual lawyers' ball in Pest, traditionally one of the most exclusive dances. Only on rare occasions was someone other than a lawyer or a law student admitted, regardless of social class. Nevertheless, this particular year, some of the liberally disposed lawyers invited Jewish students and merchants as their guests. On the whole, the Jews were received well. Only one incident marred the festive occasion, when a rather 'heavy-set aristocrat demanded the removal of "Abrahamites" '. He grabbed a certain Kunewalder, the son of one of the most important Jewish families in town, and propelled him to the entrance, saying: 'Sir, you do not belong here!' To spare an unpleasant scene, Kunewalder did not put up any resistance, but on the following day he appeared at the nobleman's quarters and demanded satisfaction – a duel with swords or pistols. 'Deeply embarrassed', reported the newspaper with relish, '[the aristocrat] acknowledged that he had acted in haste and offered his apologies.' Mollified, Kunewalder was willing to call the duel off on the condition that his rival make the apology public. The following day a notice to this effect appeared in several Hungarian newspapers.[47]

Even where the opponents of Jewish entry into society were successful, they were increasingly placed on the defensive. One Jewish lessee – 'a man of culture', the newspaper noted approvingly – applied for membership to the *Lesegesellschaft* of Orosháza in Békes county. The assembly was thrown into uproar when just as his application was about to be approved, three estate administrators rose to their feet and dramatically warned that admitting Jews would endanger the very existence of the club. 'Let us not go to extremes by taking the wording of the regulations too literally', they cautioned, 'lest it provide an excuse for someone to propose an honest and cultured peasant for membership in the Orosháza Casino.' Nevertheless, despite the fact that he had already been accepted on principle by the club, the Jewish lessee decided to withdraw with grace and instead donated his membership fees to a local hospital.[48]

There can be no denying, however, that during these years there were surprising instances of increasing social *rapprochement* between Jews and non-Jews. Describing the changes which took place in his home-town, Eperjes, in the north, Ferenc Pulszky cited the example of his own family. His uncle, Fejérváry, who in his youth had belonged to the younger generation of the Hungarian Enlightenment was a staunch liberal. His business brought him into frequent contact with Jews; his partner in the opal mines of northern Hungary was the head of Viennese Jewry, the tycoon M. L. Biedermann. Even more than his business interests, it was his hobby as a collector of antiques which formed the basis of his friendship with Leo Holländer, the owner of one of the most important coin collections in the country. Like his father, the head of Sáros county Jewry before him, Holländer, too, was to assume a prominent role as a leader of Hungarian Jewry from the 1840s on. In 1833, Fejérváry invited Holländer to join him and young Pulszky for a five-month tour in Italy to visit sites of antiquarian interest. The elder Pulszky was enraged and scandalized by Fejérváry's gesture. 'He could not curb his hatred for the Jews whom he regarded as a race of serfs; it was beyond him how his brother-in-law could befriend Holländer.'[49]

Jews, burghers and nobles

The example of Holländer was, of course, highly unusual; a young Jew on a Grand Tour in the company of noblemen was not an everyday occurrence. Nevertheless, continuous and permanent social contacts between Jews and their gentile surroundings were becoming more commonplace in the established framework of the casinos. Such was the case in Pulszky's home-town, Eperjes, cause enough for the old-school gentry to grind their teeth. Pulszky recalled that the elderly Okolicsányi, the embodiment of the narrow-minded county magistrate,

> was angered by the continuous rise of the social status of the Jews. He resented their acceptance into the Eperjes Casino where they played cards with officals, judges and even the vice-sheriff of the county [the *alispán*], himself. He believed that 'toleration was a poisonous fume emitted by faddish constitutionalism'.[50]

What struck contemporary observers was that the social stratum most willing to enter into contact with Jews was, despite men like Okolicsányi, the gentry and not the burghers. A report on the favourable change in public opinion after 1840 pointed out that not all sections of Hungarian society shared the new receptiveness towards Jews. Above all, it was the nobility who embraced progressive attitudes, often with such fervor that 'in social relations all differences fall away and Jewish families associate in friendship with the nobility'.[51] The urban population in most royal free cities was none too friendly, as a rule, noted another report in 1844. In Kassa, they were still petitioning to have the Jews expelled from the city. These sentiments, however, did not make much headway in the local *Handlungs-Kaszinó* where the request by some members to exclude Jews had been forcefully rejected by the enlightened and humane count who presided over the society. In the absence of Germans, the correspondent concluded, Magyars will generally work towards improving the lot of the Jews.[52]

These themes were echoed in another royal free city, Arad. While the burghers of the town still denied Jews permanent residential rights – the so-called *incolat* – and objected to their presence at the ball, the nobility had already elected two Jews to administrative posts in the *Leseverein*.[53] The burghers, on the other hand, were not keen on joining the *Leseverein*: of the 152 members only 31 were burghers, in contrast to 39 Jews. Although constituting a minority in the society, the land-owning nobility was clearly the element which set the tone. In this liberal climate, Jews were made to feel more than comfortable. The following year it was reported that two Jews were once again elected to the executive committee and that the library of the society subscribed to the most important Jewish weekly, the *Allgemeine Zeitung des Judentums* published in Germany.[54]

Like Eperjes, Kassa and Arad, Szeged, too, was a royal free city where Jewish integration had already begun even before 1840. Despite its privileged status, an organized Jewish community had flourished there since the end of the eighteenth century. In fact, by the middle of the century Szeged housed one of the largest Jewish concentrations in Hungary. Relations with the Christian population were exemplary; Szeged was to earn the reputation as the Hungarian city where Jewish integration had progressed the furthest.[55] As elsewhere, it was a Jewish doctor who was the first to enter the Szeged Belváros or Palánki Casino. Gábor Cájus, a surgeon who also served on the Jewish community board, was admitted in 1834, just a few years after the casino's founding. Six years later, Joseph Basch was elected to the board of directors. Like many other associations in the decade following the 1848–9 revolution, the Szeged Casino also closed down temporarily in the 1850s. When it was reconstituted as the Palánki Casino towards the end of the decade, it numbered over

250 members. Between 1858 and 1866, the new casino repeatedly elected Cájus to serve as its president. Other members of the Jewish communal elite were also represented, including four who served as successive presidents of the Jewish community: Simon Ausländer (1857), Salamon Politzer (1859), Samu Bamberger (1860) and Dr Vilmos Singer (1864) who was on the casino's board during 1857–60. Cájus, himself, was the son of yet another community president.[56]

Jewish membership in the casinos of the royal free cities was rare.[57] As a rule, it was in those provincial market towns which did not enjoy urban autonomy and where the burgher element was weak that Jews registered their greatest success in breaking through the barriers of Hungarian society. The nobility played a prominent role in these towns; in most cases, the township itself was the private property of one of the great aristocratic families and its management lay in the hands of the magnate's noble functionaries. In these towns, large Jewish communities played a dominant role in the regional economy. Three such towns – Nagy Várad, Nagy Kanizsa and Pápa – all provide good examples of social integration in the Era of Reforms.

Nagy Várad was one of the main centres of trade in eastern Hungary where its eight-hundred Jews constituted approximately 5 per cent of the population. Although the town had a burgher casino, Jews were to be found in the Bihar County National Casino. This so-called noblemen's club boasted among its ranks several 'aristocrats from the oldest and most highly influential families in Hungary'. It had been founded in 1833 and numbered between 250 to 300 members. The active presence of outstanding liberal public figures such as Ödön Beöthy who served several terms on the board of directors and was elected as president in 1848, ensured that a climate favourable to Jews prevailed.[58] Social harmony prevailed in the town and was marred only on occasion by the burgher element. Over the years several reports mentioned the casino's 'many' Jewish members – no doubt an exaggeration. In fact, only 13 of the 245 members were Jewish in 1847, scrupulously in proportion to the town's Jewish population.[59] More impressive was that Jews were elected almost from the very beginning to the highest offices in the casino. In 1839, Dr Hermann Pollak was elected as the club's vice-president; later he was repeatedly elected as its librarian and treasurer. Another Jew, Salomon Reich served in 1841 on the board of directors.[60] Even more extraordinary was the election in the fifties of Dr Friedrich Gross, the chief physician of the Nagy Várad hospital as president of the 'casino of the aristocracy'. Gross was most active in Jewish affairs both locally and on a national level.[61]

In the southwest, Nagy Kanizsa played a role analogous to Nagy Várad as a regional centre. In the 1830s, it had 8,000 inhabitants of whom about 12 per cent were Jewish. The Nagy Kanizsa community was one of the earliest in Hungary to introduce educational and religous reforms. With the communities in Arad, Szeged and later Nagy Várad, it was in many ways more acculturated than that in Pest. In 1837, a society for reading and discussion was founded by Christians and Jews 'with the aim of achieving a greater degree of social *rapprochement* between the two religious camps'. In 1839, two men stood at the head of the society, Ignatz Chernel, a Christian lawyer who served as the county assessor and Moritz Horschetzky, a much-decorated Jewish doctor who ran the Jewish hospital. Horschetzky, an amateur Jewish historian, played a pivotal role in the community. He had married into the most important family in Nagy Kanizsa, the Lackenbachers, and served as the director of the Jewish community school over many years. Like other Jewish doctors of the time, he spearheaded reforms in his community and played an active role in Nagy Kanizsa's affairs. The governing board of the society he headed was divided equally along religious lines: seven of the fourteen officeholders were Jews. This meticulous distribution of offices becomes understandable in the light of a contemporary's observation that of the 140 members in the club, 'most were Israelites'.[62] In Nagy Kanizsa then, Jews seemed to be absorbing gentiles into their society, rather than the other way around. Perhaps the reason for this lies in the unfriendly policies of the burgher casino. As late as 1863, complaints appeared in the press that Jews were still barred from membership. There were those who were quick to point out that this was true of the casino of the petit bourgeois, the *Spiessbürgerthum*, not of the intelligentsia. However, only in 1865 did the burgher casino finally decide to abandon its anti-Jewish policies, but even then within a year efforts were made to reinstate restrictions.[63]

The Pápa Casino

The reception of Jews into the Pápa Casino can be considered more representative and it is worthwhile exploring this case in depth. Pápa during the period was the fourth largest Jewish community in Hungary numbering over 2,500 Jews, about one-fifth of the total population of the town. Like Nagy Kanizsa and Nagy Várad, Pápa was a regional centre of trade in livestock and agricultural produce,

Table 1. *The number of Jews in the Pápa Casino, 1838–48*

	1838	1839	1840	1841	1842	1843	1844	1845	1846	1847	1848
					Members						
Jews	18	—	—	22	22	25	24	—	—	—	34
Uncertain	5	—	—	6	6	6	6	—	—	—	6
Total	137	—	—	121	115	116	103	—	—	—	154
% Jews	13.1	—	—	18.2	19.1	21.6	23.3	—	—	—	22.1
					Officers						
Jews	1	—	—	0	1	1	2	—	—	—	2
Uncertain	—	—	—	—	—	—	1	—	—	—	—
Total	17	—	—	17	17	17	17	—	—	—	17

and like them Pápa was not a privileged city, but a market town owned by one of the liberal magnates, Count Károly Esterházy. The town itself was governed by the iron hand of Mihály Bezerédy, Esterházy's bailiff and a leading representative of the liberal gentry in the county.

Originally the Pápa Casino was set up in 1830 by twenty noblemen as a reading society. Two years later it became a casino, and membership was opened to commoners as well. Since all members agreed that human beings were equal and that only conduct and culture determined status in society (or so the secretary of the casino maintained), it was decided in 1834 that 'any honest man, regardless of his religion, birthright, and position, was eligible to become a member of the casino'. Interestingly, despite, or perhaps because of, the open-door policy of the club, that very year a rival 'burgher' casino was established in town.[64]

By 1838, the social composition of the 137 members was a liberal mix of prominent landowning noblemen, German, Magyar and Slav burghers, as well as a considerable contingent of Jews. Somewhat more than 10 per cent of the club can be identified conclusively as members of the local gentry;[65] possibly another 10 to 20 per cent with noble-sounding Magyar names (those ending in 'y') also belonged to the nobility. Almost a third were clearly of German, Slav or Greek origin and belonged to the burgher class, as did in all probability the remaining 25 per cent with 'ordinary' Magyar names.

That year eighteen Jews were already recorded on the membership rolls and possibly there were more (see table 1), since several of the

German-sounding names are of uncertain origin.[66] The number of Jews continued to grow; a decade later, in 1848, it had nearly doubled. The ratio of Jews to gentiles increased during these ten years from approximately 13 per cent to about 23 per cent, which was slightly higher than their proportion in the town's population. Throughout this period, one or two of the seventeen club officers were Jews.[67]

The thirty-seven Jews who belonged to the casino at one time or another were recruited from the elite of Pápa's Jewry. At least nine of them can be identified as having served as presidents of the community or members of its board of directors;[68] many of the others were related to these men by blood or marriage. Another eight casino members were drawn from Pápa's Jewish *honoratiori*: all five of the community's Jewish doctors, two of its teachers and Leopold Löw who served as rabbi from 1846 to 1850.[69]

During Löw's rabbinate, Pápa became the arena of one of the most sensational and prolonged controversies between Orthodoxy and Reform in Hungary. Court trials, denunciations and imprisonment followed after the county and central administrations became drawn into the conflict. Both sides enlisted the local Hungarian press and the Jewish journals in Germany which in turn followed closely every new development. The conflict died down only when Löw departed for Szeged after the revolution and the community regained its Orthodox complexion.

Almost to a man, the Jewish casino members belonged to the small communal oligarchy which sought to impose educational and religious reforms on a reluctant majority. Conversely, only one of the leaders of the Orthodox opposition was a member of the casino.[70] The Orthodox often complained bitterly against the partisan attitudes of the local authorities, especially the bailiff Bezerédy, who consistently sided with the reform party. The casino was a convenient meeting place where patriotic, liberal noblemen could give encouragement to like-minded Jewish reformers, and perhaps even co-ordinate their strategy.[71] Löw, a passionate Hungarian nationalist, enjoyed close relations with the gentry and the aristocracy both in Pápa and in his former community, Nagy Kanizsa and could always rely on their support in times of communal conflict. Years later, he would boast of his familiarity with gentry mentality because he 'had been on the most intimate footing over many years with the most prominent party leaders of Zala and Veszprém [counties]'.[72]

In the Pápa Casino these nobles and Jewish reformers forged an informal alliance to realize their vision of a liberal transformation of Hungary. In this Pápa was not unique. In particular in the large market towns to the south, but elsewhere as well,[73] it was repeatedly a section of the provincial gentry who urged Jews to initiate religious and educational reforms in order to ease their 'social emancipation' in Hungarian society.[74]

The Pest intelligentsia

If by the 1840s, the provinces were becoming so liberal, was it possible that the capital should remain unchanged? Everywhere there were indications of a new era. The Diet of 1839–40 had been the first to discuss Jewish emancipation at length and remarkably liberal proposals were tabled in the Lower House. (The Upper House and the King had whittled them down to more modest proportions.) And despite a certain growing ambivalance, Jewish emancipation continued to be one of the issues which appeared regularly on the liberal agenda.

Hungarian Jews, too, were changing. A militant minority could be found in almost every sizeable community, trying to introduce religious and educational reforms. These attempts invariably sparked off bitter conflicts. Magyarization became the slogan of some of the reformers and a Society for the Dissemination of the Magyar Language among the Israelites was established in Pest.[75]

Although the aristocracy and the patriciate continued to exclude Jews from their casinos, more liberal societies were springing up in the forties. The most important of these was the National Circle [*Nemzeti Kör*] founded in Pest early in the decade. By 1844, the society had grown to 254 members of whom two-thirds were artists, writers and professionals. Here the leading representatives of Hungarian culture and politics were to be found.[76] The political climate was decidedly liberal, but a rather broad spectrum of opinion ranging from reform conservatism to radical democracy could be found in the club. In 1845, a sizeable minority who disagreed with the increasingly radical tendencies of the National Circle seceded and established the rival Pest Circle (*Pesti Kör*). Soon afterwards, yet another group composed of wealthy merchants, aristocrats and priests set up the more conservative Assembly (*Gyülde*), a factor which prodded the two Circles to reunite in 1847 as the new Opposition Circle (*Ellenzéki Kör*). By the autumn of that year, the club was reconstituted openly as a political party and went on to play a key role in the events which led up to the 1848 revolution.[77]

How did the cream of Hungary's liberal intelligentsia receive the Jews? One would have thought that here the conditions were ideal, since both the ideology and the social composition of the circles worked in favour of Jewish integration. These men had shaped Hungarian public opinion in the last decade into a more liberal mould and many of them also belonged to the *honoratiori*, that natural bridge between Hungary's social classes.

An informer for the secret police in the summer of 1846 confided in his report that an alliance had come into being between Jewish money and the political opposition and that 'all cultivated Israelites are members of the . . . [National] Circle'.[78] In fact, the informer could not have been more off the mark, because for a long time the National Circle 'did not want to accept Jews at all'.[79] Only three Jews could be found among the club's 254 members in 1844, a number which was to remain steady for the next three years. One must concede, however, that here the social composition of the Circle paradoxically worked *against* Jewish participation. In the provinces as we have seen, the Jewish members of the casino were recruited from the ranks of the doctors and the wealthy merchants. The National Circle, on the other hand, seems to have had an aversion to both. There were only two doctors (as opposed to eighty-one lawyers) and eight merchants among its members and there is good reason to believe that, of these, two were Jews.[80] And while it is true that at the core of the National Circle stood writers and journalists, the emphasis here was on Magyar. Most of the rather large contingent of Jewish literati in Pest, however, wrote for the German press and could barely converse in the national tongue. Indeed, it seems that the Jewish intelligentsia was socially isolated in Pest, at least until the very eve of the 1848 revolution.[81] Surely it is no coincidence that the one man who was selected from their ranks, Ignácz Barnay, the secretary of the Pest community, was fluent in Magyar.

But apparently there was also a darker undercurrent at play. When a Jewish woman showed up at the Circle's annual ball in 1845, it was noticeable that several people did little to conceal their grimaces of distaste. The following year, the newspapers were scandalized that the ball committee decided not to invite 'several, honest Israelites, just because they are Jews. What does the nineteenth century and true liberal spirit have to say about such prejudice?!' It seemed bizarre that although a handful of Jews had already been accepted as members, the rest should be excluded from the ball.[82] Even in 1847, when the founding of the Opposition Circle marked a decided turn

for the better, a police informant found it noteworthy that 'the
Opposition men expressed their hatred of the Jews openly, without
any reservations'.[83] Surprisingly, the more conservative offshoot of
the National Circle, the Assembly, seems to have been a bit more
open to Jews. Between 1845 and 1847, seven Jews were admitted:
three wealthy wholesalers, three doctors and a lithographer.[84]

Not until April 1847, just a year before the outbreak of the
revolution, did the situation begin to improve. The newly constituted
Opposition Circle now had about a dozen new Jewish members, and
significantly, nine of them can be identified as the officers of the
Magyarization Society.[85] But it was during the heady days of the
revolution that the doors were really flung wide open. In May 1848
alone, about thirty Jews were invited to join. Now, for the first time, a
sizeable group of the royal privileged wholesale merchants, the ruling
caste of the Pest Jewish community, made its appearance in the
Circle.[86] It may well be, of course, that it was not only the fault of the
Opposition Circle that these men had not joined earlier. Perhaps
caution had made these pillars of the Jewish establishment think
twice before joining such a blatantly oppositionary club.

Be that as it may, it was clear that Pest was far from leading the
provinces in integrating its Jews. On the contrary, until the
revolution Pest seemed to lag consistently behind the provinces.
Perhaps part of the explanation might lie in the very size of Pest
society. The concentration in the capital of so many outstanding
political and cultural figures may have created a 'critical mass' which
would have made Jewish participation superfluous. This was often
not the case in the much smaller provincial centres where the Jewish
economic and professional elite was much harder to ignore.

Conclusion

Count Miklós Zay's observations on the exclusion of Jews from *fin-de-
siècle* Hungarian society provided a good focus for my conclusion. Zay
had singled out the gentry as the element most hostile to Jews, in
particular the provincial gentry. He also noted that social integration
could only be gained at a heavy cost, namely the abandonment of the
Jewish community and conversion. I will, therefore, address three
issues here: the role of the gentry; Budapest in contrast to the
provinces; and community and assimilation.

The role of the gentry

If we compare the period before 1848 to the one after 1880, the
transformation of gentry attitudes towards the Jews is striking. To be

sure the gentry itself had changed in the interim. Having absorbed a large number of commoners from various ethnic backgrounds, it was clearly no longer the same class of prosperous, landowning Magyar squires who enjoyed the feudal privileges of the nobility. Although, the gentry in any period was not all cut from the same cloth, nevertheless, in *Vormärz* the dominant spirit tended to liberalism (although it was often hedged by anxious ambivalence), whereas after 1880, anti-liberal currents or at least a selective liberalism became the fashion. This was of course not particular to Hungary; throughout Central Europe, 1880 was a watershed that marked the retreat from liberal ideals and the growing exclusion of Jews from the larger society.

It is also instructive to note that the underlying motives for exclusion had also changed. In *Vormärz* society Jews were kept at bay because of the persistence of traditional religious and social prejudices which were undoubtedly reinforced by the fact that Jews for the most part did not possess the culture and manners which would have made them *salonfähig*. But by the turn of the century, the socio-economic structure and the cultural profile of Hungarian Jewry had changed dramatically and traditional religious prejudices had lost much of their appeal. After 1880, social prejudice was rationalized by a new array of arguments mobilized from the varieties of modern antisemitism. Although antisemitism in its most virulent forms remained restricted to a small, radical minority in Hungary as it was in Germany and elsewhere in Western and Central Europe, the more genteel forms of discrimination fashioned by new negative Jewish stereotypes increasingly came to pervade broad sections of Hungarian society towards the turn of the century.

Therefore, what proved singular in the social history of Hungarian Jews was the pre-1848 period, when a gentry-dominated society proved surprisingly open to Jews. For while it is true that liberalism was on the ascendant in the pre-1848 period throughout Western and Central Europe, the opportunities for Jewish integration were not uniform, but varied according to the social structure and social values of the different host societies. As Jacob Katz has noted, Jews did not enter into an undifferentiated gentile society, but rather sought entrance into a certain social segment. In *Vormärz* Germany, the 'neutral society' was decidedly a middle-class construct (although two generations earlier, the nobility had played an important role in the Berlin salons).[87] It was the middle classes which championed liberalism and set out to create a vibrant associational life with the express intention of transcending differences of estate. And indeed, the late 1830s witnessed the growing participation of Jews in various lodges, clubs and societies.[88]

In Hungary, on the other hand, it was the noblemen, not the burghers who set the liberal tone, initiated associational life and sought to overcome religious and social barriers. What implications did this have for the nature of assimilation of Hungarian Jews? At this stage of my research, I am not entirely sure. On the surface, there seems little discernible difference in the process of Jewish social integration in the two countries. For example, the timing of acceptance and exclusion coincided in both countries, bracketing a liberal half century between the 1830s and the 1880s. Nevertheless, two possible answers come to mind. First, if not for the gentry, the entrance into the casinos in Hungary would have been a much more difficult venture. In contrast to the siege mentality of the burghers who felt threatened by Jewish competition, a mood of self-confidence prevailed among the gentry in the pre-1848 era which created a certain climate of generosity towards the Jews. Tensions between Jews and gentry were minimized by the fact that they occupied separate, well-defined niches within society, thus not only averting a clash of interest, but actually fostering a division of labour. In the liberal decades this symbiosis helped to bridge differences of class and religion, and created the basis for social contacts. But when the gentry lost much of its former self-confidence towards the last decades of the century, this same division of labour readily hardened into rigid social barriers.

This brings us to the second point. Integration into a society dominated by the gentry appears in the long run to have been more tenuous than in one where the middle classes held sway. For whereas in Germany shared values and mentality formed the basis for Jews to become a part of the middle class, in Hungary, once the gentry abandoned its brief flirt with *embourgeoisement* and adopted an anti-capitalist ideology, these same middle-class values posed an obstacle to social integration. On the other hand, there seems to be evidence that by the post-emancipation era a certain social *rapprochement* with the non-Jewish middle-class was taking place. When two rival Freemason Orders were established in Hungary at the end of the sixties and the beginning of the seventies, the Jewish masons opted to join the Grand Lodge of the German bourgeoisie, rather than the gentry-dominated Grand Orient where 'the proportion of bourgeoisie and prosperous lower middle class was insignificant'.[89]

Budapest in contrast to the provinces

The concentration on Budapest has often led to distortions in Hungarian-Jewish history. All too often sweeping generalizations have been made based on the limited experience of Budapest; in particular there has been a tendency to exaggerate the extent of assimilation outside the capital. More circumspect studies have suggested that the relatively advanced state of assimilation in Budapest was not necessarily representative of the rest of Hungarian Jewry. I would certainly agree with this last view. However, one should be equally cautious about assuming the converse, namely that Budapest always served as an upper limit of assimilation for the rest of Hungary. Thus the argument has been advanced that if Jews were excluded from general society in Budapest at the end of the nineteenth century, then it followed *a fortiori* that the provincial setting could only have been worse. Here the case-study of the casinos can serve as a corrective to an overly pessimistic picture. In the pre-1848 period, as we have seen, the pace of Jewish integration in the large provincial market towns seems to have proceeded well ahead of the capital. It would be worthwhile to examine in detail the situation of the Jews in the provinces in the post-1880 period to ascertain whether they indeed suffered worse social prejudice than in Budapest. There are tantalizing reports which would indicate that their social position was not too bad.

Let us return briefly to two provincial towns, Eger and Gyöngyös, where Jews had been barred from the casinos in the pre-1848 period. A few decades later, the situation had changed remarkably. When the application of three Jews to the Eger casino was approved in 1866, a note was demonstratively entered in the minute book that 'differences of religion pose no obstacle to membership'. In the following years, Jews must have found the club so congenial that some of them dropped their inhibitions and lapsed into Yiddish on its premises! Apparently this proved too much, and a polite resolution on 25 March 1883 requested that 'the society's members should preferably converse in Magyar and not employ the corrupt Jewish-German language in their conversation'. That this incident took place during the height of the antisemitic agitation surrounding the Tisza Eszlár blood libel is testimony to the remarkable sense of security that Jews must have felt in the Eger Casino.[90] In Gyöngyös, the impact of antisemitism came to be felt only in 1925. That year, when it was decided that no Jew was to be elected to the casino's board of

directors, the seventy-two Jewish members threatened to resign.
They later backed down and as a result of this popular antisemitic
move, membership increased to 211. But this clearly implied that
until 1925, some five years into the Horthy regime, Jews still
constituted well over one-third of the membership and that even after
antisemitism had made considerable inroads within the casino,
Jewish representation continued to be disproportionately high.[91]

Even a cursory glance, therefore, reveals that the situation in the
provinces could not have been so bleak. To be sure, as antisemitism
mounted after the 1880s, Jews were increasingly excluded from local
society.[92] However, one gains the impression that even when barred
from a particular club, Jews could find their way into other more
hospitable societies. Here, too, we should exercise caution in applying
a fortiori arguments drawn from the social situation of the elite to the
rest of Hungarian Jewry. If the National and Country Casinos in
Budapest continued their policy of discrimination, this affected
Jewish society only at the very top. But it is very possible that further
down the social ladder, alternative social frameworks were available. Surely if we turn away from the elite casinos to the numerous
circles, clubs, societies, lodges and professional associations – there
were more than 600 in Budapest alone in 1922! – a more optimistic
view of social integration would emerge.[93] It is perhaps an indication
of the high expectations that Jews had at the turn of the century, that
they viewed the cup as half empty. The historian however, must not
ignore the other half.

Community and assimilation

Armed with the case histories of the casinos, we can now address two
broad problems suggested by the theme of assimilation and
community.

The first pertains to the interaction of these two factors: was there
an inverse relationship between integration into the larger society
and loyalty to the Jewish community? Did one necessarily take place
at the expense of the other? Was the casino sought out initially by
people who were alienated from and peripheral to the Jewish
community? I think the answer is unambiguous: Jewish casino
members everywhere were drawn from the commercial and intellectual elite of the Jewish community. Those who achieved the
greatest prominence in the casinos, men like Dr Friedrich Gross and
Dr Henrik Pollák of Nagy Várad, Dr Moritz Horschetzky of Nagy
Kanizsa and Leo Holländer of Eperjes, were also the ones who played
leading roles in local and national Jewish affairs both before and after

joining the casino. In the pre-1848 period, any Jew who belonged to the commercial elite – and to a lesser extent to the professions – was almost automatically mobilized by the community to play a leadership role. It was rare to encounter a Jew of prominence who remained aloof from communal affairs. But precisely their prominence in the local Jewish community made these Jews the natural candidates for the casinos. In other words, success within the community was the coin which bought entrance into the larger society.

It was typical of the *Vormärz* period that an overwhelmingly traditional Hungarian Jewry was compelled by structural factors to recruit its leadership from those elements who had become the most acculturated and the best integrated into non-Jewish society. This could create bizarre situations. For it was this same elite that was also the most vunerable to more radical forms of assimilation, namely conversion and intermarriage. Because there was almost no way at this time to detach oneself gradually from the Jewish community, there were several notable instances where men who played key roles in Jewish affairs one day, converted literally the next. (Two notorious examples were the conversions in 1843 of Moricz Bloch, the most promising intellectual among the younger generation of reformers, and in 1848 of Jonas Kunewalder, the semi-official spokesman of Hungarian Jewry.)[94]

This suggests the second question: how was the wider community affected by the entrance of Jews into the casinos? After all, only a very small fraction of the Jewish community – probably less than 5 per cent if some of the numbers cited are any indication – actually joined the casinos. One obvious answer is that it held out to the community the assurance that social emancipation was in the realm of the possible, that if the elite was accepted today, it was only a matter of time before similar opportunities would be extended to the rank and file. And indeed, this is what took place in the sixties and seventies.

The impact of the casinos was also felt in the growth of parallel associations within the Jewish community. Jewish casinos were established mostly in cities such as Pressburg, Vágujhely, Liptó Szent Miklós, Trencsén, Balassa Gyarmat, Miskolc and Székesfehérvár where Jews stood little chance of gaining entrance into the local clubs. However, even in more tolerant towns such as Eperjes, Nagy Várad, Pápa, Arad and Nagy Kanizsa not everyone was accepted into the regular casinos, and even for those who were, these Jewish counterparts served as a convenient focus for the reforming forces in the community.[95]

Indeed, the casino's greatest impact on the community derived from its role as an outside frame of reference for the communal elite. Mixing with the cream of Magyar society, Jewish casino members may have encountered sympathy, but perhaps also some prodding from impatient liberals to reform Jews and Judaism. It is difficult to imagine how these Jews could return to their community unaffected by the signals they picked up at the club. If the casino proved a strong external point of reference for the reformers, they in turn were buttressed by its prestige within the community. Status won in the community eased the way into the casino, and conversely, acceptance in the casino bolstered one's position within the community.

The interaction of assimilation and community in the *Vormärz* era was therefore quite complex. Although the two factors could work at cross-purposes, it did not necessarily follow that social integration could be won only at the expense of communal loyalty. Being a member of both the casino and the community, reinforced and mutually enhanced one's prestige and status; both served as the theatre for Jewish social aspirations.

Notes

I wish to thank Arnold Eisen, Jonathan Frankel, Jacob Katz and Ilana Friedrich Silber for their insightful comments on previous drafts of this paper. Research was funded by the American Council of Learned Societies and the Rosenfeld Project on the History of Hungarian and Habsburg Jewry, Dinur Centre, Hebrew University.

1 The Jewish salons in Germany at the turn of the eighteenth century have received considerable attention, the most recent and comprehensive study being Deborah Hertz, *Jewish High Society in Old Regime Berlin* (New Haven, Conn. 1988). Henry Wasserman, 'Jews, *Bürgertum* and *Bürgerliche Gesellschaft* in a Liberal Era (1840–1880)' (Hebrew), Ph.D dissertation, Hebrew University, Jerusalem [n.d.], pp. 43–70, explores associational life in nineteenth-century Germany. On post-emancipation Prague, See Gary B. Cohen, 'Jews in German Society: Prague, 1860–1914', *Central European History* 10 (1977), and *The Politics of Ethnic Survival* (Princeton, N.J., 1981), pp. 175–83, and also the remarks of Hillel J. Kieval, *The Making of Czech Jewry* (Oxford, 1988), pp. 75–7. On England, see Todd M. Endelman, *The Jews of Georgian England, 1714–1830: Tradition and Change in a Liberal Society* (Philadelphia, 1979), ch. 8.

2 Jacob Katz, *Jews and Freemasons in Europe, 1723–1939* (Cambridge, Mass., 1970). Katz developed the concept of 'neutral society' in his *Tradition and Crisis; Jewish Society at the End of the Middle Ages* (New York, 1961), chapter 23 and later modified it as 'semineutral society' in his *Out of the Ghetto: The Social Background of Jewish Emancipation, 1770–1870* (Cambridge, Mass., 1973), ch. 4.

3 The ban was issued in 1795 in the wake of the so-called Jacobin conspiracies and remained in effect with the brief exception of the revolutionary days of 1848 until the end of the 1860s. See Ludwik Hass, 'The Socio-Professional Composition of Hungarian Freemasonry (1868–1920)', *Acta Poloniae Historica* 30 (1974), 71–117.

4 I wish to record my debt to George Barany who in a passage on the founding of the casinos in his excellent monograph *Stephen Széchenyi and the Awakening of Hungarian Nationalism, 1791–1841* (Princeton, N.J., 1968), pp. 166–7, brought this problem to my attention and suggested the topic of this chapter. For passing mention in some of the older literature, see Imre Csetényi, 'A reformkor elsö felének konzervativ sajtója és a zsidókérdés', *Magyar Zsidó Szemle* [*MZsSz*] 42 (1925), 150–1 and Imre Csetényi, 'Adalékok a magyar zsidóság reformkorszakbeli történetéhez', *A budapesti Ferencz József országos rabbiképzö-intézet értesitöje az 1927/28 tanévröl* (Budapest, 1928), p. 19; Nikolaus László, *Die geistige und soziale Entwicklung der Juden in Ungarn in der ersten Hälfte des 19. Jahrhunderts* (Berlin, 1934), pp. 30, 34; László Simon, *Zsidókérdés a magyar reformkorban (1790–1848)* (Debrecen, 1936), p. 48. I briefly touched on the theme of this paper in a previous article. See Michael K. Silber, 'The Historical Experience of German Jewry and its Impact on Haskalah and Reform in Hungary', in Jacob Katz (ed.), *Toward Modernity: The European Jewish Model* (New Brunswick, N.J. and Oxford, 1987), pp. 140–2.

5 A handful of minute-books is now housed in the National Széchenyi Library. Some of the casinos published yearbooks which usually listed the statutes and the membership, and occasionally, even recounted the casino's history. With proper precautions, these rosters can be used to identify Jewish members. Scattered reports appear in the contemporary press, both in the general Magyar journals and in the German-language Jewish newspapers which were published in Germany and later in Hungary. Occasionally, the contemporary works on the Jewish question also yield some item of interest. Although scant research exists on the history of the casinos in general, numerous histories have been written on local casinos marking the occasion of their jubilees. However, of the several dozen I consulted in Budapest, only a handful made explicit reference to Jews (predictably, among the most informative were the ones written by antisemites). Details can also be gleaned from the numerous historical monographs on specific cities and Jewish communities.

6 There is a considerable body of literature on the subject of assimilation and its various shadings. Milton Gordon's *Assimilation in American Life* (New York, 1964) is a pioneering study on this theme. See too the introductory essay by Jonathan Frankel in this volume.

7 H. York-Steiner, 'Die Ungarn', *Die Welt* 2, no. 33 (1898), pp. 1–2. Ferenc Pulszky, a prominent public figure throughout the nineteenth century and a keen student of Hungarian society, noted twenty years

earlier that 'only rarely do we accept Jews into our society . . . [Hungary] may have given them political, but only rarely, social equality.' Ferenc Pulszky, 'A zsidókról', _Magyarország_, 26 July 1880 citing the _Pesti Napló_, 25 July 1880.

8 John Lukács, _Budapest 1900_ (London, 1988), p. 192; _Die Welt_ 1, no. 1 (1897), p. 8; Count Miklós Zay, 'Zsidók a társadalomban', _Huszadik Század_ 4 (1903), 962.

9 Moritz Zobel, 'Ungarischer Antisemitismus', _Die Welt_ 1, no. 23 (1897), p. 6.

10 Zay, 'Zsidók a társadalomban', 962; Zobel, 'Ungarischer Antisemitismus', p. 5; and _Die Welt_ 1, no. 1 (1897), p. 8. During his first term of office, Wekerle was instrumental in pushing through legislation which recognized Judaism as one of the 'received' religions of Hungary.

11 Zay, 'Zsidók a társadalomban', 960. Not one Jewish name appears on the 1883 roster of the founding members of the Country Casino. See Lajos Halász, _Az országos kaszinó ötvenéves története 1883–1932_ (Budapest, 1932), pp. 101 ff. For the statutes, see p. 20. Zoltán Horváth, _Magyar századforduló: A második reformnemzedék története (1896–1914)_ (Budapest, 1961), p. 588, n. 8, notes: 'Over the years, the [aristocratic] National Casino had altogether ten Jewish or converted Jewish members, such as Armin Vámbéry . . . or Géyza Moskowitz of Zemplén. The [gentry] Country Casino never accepted even converted Jews, and rarely did anyone who was by origin a commoner ever become its member (e.g. Sándor Wekerle).' William O. McCagg, Jr., _Jewish Nobles and Geniuses in Modern Hungary_ (New York, 1972), pp. 35–6, modifies this bleak picture: in 1913, some ten ennobled families of Jewish origin were listed in the National Casino and twenty-two in the Country Casino. 'This was not a record of overwhelming acceptance. Moreover, it is worth noting that in almost every case religious conversion preceded Casino membership, and that even Casino membership did not entail complete social acceptance.' He draws attention to the paradox that nevertheless 'the Magyar nobility accepted the Jewish community massively in terms of intermarriage'. 'Massively' is surely an exaggeration, yet the phenomenon of intermarriage between mostly (converted) Jewish women and Magyar noblemen – both gentry and aristocrats – is noteworthy and needs further exploration. On the limited access to the casinos, see also Péter Hanák and Ferenc Mucsi (eds.), _Magyarország Története, 1890–1918_ (Budapest, 1978), p. 447.

12 Paul Ignotus, _Hungary_ (London, 1972), p. 98. If this was the case during the liberal era before the First World War, it should come as no surprise that the anti-liberal climate of the interwar period brought no improvement. A recent study of interwar economic elites has noted that not one of the fifteen most prominent Jewish businessmen was a member either of the Country or the National Casino. György Lengyel, 'The Ethnic

The entrance of Jews into Hungarian society 315

Composition of the Economic Elite in Hungary in the Interwar Period', in Yehuda Don and Victor Karady, (ed.), *A Social and Economic History of Central European Jewry* (New Brunswick, N.J. and London, 1990), p. 240. See also László Márkus, 'A Horthy-rendszer elitjéröl, *Történelmi Szemle* 8 (1965), 464 and Beáta Nagy, 'Klubok, kaszinók, társaskörök: Az elit társaséletnek színhelyei', in György Lengyel (ed.), *Történeti szociológiai tanulmányok a 19.-20. századi magyar társadalomról (= Szociológiai mühely tanulmányok*, 5) Marx Károly Közgazdasági Egyetem (Budapest, 1987), pp. 3–20.

13 Zay, 'Zsidók a társadalomban', 961 and 963; Ignotus, *Hungary*, p. 97 and Andrew C. Janos, 'The Decline of Oligarchy: Bureaucratic and Mass Politics in the Age of Dualism (1867–1918)', *Revolution in Perspective: Essays on the Hungarian Soviet Republic of 1919*, ed. Andrew C. Janos and William B. Slottman (Berkeley, Los Angeles, London, 1971), pp. 38–9.

14 Zoltán Lippay, *A magyar birtokos középosztály és a közélet* (Budapest, 1919), p. 33. See Janos, 'The Decline of Oligarchy', pp. 52–3, on the ethnic composition of the gentry.

15 Albert Berzeviczy, 'A gentryröl', (1884) in his *Bezédek és Tanulmányok* (Budapest, nd), vol. II, pp. 233–53, esp. 242–6. See Péter Hanák, 'The Bourgeoisification of the Hungarian Nobility – Reality and Utopia in the 19th Century', *Études historiques hongroises 1985* (Budapest, 1987), p. 414.

16 Hanák, 'Bourgeoisification of the Hungarian Nobility', p. 407.

17 The following English-language studies give an excellent overview of Hungarian history from the end of the eighteenth century until the 1848–9 Revolution: Béla K. Király, *Hungary in the Late Eighteenth Century: The Decline of Enlightened Despotism* (New York, 1969); Béla K. Király, *Ferenc Deák* (Boston, 1975); Barany, *Széchenyi*; G. Barany, 'Hungary: From Aristocratic to Proletarian Nationalism', in Peter F. Sugar and Ivo J. Lederer (eds.), *Nationalism in Eastern Europe* (Seattle and London, 1969), pp. 259–73; Istvan Deak, *The Lawful Revolution: Louis Kossuth and the Hungarians, 1848–1849* (New York, 1979).

18 Ferenc Pulszky, *Életem és korom*, 2 vols. vol. I,(Budapest, 1880), pp. 46–8. See Barany, *Széchenyi*, pp. 166–7.

19 Memorandum of Metternich, 19 January 1837 cited in Barany, *Széchenyi*, p. 451. See also the secret police report of 1834 on the highly politicized nature of the casinos and the great influence they exercised on Hungarian public opinion in Gyula Viszota, 'A kaszinók hatása a magyar nemzeti és politikai élet fejlödésére', in his edition of *Gróf Széchenyi István iroí és hírlapi vitája Kossuth Lajosal* (Budapest, 1927), vol. I, p. XXVII.

20 Sándor Takáts, *Hangok a multból* (Budapest, n.d.), p. 359, n. 10.

21 Gyula Viszota, 'Széchenyi élete 1826–1830 közt', in his edition of *Gróf Széchenyi István Naplói* (Budapest, 1932), vol. III, p. 765.

22 7 June 1829 entry, Széchenyi, *Napló*, vol. III, p. 318.

23 Széchenyi, *Napló*, vol. III, p. LV. See also Barany, *Széchenyi*, p. 171.

24 22 October 1837 entry. Széchenyi, *Napló*, vol. V (Budapest, 1937), p. 122,

25 7 February 1832 entry. Széchenyi, *Napló*, vol. IV (Budapest, 1934), p. 241. On Ullmann's relations with Széchenyi see vol. IV, p. 597; vol. V, pp. 30, 34, 176. The 30 January 1838 entry says it all: 'Ullmann bei mir. Kopweh'. Vol. IV, p. 150.

26 Membership lists in the *Pest Casino Könyv* (Pest, 1828-) which appeared annually. The date of Samuel Wodianer's conversion is unclear. Vera Bácskai, *A vállalkozók elöfutárai: Nagykereskedök a reformkori Pesten* (Budapest, 1989), p. 160, gives 1839 as the date, but the *Pesti Hirlap* of 3 March 1841 reports that the conversion had just taken place.

27 See the secret police report on the debate in Viszota, 'Széchenyi élete', in *Napló*, vol. III, p. LV.

28 Pulszky, *Életem és korom*, vol. I, p. 48 and Barany, *Széchenyi*, p. 167.

29 Police reports, 10 February and 20 May 1830. *Napló*, vol. IV, pp. 657, 663. See also Miss [Julia] Pardoe, *The City of the Magyar or Hungary and her Institutions in 1839–40*, 3 vols. vol. III (London, 1840), pp. 2–3: 'The ball and the billiard-rooms are both extremely handsome; and the Casino known as the "National", for which only nobles or members of the learned professions are eligible, occupies the whole of the first-floor; the one above being called the *Kaufmannische Casino*, and composed of merchants and respectable individuals connected with the commerce of the city.'

30 On the history of the Pest Wholesalers Corporation, see Jakab Pólya, *A pesti polg. kereskedelmi testület és a Budapesti nagykereskedök és nagyiparosok társulata története* (Budapest, 1896). Paragraph 15 of this new association stipulated that the composition of the executive committee must always be two-thirds Christian. See the statutes in Imre Palugyay, *Buda-Pest szabad királyi városok leirása* (Pest, 1852), pp. 513–16. The *Mercantil Casino* which was founded in 1831, drew its 354 members mainly from the ranks of the merchant guilds, though it also numbered several counts and barons. See *Mitglieder des Mercantil Casino in Pesth* (Pest, 1839) cited in 'Majláth Béla adatgyüjtése a magyar kaszinók keletkezésének történeténe vonatkozóan (1829–1835)' (Majláth Collection), *Országos Széchenyi Könyvtár* (OSzK) Manuscript Collection, Quart. Hung. 2356, fol. 10r. This is a useful manuscript source collection on the histories of various casinos in the pre-1848 period.

31 Viszota, 'A kaszinók hatása', p. XXVII. Majláth lists some 60 casinos established between 1827 and 1842, as well as 14 reading circles between 1832–1837. Majláth Collection, fols. 208r-v, 270r, 271r-v, 272r-v, 273r. I have gained the impression that there were many more.

32 The incident took place in 1842. *A budavári casino-egylet félszázados története, 1841–1891* (Budapest, 1891), p. 15.

33 Gyula Antalffy, *Reformkori magyar városrajzok* (Budapest, 1982), pp. 70,

91, 101, 122, 105 respectively. The book cites extensively from contemporary newspapers.

34 Typically, the two societies reunited in 1848. See István Szücs, *A debreceni casino története* (Debrecen, 1884), pp. 10–11, 13 and Kálmán Boldisár, *A debreceni casino századéves története, 1833–1933* (Debrecen, 1933), pp. 5–11.

35 *Pesti Hirlap* 1 (1841), 723.

36 Ibid.

37 *Gyöngyösi Casino Könyv* (Gyöngyös Casino Book) (Pest, 1838), vol. II, p. 26.

38 'Izraeliták átalyában kivéve', *Gyöngyösi Casino Könyv*, vol. IV (Pest, 1840), p. 16, § 3 and § 15. The same phrase continued to appear in the following years. See *Gyöngyösi Casino Részvényeseinek névsora s a Casino alapszbályai és rendeletei 1841/42* (Gyöngyösi Casino Membership List and Casino Statutes and Regulations 1841/1842) (Pest, [1842?]) cited in Majláth Collection, fols, 188v and 122v.

39 'Cselédek és Zsidók be nem bocsájtatnak...', *Gyöngyösi Casino Könyv*, vol. II (Pest, 1838), p. 33, § 18 and vol. IV (Pest, 1840), p. 28, § 15.

40 *Pesti Divatlap* (1845), p. 1,228 and in general, László dezséri Bachó, *A Gyöngyösi kaszinó egyesület története (1836–1936)* (Gyöngyös, 1938), pp. 15, 21.

41 '... az Izraeliták, ki véven a Diplomaticusokat, s ezekre is a titkos Szavazatfennmaradván, – be nem vétetnek'. Imre Breznay, *Az egri kaszinó századéves története 1833–1933* (Eger, 1934), p. 36.

42 'Hogy mivel az Egyesületnek fenálló szabályai szerint, casinó tagja tsak hazafi lehet: vallyon a Zsidók, mint nem hazafiak, ugyan azon módon bevétethetnek é az egyesületbe? Mire végeztetett: Hogy Izraelita tsak úgy vétethetékbe a Casinóba, ha szavazás alkalmával a választottság minden tagjainak voksait elnyerte, ha tehát azok közül tsak egyis ellene szavazna, már Casinó tagjává nem lehet'. 'Komáromi Casinoi Jegyzökönyv, 1 X 1836 - 24 I 1843', OSzK Manuscript Collection, Fol. Hung. 1870, fol. 18r. See also the history of the casino based upon the society's minutebook in *Komáromi Lapok* (1883), nos. 50–1 and (1884), no. 5 as noted in the Majláth Collection, fol. 31r ff., esp. fol. 71r-v.

43 Elek Fényes, *Magyar országnak s a hozzá kapcsolt tartományoknak mostani állapotja statistikai és geographiai tekintetben*, 6 vols, vol. III (Pest, 1837), p. 207.

44 Secret report, Pressburg, 6 November 1847 *Kossuth Lajos az utolsó rendi országgyülésen 1847/48*, ed. István Barta (Budapest, 1951), pp. 230–4. Compare, however, their mixed record on Jewish legislation in Károly Kecskeméti, 'A liberalizmus és a zsidók emancipációja', *Történelmi Szemle* 25 (1982), 185–209, esp. 204–7.

45 See for example Antalffy, *Magyar városrajzok*, p. 70 on the Kaposvár Noble Casino and Pardoe, *The City of the Magyar*, vol. III, p. 2, on the Pest National Casino.

46 *Jelenkór*, 21 February 1838 cited in Imre Csetényi, 'A reformkor elsö

felének konzervativ sajtója és a zsidókérdés', *MZsSz* 42 (1925), 150–1. Many Jews attended the Pápa Casino ball later that year, volunteering even more than the entrance fee. See *Jelenkór*, 25 August 1838. In Köszeg, an interdenominational benevolent aid society for the poor was founded in 1834. By 1839, a Jewish treasurer and two Jewish committee members were elected.

47 Cited in *Allgemeine Zeitung des Judentums* [*AZdJ*] 5 (1841), 208.

48 'Man dürfe nicht über den eigentlichen Sinn der Statuten hinausschweifen, sonst könnte auch vielleicht jemand den Schein der Zulässigkeit dafür finden, dass auch ein achtbarer und gebildeter Bauer ein Mitglied des Orosházer Kasinos werden könne', *AZdJ* 6 (1842), 98–9, note based on *Agramer Zeitung*, 27 October 1841.

49 Pulszky, *Életem és korom*, vol. I, pp. 46–8. The three friends also received the Pope's blessing in Rome. See pp. 62–3. Pulszky's father must have turned in his grave when later in the century a Fejérváry married Biedermann's granddaughter and his own grandson, Agost, married into another Viennese Jewish banking family, the Figdors.

50 Ibid., p. 46. see also Ladislas Tóth, 'La société hongroise de Presov', *Revue d'Histoire Comparée* 25 (1947), 50–8.

51 *Israelitischen Annalen* 3 (1841), 149.

52 *Orient* 5 (1844), 132. Kassa spearheaded the opposition to the 1840 Law XXIX which permitted Jewish settlement in the cities. More than 250 burghers signed a petition against the Jews in 1841 and submitted it to the Emperor in Vienna. There were nevertheless some burghers who were sympathetic to Jews. See Imre Csetényi, 'Adalékok a magyar zsidóság reformkorszakbeli történetéhez', *A budapesti Ferencz József országos rabbiképző-intézet értesitöje az 1927/28 tanévröl* (Budapest, 1928), 13–14 and György Kerekes, *A kassai kereskedök életéböl: Harmad félszázad 1687–1913* (Budapest, 1913), pp. 97–113, 176.

53 *AZdJ* 5 (1841), 88. Actually relations could not have been so bad in Arad since that same year some of the burghers contributed towards the purchase of an organ at the Purim ball.

54 *AZdJ* 6 (1842), 701–2.

55 *Ellenör*, 15 September 1880, pp. 112–13.

56 Károly Czímer, *A Szeged-Belvárosi kaszinó százéves története (1829–1929)* (Szeged, 1929), pp. 26, 28, 87–9, 97. On Cájus, see also Immanuel Löw and Zsigmond Kulinyi, *A szegedi zsidók 1785–töl 1885–ig* (Szeged, 1885), pp. 82–3. The two Dr Steinhardts admitted along with Cájus to the casino in 1834, do not appear to have been Jewish, since Löw and Kulinyi make no mention of them.

57 We can also add Debrecen to the list. By 1847, we find in the Debrecen Casino, Dr H. Pollák who was also the local *Védegylet* treasurer and Ignác Klein, the community's president over many years, who was 'one of the earliest members of the casino'. Henrik Pollák, 'Adatok a magyar

izraelita statistikájához', *Elsö magyar zsidó naptár és évkönyv 1848–ik szököévre* (Pest, 1848), p. 121 and Ignatz Einhorn, 'Visszapillantás', ibid., p. 247. On Klein see [Ferenc]z [Meze]y, 'Klein Ignác emlékezete', *MZsSz* 3 (1886), 69–70.

58 *Bihar Vármegye és Nagyvárad: Magyarországi Vármegyei és Városai*, ed., Samu Borovsky (Budapest, [1901?]), p. 348.

59 See for instance Einhorn, 'Visszapillantás', pp. 247–8. Pollák, 'Adatok a magyar izraelita statistikájához', ibid., p. 121 gives the precise figure of thirteen.

60 Borovsky, *Bihar Vármegye*, pp. 348, 442–3; *AZdJ* 5 (1841), 87 and the membership list in the *Bihari Casinokönyv* 12 (1844).

61 Ignatz Reich, 'Friedrich Gross', *Beth-El*, 2nd edn vol. 1 (Pest, 1878), p. 110. It must have been in the fifties (Gross died on 2 January 1858), because otherwise it would have received prominent mention in the pre-1848 surveys of Jewish advances in Hungary.

62 H. Rosenmark, 'Die Israeliten-Gemeinde zu Gross-Kanischa in Ungarn', *AZdJ* 6 (1842), 98 and Ignatz Reich, 'Dr Moriz Horschetzky', *Ben Chananja* 3 (1860), 74–7.

63 *Ben Chananja* 6 (1863), 46, 200–1; 9 (1866), 505.

64 Illés Vermes, 'Elöirat', in *Pápai Casino Könyv 1838* (Pápa, 1838), p. 5. Indeed, even as late as 1845, the *Pesti Divatlap* (p. 640) reported that the 'Burgher' casino still excluded Jews.

65 They belonged to the Barcza, Békássy, Bezerédy, Cseresnyés, Kenesey, Pálffy, Pap, Rába, Szakonyi and Vigyázó families which were listed among the gentry of Veszprém county. See Fényes, *Magyar ország . . . statistikai és geographiai tekintetben*, vol. 1, (Pest, 1836), p. 432.

66 The names of uncertain origin were: Sándor Falk, Ignatz Frank, Antal Freund, János Freund, Ignácz Fridrich, Ignácz Grosz, Leopold Ofner, Ferenc Szauer, István Szauer, Móricz Schnell, Dániel Schvarz, Antal Steiner, Antal Strausz and Leopold Vitmáyer, Jr.

67 *Pápai Casino Könyv* (Pápa, 1838–48). Jewish-sounding names among the membership lists were compared with lists of definitely identifiable Pápa Jews, the most important of these being the list of contributors to the Pápa Jewish school (who I assume are all Jewish) which is appended to Lipót Löv, *Jeremiás prófétának négy aranyszabálya a valódi hazafiságról* (Pápa, 1847), pp. 15–16.

68 Hermann Fromm, Adolf Herczfeld (1845), Samu Hirschler (1841), Albert Neumann (1841), Hermann Neumann (1845), Salomon Neumann (1841, 1845), Móricz Rechnitzer, Samu Schlesinger (1845) and Adolf Spiczer (1845).

69 The two teachers were Mano Singer and Ignácz Bleur. The latter was the author of a reader, *Magyar Olvasokönyv* (1848), and translated the prophet Joel for Löw's *Magyar Zsinagoga* (1847). The five doctors: József Deutsch, Dávid Dietrichstein, Móricz Feitel (a relative of one of the

community's presidents, Herzfeld), Ignácz Lamberger and Samu Pserhofer. Pserhofer, who had been a member as early as 1838 and had served
several years on the board of directors, also wrote a book on the
relationship between religion and medicine, and contributed a piece on
religious education of children in *Magyar Zsinagoga* (1847). Feitel was the
leading spirit in the campaign to reform the community; it was he who
persuaded the communal leaders to invite his friend Löw to Pápa.

70 For instance, 24 of the 37 casino members appeared among the
contributors to the Pápa school. See Löv, *Jeremiás*, pp. 15–16. For the
names of the Orthodox opposition see Magyar Országos Levéltár. C55
Helytartótanácsi levéltár. Dept. Judaeorum. 1846–2–19. Of these, only
József Sauer was a casino member (from 1841 to 1848). It is also
significant that the previous rabbi, R. Feivel Horowitz (d. 1845) was *not* a
member. The dynamic Horowitz, a flexible Orthodox rabbi who
recognized the need for moderate change, had come to Pápa at the
invitation of Count Esterházy who sought to give the community a more
modern and Magyar complexion. Horowitz was apparently one of the
first Hungarian rabbis to deliver a sermon in Magyar. (The Orthodox
were to claim that he had been pressured by Esterházy and that soon
after he went to the grave heartbroken.)

71 A similar situation obtained in the Freemason lodge in Frankfurt. See
Katz, *Jews and Freemasons*, pp. 92–4.

72 Leopold Löw to Ignác Hirschler, 26 October 1864, in [Ferenc Mezei],
'Löw Lipót levelei dr. Hirschler Ignáczhoz', *MZsSz* 8 (1891), 262. It was
during his rabbinate in Nagy Kanizsa that Löw became acquainted with
Ferenc Deák, one of the leaders of the liberal opposition in Hungary.
Deák lived nearby. When Löw decided to leave for Pápa, he was warmly
recommended as a loyal Magyar patriot by the liberal Count Leó
Festetics to the equally liberal Count Károly Esterházy. See the various
letters in Löw and Kulinyi, *A szegedi zsidók*, pp. 182–4. Later, after Löw
was denounced by his Orthodox enemies and was arrested for his part in
the revolution, Bezerédy wrote to Festetics (24 October 1849) urging
him to intervene on Löw's behalf with the military authorities.

73 The casino of Aszod in Pest county had 'a large number of Jewish
members' in 1848. *Ungarische Israelit*, vol. 1 (1848), pp. 35–6. More
surprising is the explicit declaration of the Bereg County Casino in 1841
that membership was open to Jews. A Jew, David Berger, was elected
treasurer in 1843, but he declined because he was not a member. The first
Jewish member appears in 1849. György Kozma, *A beregmegyei kaszinó
százéves története* (Budapest, [1941?]), p. 39. Similarly, *Életképek* 9 (2
January 1848) reports that the Ungvár Casino, founded in 1842, accepts
Jews and that a Jewish doctor, a certain Henrik B., has already been
kicked out of the club for cheating at cards. Located in the northeast
region of Hungary, Bereg county Jewry was dominated by a large

Hasidic population. At this time there were hardly any signs of acculturation among the local Jews.

74 The best-known call for 'social emancipation' was made in the article of Gábor Fábián of Arad and in the editorial of Kossuth in *Pesti Hirlap* 3 (1843), 299–300. The idea of social emancipation, as opposed to purely legal emancipation, was much discussed during those very years in Germany.

75 For a good contemporary overview see Márton Diósy's history of the Magyarization society and Einhorn's 'Visszapillantás' both in *Elsö magyar zsidó naptár és évkönyv 1848-ik szököévre*, pp. 83–93 and 241–58.

76 Among the members one found several future ministers, outstanding political figures, and some of the most important poets and writers of the time (e.g. Kossuth, Deák, Eötvös, Trefort, Pulszky, Teleki, Ráday, Rottenbiller, Vörösmarty, Josika, etc.). See Lajos Nagy, 'Budapest története, 1790–1848', in Domokos Kosáry (ed.), *Budapest története*, 5 vols. vol. III (Budapest, 1975), p. 470.

77 Ibid., pp. 470–1.

78 Secret report, Pest, 16 June 1846. *Kossuth Lajos az utolsó rendi országgyülésen 1847/48*, ed. István Barta (Budapest, 1951), p. 258.

79 'Pesten a kör elöbb a zsidókat fölvenni sem akart . . . ' Einhorn, 'Visszapillantás', pp. 247–8. He goes on to say that now, that is, 1847, three of the Circle's Jewish members – Barnay, Kanicz and Rosenfeld – have been elected to the executive committee.

80 Nagy, 'Budapest története, 1790–1848', p. 470. Although I have not seen the names of the three Jews, I am certain that Manó Kanicz, a wealthy wholesale merchant, was one of them. Kanicz was by far the most politically active Jew in the forties, participating in almost every one of the numerous societies set up by the opposition. He was equally active within the community. See also the previous note and Bácskai, *Vállalkozók*, pp. 97–8.

81 Mór Mezei, 'Az izraelita-magyar-egylet története és célja', *Elsö magyar-izraelita naptár és évkönyu 5622-dik évre. Második évfolyam* (Pest, 1861), p. 11, hints at this.

82 *Pesti Hirlap* 30 January 1845; *Pesti Divatlap* 1846 cited in Gyula Farkas, *A 'fiatal Magyarország' kora* (Budapest, 1932), p. 100 and *Budapesti Hiradó* 15 February 1846.

83 Secret report, Pest, 10 June 1847 in *Kossuth Lajos az utolsó rendi országgyülésen 1847/48*, ed. István Barta (Budapest, 1951), p. 281.

84 For membership lists in 1845, 1846 and 1847 see 'A "Gyülde" alapszabályai és tagjainak névsora (1845–1848),' OSzK Fol. Hung. 1217, fols. 6r-12v; *A közhasznu gyülde tiszteleti, helybeli és vidéki rendes tagjainak névsora betürenddel s alapszabályai* (Pest, 1846–7), vols. I and II. Frigyes Eckstein, Fülöp Jacobovics and M. Moricz Jacobovics were the doctors; Manó Kanicz, M. L. Koppel and Fülöp Kunewalder were the merchants; and Ignatz Mandello, the lithographer.

85 See the May 1847 membership list in 'Az Ellenzéki kör pénztári könyve', OSzK Fol. Hung. 980, fols. 7v-34v and the Magyarization Society's list on *Elsö magyar zsidó naptár és évkönyv 1848-ik szököévre*, pp. 39–40. The officers were Dr József Rosenfeld, the vice-president of the society, Márton Diósy and Mór Szegfy, the two secretaries and Manó Tettinger, the controller. Barnay, Kanicz, Dávid Kain, Armin Klein, the editor of the *Ungar* and Salomon Rosenzweig, a teacher at the Jewish school, were on the executive committee. Interestingly, neither the president of the society, Dr Jacobovics, nor its librarian, Ignácz Einhorn (who later achieved fame as the rabbi of the radical Reform society in Pest and toward the end of his life as the first Jew to attain the rank of state secretary) seem to have become members. Jacobovics preferred the *Gyülde*.

86 'Az Ellenzéki kör pénztári könyve', OSzK Fol Hung 980, fols. 36v-42v. Another dozen or so Jews were accepted in the subsequent months. (See fols. 44v-64v.) Of these new members, Jacob Kern, David Fleischl, Jacob Lackenbacher, J. Baumann, Károly Boscovicz, Sr., Lipót Ponczen, Armin Engländer, Mano Breisach, Károly Hürsch, etc., all played important roles in the communal life. See the community's list of officers in *Elsö magyar zsidó naptár és évkönyv 1848-ik szököévre*, pp. 37–9. There is much useful information on these men in Bácskai, *Vállalkozók*. Jonas Kunewalder, who served as the president of the Pest community and as the unofficial head of Hungary's Jewry over a period of several years finally makes his appearance in the Circle with his brother Fülöp, but by this time both brothers and their brother-in-law, Manó Kanicz, had converted.

87 Referring to the changes which took place at the end of the first decade of the nineteenth century, Arendt writes, 'The nobles had been the first to admit the Jews to a degree of social equality, and it was among the nobles that systematic antisemitism first broke out. Social prejudices were taken up once more, and intensified to the point of crass, brutal exclusion'. Hannah Arendt, *Rahel Varnhagen: The Life of a Jewess* (London, 1957), pp. 99–100. See also Hertz, *Jewish High Society*, esp. pp. 114–15, 253–9.

88 On the decisive role of the middle class in German associational life, see Thomas Nipperdey, 'Verein als soziale Struktur in Deutschland im späten 18. und frühen 19. Jahrhundert', in *Geschichtswissenschaft und Vereinwesen im 19. Jarhundert* (Göttingen, 1972), pp. 13–44. On Jews in German societies see Katz, *Jews and Freemasons*, pp. 82–127 and Wasserman, 'Jews, Bürgertum and Bürgerliche Gesellschaft', pp. 43–70.

89 Hass, 'Hungarian Freemasonry', 79. See also Róbert Iván Gál, 'A dualizmuskori szabadkömüveség foglalkozási öszzetétele', in György Lengyel (ed.), *Történeti szociológiai tanulmányok a 19.-20. századi magyar társadalomról* (=*Szociológiai mühely tanulmányok* 5) (Budapest: Marx Károly Közgazdasági Egyetem, 1987) pp. 21–43. Unfortunately, beyond a

few scattered references, neither Hass nor Gál spell out the religious composition of the Freemasons in detail.

90 '[A]z egyesület tagjai lehetöleg magyarul társalogjanak s az elrontott zsidó-német nyelvet társalgásuk közben ne használják.' Breznay, *Az egri kaszinó százéves története*, pp. 71, 102.

91 Bachó, *A Gyöngyösi kaszinó*, pp. 15, 21.

92 Even this was not an irreversible process. In Liptó-Szent-Miklós, a town located in the Slovak uplands, antisemitism began to spread in the 1880s. 'Jews were excluded from certain social circles . . . Slowly, slowly the Jews withdrew from social life.' In 1891, however, the recently appointed county high sheriff, the *föispán* Lajos Kürthy, decided to uproot antisemitism altogether. He politely insisted that at the forthcoming county ball, both Jews and the city burghers take part. At the ball, the most striking partners were Dr Náthán Schlesinger who danced with the wife of the *föispán* (neé Countess Ludovika Zichy) and the *föispán* with Mrs Schlesinger. The week after the ball the *föispán* and his wife paid a call on several Jewish families. 'Following this incident, the social situation of the Liptó county Jews totally changed as if struck by magic. Once again, they began to meet and still meet their fellow non-Jewish citizens in every area of social life.' Emil Herzog, *A zsidók története Liptó-Szt.-Miklóson* (Budapest, 1894), pp. 293–6.

93 On the rich associational life in Budapest see József Zoltán and László Berza (eds.), *Budapest történetének bibliográfiája* vol. IV (Budapest, 1965), pp. 391–409. It was of course well known that the Lipótváros casino was overwhelmingly Jewish. Of its 1800 members only 675 survived the Second World War (ibid., p. 396, item 9,458). But the Jewish membership of other societies such as the *Fészek* club of the artists and writers, or the *Unio* and *Park* clubs, still remains to be explored.

94 See William O. McCagg, 'Jewish Conversion in Hungary in Modern Times', in Todd M. Endelman (ed.), *Jewish Apostasy in the Modern World* (New York and London, 1987), pp. 150–3 and Silber, 'German Jewry and its Impact . . . in Hungary', p. 138. Bloch was elected as a corresponding member into the Hungarian Academy of Sciences in 1841, while he was still Jewish. Kunewalder was named in 1844 to the board of directors of the *Védegylet*, the patriotic Society for the Protection of Hungarian Industry founded by Kossuth.

95 On the Jewish casinos, see Einhorn, 'Visszapillantás', pp. 254–5.

Modernity without emancipation or assimilation? The case of Russian Jewry

ELI LEDERHENDLER

It is notoriously difficult to define modernity, and Jewish historians have had to wrestle with this question as much as anyone else. But certain generalizations have gained currency in Jewish historiography, allowing for periodization and the use of abstract concepts as shorthand labels. Among the terms which modern Jewish historians have used most often as such analytical constructs are Enlightenment, emancipation and assimilation. The bicentennial of the French Revolution reminds the Jewish historian how much the periodization and conceptualization of modern Jewish historiography have been shaped by the issue of Jewish emancipation and its attendant social phenomena.

If these concepts are indeed taken as the criteria required to define Jewish modernity, Russian Jewry cannot be said to have become modern until February 1917. The process of emancipation and assimilation were highly retarded in the Russian-Jewish context; and Enlightenment, or Haskalah – insofar as it affected Russo-Polish Jewry – remained a limited intellectual phenomenon whose impact on the daily lives of most Jews was marginal up until the 1880s (and, arguably, beyond). It would seem to follow that Russian Jewry from 1772 to 1917 constitutes a separate episode in Jewish history that ought not to be examined in the same conceptual context as the rest of European Jewry.

But what if – as has been suggested by Todd Endelman's work on English Jewry[1] and by Jacob Katz's critique of the dominant Germanocentric tradition in modern Jewish historiography[2] – it is really the classic historiographical concepts that ought to be re-examined and revised? Endelman argues that the English case was exceptional in that Enlightenment and emancipation, on the German model, are really inappropriate as keys to understanding social change in English Jewry.[3] The American case provides us with yet another exception. Indeed, if we examine the modern development of Jewish communities, country by country, we will find that few communities anywhere adhere very closely to the ostensible paradigm. Emancipation took a different course in Germany than in France or Italy.

Assimilation, too, has become something of a liability rather than an asset in historical analysis. In the 1960s Milton Gordon refined the concept by showing that not all culturally assimilated people were likely candidates for complete social integration.[4] More recent studies suggest that because cultural adaptation has taken place without the elimination of either the social distance between ethnic groups or the distinctive patterns of, for example, economic activity, urban residence and educational strategy, 'assimilation' has not meant in reality what it was once taken to mean: a one-directional process of group disappearance.[5] Recognition of this has led to a preference for the word acculturation over the term assimilation.[6]

Research into such areas as Jewish political activity has also highlighted the inadequacy of 'assimilation' in defining the programme of those Jews who publicly pursued the goal of Jewish equality and social integration.[7] 'Integration and identity', as Uriel Tal argued, were the twin aims of the Jews in Imperial Germany.[8]

If the historical differences among the emancipated Jewries and the breakdown of the classic equation between emancipation and assimilation have led to a critique of an older historiography, Enlightenment as a criterion for Jewish cultural modernization has also suffered. The studies by Endelman and Rozenblit have persuasively indicated that cultural, economic and social change developed, to a large extent, independently of the intellectual issues of the Haskalah, at least in certain countries and social settings. The primacy of social rather than intellectual factors also informs Leon Jick's study of synagogue reform in America, where (he contends) that ideological programme and intellectual leadership followed rather than preceded institutional change.[9]

Thus, when we examine specific chapters in modern Jewish history, we find that the basic terms popular in the past are too abstract to serve as sharp analytical tools.

However, the departure from an archetypical model, the qualifications attached to the meaning of assimilation and the restriction of Haskalah to more modest proportions in historical analysis – these

quite considerable revisions in the basic criteria used to measure
Jewish modernity – make it feasible to treat Russian-Jewish history
before 1917 not as an exception to the rule in the history of modern
European Jewry, but as part of the same historical process. This
possibility has been most fruitfully explored by Steven Zipperstein,
whose study of Odessa Jewish society places the history of this rather
cosmopolitan Jewish community squarely in the modern European
framework.

However, the example of other major cities – Warsaw, for instance
– suggests that modernization and secularization cannot be automatically equated with urbanization as such. Zipperstein has clearly
argued that the socio-economic and cultural context of Odessa was
different from that obtaining elsewhere in the Pale. One question that
remains to be answered is whether Odessa is not simply an
exceptional case (an exception within an exception – altogether too
daunting a prospect for historiographical comfort) paralleled, perhaps, by only a handful of other Eastern European cities, containing
but a small part of Eastern European Jewry before the 1880s (Brody,
Riga, St Petersburg and Moscow). Or can nineteenth-century
Russian Jewry as a whole be profitably studied in relation to modern
development? What modern indicators existed in the history of
Russian Jewry in the nineteenth century?

As I have argued elsewhere, one area in which modernizing
trends can indeed be discerned in Russian Jewry (roughly from the
1840s to the 1870s) is that of political relations.[10] A transitional period
(from the Polish partitions to the middle of the nineteenth century)
had been marked by a deterioration in the established structures of
the community, by a loss of its political rationale and by a
fragmentation of its leadership echelon. And, in consequence, new
claimants to communal responsibility had emerged. These latter –
who included prominent rabbis, Russified notables and *maskilim* –
vied with each other for legitimacy and power in ways that indicated
the passing of the traditional Jewish political order, and the
development (by 1880) of something recognizably modern, based on
such concepts as public opinion, peoplehood and social
responsibility.[11]

Much of my argument rests on the activity of the *maskilim* – not
as literary figures primarily, but as actors in the political
sphere – and as such is open to legitimate questions regarding the
gap between their self-appraisal as the avant-garde of Russian
Jewry and their real situation as a modernized but marginal

intelligentsia in the Pale. In other words, for all the innovation that their activity brought to the field of Jewish politics in Russia (most noticeably, perhaps, in the development of Jewish journalism there), did their actual impact exist more in their own minds than in anyone else's? And if that is the case, how valid is it to speak of political modernization with regard to Russian Jewry as a whole, at least in this pre-twentieth-century period? Do our findings have to be carefully hedged in, confined to peripheral groups and exceptional communities? Does the historian have to particularize as much as possible and generalize as little as he can? Is modernity, in a word, marginal or basic to the Russian-Jewish experience before 1881?

Leaders or peripheral figures?

The Western-oriented Jewish intelligentsia in mid-nineteenth-century Russia was by all standards a tiny segment of the Jewish population. The fact that such people became increasingly visible, even conspicuous, in the period of Nicholas I and, particularly, of Alexander II, should not be mistaken for massive socio-cultural change. To some extent, their notoriety and their assumed influence in Jewish affairs may be said to have been a function of perception rather than reality: of their own self-perception, first of all, and the perception of their traditionalist opponents, who believed them to be more influential than they in fact were. Yet, their social and political role cannot be dismissed lightly, for perceptions of power and leadership may sometimes, as in this case, help to alter reality.

Accounting for the role of *maskilim* in Russian Jewry is a complex matter. It cannot be entirely subsumed under the rubric of 'leaders from the periphery' – a label applied to those situated on the margins both of their own minority group and of the majority culture – and who therefore base their claims to political leadership on their mediating role between the two groups. Some of the more prominent of the non-traditionalist figures indeed do fall under this definition. Those who won a measure of Jewish recognition by virtue of their standing in Russian economic life or by virtue of their co-optation by official circles did often become semi-official spokesmen for their community. Among them were the men of Baron Joseph Guenzburg's circle who were drawn in the early 1860s into the Society for Promoting Jewish Enlightenment (OPE) for example, or certain crown-appointed rabbis and other public figures who were appointed to posts as ministerial or provincial Jewish advisers to the government (so-called 'learned Jews' – *uchonye evreii*).[12]

Others, such as Isaac Ber Levinsohn, Mordecai Aaron Guenzburg, Avraham Ber Gottlober, Eliezer Silbermann, Alexander Zederbaum, Ilya Orshansky – to name but a few – held no official office, were not among the wealthy notables, but still asserted a leadership role in Jewish society. Their decision to play a vocal part in Jewish affairs stemmed not from their occupying a borderline position *vis-à-vis* Jewish society, on the one hand, and Russian society, on the other. Rather, they developed an ethos of communal responsibility that was based partly on their early training for membership in the rabbinic elite; partly on their perception of the breakdown of traditional communal leadership and partly on a need to assert and objectify (in the face of traditionalist opposition) their personal sense of having achieved a superior socio-cultural perspective.

Thus, in 1804 one of the first Russian maskilim, Lev Nevakhovich, confessed that he felt 'called', by virtue of his education and his literary competence in Russian, to serve as his people's advocate.[13] From the 1830s until his death in 1860, Isaac Ber Levinsohn dedicated himself to countering slanders against the Jewish people.[14] Avraham Ber Gottlober outlined in 1859 what he felt were the key contributions of his fellow *maskilim* to Jewish society:

> Everyone should realize that Israel has not been abandoned. In all its habitations there are *maskilim*, people of discernment and learning, who are working for the good of our people . . . 'God has done great things for us', for He has not withdrawn His graciousness from His chosen people. He dwells in the hearts of our *maskilim* so that [they may] succour the remnant [of Israel], either through being their shield and defender against their enemies and defamers, or by suggesting ways to correct their inner lives so that they may walk the straight path and earn respect in the eyes of God and King.[15]

A decade later, Shmuel Yosef Fuenn, publisher of the Vilna journal, *Hakarmel*, enunciated his own credo of public responsibility when he contrasted the task of the Jewish journalist in Russia with his counterpart in countries where Jews were already emancipated:

> The [writer] who endeavours to observe the affairs of his brothers in a place where they are still only taking the first steps on the road toward citizenship – in a place, that is, where [modern] concepts are still only vaguely perceived or defined, the system is not firmly established and there is disarray instead of public order – there [the writer's] task is difficult indeed. He must distinguish [for his readers] between good and evil, the sacred and the profane. He must cope with intimidation by those who have not acquired wisdom, who revile and attack him for

his questioning of customs which, through habit, have acquired an aura of sanctity . . . Who is he to act as teacher and public benefactor? Why should he presume to offer [advice] that has not been required of him? . . . but we have been summoned to make our best effort, to honour our obligation as far as we are able, and we are 'not free to desist' from [this labour].[16]

And in 1872, Lev Levanda declared, 'A great and sacred mission has been given to us: to transform, re-educate, our co-religionists, to set them on the high road to walk hand in hand with all humanity. We must be the rabbis, teachers, writers and intellectuals.'[17]

Their example of self-assumed leadership was closely paralleled by that of prominent traditionalist rabbis, who themselves claimed to speak authoritatively for the community and who often challenged, but sometimes also accepted, the right of the 'assimilated' *maskilim* to speak for and to instruct the Jewish public at large. To the extent that the traditionalists did on occasion look to the *maskilim* or to the notables for political intercession or support, and did then expect them to represent the community, to that extent we can legitimately speak of the non-traditionalists as playing a part within the national leadership of Russian Jewry in fact, and not merely in fantasy.

Jewish political history is full of examples of court Jews and other such 'leaders from the periphery' – so that in a sense, we can see here an example of historical continuity. However, when intellectual figures who did not fit the mould of the court Jew aspired to the role of communal spokesmen (and sometimes achieved it, as will become clear), the old patterns underwent an acknowledged transformation.

Let us take, first, the 'leaders from the periphery'. Here we may take as a prime example the group of *shtadlanim* (political advocates or 'lobbyists'), wealthy entrepreneurs and government-recognized intellectual figures who formed the leadership of the OPE, founded in the autumn of 1863. This was an intentionally elitist group whose combined financial and intellectual resources would, it was hoped, effectively further the modernization of Jewish education and the Jewish economic structure – and thus earn for Russian Jewry an honourable place in a progressive Russia-in-the-making.

The OPE supported modern Jewish schools, libraries, publication projects, scholarships for university and professional education and stipends for teachers. But, because of the involvement of the Guenzburgs, father and son, the organization was widely viewed as an extension of their own *shtadlan* activities. Moreover, because of the society's location in St Petersburg and, finally, because of the fragmentation earlier in the century of the Jewish communal leadership, the OPE was widely perceived by Russian Jews as a political lobby and a defender of Jewish interests in general.

Confirmation that the OPE was viewed by many Jews – by average, traditional Jews and not only by acculturated merchants or by intellectuals – as a political instrument may be seen in the following report by a militantly anti-maskilic Orthodox memoirist:

> In the most recent past, ever since there arose among our people the great ones [that is, men with access to high government circles] and the Enlightened ones, the people have begun to say: 'Now we have brothers in [that is, close to] the palace' . . . so that only they are deemed fit for public activity, and it is to them that the people look for salvation.[18]

In the course of its first five years, the society was requested on numerous occasions to intercede with the authorities on behalf of individuals and groups of Jews: authors whose manuscripts had not seen the light of day since their submission months earlier to the censors; merchants who sought relief from residential restrictions close to the border; civic-minded men who desired to play a role in municipal affairs; trained surveyors hoping to circumvent the near-total ban on Jews in the civil service; destitute farmers and outraged readers of scurrilous anti-Jewish articles in the Russian press.[19] But an indication that the OPE, and Baron Guenzburg in particular, were seen as representing more than a limited constituency of wealthy merchants and of *maskilim* is the fact that in 1873 the most active Orthodox leaders of the time (the rabbis, Isaac Elhanan Spector and Israel Salanter) appealed for the Baron's help in a matter touching on the heart of traditional Judaism: the welfare of the *melamdim* (teachers) in the traditional religious schools.[20]

The episode of the appeal for the *melamdim* is instructive in that it demonstrated both the flexibility in the concept of leadership in Russian Jewry and the limits to the role the Orthodox would concede to 'leaders from the periphery'. For Baron Guenzburg wished to do more in the matter of the *melamdim* than simply lodge a personal petition on their behalf with the education ministry, as he had been asked to do. The Orthodox leaders believed that he could easily and legitimately perform the role of their agent within the traditional parameters of private diplomacy which had always been entrusted to peripheral figures with access to those in power. But Guenzburg had urged that the entire matter of the traditional Jewish schools be taken up by a committee to be made up of scholars on the board of the OPE.

The Orthodox leaders balked at this encroachment on their territory, something that was unacceptable under the old system of the *shtadlanim.*[21]

This was perfectly in keeping with the traditional, strictly utilitarian approach to men of Guenzberg's ilk. Their usefulness to the main body of Jewry was defined by and restricted to their ability to seek favours from the authorities. This utilitarian thinking was breached by a number of moderate modernizers among the Orthodox rabbinate, led by Rabbi Shmuel Mohilever of Radom. Mohilever and some of his colleagues actually proposed a type of entente between moderates on both sides of the Orthodox–maskilic divide in order to co-operate on school reform and other issues of common interest. Such negotiations were evidence of the differentiation within the Orthodox camp itself, and of the attempts of those like Mohilever to use moderate–maskilic alliances as a means to bolster their own positions.

Specifically, what the moderate rabbis sought at this juncture, in 1873–4, was maskilic help in convening an official rabbinical conference to lend authority to their proposed programmes of educational reform.[22] This proposal, which was rejected by the OPE board itself as unfeasible, given the disunity among the rabbis and the improbability of government approval,[23] demonstrated that some rabbinic leaders were willing to acknowledge a greater role for the *maskilim* – subordinate to the rabbis, to be sure, but also beyond mere *shtadlanut.*

As for the maskilic writers who were not themselves highly connected or wealthy, they constantly asserted their own competence to advise Russian Jewry and to guide its public affairs, in concert with the notables, with the rabbis, or with Western European Jewish organizations (chiefly the French-Jewish Alliance Israélite Universelle). The fact that *maskilim* pioneered the Jewish press in Russia gave them a distinct advantage in assuming the roles of observers, commentators, preachers and social critics. Here we are not dealing with leaders from the periphery. The Hebrew and Yiddish newspapers, in particular, played an entirely internal role in broadening as well as deepening the sphere of public discourse in Jewish society, in legitimizing the concept of public opinion – a radical innovation at the time – and in fostering a sense of 'the Jewish interest' that transcended purely local concerns. 'Thus have these *maskilim* increased in strength and influence, through the power of their writings in our country', complained an Orthodox polemicist.[24]

Perhaps as important, the press became an arena where traditionalists and modernizers addressed each other directly. (This was true
above all of the journals *Hakarmel* and *Hamagid*.) In the debate over
communal leadership, social welfare, religious reform and the
rabbinate that erupted in 1868–9, writers from both sides used the
pages of the Jewish press to trade charges of incompetence and social
irresponsibility and to challenge leading rabbis and lay figures to pay
closer attention to the community's inner life (discussed below).
Reflecting on the role played in Jewish affairs by the press, the
moderate traditionalist, Yehiel Mikhl Pines, wrote:

> I have seen how necessary *Hakarmel* is, for in truth, without it we in
> Lithuania would have no vehicle for expressing the public opinion
> through which we must discuss and weigh honestly . . . civic and
> political issues.[25]

As an arena for public debate, the press re-defined Jewish politics.
Added to the external dimension that was traditionally handled by
shtadlanim and the domestic aspects of local community affairs, there
was now a new internal factor that was independent of both the local
communal structure and the notables in St Petersburg. Though their
programme was rejected by the majority of Jewish society, the
maskilim commanded the attention, through their journals, of a much
wider segment of Russian Jewry than they themselves comprised. The
modernization of communication techniques was essential to the
modernization of politics, and the new tools were rapidly imitated by
the traditionalists.

Maskilim and rabbis in years of crisis

The programme of the *maskilim* demanded a large measure of
acculturation. That is to say, they tended to favour the social
integration of Jews within the dominant culture, along roughly
Western European lines. To that end, they deemed it necessary for
the Jews both to acquire facility in the native language of the country
and to modernize Jewish culture itself.

The character of Jewish society and the nature of the remedial
changes required were issues sharply debated within the maskilic
camp, of course. But the distance between *maskilim* – of all categories –
and traditionalists was much greater, and became virtually unbridgeable by the middle of the century. This fact found political expression,
for example, in the dual rabbinate system (crown-appointed officiating rabbis working side by side with non-official but popularly

recognized and truly functioning 'religious' rabbis); in the ties with the authorities which the *maskilim* cultivated; in the conflicts between *maskilim* and traditionalists over the new crown schools for Jews and the two state rabbinical seminaries and in the emergence of a militant Orthodoxy to resist maskilic influence.

Under these circumstances, the question of who would represent the Jews politically became of crucial importance. As already noted, Orthodox leaders were not averse to being represented by non-Orthodox personages (*shtadlanim*), but they drew the line when matters of religious life were at stake. In 1843, two of the leading rabbinical figures of the time – Menahem-Mendl Schneerson of Lubavich and Yitzhak of Volozhin – personally experienced the kind of pressure that could be brought to bear when *maskilim* acted as communal leaders under government auspices. It was on that occasion that the Ministry of Education (or 'National Enlightenment'), under Count Uvarov, summoned Jewish representatives to St Petersburg in order to discuss and accept the government's plan to reform Jewish education. The conference brought the two rabbis together with a number of prominent *maskilim*: Bezalel Stern of Odessa, Max Lilienthal and Lev Mandelstamm (the last two having been commissioned by Uvarov for the task).[26] Although the traditionalists won certain concessions at the time, it was clear that they were thrown on the defensive and would henceforth make every effort to counter what they felt was undue interference by the *maskilim* in Jewish life. By the same token, however, though they were backed up by Uvarov, the claim by the *maskilim* to communal authority was largely a matter of their own self-perception. They did not win popular acceptance.

And yet we do know that, beginning in 1856 (with the appearance of *Hamagid*) the new Jewish journals provided the leading maskilic writers with a wider influence on the structure and development of Jewish affairs. If by 1873 Rabbi Mohilever believed it worthwhile to pursue a *modus vivendi* with the OPE (and he was not alone in this), we must ask whether it would not be hasty to conclude that the *maskilim* were merely an isolated group in Jewish society – a group whose leadership potential was apparent only to themselves. Again, perceptions have a great deal to do with this question. It was assumed that *maskilim* had political advantages – advantages that might accrue to the traditionalists in the Jewish community if they could reach an understanding with the modernists. But in acting on that perception, the Orthodox mainstream made it self-fulfilling.

To shed further light on this issue, and to help explain why power-sharing with *maskilim* was even conceivable to some rabbis in the 1870s, let us examine the crisis of 1868–9. The emergency situation faced at that time, chiefly by the Jews of Lithuania, comprised two aspects. First, the famine that struck the region in those years seriously overburdened the existing social-welfare arrangements in the communities, and set in motion a process of internal migration as well as westward emigration. (The mass emigration to America, often dated to the years following 1881, had its roots twelve years earlier.) Second, in this same period of time, Jewish communal affairs were subjected to close and hostile scrutiny by a commission appointed by the governor-general of the northwest (Vilna) district, Konstantin von Kaufmann.

The famine exacerbated the problem of pauperization and highlighted the ineffectual procedures for organizing Jewish community action. The maskilic press was extremely critical of the local lay and rabbinic leadership for failing to face up to the crisis and for its impotence in general. This criticism was, for the first time, also levelled at the notables who lived in far-off St Petersburg.[27]

Indeed, although there were clearly external economic causes behind the critical social situation, the debate in the Jewish press raised two basic questions. Was the traditional religious culture guilty of maintaining a primitive system of education, of promoting early marriage and thus perpetuating economically unviable households, and so creating a distorted, 'non-productive' occupational structure patently unable to meet the needs of a growing population?[28] And, beyond that, who if anyone in the Jewish community of Russia and Poland had the authority to effect the changes in the religious, educational and communal-organizational spheres so desperately needed in order to grapple with poverty, hunger and unemployment?[29]

Some writers (the Orthodox Yehiel Mikhl Pines, the moderate Eliezer Silbermann and the more radical Moses Leib Lilienblum, for example) believed that adaptation to modern conditions was being effectively blocked by religious leaders, and that the solution, therefore, lay in a mobilization of the moderate rabbinate which could, with the aid of *maskilim*, reform Jewish education and customs. Others (including, again, both Orthodox and some anti-traditionalist writers) denied that the rabbis were in any position – politically, socially, economically or morally – to effect the kind of social changes in Jewish society that would allow it to meet the challenges of the day.[30] Under no circumstances, however, were the

Orthodox willing to accord to the *maskilim* any standing in deciding matters directly related to religious practice.

Out of this debate, which appeared to thwart the idea of religious reform, one proposal did emerge that appealed to both Orthodox and maskilic spokesmen: the establishment of some co-ordinating agency for Russian-Jewish affairs nationwide, modelled either on the French-Jewish Consistory or on the Alliance Israélite Universelle. Many writers hoped that the OPE would assume this role.

This was rather startling in view of the accusation made at that time that the Alliance constituted the core of a secret international Jewish brotherhood, and that this world-wide Jewish society functioned locally through the *kahal* – the individual community – which perpetuated Jewish exclusiveness. That was the gist of the case made by Jacob Brafman of Vilna, a convert from Judaism, who in 1868–9 played a central role in the Vilna Commission set up to examine the truth of his claims.[31] The commission proceeded to subject Jewish religious and communal life to a painstaking review, and to draw up a proposal that would do away with the separate Jewish government schools, tax rolls and registration of population. In addition, small prayer halls (*shtiblekh*) were to be forbidden, leaving only crown rabbis and supervised synagogues to function. Jewish divorce laws were to be amended; ritual baths placed under medical supervision and the number of voluntary associations (*hevrot*) vastly reduced.[32]

The Jewish community was invited to send representatives to this commission, and a number of Jews with official standing were also invited. The result was that, together with Rabbi Yaakov Barit of Vilna, a prominent Orthodox figure (albeit one known for more advanced ideas), a number of well-known *maskilim* attended the commission's discussions: Lev Levanda and Jonah Gerstein (both 'learned Jews' – advisers – assigned to the provincial administration), Emanuel Levin (a member of the OPE), Hirsh Shapira (a prominent Kovno *maskil*) and Zalkind Minor (the crown rabbi of Minsk).[33]

The Jewish spokesmen, who might have been expected to split along ideological lines, given the vociferous debate over communal priorities and authority then being waged in the press, achieved a remarkable degree of unity under the leadership of Barit. The memorandum they submitted on the commission's recommendations made it clear that there could be no question of interference in the internal religious life of the Jewish community. The new governor-general, Alexander Potapov, accepted their arguments, and a major Jewish victory was scored.[34]

What is especially relevant in the present context is the role played by the *maskilim* in the Jewish delegation. In contrast to the episode of 1843, when the *maskilim* had clearly aligned themselves with the authorities and overwhelmed the traditionalist representation, they now were (and were seen to be) active supporters of Orthodox rabbi in the group and of the sanctity of Jewish religious freedom. The possibility existed, then, of a common ground between the Orthodox leaders and moderate *maskilim*, particularly with regard to political representation. (This, evidently, was the background to Mohilever's appeal to the OPE four years later, asking for co-operation over school reform and for a more sensitive policy with regard to religious issues.) The maskilic representatives who appeared before the Vilna Commission had gained a measure of credibility as community spokesmen that their predecessors a generation before so clearly had lacked.

Several factors contributed to this development. First, Jewish society in the late 1860s and 1870s was already caught in the throes of a serious socio-economic crisis that challenged the authority and security of the more traditional leaders. The *maskilim* were the ones who advocated explicit social and economic reforms, which seemed to address the needs of the moment. Second, the attitude towards Jewish communal interests taken by *maskilim* of the 1860s and especially the 1870s had matured, and was more sympathetic and protective than had been the case under Nicholas I. The relationship of Jewish writers and intellectuals towards the Russian government had become less trusting, more critical.[35] Finally, maskilic politics – in keeping with the idea of public opinion developed by the press – had undergone a conceptual reorientation, looking to 'the people' rather than to the state as the source of political legitimacy.

Ten years after the crisis of 1869, the maskilic and rabbinic leaders were once again at loggerheads over a question of political represent-ation. The occasion was the convening of an official Rabbinical Commission at the capital, under the auspices of the Department of Foreign Cults of the Ministry of Internal Affairs. Such a body had not met in seventeen years, although when first mandated by law the Rabbinical Commissions were meant to meet regularly and frequently.[36]

The announcement in 1878 that the ministry was summoning a new Rabbinical Commission for the early part of the following year aroused speculation in Jewish circles that the government had decided to effect the emancipation of the Jewish population (or, at the very least, to put such a process into motion through the establishment of a Jewish consistory in St Petersburg). These expectations gained currency against the background of the Russo-Turkish war, just then concluded, in which Russian Jews in the ranks of the army had passed the test of battle. Moreover, at the end of the war, Jewish emancipation in Romania had been part of the agenda of the great powers at the Congress of Berlin.[37]

A struggle ensued in the Jewish communities of the Pale over who would appear on the list of nominees to the Rabbinical Commission; the final choice of delegates was up to the ministry. Rabbis were the natural choice for such a body, perhaps, but Russified and socially prominent members of the intelligentsia or Jewish upper classes were more likely to be able to function as political representatives (if only because of their facility in the Russian language). Moreover, the composition of such commissions had in the past leaned heavily towards *shtadlanim*, 'learned Jews', crown rabbis and the like. Writers from the modern camp expressed their conviction in the press that, this time as well, it made more sense for the communities to choose *maskilim* to represent them.[38] After all, *maskilim* in the late 1870s could legitimately claim a wider credibility as communal spokesmen than their predecessors from the previous generation.

The fact that the agenda of the commission was thought to be essentially civic or political in nature probably weighed heavily in favour of the *maskilim*. On the eve of the commission's first session, *Hameliz* triumphantly announced the coming act of emancipation; *Hamagid*, though more circumspect, held out the hope that such, indeed, was the government's intention. It should therefore come as little surprise that, in the end, many Jewish communities chose *maskilim* together with respected rabbis to represent them.[39]

The Rabbinical Commission of 1879 adjourned within a month without having undertaken any serious business – let alone the emancipation of the Jews. But the considerable political victory scored by the *maskilim* within some of the major communities demonstrates how far their role as a leadership group (in opposition to, but still not completely ostracized by, the Orthodox camp) had expanded and won a measure of acceptance beyond their own immediate circle.

Most Jews in Central and Western Europe remained somewhere between the poles of total assimilation and communal introversion, because emancipation did not resolve the issues of Jewish social and religious particularism. The debate over emancipation, in fact, gave birth to the 'Jewish question'. Likewise, assimilation (in the extreme sense) could not – by definition – offer the community as such a path to social integration. In Western and Central Europe, therefore, modern Jews often redefined Jewishness in terms which embraced both community and assimilation (or, at least, a high degree of acculturation).

In Russia, where assimilation as a strategy for social mobility was hardly conceivable and where the government did not seriously consider emancipation, traditional communal life was altered by the fragmentation of the Jewish community into local units and competing regional, religious and class groupings. To Russian Jews, too, therefore, the nineteenth century brought change and even dislocation. Issues of communal authority, continuity and leadership agitated Jewish society. Where community remained so central an issue, those who advocated a Western-type accommodation combining integration and identity also articulated a strong commitment to community.

My intention has not been to argue that the *maskilim* in Russia, with their programme of modernization, constituted anything more than one small group within Jewish society before 1881. Despite their ethos of communal leadership, they were far from achieving anything like hegemony. (Indeed, the nationalist *maskilim* who did so much to establish the Hovevei Zion organization in the 1880s found that they had to struggle for supremacy even within that group against traditionalist rivals.)

However, it would not be inaccurate to say that by the 1870s the influence of the *maskilim* in Jewish life was considerable, even disproportionate. After the crisis of 1868–9, little remained of the would-be alliance with the government which they had sought in the 1840s, but they had gained in credibility as spokesmen for the Jewish people. And those who refused to grant them this status still imitated their techniques of mobilization and communication.

Of course, Russo-Polish Jewry, a society undergoing modern transformations *even while producing a numerically preponderant conservative mainstream*, did experience the nineteenth century in ways which were distinctly Eastern European. However, a theory of Eastern European exceptionalism – one that would consign the story of Jewish acculturation and ideological modernization to the margins of Russian-Jewish history – turns out to be erroneous when applied to Jewish political development. The Jewish experience in Tsarist Russia was different, but not divorced from that of Europe to the west.

Notes

This chapter summarizes and extends a discussion contained in my book, *The Road to Modern Jewish Politics: Political Tradition and Political Reconstruction in the Jewish Community of Tsarist Russia* (New York and Oxford, 1989), and is published with the permission of Oxford University Press. Some of the historical data I have discussed here was first presented in the book, chiefly in ch. 5. I would like to thank Steven Zipperstein and Jonathan Frankel who read earlier drafts of this essay and suggested improvements.

1 Todd M. Endelman, *The Jews of Georgian England: Tradition and Change in a Liberal Society* (Philadelphia, 1979).

2 Jacob Katz (ed.), *Toward Modernity: The European Jewish Model* (New Brunswick, N.J., 1987). See also, in that volume, the essay on Vienna by Robert Wistrich and on Prague by Hillel Kieval.

3 Endelman, *Jews of Georgian England*, pp. 6–11.

4 Milton Gordon, *Assimilation in American Life: The Role of Race, Religion and National Origins* (New York and Oxford, 1964).

5 See, for example, Marsha Rozenblit, *The Jews of Vienna, 1867–1914: Assimilation and Identity* (Albany, N.Y. 1983); Calvin Goldscheider and Alan S. Zuckerman, *The Transformation of the Jews* (Chicago and London, 1984); Calvin Goldscheider, 'Self-Employment and Jewish Continuity', *Studies in Contemporary Jewry*, vol. II (1986), ed. P. Medding, pp. 191–207; Victor Karady, 'Jewish Enrollment Patterns in Classical Secondary Education in Old Regime and Inter-war Hungary', *Studies in Contemporary Jewry*, vol. I (1984), ed. J. Frankel, pp. 225–52; and see the volume of essays on the interplay of modern social conditions and ethnicity in the case of Soviet nationality groups in the Baltic region: *Nationality Group Survival in Multi-ethnic States: Shifting Support Patterns in the Soviet Baltic Region*, ed. Edward Allworth (New York, 1977), including my essay on Soviet Jews in Latvia and Lithuania ('Resources of the Ethnically Disenfranchised', pp. 194–227).

6 For example, in Endelman, *Jews of Georgian England*; Steven J. Zipperstein, *The Jews of Odessa. A Cultural History, 1794–1881* (Stanford, 1985); Steven J. Zipperstein, 'Haskalah, Cultural Change, and Nineteenth-Century Russian Jewry: A Reassessment', *Journal of Jewish Studies* 35, no. 2 (1983), 191–207.

7 This is suggested, for example, by Ismar Schorsch's *Jewish Reactions to German Anti-Semitism, 1870–1914* (New York, London and Philadelphia, 1972) and Jehuda Reinharz's *Fatherland or Promised Land: The Dilemma of the German Jew, 1893–1914* (Ann Arbor, Mich. 1975).

8 Uriel Tal, *Christians and Jews in Germany, Religion, Politics and Ideology in the Second Reich, 1870–1914* (Ithaca N.Y. and London, 1975).

9 Leon Jick, *The Americanization of the Synagogue, 1820–1870* (Hanover, N.H., 1976).

10 Lederhendler, *Modern Jewish Politics*.
11 Ibid., chs. 3–5.
12 The institution of the crown rabbinate (officially recognized and legally
    defined by statute) grew up in Russia in tandem with an unofficial or so-
    called 'religious' rabbinate. Among the official rabbis were several
    outstanding *maskilim*, such as Zalkind Minor, the rabbi of Minsk, and Dr
    Abraham Neumann, rabbi of Riga and subsequently of St Petersburg.
    Other prominent *maskilim* served as Jewish advisers – known as 'learned
    Jews' (*uchonye evreii*) because of their European education – attached to
    provincial administrations, school districts, or state ministries. Shmuel
    Yosef Fuenn and Lev Levanda were *uchonye evreii*, as were Yaakov
    Gurland, Herman Baratz, Moisei Berlin, and others. Finally, the heads
    of the crown rabbinical seminaries in Vilna and Zhitomir served as
    censors of Hebrew and Yiddish publications, along with other *maskilim*
    and Christian converts from Judaism. Thus, Haim Selig Slonimskii was a
    censor, as were Wolf Tugendhold, Joshua Steinberg, Iosif Seiberling and
    others. See tables 2 and 3 in Lederhendler, *Modern Jewish Politics*, ch. 4.
13 Lev Nevakhovich, introduction to 'Kol shav'at bat yehuda' (Shklov,
    1804), reprinted in *He'avar* 2 (1918), separate pagination.
14 On Levinsohn's role as an apologist, see Lederhendler, *Modern Jewish
    Politics*, ch. 4. Levinsohn's best-known works in defence of Judaism
    include: *Efes damim* (Vilna, 1837), *Yemin tsidkati* (Warsaw, 1881) and
    Zerubavel (Odessa, 1863; Warsaw, 1875). Levinsohn linked his work as an
    Enlightener and as a champion of the Jews in the epitaph he composed
    for himself:

    > With the enemies of God I have engaged in battle, with words, not
    > weapons of iron. The innocence of Jeshurun have I revealed to the
    > nations, bear witness, *Zerubavel* and *Efes damim*.

    See D. Natanson (ed.), *Sefer hazikhronot, divrei yemei hayei . . . Yitzhak Ber
    Levinsohn* (Warsaw, 1875).
15 Avraham Ber Gottlober, in *Hamagid* 33 (1859), 132.
16 Shmuel Yosef Fuenn, in *Hakarmel* 1 (1868), 1.
17 Lev Levanda, *Goriachee vremia*, part 2, in *Evreiskaia Biblioteka* 2 (1872), 34.
18 Yaakov Halevi Lifschitz, *Zikhron Ya'akov* (Frankfurt-am-Main, 1924),
    vol. II, p. 188.
19 Leon Rosental (ed.), *Hevrat marbei haskalah beyisrael* (St Petersburg,
    1890), vol. I, pp. 2, 9, 27, 65, 109; ibid., vol. II, pp. 7, 21, 27, 30–1, 46–7
    50–1, 119–20, 167–76, 198–201.
20 Lifschitz, *Zikhron Ya'akov*, vol. II, pp. 124–6; cf. Yaakov Halevi Lifschitz,
    Toledot Yitzhak (Warsaw, 1896), pp. 85–6.
21 Lifschitz, *Zikhron Ya'akov*, vol. II, p. 127; see the plan outlined by
    Mohilever in St Petersburg in Rosental, *Hevrat marbei haskalah*, vol. I, pp.
    101–2. On the involvement of Guenzburg and the OPE in education and

reform, see Zipperstein, 'Transforming the Heder: Maskilic Politics in Imperial Russia', in A. Rapoport-Albert and S. J. Zipperstein (eds.), *Jewish History: Essays in Honour of Chimen Abramsky* (London, 1988), pp. 87–109.

22 Rosental, *Hevrat marbei haskalah*, vol. I, pp. 87–90, n.; ibid., p. 97; Lifschitz, *Zikhron Ya'akov*, vol. II, p. 128; *Hazfirah*, 2 (1874), 11–12.

23 Rosental, *Hevrat marbei haskalah*, vol. I, pp. 93–4, n.

24 Lifschitz, *Zikhron Ya'akov*, vol. II, pp. 42–4.

25 *Hakarmel*, 15 (1868), 113.

26 See B. Mandelstamm, *Hazon lamo'ed* (Vienna, 1877); M. Lilienthal, *Magid yeshu'ah* (Vilna, 1842); Hayim Meir Hilman, *Beit rebbi* (Berdichev, 1901–2), part 3, ch. 3, pp. 9–20; Lifschitz, *Zikhron Ya'akov*, vol. I, pp. 82–3, 101–2; David Philipson, *Max Lilienthal, American Rabbi: Life and Writings* (New York, 1915), pp. 159–367; M. Morgulis, 'K istorii evreiskoi obrazovaniia russkikh evreev', in his *Voprosy evreiskoi zhizni* (St Petersburg, 1889), pp. 1–71; A. B. Gottlober, *Zikhronot umasa'ot* (Jerusalem, 1976), vol. II, pp. 127–45; Immanuel Etkes, 'Parashat hahaskalah mita'am vehatemurah bema'amad tenu'at hahaskalah berusiah', *Ziyòn* 43 (1978), 264–313; Michael Stanislawski, *Tsar Nicholas I and the Jews: The Transformation of Jewish Society in Russia, 1825–1855* (Philadelphia, 1983), pp. 77–82.

27 *Hakarmel* 3 (1868), 18; ibid. 4 (1868). 25; *Hameliz* 9 (1868), 67, 69; *Hamagid* 7, 13–14, 16–19, (1868); ibid., nos. 8, 15, 25 (1869); Lifschitz, *Zikhron Yaakov*, vol. II, p. 70.

28 See S. Braiman, 'Pulmus hatikunim badat basifrut ha'ivrit baemza hameah ha 19', *He'avar* 1 (1952) 115–31; H. Hamiel, 'Bein haredim lemaskilim berusiah bishnot ha-60 veha-70', *Sinai* 59, nos. 1/2 (1966), 76–84; G. Katznelson, *Hamilhamah hasifrutit bein haharedim vehamaskilim* (Tel Aviv, 1954); Azeril Shochat, *Mosad harabanut mita'am berusiah* (Haifa, 1976), p. 20–1, 61–3, 70–104, 134–43; cf. Moshe Leib Lilienblum's essays, 'Orhot hatalmud' and 'Nosafot lehamaamar orhot hatalmud', serialized in *Hameliz* (1868–9). On Lilienblum, see Z. Epstein, *Moshe Leib Lilienblum: shitato vehelekh mahshevotav besheelot hadat* (Tel Aviv, 1935); H. Hamiel, 'Pulmus M. L. Lilienblum', *Sinai* 60, nos. 5/7 (1967), 299–310; Zipperstein, *Odessa*, pp. 141–2.

29 *Hakarmel*, suppl. to 8 (1869), 10; *Hamagid* 17 (1869) ("Al devar matsav benei yisrael berusiah vetikuno'); ibid. 28 (1869), 217–18; ibid., 42 (1869), 288–9; *Den*, 1, 8, 11, 12 (1870); *Razsvet* 20, 22–4, 28 (1870); Yehuda Slutsky, *Ha'itonut hayehudit-rusit bameah hatesh'a 'esreh* (Jerusalem, 1970), pp. 78–9; D. Feinberg, 'Zikhronot', *He'avar* 4 (1956), 26–36.

30 *Hakarmel* 13 (1869), 98–9; Zvi-Hirsh Jonathansohn in *Hameliz* 49 (1868), 364; *Hakarmel* 14 (1869); 106–7; Silbermann in *Hamagid* 21–3, 26–7 (1869); ibid, 48 (1869), 383–4; *Hakarmel* Russian supplement to 38 (1869), 149–51.

31 Isaac Levitats, *The Jewish Community in Russia, 1844–1917* (Jerusalem, 1981), pp. 193–4; I. M. Tcherikover, *Istoriia obshchestva dlia rasprostranenia prosveshchenia mezhdu evreiami v rossii . . . 1863–1913 gg.*, edited by S. Ginsburg (St Petersburg, 1913), p. 94; cf. J. L. Gordon's response to Brafman on behalf of the OPE, *Evreiskaia Biblioteka* (1873), 284–91.

32 *Hameliz* 24 (1868), 174; ibid. 45 (1869), col. 310; ibid., 2 (1878), cols. 29–32 and 3 (1878), cols. 49–52; S. An-sky, 'Evreiskaia delegatsiia v vilenskoi komissii 1869 goda', *Evreiskaia Starina* 5 (1912), 190–5 (minutes for the session of 11 October 1869).

33 *Hameliz* 45 (1869), col. 310 and 2–4, 6–9, 13, 17 (1878); *Den'*, 2, 4, 11, 21 (1870); *Hamaggid* 41 (1870), 323; ibid., 5 (1870), 34, and 6 (1870), 42. See also P. Rabinovich, 'Geon Ya'akov', *Kneset yisrael* 2 (1887), cols. 159–60; An-sky, 'Deputatsiia', pp. 187–201; Iulii Gessen, 'Vilenskaia komissiia po ustroistvo byta evreev', *Perezhitoe* 2 (1911), 306–11; M. Knorozovskii, 'Eshche o vilenskoi komissii 1869 goda', *Perezhitoe* 3 (1912), 385–92; Lifschitz, *Zikhron Ya'akov*, vol. II, pp. 113–14.

34 Minutes (Vilna Commission), no. 7 (pp. 197–9) and petition of the delegates to Potapov, are found in *Evreiskaia starina* 5 (1912) 200–1; cf. *Hameliz* 9 (1878), cols. 179–80; ibid., 13 (1878), cols. 249–51; ibid., 17, (1878), cols. 321–3 and 45 (1869), 311; Rabinovich, 'Geon Ya'akov', p. 160.

35 See Israel Bartal, 'Halo-yehudim vehevratam besifrut 'ivrit veyidish bemizrah eiropah bein hashanim 1856–1914' (Ph.D. dissertation, Hebrew University, Jerusalem, 1980), pp. 15–22, 45–51, 90–5, 130–1; Israel Bartal, 'Bein haskalah radikalit lesozializm yehudi', *Proceedings of the Eighth World Congress of Jewish Studies* (Jerusalem, 1984), Panel Sessions: Jewish History, pp. 16–17; Jonathan Frankel, *Prophecy and Politics: Socialism, Nationalism and the Russian Jews* (Cambridge, 1981), p. 32; Lederhendler, *Modern Jewish Politics*, ch. 5.

36 For the law of 1848 mandating the commissions, see *Polnoe sobranie zakonov rossiiskoi imperii*, second series, vol. XXIII, part 1, no. 22,276. Cf. Shimshon Dov Yerushalmi, 'Va'adot uve'idot harabanim berusiah', *He'avar* 3 (1955), 86–94; Morgulis, 'K istorii obrazovaniia', pp. 148–51; Levitats, *Jewish Community*, p. 103. In the nineteenth century the commission met in 1852, 1857, 1861–2, 1879 and 1893–4. It met for a final time in 1910.

37 Lifschitz, *Zikhron Ya'akov*, vol. II, pp. 203–4; Nahum Sokolov, 'Hayehudim beyihus hashitot hamediniot', *Hameliz* 19 (1878), col. 371; Mordecai Ben-Hillel Hacohen, 'Tikvah nikhzevah', *Hakol* 30 (1879), cols. 449–50.

38 M. L. Lilienblum, 'Petah tikva', *Hakol* 22 (1878), col. 157.

39 Hacohen, 'Tikvah nikhzevah', *Hakol* 33 (1879), cols. 493–5. On the bitterly contested election in Kovno, see Lifschitz, *Zikhron Ya'akov*, vol II, p. 206. On the role of non-rabbinic figures in the commissions, see

Morgulis, 'K istorii obrazovaniia', p. 193. Cf. the correspondence from St Petersburg by I. B. Halevi Ish Hurwitz in *Hamagid* 8 (1879), 61; *Hamagid* 11 (1879), 84; *Hameliz* 4 (1879), col. 71 (and also 10 (1879), col. 202); 'Petersburger Briefe', *Allgemeine Zeitung des Judentums* 10 (4 March 1879), 147–50 and 13 (25 March 1879), 193–5, 203.

Ahad Ha'am and the politics of assimilation

STEVEN J. ZIPPERSTEIN

'Only antisemitism had made Jews of us', Theodor Herzl and Max Nordau admitted in 1895 over glasses of beer, shortly before the launching of Herzl's Zionist movement.[1] The half-frivolous, but also deadly earnest, assertion highlighted one of the central themes in the thinking of both European literati and would-be Jewish leaders. Had their prudish, stern Russian nemesis, Ahad Ha'am (the pen-name of Asher Ginzberg, 1856–1927), been there to contribute to the Vienna beer-hall conversation and had he been coaxed (which is even less likely) to disclose what fear most animated his Jewishness, he probably would have said assimilation.

Why he remained Jewish, he wrote a few years earlier in a brilliant and sardonic article, 'Avdut be-tokh herut' (Slavery in Freedom), was no more an issue than why he remained his father's son. But, as the leading spokesman of what came to be known as 'spiritual Zionism' claimed in the same essay, which has proved to be one of the most influential Jewish statements on the subject, if Jews were to address their more pressing problems they would have to begin with assimilation – the most fundamental of all.[2] Indeed, he said that all else that was important in Jewish life – nationalist politics, the colonization of Palestine, reform of Jewish linguistic and educational life – represented bulwarks against this threat, which, if left un-checked, could undermine not only Jewry's ancient and expansive dreams but its very existence. An examination of Ahad Ha'am's preoccupation with assimilation will go far to explain the otherwise ambiguous character of his politics. It should also clarify an important facet of modern Jewry's understanding of assimilation; in this area, unlike many others, Ahad Ha'am's much-debated cultural Zionist legacy has become an integral feature of contemporary Jewish thought.

To study this aspect of his thought, indeed, almost any feature of his biography, it is necessary to look at it in the context of his politics. Until very recently, this dimension of his biography was overlooked in the vast body of secondary literature on him (some 430 items appear in a bibliography compiled as early as 1935–6),[3] which saw Ahad Ha'am mainly as an essayist, as Hebrew literature's grand man of letters.[4] Nearly all his contemporaries (and his biographers) agreed that he was not a politician. He was too frank, modest, impatient or unyielding to be effective, or even seriously interested in politics and power, they said. 'Herzl was the leader of the generation, Ahad Ha'am its teacher', wrote the latter's first biographer. The statement was considered authoritative, and it constitutes a much-sanitized gloss on a contentiously political career.[5] This distinction was, of course, crucial for many Zionists, especially Eastern European ones, who admired Ahad Ha'am but embraced Herzlian politics, which Ahad Ha'am repudiated unequivocally. And this view of him was lent authority by virtue of the fact that Ahad Ha'am himself readily spoke of his lack of administrative aptitude, of his disinterest in shaping the will of others, of his deference.

But starting with his first essays, nearly all of Ahad Ha'am's writing was animated, even dominated, by political concerns.[6] Among the most politically preoccupied were Ahad Ha'am's early midrashic-like expositions of the 1890s which have frequently been misread as abstractly philosophical but which represented, if rather obliquely, the public face of his semi-secret nationalist society, the Bnei Moshe.[7] The cultural aims of his group emphasized the need to educate properly those Jews responsible for the rebuilding of Palestine, a pedagogic strategy which seemed to many Jewish nationalists a pale substitute for emigrationist and diplomatic initiatives. For them Ahad Ha'am appeared to lack a coherent agenda, a political focal point, or even a set of clearly designated tasks suitable for more than a small coterie of like-minded intellectuals.

The elusive character of his politics must be viewed, as we shall see, as part and parcel of a traditional idiom that he endeavoured to secularize; its key concern was assimilation. A re-reading of his articles, against the backdrop of his public life, makes it clear that, to the extent to which he believed that Jews themselves could contribute towards solving their collective problems, it was by addressing this goal. Assimilation was the central focal point of his publicistic and political career. The terms assimilation (*hitbolelut*) or, what constituted its close counterpart in his opinion, fragmentation (*hitpardut*), appear no more than nine times in the annotated index compiled by

Ahad Ha'am for his four-volume collected essays, but the issues run throughout. This chapter will study the most active political and literary period of his life – until Herzl's death in 1904 – which was followed within two years by Ahad Ha'am's own rather sudden semi-retirement from political life. It was within a short span of seventeen years, from 1889 to 1906, that he established his reputation and intellectual pre-eminence, and to the extent to which a single theme could be said to unite his work, it is the politics of assimilation.

Ahad Ha'am was the son of a rich Hasid. His father saw to it that he was supplied with the best tutors, a well-stocked library (the family lived from the time that Asher was twelve on a Ukrainian rural estate) and, once the appropriate time came, with a well-pedigreed wife related to two eminent Hasidic dynasties, including the distinguished Schneersohns. His pious scholarly father was distant and morbidly disapproving and the reclusive, cerebral only son rebelled at first by reading forbidden books, but avoided open confrontation with his father until he was well into his thirties. Long after he found the cloistered piety of his parental home stifling, he was unable to cut himself away from it. He lied about his goals, for instance, when, at the age of twenty-eight, he left to study abroad at university (he returned home in a few weeks) and he stayed in business with his father even after they had moved together to Odessa and Ahad Ha'am emerged as the *enfant terrible* of the hebraic world. Their partnership dissolved only when the business failed.[8]

From the outset, then, Ahad Ha'am's rebellion was moderated by strong filial attachments (when his father died in 1899, he fell into one of his deepest depressions), by warm associations with an all-pervasive Judaism, by a feeling of insurmountable provincialism and by a disinclination to take anything to extremes. Though he would later argue that one of Judaism's central features was the fanaticism (for justice, above all) of its heroic figures, such manifestations were alien to his temperament and ideology. Once he encountered British thinkers like John Stuart Mill and especially Herbert Spencer his inclination to see change as gradual rather than abrupt was provided with modern philosophical foundations, buttressed by his lifelong admiration for the doyen of medieval Jewish philosophy, Moses Maimonides.[9]

In a semi-autobiographical essay written sometime between 1881 and 1884, entitled 'Ketavim balim' (Tattered Manuscript'), Ahad Ha'am described the anguish and beauty of abiding religious

attachments in a transitional maskilic figure caught between conflicting worlds:

> But what am I now? A maskil? I cannot say that with certainty. Still
> now, in the moments before the end of the sabbath, between the time
> that the sun sets and one begins lighting candles once again, I love to sit
> in a corner in the dark to examine the range of my feelings. In such
> moments I feel my soul rising heavenward, as if my spiritual elation has
> emerged from within me to the sound of heavenly voices, and I recall
> various memories from the days of my youth, memories that make me
> laugh, pleasant recollections – recollections that please me very much
> . . . Sometimes my lips will open as if by themselves and I find myself
> chanting some well-known melody in a hushed voice . . . During those
> long winter evenings, at times when I'm sitting in the company of
> enlightened men and women, sitting at a table with *tref* food and cards,
> and my heart is glad and my face bright, suddenly then – I don't know
> how this happens – suddenly before me is a very old table with broken
> legs, full of tattered books [*sefarim balim*], torn and dusty books of
> genuine value and I'm sitting alone in their midst, reading them by the
> light of a dim candle, opening up one and closing another, not even
> bothering to look at their tiny print . . . and the entire world is like the
> Garden of Eden.[10]

By the time this article appeared in print, in 1890 in a slim volume
called *Kaveret* (Beehive), published and edited anonymously by Ahad
Ha'am, he was a public figure and the leading member of the Jewish
nationalist *Bnei Moshe* society (Sons of Moses), whose platform was
inspired by the symbolic leadership of the Lawgiver. The kernel of
Ahad Ha'am's anti-assimilatory politics was contained in two essays –
'Lo zeh haderekh' ('This is not the way') and 'Derekh heḥayim'
('The way of life'), dating from 1888 and 1889. The first was written
for public consumption and the second (along with several addenda)
distributed exclusively to members of Bnei Moshe. Assimilation had,
of course, been closely examined earlier by other Jewish nationalists
(in the pioneering work of Peretz Smolenskin, for instance) but Ahad
Ha'am's attempt to fashion a movement, an ideology and even a
distinct leadership style built around this issue was unique.[11]

It was not mounting Judeophobia (as argued by other Jewish
nationalists) but the threat of assimilation – individualism, or
rampant egotism is how Ahad Ha'am first referred to the threat – that
demanded Jewry's restoration to Zion. The return of the Jews to their
original home would be accompanied by a return to the original
Jewish language and also by a rebirth of political instincts and

institutions supplanted by theology after the Roman conquest of Palestine. Until emancipation, Jewry's viability as an exilic community had been ensured but modern trends had now weakened Jewry's ability to integrate outside influences, as it had always done, into a framework that retained national cohesion. Before the emancipatory movements of the late eighteenth century, Jewry was sustained by its commitment to collective life but modern developments and the prospect of political freedom had isolated Jews from the natural community of Jewry, fragmented them by virtue of their citizenship (real or anticipated) in the European states, and readied them for assimilation. Moreover, individualism nourished assimilation in the West and contributed toward the disintegration of an already beleaguered Eastern European Jewry. Such individualism constituted a far greater threat than either antisemitism or poverty and it had even seeped into the Palestinophile Hovevei Zion, based in Russia, which sought to induce immigration by promising social mobility in raw, restive Palestine. Such ill-conceived tactics had halted the movement's initial momentum, bewildered its constituency (who found its reports unreliable) and strengthened the very atomistic inclinations that nationalism, according to Ahad Ha'am, was designed to check.[12]

His first two articles were intended to complement one another: 'Lo zeh haderekh' demonstrated what Zionism ought not to do and 'Derekh hehayim' pointed in what Ahad Ha'am believed was the right direction. They must be read as two sides of the same coin, as he had intended. In 'Lo zeh haderekh', he preferred to remain evasive, leaving his most concrete recommendations to the other, privately circulated declaration. For instance, he admitted in the first essay that, 'It is difficult to say whether at any period our people as a whole really entertained the sentiment of national loyalty in this high degree or whether it was only a moral idea cherished by the most important sector of the people.' Throughout Jewry's history, he contended, national consciousness had waned, 'until it all but disappeared from the consciousness of the great mass. It continued to pulsate, feebly, but only in a remnant, who would be stimulated now and then to unite for the sake of the common welfare.'[13] In 'Derekh hehayim' he made it clear that, in his expectation, the Bnei Moshe would now serve this austere function.[14]

He set out an agenda (reminiscent of the Russian populist Peter Lavrov) designed to encourage Jews to transcend their personal needs for the sake of larger collective concerns, to become true nationalists who refused to close their eyes to the bombast of the Hovevei Zion and who recognized that a nationalist movement had to be grounded on solid, ideologically coherent foundations. In language that belied the standard image of him as distracted, sceptical, and unable either to inspire others or move himself to the point of inspiration, Ahad Ha'am outlined in 'Derekh hehayim' a political programme aimed at reclaiming assimilated Jews. What he proposed was to replace Judaism's theology with a national-cultural framework which would, he hoped, alienate neither the assimilated nor the religiously inclined, both of whom were represented in Bnei Moshe. The burden of maintaining this all but impossible balance caused great friction and contributed towards the society's closure some eight years later. As he argued in 'Derekh hehayim':

> 'National' must be raised to the level of a moral concept, a designation well-regarded in the eyes of the people, one which not every man is worthy of bearing, one which imposes an obligation of guarding scrupulously the honour of the flag to ensure that there is no danger of its being desecrated either by the person who bears it or by those outside its ranks. Little by little the society will enlarge its sphere of influence. It will include [among its tasks] the education of the young, and measures to bring back to the fold the sons and daughters of our people whom we have given up to other nations. In general, wherever improvement is needed, it will set about improving things. In the end, and it does not matter when this is attained, there will arise the sort of revitalized generation that we are seeking – a generation that will refuse to bow down before Baal and grovel in the dust before its enemies, that will take pride in its people, glory in the honour of its nation . . . Such a generation will save Israel, it will carry it to Zion, it will act, it will succeed.[15]

What he envisioned, then, was the creation of a core of receptive and devoted nationalists within the Hovevei Zion who would help ensure that the Bnei Moshe's vision had a sympathetic hearing. Its devotees would make certain that the folk was reschooled in its image, by virtue of their pristine personal behaviour, their commendable activist *élan*, and their cohesive and integrated vision of the Jewish past and future. In creating the Bnei Moshe, Ahad Ha'am attempted to translate into modern Jewish political idiom methods used to inspire and rule traditional Jewry: Bnei Moshe was to perform a function comparable to that of the eminent Volozhin yeshiva outside Vilna or a distinguished Hasidic court – it was to serve as a fulcrum, a focal point which would inspire Jews elsewhere by virtue of the austere and exemplary behaviour of its members, and especially its leaders. This is why Ahad Ha'am blithely dismissed criticism from Bnei Moshe members who insisted on knowing what they were expected to do, what actions they were expected to perform as members of this elite society. If, as Ahad Ha'am felt, they did not understand what was expected of an elite in times of crisis – if they were unable to appreciate that their service to the community had less to do with concrete activity than with inspiration – they were unworthy of membership.[16]

The need to affirm the authentic values of Jewry's elite (now secularized but, Ahad Ha'am felt, fundamentally the same as always) contributed to the reverent, even obsequious way in which he was treated by his circle. His special status was formalized once the Bnei Moshe was established with a highly ritualized system in which he functioned as the all but dictatorial leader.[17] For his constituency (and for Ahad Ha'am himself) this was part and parcel of the same attempt to stem the tide of Jewry's assimilation by inspiring a new cadre of leaders headed by a charismatic and exemplary totem. He and his entourage sought to replace the charisma of one set of hegemonic symbols with another and stressed the need to substitute the waning primacy of Hasidic and rabbinic masters with a leadership in the same mould but which, they claimed, was both modern and authentic.[18]

Those viewed by the Bnei Moshe as 'assimilated' were made up of a mixed multitude of university and gymnasium students, commercial magnates, clerks, shopgirls and youth fresh from the provinces who arrived in Odessa, and other cities of the south, in search of schooling, jobs, publishers and a more expansive style of life. Frequently they were disdainful of Jewish nationalism which, as they saw it, resembled their recent provincialism.[19] Moreover, the vast majority of Odessa's native Jewish intelligentsia – Russified, secularly sophisticated, cultivated in ways that the Hebraists around Ahad Ha'am could never be and considerably more distant from the rhythm of traditional Jewish life – ignored, or, at best, patronized Hebraists who knew this and resented it deeply.[20]

The first book financed and distributed by the Bnei Moshe was produced to attract such Jews to the nationalist camp. Entitled *Khanukah*, and written in Russian, it was expected that this would be the first of a series of similar books that would highlight the salient nationalist symbols that retained their relevance even as the religious character of Jewry's holidays was losing its importance to most Jews.[21]

Written by Boris Brandt, a nationalist sympathizer but not a member of the inner circle of the Bnei Moshe, and closely supervised by Ahad Ha'am, the publication saw Hanukah as the Jewish nationalist festival *par excellence*:

> Hanukah! So many glorious deeds, so many marvellous memories are associated with it. Next to Passover no other Jewish festival has such profound national-historical meaning . . . We celebrate not only the consecration and renewal of the Temple, some two thousand years ago . . . but also the renewal and revival of this same Jewish nation, reviving its soul once again for a new life and new and glorious historical activity.[22]

The festival was viewed in this pamphlet as an inspirational tale of Jewry's struggle against the seemingly insurmountable assimilatory forces of Hellenism. Its message was particularly significant today, affirmed Brandt, in what he called the 'third epoch' of Jewish history (following on the heels of the Mosaic and rabbinic ones), and Hanukah constituted proof of Jewry's special genius for survival and renewal: 'Mattathias, the Hasmonean, and his five sons, especially his third son Judah, heroes of the most elevated and idealistic sort, are rarely found in history and then only when produced by the genius of the Jewish nation.'[23]

It is within the context of the Bnei Moshe's preoccupation with assimilation – a preoccupation fuelled by the condescension of local Russified Jews and by the uniquely acculturated tenor of Jewish life in Odessa, where the Bnei Moshe originated – that Ahad Ha'am's "Avdut betokh ḥerut' (Slavery in Freedom) must be read. The essay, published in 1891, launched a lifelong and fertile dialogue between historian Simon Dubnov and Ahad Ha'am; it was a reply to a review written by Dubnov in *Voskhod*, the respected, liberal Russian-language Jewish monthly, based in St Petersburg, and known for its critical attitude towards Jewish nationalism.[24]

In his article, Dubnov contrasted two recent publications – the Bnei Moshe's *Kaveret* (whose sponsorship by the Bnei Moshe and editorship, and financial help, by Ahad Ha'am, were not known) and the *La Gerbe* (published by the *Archives Israélites*). Dubnov's criticisms of the former were withering. Although it was designed to showcase the major Russian Jewish nationalist talent (Ahad Ha'am, for instance, had three pieces in the volume, more than any other contributor), Dubnov described it as provincial, narrowly conceived and promoting an image of Judaism thoroughly inferior to that

presented in the expansive, universalistic *La Gerbe*. Dubnov particularly castigated the well-known Hebrew secularist publicist Moses
Leib Lilienblum, who, inexplicably in Dubnov's view, affirmed in
Kaveret the archaic strictures of the guide to traditional Jewish
practice, the *Shulḥan Arukh*, a surprising reversal of his former
enlightened maskilic commitments. Ahad Ha'am's own essays,
Dubnov noted, were vague and surprisingly pessimistic for a
supporter of Jewish nationalism.[25] It was the contrast made by
Dubnov between the cultivation of the politically free Western Jew
and the moral as well as civic subjugation of those in the East that so
enraged – and probably also bruised – Ahad Ha'am, who was
especially sensitive to the charge that his Hebraist entourage had not
transcended their cloistered pasts:

> The opponents of the Hovevei Zion in the Russian Jewish press think
> that they have no more formidable weapons at their disposal than the
> same ones that they used when they fought the battle for 'culture'
> against the 'obscurantists'. That is to say, instead of examining our
> views and proving us wrong on the basis of arguments drawn from facts
> and reason, they think that they can put us out of court by an array of
> distinguished names; they think that they can frighten us by pointing
> out how widely we differ from the Jewish thinkers of Western Europe.
> They forget that their new opponents include many who are no
> strangers to Western culture, and we are aware that even professors
> sometimes make mistakes and that even members of Academies have
> been known to cling to obsolete beliefs.[26]

'Slavery in Freedom' was the most apt way to describe the condition of *La Gerbe*'s contributors, the cream of French Jewry, so
unperceptively celebrated by Dubnov but who were, in fact, a sadly
disquieted and perplexed group. Their claims that the revolution was
sacrosanct and Jewish peoplehood without real relevance were
belied, Ahad Ha'am detected, by their thinly veiled pessimism and
their still-resilient Jewish ethnic-cultural attachments. These were
still evident, despite their hollow protestations to the contrary. They
could not acknowledge such feelings for fear of appearing unpatriotic;
they sacrificed their authenticity as Jews and human beings for the
sake of emancipation. What Dubnov had mistakenly identified as
'spiritual exaltation' was self-denial and even an abiding, raw fear.
'We hear cries of defeat, not paeans of triumph . . ., an undercurrent of grief and a dark thread of lamentation.'[27]

Fear of antisemitism, the need to hide their (often quite intense)
Jewish attachments, and indeed to obscure all that was instinctive

and authentic, was the terrible price that they paid for their 'freedom'. 'Try as they will to cancel [their Jewish feelings], seek as they will for subterfuges to deceive the world and themselves, it lives on none the less; resent it as they will, it is a force that is at the very centre of their being.'[28]

The essay was a passionate, unyielding *tour de force*, one which expressed Ahad Ha'am's views in far more definitive and obstinate terms that he would subsequently employ. But his denunciation did not provide a guide as to how Jews were expected to live in the modern world while retaining their Judaism. In general, while his earliest essays were powerful, even beautiful in parts, they declaimed more than they analysed. This changed after the publication of his controverisal 'Emet meereẓ yisrael' ('The Truth from Palestine'), which appeared in 1891 after his first Palestinian visit. His reputation as Zionism's main internal critic dated from this point. His earlier essays had been contentious, especially when viewed against the backdrop of the author's active political involvements, but 'Emet' was the most detailed attack on the movement to date, certainly the most vehement piece of criticism from within. In turn, it precipitated fissures in the Bnei Moshe that freed Ahad Ha'am from some of the constraints he had felt before and which had stopped him from airing his views with the clarity he might have preferred.[29]

By 1893, when he published 'Ḥikui vehitbolelut' ('Imitation and Assimilation'), the delicate compromise that he had fashioned in the Bnei Moshe between the religious and non-religious was under irreparable attack from both within and outside the organization. He now set his sights unreservedly on attracting Russified, non-religious, even otherwise 'assimilated' Jews. His latest battle with the religious members of Bnei Moshe had, in fact, been prompted by his support for precisely such a figure – the Russified engineer Vladimir Tiomkin, in a Jaffa-based controversy that pitted Tiomkin against considerably more traditional opponents whom Ahad Ha'am summarily expelled from the organization. In 1893, the Bnei Moshe dropped a clause in its constitution that asked members to respect even those dictates of religious Judaism that might conflict with their inclinations; in supporting the deletion of this item, Ahad Ha'am explained that it hindered the recruitment of Russified Jews.[30]

His analysis in 'Ḥikui vehitbolelut' of the dynamics of assimilation was considerably more nuanced than that of his earlier pieces and here he relied on the most original concept in his repertoire – the notion of a 'spiritual centre', first used in 1891 after his return from

Palestine. In formulating this idea he based himself on the Spencerian
French psychologist Frédéric Paulhan who taught – as Ahad Ha'am
explained in the introduction to the first edition of his collected essays,
published in 1895 – that for both the individual and the collective
alike it is inevitable that, 'a particular spiritual factor in the depths of
the soul [gains] predominance over all other forces, until such time
that it succeeds, even imperceptibly, in uniting all of these around
itself, in making them subservient to its own purpose, and in changing
the character of all of them in accordance with its needs'. Such
concentration of spirit was a psychological principle and he cited in
particular Paulhan's well-known *L'Activité Mentale*, where he sought
to substantiate empirically the principle of the concentration of the
spirit by tracing it in the biography of Charles Darwin. Ahad Ha'am
applauded Paulhan's achievement: 'He succeeded in providing a
lucid portrait, based on the process of concentration as employed in
the soul of this great man. And what is possible for the life of a single
individual cannot be said to be impossible for the spiritiual life of a
nation.'[31]

In 'Ḥikui vehiṭbolelut' he maintained that all aspects of social life
were the products of imitation of one sort or another; the way in which
social forces were moulded into coherent units was by virtue of their
attraction to 'some centre . . . which thus becomes the single or chief
object of universal imitation'.[32] Such imitation was an inevitable and
healthy feature of society. Only when this led to 'self-effacement' and
to the repression of a nation's natural inclinations could one speak of
assimilation. Using mechanistic terminology drawn from Herbert
Spencer (this essay was considerably more sophisticated than "Avdut
betokh ḥerut' but far less successful as a literary performance), he
explained rather ponderously that, 'it is not imitation as such that
leads to assimilation. The real cause is the original self-effacement
which results in assimilation, through the medium of imitation.'[33]

To avoid such cultural submergence required of nations, quite
simply, 'to love themselves'; they would thus reinvigorate their innate
strengths, attaining renewed self-confidence and national vitality.
And though Jewry's ability to renew itself had been blunted in recent
times, this attribute was not lost and was evident even in a flawed
movement like Reform Judaism which, despite itself and contrary to
its public statements, embodied at least a kernel of nationalist
longing. Consequently, widespread assimilation was unlikely – at
least in the short run – since even in the least nationalistically inclined
Jews fires continued to simmer. None the less, if current trends among

Jews were left unchecked, they could well result in the permanent
fragmentation of Jewry, rendering Western and Eastern Jews discreet
entities comparable to the tribes of ancient Israel.

This was why there was a crucial need for a centre. In the past,
outstanding kings (David or Solomon) had succeeded in creating
around themselves, by virtue of military prowess or brilliance, a
central focal point for their nation. Now, in the absence of such
leaders, a geographically coherent centre was all the more essential in
order to reclaim Jewry's fragmented allegiances, to redevelop its
national individuality and to purify it:

> today, in [Jewry's] old age, neither strength nor wisdom, nor even
> wealth, will succeed in creating a centre anew. And so all those who
> desire to see the nation reunited will be compelled, despite themselves,
> to bow before historical necessity and to turn towards the east, to the
> land which was our centre and our essential framework in ancient
> times.[34]

Even before he formulated his concept of a spiritual centre, Ahad
Ha'am had argued in 1891 in "Avar ve'atid' (Past and Future) that a
preoccupation with the future, which had always been the hallmark
of Jewry, should now dominate the thinking of nationalists who held
the key to their people's destiny. The Jews had not succumbed to the
'verdict of history' and disappeared like other ancient nations because
of the way in which this image of the future retained so central a place
in their national consciousness. This fact, above all, had ensured their
survival, while other nations – even those with considerably more
brilliant pasts – had perished.[35]

A preoccupation with the past was to be found in Judaism's vast
corpus of rabbinic laws whose observance, said Ahad Ha'am, had
frequently, and quite incorrectly, been credited with sustaining
Jewish life. If a connection existed between Jewish survival and
rabbinic ritual it was, he argued, due not to the laws that Jewry
obeyed *per se* but rather to the primacy which so many of those laws
place on life in Palestine, thereby reinforcing Jewish faith in the
future. Rituals, then, with a Palestinian focus and without any
immediate relevance to the present had more impact on preserving
Jewry than did those with clear applicability.[36]

Ahad Ha'am's belief that Jews owed their collective existence to an
ability to concentrate their spiritual resources on the rebuilding of a
future Palestine helped determine for him the most immediate task on
the national agenda. There was an urgent need to sustain and
reinvigorate Jewry's spiritual resources until such time that Jews were

sufficiently equipped, Palestine appeared, and objective conditions suitable for a still grander undertaking. What he proposed was a renewal of the spiritual politics that he believed Jewry had employed through the ages. His tactics, as he saw it, possessed an authenticity and proven effectiveness.

The concept of a 'spiritual centre' was Ahad Ha'am's reply to the sustained pessimism of his essay 'Emet meerez yisrael'; there he left little room for meaningful action, except for whatever contributions (technical or financial) might be made by Western Jews committed to the Jewish nationalist cause. Russian Jews, however, the bulk of his readership and Zionism's constituency, could contribute, he said, little as pioneers (land was scarce in Palestine and prohibitively expensive), and even less as politicians (the Hovevei Zion's government-approved charter, of 1890, permitted fund-raising, not politics). With his 'spiritual Zionism', Ahad Ha'am sought to demonstrate that he was something other than a mordant critic and that he was interested in providing concrete solutions to Jewry's problems.

At the same time, he was intent upon putting himself forward – always with the option to retreat if he met with resistance – as Pinsker's heir and as the leader of Russian Zionism. Consequently, he first used the term 'spiritual centre' in an essay written to commemorate Pinsker's achievements, published soon after his death in 1891. The essay's purpose was, as Ahad Ha'am explained, to clarify Pinsker's legacy and in it he summarized the latter's seminal tract, *Autoemancipation*. He then revealed that near the end of his life Pinsker had lost hope that the legalization of the Hovevei Zion's activities would solve its daunting problems, an assumption that Pinsker had cherished since the birth of the group in the early 1880s. Ahad Ha'am's readers were thus introduced to a Leon Pinsker who sounded, rather improbably, just like Ahad Ha'am – who was similarly obsessed with the insurmountable obstacles confronting Palestinian Jewry, and, above all, with the need to revive Jewry's national identity in the Diaspora:

> What was there left for him to do once experience had taught him that it was extremely difficult to put his ideas into practice in [Palestine] and that the members of the Hovevei Zion too were 'only Jews', [and not yet prepared for nationalist tasks]?

Pinsker had concluded, and told Ahad Ha'am just before his death, that Zion could serve Jews, at least in the short run, as a 'secure haven not for Jews, but for Judaism'.[37]

This was, he said, Pinsker's 'nationalist testament' (*zava'ah leumit*),[38] as commanded, significantly, to Ahad Ha'am. In the end, Ahad Ha'am never managed to wrest control of the Hovevei Zion – though for several years following Pinsker's death he was, along with one or two others, among the most influential figures in the movement – but he would now, and unreservedly, identify the true ideals of Hovevei Zion with those of his own Bnei Moshe. Within a few years, once he was confronted with Herzlian Zionism, he fought it in the name of the original Russian-Jewish nationalist movement whose goals he now purported to personify and which, ironically, in its prime and during Pinsker's lifetime he had criticized mercilessly.

Before Herzl's appearance in the mid 1890s, Palestinophilism was represented by a patchwork of rather small, mostly Russian-based groups (with a membership of some 14,000 at their height), inspired by the pogroms and by the secularized Messianism of the 1880s. Herzl gave the movement a semblance of international recognition and he supplanted its medley of maskilic, rabbinic and provincial plutocratic leaders. Earlier, the Hovevei Zion had organized the main thrust of its activities (much to Ahad Ha'am's dismay) around the haphazard collection of funds for Palestinian Jewish settlers. Now Herzl's goals were a charter, international recognition, and eventually the mass movement of Jews to the land that he called, in his utopian novel of 1902, *Altneuland*.[39]

The relationship between Herzl and Ahad Ha'am was complex, vituperative, laced with condescensions on both sides, and replete with repeated misunderstandings and both conscious and unconscious slights. By 1897, when Herzl first consolidated his movement, Ahad Ha'am was editor of the leading Hebrew monthly *Hashiloach*. He had lost his small fortune in bad investments and disbanded the Bnei Moshe, but his journal provided him with an important forum, enhancing his already formidable credentials. Ahad Ha'am refused to join the new Zionist movement, criticized those in his entourage who did (which included most of his closest colleagues) and, as Ben Halpern has observed, acted 'virtually as a coeval institution in himself'.[40]

In 1902, when Herzl was faced by a visible opposition within the movement (spearheaded by Russian Zionists sympathetic to Ahad Ha'am) and when his diplomatic negotiations in the Ottoman Empire had proved abortive, Ahad Ha'am launched a series of spirited attacks on him aimed at winning back the movement to what he called the ideals of the Hovevei Zion. Hovevei Zion, he had said in one of his first forays against Herzl, 'begins with national culture,

because only through the national culture and for its own sake can a
Jewish state be established in such a way as to correspond with the
will and needs of the Jewish people'.[41] Here too he stressed that the
central goal of Zionism must be the emancipation of Jewry from the
inner slavery brought on by assimilation. His most important essays
of this period on the dangers of assimilation were his 1902 review essay
on Herzl's *Altneuland* and his speech to the Minsk congress of Russian
Zionists of the same year, 'Teḥiyat haruaḥ' ('Spiritual Revival').

His review of *Altneuland* sparked a major Zionist battle, arguably
the most important to date between Eastern European and Western
Jewish nationalists, though much more was at stake than regional
antagonisms. That Ahad Ha'am's bitterly sardonic and well-timed
essay elicited such a strong response was unsurprising; what was
puzzling was Herzl's maladroit behaviour in the debate that brought
to the surface precisely the sort of tensions (East versus West, religious
versus secular) that he had so assiduously, and successfully, reduced
since his appearance as the leader of Zionism. For Ahad Ha'am
Altneuland was God-sent, published at a particularly vulnerable
moment in Herzl's tenure and publicizing, for the first time, the flat,
characterless, Jewishly illiterate vision of his prospective state. The
fact that this was the image that presented itself to an assimilated
Central European Jew was, he felt, virtually inevitable; that others,
much closer to their people, acclaimed it was tragic.

Ahad Ha'am treated *Altneuland*, not unreasonably, as a social
blueprint rather than as a novel (aesthetic considerations bored him,
as he acknowledged frequently). Had not Herzl made it clear that
what he hoped to create was a pluralistic, anti-clerical, Western state
where all but the deracinated remnants of Central European Judaism
(like a Reform-style temple atop, or near, the Temple Mount) were
eliminated from its national culture and where the chief influences
were English, French, German, but not Jewish?

> And since everything to be found in Eretz Israel [Palestine] was
> actually created not there, but rather in England, America, France,
> and Germany, consequently all that happens to be there belongs not to
> Jewry alone but to all the nations of the world. The fundamental
> principle of the new society is, as a result, 'Without any distinction for
> reasons of either religion or nationality'.[42]

Herzl's Jewish world was one in which the hotly contested 'language
question' – which pitted Yiddish against Hebrew in one of the most
significant debates of the period – had no resonance. In Herzl's

Palestine Jews studied French and German in schools, spoke, most probably, German on the street, although the question held so little interest for Herzl that he did not even feel it necessary to spell out the preferred tongue. Hebrew wasn't even taught or, if it was, Herzl did not mention it. To the extent to which a national culture existed, it was an unambiguously Western import – English games, German or French theatre, continental conviviality.[43]

The only truly discordant voice in the novel was that of the fanatic Geiger – formerly an ultra-Orthodox anti-Zionist, now a fervent nationalist, self-seeking, pompous and repulsive. He vied for leadership of the Palestinian society and won some popular support but, in the end, the rabbis managed to win the masses over to the side of moderation and good sense. The disreputable Geiger, then, was the only evidence in the novel of a self-consciously Jewish voice, and his was provincial, indeed hatefully narrow.

How inferior, observed Ahad Ha'am, was Herzl's Utopian novel to that of a lesser-known novel by a member of Ahad Ha'am's Hebraist entourage, Elhanan Levinsky, whose work written ten years earlier was one of true Jewish authenticity. Ahad Ha'am managed in this way to contrast two very different perspectives on Jewry, one represented by Herzl and the other, the superior one, by an Eastern European Jew and one of his friends and co-workers:

> How much greater is the Zionist ideal of the Hebrew writer than of the German leader. In the former, there is authentic national freedom and life based on general human principles; in the latter case – an ape-like mimicry devoid of any specifically national character; replete with a spirit of 'slavery in freedom', a daughter of exile.[44]

Only a few months before the publication of Ahad Ha'am's review, he was the star speaker at the first countrywide national Russian Zionist conference since the start of Herzl's movement, held in Minsk in September 1902. The speech, reproduced in *Hashiloach* as 'Tehiyat haruah', was among his lengthiest – it took him some two hours to read it to an audience accustomed to short, pithy Ahad Ha'amist statements.[45] It was uncharacteristic in other respects, as well. For all its anti-Herzlian content, it was surprisingly diplomatic in its acknowledgement of the legitimate (if subordinate) tasks of the Herzlian movement though this was said in the context of a proposal that would have split the Zionist camp in half, with all those interested in cultural affairs joining a new group whose creation was proposed in Minsk by Ahad Ha'am.

Employing both irony and more than a hint of cruelty, Ahad
Ha'am argued that proof of Jewry's genius was to be found in the
achievements of precisely those Jews who had earned their fame
outside their community. In contrast, those prominent within the
Jewish community were today typically mediocre and pale by
comparison. It was the others – obviously neither among his listeners
at Minsk nor the readers of *Hashiloach* – who 'embody in their work
the natural spirit' of Jewry, and, despite themselves, 'the spirit of
Judaism comes to the surface in all that they attempt and gives their
work a special and distinctive character, which is not found in the
work of non-Jews working in the same fields'.[46]

In line with this argument, the speech was replete with biological
and organic allusions.[47] Jewish exile was compared to a fruit tree
sustained by artificial means in alien soil; one's native language, said
Ahad Ha'am, was the most natural of all and he reported that in cases
where the afflicted forgot how to speak and could only remember
words in one language, it was invariably their native tongue that they
remembered and not the language in which they were most fluent at
the time of their illness. This represented proof of 'the natural, organic
link between a human being and his own language' and his 'natural'
community.

It was the attraction of Jewry's best minds to alien cultures that
was, or at least should be, the chief item on the communal agenda.
Culture was sustained by geniuses who constituted the hallmark of
national cultural achievement, he argued, and the mere existence of
widespread literacy could not, in itself, ensure the vitality of a nation.
Take the Swiss, for example, who maintained an otherwise
exemplary life but had not produced any extraordinary minds and
therefore were justifiably criticized for their lacklustre culture. Jews
could well suffer this fate. A good example of the sort of outstanding
figure who was drawn, rather inexplicably, to the larger cultural
realm and away from Jewry was the sculptor Mark Antokolsky.
When Antokolsky conjured up images of monastic purity, he thought
of eleventh-century monks rather than of those with 'much broader
human appeal and much closer' to his own experiences, such as Elijah
the Gaon of Vilna, the eighteenth-century sage who lived in
Antokolsky's native city. Since, according to Ahad Ha'am, nationalism, when successful, achieved the 'recentralization of . . . spiritual
potential', he argued that, 'It is beyond dispute . . . that if these
scattered forces had been combined in earlier times, [our] culture
would be today one of the richest and most original in the world.'[48]

In the absence of such a 'recentralization' programme, or any coherent campaign to revitalize and refocus Jewry's cultural energies, those who remained most visibly Jewish were unimpressive, derivative, in effect, those incapable of embracing a larger and more magnetic spiritual world. If this decline were not checked, rot would soon set in and things would degenerate beyond repair. This would constitute a tragic loss for Jews and also for the larger society, since assimilation extracted a huge price in terms of the quality and viability of cultural achievement:

> In the one case, a man works among his own people, in the environment which gave birth to him, which endowed him with his special aptitude, which encircled the first slow growth of his faculties and implanted in him the rudiments of his human consciousness, his fundamental ideas and feelings, thus helping to determine in his childhood what would be the character of his mind throughout his lifetime. In the other case, a man works amidst an alien people, in a world that is not his own, and in which he cannot be at home unless he changes artificially his own nature and the basic cast of his mind, unless he tears himself into two disparate halves, ensuring that all his work, along with his very character, are devoid of either harmony or wholeness.[49]

The tens of thousands of Jews criss-crossing the Western world in search of bread and safety, the main focal point of Zionist politics, would eventually find homes, he argued. But unless Zionism came to be seen as something more than merely 'a romance of diplomatic embassies [and] interviews with prominent personages', it would not be able to inspire the much smaller number upon whom the Jewish future truly depended. Issues of peripheral importance – migration, Palestinian land acquisition, the vain search for a charter – occupied Jewish nationalists, to the detriment of far more pressing concerns that, if left unaddressed, would leave the destitute Jewish masses without leadership, moral direction or a firm national foundation for continued existence. And while other nations might first concentrate their attentions on diplomacy before busying themselves with cultural politics, 'Jews are different.' The Jewish nation could be compared to a grown man, who, having long before emerged from childhood, was now asked to return to the regimen of his infant years:

> Jews climbed the lower rungs of the ladder thousands of years ago, and then, once they had achieved a high stage of culture, their natural progress was forcibly arrested, the ground was cut from under their feet, and they were left hanging in mid-air, burdened with a heavy pack of valuable spiritual goods but robbed of any basis for a healthy existence and free development.[50]

Pre-modern exilic life did not need (nor would it permit) such conditions to be corrected; contemporary Jewish life would be untenable unless they were corrected with the reconstruction of Jewish life in its original Palestinian home.

Though Ahad Ha'am was, as his critics charged, frequently evasive about his agenda, refusing to acknowledge his hunger for power, the full extent of his elitism, the goals or even the existence of his Bnei Moshe, he was never vague about the role that the politics of assimilation played in his thinking. That this theme has never been systematically examined before is because politics have not been given due weight in studies of him.

He argued that assimilation threatened not only Western Jewry but the viability of Jewish life everywhere, even in the seemingly cloistered confines of the Russian Pale of Settlement. The decline of the theological foundations of Judaism even in Eastern Europe (not yet recognized by most Jews, he knew, but inevitably in view of the compelling influences of modernity), the loss of Jewry's best minds to gentile culture, and the fragmentation of the Jewish world in the wake of emancipation with its potent allure – all these factors had disfigured the life of the Western Jews but their impact would not stop there. Hovevei Zion, as he understood it, constituted the natural heir to the exilic legacy of the Jewish people and the focal point of Jewish identity in a world where both the refusal to assimilate outside influences and an unchecked eagerness to do so could result in the disappearance of Jewry. What was essential was the creation of a spiritual centre in Palestine which would contribute a suitably rich and nuanced foundation for a modern Jewish secularized culture.

Crucial to this process of cultural reconstruction was the reassertion of the values of Jewry's rightful elite. It was, of course, common for Eastern European nationalist movements to insist, as Raymond Pearson has observed, that their formative, preliminary phases should be devoted to a 'national education programme [and] and the creation of a "culture-community", a consciousness-raising exercise by the intelligentsia to invest territory which was otherwise ethnically deficient or inert with an identity which the populace could embrace'.[51] But for Ahad Ha'am, and perhaps uniquely so, the creation and recognition of an authentic national leadership would provide a decisive bulwark against the degenerative forces of assimilation. The rightful spiritual mentors would reorient the masses, win back the best minds of Jewry, and refocus attention on the exemplary cultural centres where the stage would be set, as in the past, for all that was truly significant in Jewish life.

Notes

This chapter is drawn from my forthcoming biography of Ahad Ha'am that will be published by Peter Halban/Weidenfeld. I am grateful for research assistance and travel grants to Jerusalem from the Committee on Research of the Academic Senate at the University of California at Los Angeles. The term 'politics of assimilation' is, of course, drawn from Michael Marrus's important study, *The Politics of Assimilation: A Study of the French Jewish Community at the time of the Dreyfus Affair* (Oxford, 1971).

1 *The Complete Diaries of Theodor Herzl*, ed. Raphael Patai, trans. Harry Zohn, vol. I (New York, 1960), p. 196.
2 'Slavery in Freedom' appears in English translation in Leon Simon, (trans.), *Selected Essays by Achad Ha-'am* (Philadelphia, 1912), pp. 171–94. Most of the material quoted in this chapter from Ahad Ha'am's work is translated from the original Hebrew as it appears in *Kol kitvei Ahad Ha'am* (Jerusalem, 1956).
3 A bibliography, compiled by Yohanan Pograbinski, may be found in *Kiryat sefer*, vols. XI and XII, 1934/35 and 1935/36. The standard biographies of Ahad Ha'am are M[oshe] Glickson, *Ahad Ha'am: Hayav ufo'olo* (Jerusalem, 1927); Aryeh Simon and Yosef Heller, *Ahad Ha'am* (Jerusalem, 1955); and Leon Simon, *Ahad Ha-am: A Biography* (Philadelphia, 1960).
4 For remarks on the literary dimension of Ahad Ha'am's legacy, see Dan Miron, *Bodedim bimo'adam* (Jerusalem, 1987), pp. 343–5.
5 Glickson, *Ahad Ha'am*, pp. 2–3.
6 For a persuasive analysis of Ahad Ha'am's politics, see Yossi Goldstein, 'The Zionist Movement in Russia (1897–1904)', unpublished Ph.D. dissertation, Hebrew University, Jerusalem, 1982, pp. 107–13.
7 A recent example of the way in which Ahad Ha'am's early political essays have been misread may be found in Alan Mintz's otherwise perceptive 'Ahad Ha-am and the Essay: The Vicissitudes of Reason', in Jacques Kornberg (ed.), *At the Crossroads: Essays on Ahad Ha-am* (New York, 1983), pp. 3–11. Mintz writes (p. 3): 'I limit my discussion to the essays written in the early 1890s, which were included in the first edition (1895) of *Al parashat derakhim* (At the Crossroads), among these I exclude the overtly political essays. What we are left with is about a dozen essays, the best known and most frequently anthologized and, I believe, the most influential.' Included in his list are essays that are, in fact, central to Ahad Ha'am's analysis of the politics of assimilation, for example, 'Avar ve'atid' and 'Hikui vehitbolelut'.

8 Ahad Ha'am provided information on his early years in memoirs published in Ahad Ha'am, *Pirkei zikhronot veigerot* (Tel Aviv, 1931). His sister wrote a memoir which contains important information on their parental home. See 'Akhad Ga'am v dome ego roditelei v derevne Gopchitse', in the Central Zionist Archives, Jerusalem, no. 4, 791, 1917.

9 For a discussion of intellectual influences on Ahad Ha'am see the chapters written by Heller in L. Simon and Y. Heller, *Ahad Ha'am*, pp. 127–247.

10 *Kol kitvei*, p. 115; in *Kaveret* (Odessa, 1890), the quote appears on p. 83.

11 Both 'Lo zeh haderekh' and 'Derekh heḥayim' are republished in *Kol kitvei*, the latter as part of an article entitled, 'Nisayon shelo hizliaḥ'. For a collection of the addenda to 'Derekh heḥayim', along with other documents relevant to the early years of Bnei Moshe, see the pamphlet no. 1882 in the Ahad Ha'am archives, Jewish National and University Library.

12 'Lo zeh haderekh,' *Kol kitvei*, pp. 11–14.

13 Ibid., p. 12.

14 'Derekh hehayim', *Kol kitvei*, p. 438.

15 Ibid., p. 439.

16 See the discussion of Ahad Ha'am's response to such complaints in Sh[muel] Tchernowitz, *Bnei Moshe utekufatam* (Warsaw, 1914), pp. 62–5. Also see *Igrot Ahad Ha'am*, vol. VI, p. 84.

17 For among the most vivid descriptions of this circle, see Chaim Tchernowtiz (Rav Tsair), *Masekhet zikhronot* (New York, 1945) and Simon Dubnov, *Kniga zhizni*, vol. I (Riga, 1934). Also see Yehoshua Barzilai, 'Ekh ne'asoh Asher Ginzberg le-Ahad Ha'am?' *Hashiloach* 30 (1914), 302–5. A useful source of biographical information on figures in Ahad Ha'am's immediate entourage is S. L. Zitron, *Leksikon ziyoni* (Warsaw, 1924).

18 My interpretation of the transmutation of traditional leadership patterns in Ahad Ha'am's circle has been informed by arguments made in a stimulating paper by Eli Lederhendler, 'Interpreting Messianic Rhetoric in Russian Haskalah and Early Zionism' (*Studies in Contemporary Jewry*, vol. VII: *Jews and Messianism in the Modern Era: Metaphor and Meaning*, ed. J. Frankel (New York, 1991).

19 Dubnov, *Kniga zhizni*, vol. I, p. 286.

20 See Steven J. Zipperstein, *The Jews of Odessa: A Cultural History 1794–1881* (Stanford, Calif. 1985), esp. pp. 129–54; Dubnov's *Kniga zhizni* is among the best accounts of relations in the late 1880s and 1890s between Odessa's Russified Jewish intellectuals and the Hebraists; see ch. 26.

21 B[oris] Brandt, *Khanuka: istoricheskii ocherk* (Warsaw, 1890).

22 Ibid., p. 3.

23 Ibid., p. 5.

24 See Robert Seltzer, 'Ahad Ha-am and Dubnow: Friends and Adversaries', in Kornberg (ed.), *At the Crossroads*, pp. 60–72.

25 Dubnov summarized his essay, published in *Voskhod*, 1890, no. 12, in *Kniga zhizni*, vol. 1, pp. 247–9.
26 *Kol kitvei Ahad Ha'am*, p. 64.
27 Ibid.
28 Ibid., p. 67.
29 This period is discussed at length by Ehud Luz in *Parallels Meet* (Philadelphia, 1988), trans. by Lenn T. Schramm, pp. 63–104.
30 Tchernowitz, *Bnei Moshe utekufatam*, pp. 92–126.
31 *Kol kitvei Ahad Ha'am*, p. 2.
32 Ibid., p. 86.
33 Ibid., p. 88.
34 Ibid., p. 89.
35 Ibid., p. 88.
36 Ibid.
37 Ibid., p. 45.
38 Ibid., p. 46.
39 The first two volumes of David Vital's magisterial three-volume history of Zionism – *The Origins of Zionism*, and *Zionism: The Formative Years* – contains a particularly incisive portrait of Herzl and his diplomatic activity.
40 Ben Halpern, 'The Disciple, Chaim Weizmann', in Kornberg (ed.), *At the Crossroads*, p. 158.
41 *Kol kitvei Ahad Ha'am*, p. 142.
42 Ibid., 317.
43 Ibid.
44 Ibid., p. 320.
45 Mordecai Nurock (ed.), *Ve'idat ziyonei rusiah beMinsk (August–September 1902)* (Jerusalem, 1962).
46 *Kol kitvei Ahad Ha'am*, p. 176.
47 Ibid.
48 Ibid.
49 Ibid.
50 Ibid., p. 181–182.
51 Raymond Pearson, *National Minorities in Eastern Europe, 1848–1945* (London, 1983), p. 36.

Index

Made in the USA
Las Vegas, NV
29 January 2022

42609194R00236